HOW TO HANDLE YOUR OWN CONTRACTS

REVISED EDITION

HOW TO HANDLE YOUR OWN CONTRACTS

REVISED EDITION

A Layman's Guide to Contracts,
Leases, Wills, and Other
Legal Agreements

Christopher Neubert & Jack Witham, Jr.

GREENWICH HOUSE
Distributed by Crown Publishers, Inc.
New York

This 1984 edition is published by Greenwich House, a division of Arlington House, Inc., distributed by Crown Publishers, Inc., by arrangement with Sterling Publishing Co., Inc.

Legal forms supplied courtesy of Julius Blumberg, Inc.

Manufactured in the United States of America

Library of Congress Cataloging in Publication Data

Neubert, Christopher.
  How to handle your own contracts.

  Bibliography: p.
  Includes index.
  1. Contracts—United States.   I. Withiam, Jack.
II. Title.
KF801.N48   1984   346.73′02   84-10132
347.3062

ISBN: 0-517-378728
h g f e d c b a

Table of Contents

Preface

Any attorney or student of the law comprehends the complexity of contract law. To say that the topic is voluminous is an understatement. The layman, however, does not have the opportunity to study contract law and cannot expect to understand fully the consequences of his written or verbal acceptance of an offer.

Unquestionably, an attorney's function is to assist the layman in his legal transactions, and it would be ludicrous to suggest that this book, or any publication, could competently replace an attorney's advice. The authors do not make that claim. This book is not a formal legal treatise, but rather a guide to the layman. Where an attorney offers solutions, this book instead hopefully highlights problem areas in contract law. If this objective is accomplished, then armed with an awareness of his rights the layman can seek the advice of counsel, trained to advocate the law as it applies to the layman's particular situation. It cannot be stressed adamantly enough that in any individual case an attorney should always be consulted.

In closing, the authors offer this thought from the New York State Bar Association Lawyer's Code of Professional Responsibility, Canon 2, EC2–5:

> A lawyer who writes or speaks for the purpose of educating members of the public to recognize their legal problems should carefully refrain from giving or appearing to give a general solution to all apparently similar individual problems, since slight changes in fact situations may require a material variance in the applicable advice; otherwise, the public may be misled and misadvised. Talks and writings by lawyers for laymen should caution them not to attempt to solve individual problems upon the basis of the information contained therein.

The book was written in this spirit and the reader should keep this in mind while reading it.

Introduction

Mephistopheles: . . . But tell me Faustus shall I have thy soul?
And I will be thy slave, and wait on thee,
And give thee more than thou hast wit to ask.
Faustus: . . . . .Ay, Mephistopheles, I give it to thee . . .
Mephistopheles: . . . .But Faustus, thou must write it in a manner of a deed of gift . . .
Faustus: . . . . .Now I will make an end immediately. (Writes)
Mephistopheles: . . . .O what will not I do to obtain his soul? (Aside)
Faustus: . . . . .Consummation est: this bill is ended,
And Faustus hath bequeathed his soul to Lucifer.

"Dr. Faustus" (Marlowe)

What appeared to Dr. Faustus to be an intelligently conceived deal at the outset, moved inexorably into a nightmare. Although the doctor possessed a sense of his commitment at the time of signing his contract with Mephistopheles, it was the Devil who later possessed the more favorable position and in the end possessed Faustus himself.

Not all contractual agreements result in obligations as onerous and unforeseen as the pact between Lucifer and Faustus, but the signing of a contract where one party unwittingly commits himself beyond his immediate comprehension of the event is not an infrequent occurrence. Except under particular circumstances forbidden by statute or after-the-fact, court-imposed nullifications, parties can contract to perform or not perform any act. A person's promise, in return for a promise or an action on the part of another, binds the parties securely to each and every implied or expressed covenant in the agreement.

In today's world, people are required more and more often to put their signatures on the dotted line. Although a written contract is in most cases a mutual safeguard, since it may explicitly define duties and rights, it can just as effectively be an inescapable snare for the layman. The "fine print" or legal interpretation of the contract's bold-faced language can entrap the unwary and obligate him far in excess of his original intention.

Attorneys spend lifetimes mastering the law. The layman cannot expect to understand the complete legal ramifications of his actions, and yet so often he is in a position which demands a legal action on his part. Although the most prudent course to follow is to consult an attorney before entering into a contract, time or cost might not permit this—what some may consider a luxury. In the long run, however, the situation may become so burdensome that legal advice must be procured.

It would be propitious to avoid any position of having to seek legal assistance after the event in order to resolve the dilemma of an oppressive contract. The purpose of this book is to that end. By alerting the layman to his rights and to the patent dangers that can be inherent in legal provisions and clauses, before he subscribes to them, the expense and headaches associated with extricating himself from the entanglement can be averted. The layman, aware of his rights and possessing a perfunctory knowledge of the applicable law, will be able to avoid many problems by refusing to commit himself or by obtaining legal counsel to bolster his bargaining status and to protect his rights through a more equitable agreement.

This book attempts to outline the basic legal complications of contracts and certain other documents. The book is not an exhaustive or definitive treatise, nor does it purport to be. It is a guide which explains the layman's rights and translates "legalese" into the vernacular, so that the next time he is confronted with a legal instrument, a dotted line and a pen, he will not sign in wonderment, or out of embarrassment.

Because the law is a constantly evolving discipline and because vagaries exist between states, the thrust of the legal conclusions in this book are general. The authors are themselves New York-schooled, but clearly indicate where reference is made to peculiarities in their own State's law. In any event, because of these differences, where specific information is required, it is always recommended that the layman consult local law. Also, if the risk is great and the danger of later legal complications imminent, the layman should never hesitate to consult an attorney.

The first chapter will discuss the basic concepts of contract law. It is not intended to be exhaustive, but it is a guide to help the reader familiarize himself with the elements of contract law.

HOW TO HANDLE YOUR OWN CONTRACTS

REVISED EDITION

CHAPTER 1

General Principles of Contract Law

What is a contract? There are many definitions of a contract—the following is typical of most: A contract is a *promise*, or a set of promises, for breach of which the law gives a remedy, or for the performance of which the law in some way recognizes a duty. There are certain essential elements that are found in all valid contracts. These elements will be discussed in more detail later, but a quick mention of them here is helpful. They are as follows:

(1) Offer
(2) Acceptance
(3) Consideration
(4) Legal capacity of the parties to the contract
(5) Legal subject matter
(6) A writing if required by law

Other factors might be taken into account in determining the validity and scope of the contract, but the above elements are essential for an enforceable contract and should serve as a good reference point for recognizing the existence, or absence, of a contract.

Elements (1) and (2) are dealt with together, since in order for an offer to culminate in a contract, there must be an *acceptance* of that particular *offer*. The theory underlying offer and acceptance is termed *mutual assent*. Mutual assent is frequently referred to as a "meeting of minds" of the parties to the contract. In essence, it means that the parties are both agreeing to the same thing. This is an important aspect for the party of a contract to remember; that is, it is not his subjective intent that governs the contract but rather the outward, objective expression of the intent that is looked to and is controlling. Just as a child cannot run until it begins to walk, the parties cannot have a contract unless there is an offer and an acceptance of that offer. It is most important that a person fully understands an offer and all of its ramifications, before accepting it. Subjective interpretations of the offer are not the controlling factor. If one is not sure of what is being offered, then the intelligent response is to ask "What does this mean?" and not to sign the dotted line and ask questions later.

Offer

What is an offer? An offer is a promise conditional upon an act, forbearance or return promise, which is being given in exchange for the promise of its performance. The essential components of an offer are:

(1) Intent to contract
(2) Definite and certain terms
(3) Communication to the offeror

When these components exist, the person to whom the offer is made has the ability to accept, and thereby create a contract.

An agreement to agree is not a contract, because components (1) and (2) are lacking. However, there are instances whereby parties have entered into a binding contract orally, agreeing to reduce the oral agreement to writing at a subsequent date. The mere fact that one party cannot force the other party to sign the written contract at a later date does not render the oral contract unenforceable.

Once the offer is made, it is binding on the offeror until an agreed-upon time expires, or until a reasonable amount of. time passes. Generally, an offer may be revoked at any time before it is accepted. But if the offeror grants another party an option in writing, for a specified duration, the offer must remain open and cannot be revoked until that time has passed. The revocation may be effectuated by:

(1) An offeror's revocation, which puts the offeree on notice of the revocation;
(2) The offeree's rejection of the offer;
(3) The offeror's death or insanity; or
(4) The proposed contract becoming illegal due to some third-party intervention, e.g., a statute passed by a government.

Except for (2), the forms that revocation can take are self-explanatory. Let us briefly consider (2). An offer may be rejected in three basic ways:

(a) Express rejection;
(b) Counter offer—this changes the terms of the original offer, and as such, is regarded as a rejection of it;
(c) An acceptance which is conditional upon some act or promise which is not included in the original offer. Again, it works as a rejection of the original offer.

We now have proffered a general explanation of what is an offer, and how it may be terminated or rejected. Our focus should next be centered upon the acceptance of the offer.

Acceptance

Acceptance is simply saying "yes" to an offer—assenting to the terms of the offer. The terms of the acceptance must comply with the offeror's fequirements of method of acceptance. Acceptance, like offer, has three essential elements that are necessary for it to be valid:

(1) It must be absolute on its face;
(2) It must conform to the conditions set out in the offer; and
(3) a.In the case of a bilateral contract, the offeree must inform the offeror of the acceptance or
 b. The undertaking and completion of the act requested for in the offer where the contract is unilateral.

A quick review of what has been discussed might now prove helpful. Offer and acceptance have been explored along with the essential elements of both. But what is this talk about "bilateral" contracts and "unilateral" contracts? A quick definition of these two terms might help in understanding what is expected of the offeree who is responding to an offer. A *unilateral contract* is one in which the promisor does not receive a return promise as consideration for his promise, generally performance of some act by the other party. A *bilateral contract*, which is the type with which the book will mainly concern itself, is one in which there are mutual promises between the two parties to the contract.

Consideration

The third element of a contract is consideration. A promisor (offeror) promises to do something for the promisee (offeree) and in return expects a return promise or performance. This return promise or performance is the consideration. Consideration takes the form of a legal benefit to the promisor or a legal detriment to the promisee. The consideration may be represented by something other than a promise; it may be a forbearance or the creation, modification, or destruction of a legal relationship; or simply a return promise.

Generally, a court will not inquire into the adequacy or fairness of the consideration in the contract unless it is unduly inadequate on its face. If this is found to be the case, the contract may be unenforceable. If the court finds that the parties bargained fairly and from equal positions, the parties will be bound by the consideration contained in the contract. Therefore it is imperative that a contracting party demand a fair return for his promise or performance.

Generally, the consideration is given to the party who is making the promise or performance. However, consideration given to, or by a third person will constitute valid consideration and support a promise and impose contractual liability. An example will be helpful. **X** promises to pay **Y** $1,000 in consideration for **Y**'s transferring title of his car to **Z**, a third party. **Y** transfers the title to **Z** and demands the $1,000 from **X**. **X** refuses. **Y** can sue **X** on the contract because the promise is enforceable. As a rule, one promise is valid consideration for another promise. In a bilateral contract, legal enforceability of both promises must be present or the contract might be unenforceable.

Consideration can be viewed as the bargaining objective of the parties: "I promise to do something for you and in return for this undertaking, you promise to do something for me." In most instances, money is the consideration for the promised act. "I promise to transfer title of my car to you and in return for this transfer, you promise to pay me $1,000." Simply stated, the offeror will sell his car to the offeree for $1,000. When viewed from a contractual point of view, it is the exchange of two promises. The consideration given the seller for his promise to transfer title is the $1,000. The consideration given to the buyer for the $1,000 is the car.

There are some pitfalls of which the contracting party should be aware. Some promises on their face appear to be consideration but really are not. A moral obligation to do something is not consideration. However, a *moral duty* to pay, in addition to a pre-existing debt, will support a promise. An example would be a debt that has been discharged in bankruptcy. After being discharged in bankruptcy, the debtor makes a promise to pay the debt. It is valid and enforceable. This should be distinguished from a situation where a promise to do an act which is legally enforceable does not constitute consideration. The logic underlying this theory should be evident. If a person is legally obligated to do something anyway (if the act is legally enforceable), that person is not deemed to be giving any consideration in return for an additional promise. The original and legally enforceable promise (duty) is binding without the new contract. The party has given no new consideration for the return promise. However, if that once-legally enforceable promise is no longer viable, due to some reason such as discharge in bankruptcy, then we have the originally cited situation. The promise to pay, which is no longer legally enforceable, is new consideration for a return promise or performance. It is a unique situation, and one should be aware of its existence.

Capacity of the Parties

This fourth element of a contract (see list at the beginning of the chapter) is generally overlooked by contracting parties. Most parties impetuously sign their names on the dotted line and ask questions later. This practice should be avoided. Before signing any contractual agreement, a party should ask pertinent questions first and make the proper inquiries as to with whom he is doing business. Generally, persons who are minors (in New York, under the age of 18), mentally ill or defective, under guardianship, or intoxicated are deemed incapable of entering into an enforceable contract. But, how can it be determined that a person is mentally ill or defective? There is no formula to be applied whereby it can be determined if someone is lacking capacity in some way. This fact is true and can be unfortunate. The result could be a contract that is unenforceable. The contract is voidable, or at least the parts of the contract that have not yet been performed are voidable. The rationale underlying the law is that the party does not have the capacity to understand the full nature of the transaction into which he or she is entering. In reality, the law is stepping in to protect the innocent parties.

In regard to capacity of the parties to the contract, the only concepts that will be covered are *void* and *voidable* contracts. If the contracting parties do have capacity and the other essential elements are met, there is a valid and enforceable contract. However, at times, one party may lack capacity. A voidable contract is a contract that one or more of the parties can get out of simply by electing to do so. Of course, the party may elect to honor the contract (ratification) and the parties will be legally obligated to perform. The latter situation causes no problem. It is when the party wants to avoid the legal relations created by the contract, due to lack of capacity, that a problem arises. Unfortunately, there is not much a party can do if he contracted with a person who lacks capacity. The contract is voidable and the party is out of luck. However, if the party who contracted with the party lacking capacity has already partially performed the contract, the court may award him the reasonable compensation for his services, especially in the case of supplying necessaries.

A void contract is a misnomer, because actually no contract ever existed. It is more like an unenforceable agreement. A void contract imposes no liability whatsoever on the incapacitated party making the contract. This differs slightly from the voidable contract in that a voidable contract can be ratified and treated as an enforceable contract. Even if the contract is deemed void, a party might be able to recover some compensation for services rendered. In summary, a voidable contract can be ratified (at least you have a slim chance); a void contract cannot be ratified.

Legal Subject Matter

The fifth element essential to a contract is a simple, logical concept dealing with the legality of the subject matter. In essence, what is meant is that two parties cannot contract to do something that is illegal. To put it another way, the parties may enter into a contract to do something illegal (e.g., sell marijuana), but it is not enforceable. The performance of formation of the contract is illegal, if what is contracted (bargained) for, is tortious, criminal or contrary to public policy. If there is a statute that prohibits certain conduct, then the conduct is unenforceable, by virtue of the statute. Public policy is more of an interpretation by the courts, and if the courts deem a transaction to be against public policy, then the contract is illegal and unenforceable. Common examples are gambling transactions. If a contract has been entered into and the subject matter is illegal, or is subsequently declared illegal by statute, the contract is illegal and unenforceable.

A Writing If Required by Law: The Statute of Frauds

This sixth and final element is self-explanatory. If a writing is required by law, there must be a writing or else the contract is unenforceable. For all practical purposes, a contract should always be reduced to writing and signed by the parties whenever possible. However, this does not mean that an oral contract is not enforceable. It might be harder to prove, but it still can be enforced by either party. But if the agreement can be reduced to writing and signed by the contracting parties, do it. Then, this element, the statute of frauds, will be automatically satisfied.

There are two general principles indicating whether or not a written contract is necessary. The two principles are: when the transaction involves (a) real estate or (b) a contract which will not be completed within one year from the date of the contract, a writing is required. Principle (a) is always applicable—any transaction involving real estate must be reduced to writing to be enforceable. Principle (b) is more of a rule-of-thumb which is used to judge the enforceability of an oral contract. Remember, an oral contract is as enforceable and as legally binding as a written contract, if the contract is not required to be in writing and can be performed within one year.

The six essential elements of a contract have been discussed briefly. These elements should be considered as a skeleton or foundation of basic contracts. As will be seen in our discussion and use of the blank contract provided in the text, sometimes other elements are contained within the contract that do not directly make up the framework of the basic skeleton.

Contract law is voluminous, and it is not the objective of this book to furnish a detailed history and all the legal ramifications of contract law. Rather, the book, and this initial section, in particular, have as the main objective, to describe the basic elements of any contract, so that the reader may understand his or her position more fully when entering into a contractual arrangement with another party.

We now take up some of the problems that will confront a contracting party. Usually, a person has certain rights and/or obligations of which he or she is not aware. The remainder of this chapter deals with some of these.

A Sample Contract

Let us begin by briefly looking at a blank contract, and let us fill it in with a hypothetical transaction, in order to see that the six basic elements are satisfied.

In the sample, the two contracting parties are identified at the outset of the form. The offer and acceptance, which have been reduced to writing, are present. John Smith offers to transfer a title of an automobile to Mary Jones, who accepts this offer, as is evidenced by her signature on the contract. The consideration given by John Smith is the transfer of title of the automobile. The consideration given by Mary Jones is the $1,000. Therefore, mutual assent exists (offer and acceptance), supported by consideration from both parties. It is assumed that both parties have the legal capacity to enter into the contract and that the contract's subject matter (i.e., transfer of title for $1,000) is not illegal or void by statute. Finally, since the contract is in writing, and is signed by both contracting parties, the six elements are met.

On its face, the contract is enforceable. However, something might happen. Suppose the car is stolen before delivery? What happens if the parties want to get out of the contract because fraud was involved? What happens if the parties left some element of the agreement out of the contract and have now realized this fact? These and other problems can and do arise. These problems are covered in the book.

A good starting point is to refer to the last sentence of the sample contract, above the clause "IN WITNESS WHEREOF." The sentence states, "This instrument may not be

Articles of Agreement,

Between JOHN SMITH, WHO RESIDES AT
10 XYZ STREET
NEW YORK, N. Y.

of the first part,

and MARY JONES, WHO RESIDES AT
20 ABC STREET
NEW YORK, N. Y.

of the second part.

The party of the first part, in consideration of

ONE THOUSAND DOLLARS ($1,000.00)

covenants and agrees to

SELL TO THE PARTY OF THE SECOND PART A 1970 BLACK FORD
AUTOMOBILE. PARTY OF THE FIRST PART WILL TRANSFER TO
THE PARTY OF THE SECOND PART THE CERTIFICATE OF TITLE
AND ANY OTHER DOCUMENTS NECESSARY TO EFFECTUATE A
COMPLETE TRANSFER OF TITLE FROM PARTY OF THE FIRST PART
TO THE PARTY OF THE SECOND PART.

The party of the second part, in consideration of COMPLETE TRANSFER OF TITLE
OF THE 1970 BLACK FORD AUTOMOBILE FROM THE PARTY OF THE FIRST
PART TO THE PARTY OF THE SECOND PART.

covenants and agrees
TO TENDER PAYMENT OF ONE THOUSAND DOLLARS ($1,000.00) TO THE
PARTY OF THE FIRST PART. THE TENDER SHALL BE IN THE FORM OF
CASH AND WILL BE DUE ON THE DATE OF DELIVERY OF SAID AUTOMOBILE.

This instrument may not be changed orally.

In Witness Whereof, *the parties hereunto have set their hands and seals the*
day of *in the year one thousand nine*
hundred and

Sealed and delivered in the presence of

_____

_____

changed orally," which leads us to the *Parol Evidence Rule*.

Parol Evidence Rule

The Restatement of Contracts, § 237, states the parol evidence rule in this manner:

> . . . the integration of an agreement makes inoperative to add to or vary the agreement all contemporaneous oral argeements relating to the same subject matter; and also, unless the integration is void, or voidable and avoided, the integration leaves the operation of prior agreements unaffected.

What does this mean? When a contract is expressed in a writing which is intended to be the complete and final expression of the rights and duties of the parties, parol evidence of prior oral or written agreements of the parties, or of contemporaneous oral agreements, which varies or contradicts the written contract is not admissible. *Parol evidence* means evidence *not* contained in the particular written contract. Think about it for a minute. The purpose of the parol evidence rule is to have all the elements of the contract contained within one document. The rule is attempting to eliminate the possibility that there will be two parties presenting numerous agreements which contradict each other. The purpose of the parol evidence rule is to provide a means by which parties to contracts can secure certainty and finality in defining their rights and obligations, and exclude fraudulent claims.

Does the rule accomplish its purpose? Yes and no. It accomplishes its purpose in so far as prior and contemporaneous agreements are concerned, if the contract meets certain requirements. These requirements are: (1) there is a writing; (2) it has legal efficacy (effectiveness of the contract itself); (3) the writing must be an integration (the writing is adopted as incorporating within itself finally and completely all prior and contemporaneous plans, deliberations, negotiations and agreements); (4) and it is the intention of the parties that all terms of the agreeement are included within the contract that were intended to be included. With these requirements met, no other prior oral or written agreements on the subject matter are admissible.

Here is an illustration of this principle. In fact, the reader might have had this unfortunate experience already. Peter Purchaser wants to buy a used car. He goes to Shakey Sam the Used Car Man. Peter informs Sam that he wants a 1979 Ford. Sam says, "I have just the car for you." In fact, Peter and Sam converse for the better part of an hour discussing white-wall tires, radio, air conditioning and other "so-called" extras for the car. The extras discussed are never reduced to writing. Peter and Sam finally agree to the price. Sam asks Peter to step into the office where he produces a written contract. The essential element needed is Peter's signature on the contract and the car will belong to him. Peter is excited. All he can think about is the car and the drive-in movie that night with his favorite girl friend, Sally Sweetlips. Peter does not take the time to read the contract; he just signs it. Unfortunately, the contract that Peter signed with Shakey Sam is an agreement that requires Sam to transfer to Peter a 1979 Ford and nothing else. None of the extras are included in the contract that Peter believed would be included. On the bottom of the contract, above the signatures, is a clause which states ". . . the parties agree that this agreeement is intended to merge all prior agreements as to the sale of said automobile. The contract is deemed to be a total and complete integration of all the intentions of the parties . . ."

Sam produces a 1979 Ford and says to Peter, "Here is the car. Where is my money?" Peter is shocked. He shouts, "This is not what I wanted; where are the extras that we discussed and agreed upon?" Sam pulls out the contract which calls for transfer and delivery of a 1979 Ford and says, "We contracted for a 1979 Ford, nothing more, and this is what you get." Peter is out of luck under the parol evidence rule. However, under the UCC dealing with the sale of goods, he might be afforded a remedy. In a later chapter the rights and remedies of a purchaser of goods in a sales transaction will be discussed.

But what about subsequent agreements by the parties? Referring back to our sample contract between Smith and Jones, the clause "This instrument may not be changed orally" is contained within the contract. What effect does the rule have on the clause? In general, the parol evidence rule does not prevent proof of an oral or written agreement which varies or contradicts the terms of a prior written agreement. Just because parties enter into a contract does not mean that they cannot get out of it if they desire to. Parties should be allowed to change prior contracts if they wish. So the rule fails in its purpose when dealing with subsequent agreements. Some states (e.g., California, Montana, and others) have enacted statutes to secure complete finality by providing that contracts can be changed only by another written contract or by a completely performed oral agreement. So, in the above example, a subsequent written modification, signed by the parties to the original contract, would be admissible. Again, statutes of the particular locality must be consulted to determine if and when the rule is applicable.

The purpose of briefly discussing the parol evidence rule is so that the reader will be aware that an oral modification of prior contracts is very dangerous. If the parties desire to modify the contract, then it should be done in writing and should be signed. This subsequent writing is admissible and will effectuate a modification of the original contract terms.

In concluding discussion on the parol evidence rule, it is worth noting that there are situations which could be classified as exceptions to the rule; more accurately, they can be said to be outside the scope of the rule. For example, parol evidence is admissible to show that no contract was made or that the contract executed by the parties was voidable for fraud, mistake, duress, undue influence, incapacity, or illegality. Parol evidence also is admissable to show that the writing to which the parties assented was only a part of their complete contract. If it is established that this is true, a collateral oral agreement is provable and enforceable, even without additional consideration.

Ambiguity of expressions contained in the contract can be interpreted by the use of parol evidence. Parol evidence also is admissible to prove usage and custom, to define the meaning of words used in the writing and to add terms of performance in accordance with usages not inconsistent with the terms expressed in the writing.

This section by no means covers the parol evidence rule in depth. However, there are two important points that the reader should retain:

(1) A writing that is legally effective, integrated and intended as such by the parties will not be affected by prior oral or written agreements between the parties. That writing (contract) will be deemed complete on its face. So make sure that all the duties and obligations of the parties are contained in the contract.

(2) Subsequent oral agreements affecting the contract and its subject matter should be entered into only if the party knows that it is enforceable. If confronted with this problem, a person should consult an attorney since enforceability of the oral modification is governed by state statute. The safest approach is to have the subsequent agreement reduced to writing and signed by the parties.

Duress, Unconscionability, and Fraud

A contract induced by *duress* is either void or voidable and therefore unenforceable. Duress basically consists of threats of bodily or other harm, or means which coerce the will of another, inducing him to do an involuntary act. Duress also can consist of illegal imprisonment or legal imprisonment used for an illegal purpose which induces a person to act against his will.

One must be exercising free will when a contract is entered into. The parties must be acting voluntarily. Duress is concerned with the state of mind of the party who is entering into the contract. Certain situations are not considered to be duress. For example, where a party enters into a contract on account of embarrassment, this emotion will not be deemed duress and the contract is valid. Moreover, a person entering into a contract because he feels that there is a moral obligation to do so is not under duress. One last point to remember is that agreements procured by duress may be ratified, but not while the duress which induced the original transaction is still present. A species of duress—undue influence—is very similar and is another expression for the restraint of free will. Generally, in order to invalidate a contract, undue influence must operate to deprive a party of his free agency or will.

Unconscionability is an elusive concept. Conduct could be considered unconscionable if it appears that one party is at a considerable disadvantage in bargaining with another who takes advantage of his superior bargaining status. If a court deems that a contract is unconscionable, it will refuse to enforce the contract. In the absence of any mistake, fraud, or oppression, however, the courts are not interested in the impolicy, or injudiciousness, of contracts voluntarily entered into between the parties. Such parties have the right to insert any stipulations they wish to, provided that the contracts are not inconscionable, illegal or against public policy. Just because the bargain entered into appears onerous, it is not invalidated, if entered into voluntarily and fairly.

Unconscionability concerns itself with the fairness of the bargaining positions of the parties to the contract. For example, Mrs. Jones is on public assistance and receives $200 monthly from the government. She purchases a $1,000 refrigerator and freezer from Mr. Smith who owns a retail store. She puts $10 down and signs a retail installment agreement whereby her furniture is pledged as security for the loan. Mr. Smith knows that Mrs. Jones is on welfare and knows what her monthly income is. The retail installment agreement calls for $100 monthly payments and in the event of default (of payment), Mr. Smith may take all of her furniture. The court might find this agreement unconscionable and unenforceable due to the unfairness of the bargaining position of the parties. (Note: in New York, price alone can be deemed unconscionable in a retail installment agreement.)

The general theme which runs throughout contract law, is that there must be full and free consent between the parties to the contract. The law will generally not inquire into a contract to see if it is a wise and reasonable bargain. However, the courts will inquire into whether fraud was present and material to the signing of the contract. Fraud is material where the contract would not have been made if the fraud had not been perpetrated.

Fraud means misrepresentation, concealment, or non-disclosure where there is no privilege to withhold information. If a material element of the contract is concealed, or misrepresented to a party when there is a duty to disclose, that party has been defrauded—the contract is voidable and unenforceable. The facts surrounding the contract are the determining factor to which the courts look. If the courts feel that a material element relating to the subject matter of the contract has been misrepresented, concealed or not disclosed when there was a duty to do so, the courts may deem this conduct to be fraudulent, in which instance the contract is unenforceable.

Impossibility of Performance

The general rule is that impossibility of performance is not a defense for one under a contractual duty. There have been a great many cases in which courts have inquired into the question of impossibility of performance and acted to resolve it. Impossibility of performance is generally divided into two areas: *original impossibility* and *supervening impossibility*. Original impossibility exists where the contract entered into was impossible to perform from the outset. Supervening impossibility develops sometime after the inception of the contract.

There are two other distinctions between the kinds of impossibility of performance—*subjective impossibility* and *objective impossibility*. Impossibility of performing a promise that is due wholly to the inability of the individual promisor is subjective. Subjective impossibility neither negates the validity of a contract nor discharges a duty created by the contract, and the party may be held liable under the contract. Objective impossibility is distinguished by the fact that the promise of performance contracted for cannot be done by anyone and is not due to the fact that only the promisor cannot do it.

Impossibility of performance, if it is to release a party from his obligation to perform, must be real and not just an inconvenience. If a party is excused for the reason of impossibility of performance, it is imperative that the performance contracted for cannot be accomplished by any means.

Generally, facts existing when a bargain is entered into or occurring subsequently and making the performance more difficult or expensive than originally anticipated by the parties, do not discharge the parties from their obligations to perform.

There are exceptions to the general rule and in such instances, impossibility of performance is a defense for non-performance of the contract. This transpires where the contract subject matter has been destroyed or ceases to exist through no fault of the performing party to the contract. Also, if the contract is for personal services, then death, illness, or incapacity of that essential person will constitute a defense for non-performance. Suppose a lawful contract was entered into, but subsequently has been deemed illegal, by statute or as against public policy. Future events prevent the intended purpose of the parties to the contract. The classic case dealing with this last exception is where **X** rents **Y** a room in her house. **X** and **Y** both believe that a parade will be along the road on which **X**'s house is located. The room is rented so that **Y** can see the parade. That is the purpose of the rental agreement. However, the parade's route is altered and does not proceed on **X**'s street. **X** wants the rental money and **Y** claims the accomplishment of the purpose became impossible. This is valid defense for **Y**'s non-performance.

Temporary impossibility of performance may not excuse a party from performing; his performance might be delayed only temporarily. These are questions of fact to be evaluated by the courts.

Similar to the other sections of contract law which have been covered here in this chapter, impossibility of performance is investigated on a very elementary level without going into depth. The main purpose has been to familiarize the reader with these areas so that he may understand more fully his contractual position. Impossibility of performance is a difficult concept of contract law, and as such, is based on interpretation of each individual set of facts. However, in conclusion, a couple of points might be worth noting:

(1) Upon entering into a contractual situation, the parties should always ascertain that

the performance for which the contract calls is possible at the time the contract is signed.

(2) There is nothing illegal with placing a "saving" clause in the contract. The "saving" clause is an added protection for the contracting party and simply states that if performance of the thing or act contracted for is rendered impossible due to some act, event, or other intervening factor not caused by the fault of the performing party, such party will be discharged of this duty to perform.

Statute of Frauds

The Statute of Frauds is operative in procedural law rather than in substantive law. A contract which fails to comply with the statute of frauds is not void, but merely unenforceable (in some states the contract is void).

The Statute of Frauds concerns itself with the requirement of a writing in certain contractual situations. Where a writing is required, absence of such writing violates the Statute of Frauds and the contract is unenforceable.

Below is a list of major classes of cases covered by writing requirements (UCC excluded; some of these types of contracts will be covered later in the book) in New York State:

(1) Promise to answer for the debt, default, or miscarriage of another. (General Obligations Law Sec. 5–701 (2)).

(2) Promise of an executor or administrator to answer for damages or debts owed by decedent out of his own pocket. (Estates, Powers and Trust Law Sec. 13–2.1).

(3) An executory contract to establish a trust, make a will, or a testamentary disposition. (Estates, Powers and Trust Law Sec. 13–2.1).

(4) A promise made in consideration of marriage except mutual promises to marry (mutual promises to marry are unenforce-able in N.Y.). (General Obligations Law Sec. 5–701 (3)).

(5) A contract to pay a commission or finder's fee for negotiation of a loan or of a sale of real estate, or of the sale of a business or business opportunity. (General Obligations Law Sec. 5–701 (10)). (Not applicable to auctioneers, lawyers, and licensed real estate brokers.)

(6) A contract to transfer an interest in real property, or an actual transfer. So also is a lease for more than one year. (General Obligations Law 5–703).

(7) A contract which, by its terms, is not to be performed within one year from the making thereof. (General Obligations Law Sec. 5–701 (1)).

(8) A contract which, by its terms, is not to be completed before the end of a lifetime. (General Obligations Law Sec. 5–701 (1)).

Accord and Satisfaction

One last area of consideration that the reader should note is *accord and satisfaction*. At common law, an accord and satisfaction was a technical instrument. It was not until the 1800's that an executory accord, based on sufficient consideration came to be recognized as a valid contract. In operation, an accord and satisfaction replaces the obligation of the original contract with a new contractual obligation. The accord and satisfaction becomes effective when there is:

(a) an accord (which is the new agreement the parties enter into);
(b) subject matter of the accord (generally the amount of money owed); and
(c) an obligee who accepts the tender by the obligor.

Upon satisfaction of the accord, the original contract is discharged and the obligor is no longer liable on either contract. This is not an easy concept. The reason for mentioning it is that accords and satisfactions are used every day by people who do not realize that they are involved in such a transaction. An example might illustrate the point. **X** has a legitimate claim against **Y**. **Y** agrees to pay **X** $1,000 and **X** agrees that when he receives the money, he will accept it in satisfaction of his legitimate claim. The agreement is in writing, signed by the parties. **Y** gives the $1,000 to **X** and **X** accepts the money. In New York State this is an accord and satisfaction. As stated in the beginning of the book, many of the rules of contract that are discussed in the book might be unique to New York. The reader should always consult the laws of his locality to determine if the rules are similar.

Upon breach by the party who promises to pay or render performance, the promisee has two options. The promisee may elect to enforce the accord or sue on the original obligation. The written accord only suspends, it does not discharge, the original claim. As an example of accord and satisfaction in daily affairs, consider this situation (which does occur frequently): there is an unliquidated amount owed to one party. The debtor sends a check to the creditor, marking on the check "payment in full." If the creditor cashes the check, an implied accord and satisfaction occurs, in which case the creditor is *estopped* from asserting that his claim is not discharged. So, one should be wary, if a check is received on a debt in which the amount is still in dispute, and if the debtor has added to the notation "payment in full" on his check. The check should not be cashed before consulting an attorney.

The "Plain English" Law

For years, a contractual document, particularly the "fine print" imbedded somewhere in the foundation of an agreement, has been a bane to the common man, be he consumer, renter or debtor. Typical contractual provisions were written in such technical language that only a lawyer, well-versed in the law governing the subject matter, could fully decipher and comprehend their meanings. Attorneys, of course, drafted agreements in "legalese" for a sound reason; they knew what certain time- and court-tested phrases and terms meant. Still, the layman was faced with a dilemma. He either had to hope the party with whom he was dealing would treat him fairly, or he had to expend time and money to consult an attorney to explain the significance of the contract he planned to enter into.

In an attempt to alleviate this problem, state legislatures have been considering the passage of bills requiring that specific consumer contracts be written in a manner that can be read and easily understood by the layman. Two years ago, in 1977, New York State passed its first "plain English" statute, a law so controversial that it had to be amended one year later to clarify its confusing points. Although it does not appear that the New York statute will serve as the paragon for other state governments, it would be useful to examine the law in order to be familiar with the concept of legislating a requirement that certain technical dealings be written in the vernacular.

General Obligations Law Sec. 5–702, as amended, states that after November, 1978, a written agreement for residential leases or money, property or services for personal or household purposes involving sums less than $50,000 must be:

1. Written in a clear and coherent manner using words with common and everyday meanings;
2. Appropriately divided and captioned by its various sections.

If someone fails to comply with the statute, he becomes liable for any *actual* damages incurred by the consumer, and he must pay the consumer an additional $50 as a penalty. The penalty provision limits to $10,000, however, the total amount that any one violator need pay to a class of aggrieved people. Thus, a landlord who continues to use a "legalese" lease (to date only applicable to vacancy leases) must make recompense to his tenants for any losses they suffer, presumably as a result of violating a technically written lease, plus $50 to each tenant. However, if the landlord has more than 200 tenants, the $50 penalty per tenant, in this instance $10,000, will be pooled and pro-rated among the number of tenants comprising the class. You should be aware, however, that the law does not permit you to walk away from a lease or contract because it is not in "plain English." It serves only as your protection against damages or losses which you suffered because you were unable to understand an expressed provision in the contract and hence failed to abide by it.

What does all this mean? It is too early to tell how significant the law will prove to be to the unwary consumer, since the theory behind the statute (to protect someone who is unable to comprehend what he is signing from a party who is in a stronger bargaining position and who has the advice of a team of lawyers) has long been a principle of common law. Where the facts of a particular case warranted such action, courts have intervened to preclude the enforcement of patently unfair contracts (see Unconscionability, page 17). Thus the law may prove to be only a codification of existing common law, with the addition of government-mandated penalites where violations are found. Furthermore, the defen-

dant in any action under the law has a defense against a claim for penalties, if he can show he made a good-faith attempt to write his contracts in conformity with the law.

It would seem that in the end the courts will have to interpret the law on the basis of reasonableness, perhaps calling into play the fictional "reasonable man" of torts law. Instead of asking what the reasonable man would have done in a certain situation, courts will ask whether a reasonable man would have been able to understand the expressed terms of the contract in question. If the reasonable man could have grasped the meaning of the contract, then, arguing backwards, the contract is "written in a clear and coherent manner. . . ." In the end, practicality should prevail.

Conclusion

Other aspects of contract law, such as breach of contract, remedies, and discharge of the contract will be discussed in later chapters. We hope the reader has gained an understanding of basic contract law from this introduction. An attempt should be made to apply these concepts while reading the book. Through application of any principles discussed, the reader may better understand his position when he enters into a contract and will not find himself in a situation as unfortunate as that of Dr. Faustus.

CHAPTER 2

Leases . . . The Renter's Predicament

Introduction

Of all legal agreements, the one that is perhaps most steeped in history is the lease. Although in essence a contract for personal property, its roots are so intertwined with real property law that a lease possesses problems peculiar unto itself which cannot be cured solely by contract law remedies. For this reason, a prospective lessee should be most cautious when signing a lease, scrutinizing every paragraph for clauses which later could result in unanticipated hardships. This is not to say that recognition of an unfavorable sentence and a curt request to the landlord to erase the undesired language will be your panacea. In most urban areas, apartment letting is a seller's market, and little can be done to secure the upper hand on the landlord. If you will not sign, another lessee awaits in the hall, ready to accept the landlord's terms.

However, all is not lost. Ideally, you wish to keep disagreeable clauses out of the lease entirely, and your awareness of possible problems is to your advantage. Depending upon the city or state in which you reside, you may not need to resort to the courts for relief. State or municipal agencies will often assist an apparently tortured tenant. In many instances, tenant unions and associations have been formed by irate lessees to better promote their bargaining position in disputes. If all else fails, one can always turn to the judicial system, but legal relief can prove to be both time-consuming and expensive. A wary, alert and informed lessee can sidestep many of the common lease pitfalls without resorting to outside assistance.

To put the situation in proper perspective, a cursory comprehension of landlord-tenant law, its common-law origins and its current statutory status, is helpful. At its incipience, the concept of a leasehold was both contractual and personal. By creating convenants the landlord and tenant agreed to the performance or nonperformance of certain acts, the most obvious examples being the tenant's promise to pay a predetermined rent for which the landlord pledged not to oust the tenant from the leased property. As law progressed, the tenant's rights became more extensive until his defensible rights stemmed not just from the covenants, but from the possession of the land. Thus if the landlord sold the property to a third person or if an outsider forced the lessee from the leasehold, the tenant could maintain an action to recover possession against the third person, since his lease had developed into an estate, albeit a non-freehold estate.

It was this recognition by the law of a lease as an estate in land and not a contract in personalty that was the foundation of modern landlord-tenant law. The tenant now obtains an estate in the leasehold for a specified term; a position just short of actual ownership. For the length of the term the tenant has absolute control over the property—control so absolute, in fact, that it is good even against the landlord.

If this be the case, however, then why is the present-day tenant at such a disadvantage? The answer lies in supply and demand. Because of the serious shortage of adequate housing in most metropolitan areas, lessees are willing to subscribe to a lease with covenants granting the landlord the ultimate upperhand. In this sense, contract law does prevail, and a tenant, suddenly oppressed with a typical leasehold disaster, will find that he has unwittingly signed away his rights, under the lease. Although the time may not be too late to secure a final resolution in his favor, prevention at the outset could prove to be the saving grace in time, money and aggravation.

One covenant which any prospective tenant must sign is the one stating the rent which he must pay in order to have the possession of the property pass to him. The covenant to pay rent is usually the thorn in the tenant's side when a dispute arises. The reason for this is that the rent payment is not conditioned upon performance by the landlord under any of the other lease provisions. In most states, as long as the landlord has delivered the leasehold and thereafter does not commit any act of absolute or constructive eviction, the tenant is compelled to pay rent to the landlord as it accrues. The tenant, in other words, cannot rescind the lease once he commits himself to a term, whatever the period of time might be.

At one time, because the covenant to pay rent was independent in its own right, the landlord enjoyed the privilege of collecting rent from a vacated tenant without any responsibility to mitigate damages by seeking a replacement tenant. In fact, unless the lease specifically provided to the contrary, the landlord did not need to accept a third party offered by the original tenant, regardless of the reasonableness of the request. The tenant had contracted to pay a predetermined amount of rent for possession of the leased premises and pay it he must.

Although these tenets still prevail theoretically, in many jurisdictions state legislatures have intervened to alleviate this otherwise overly harsh rule of law. This result has been achieved by the statutory right of tenants to withhold rent from the landlord where the landlord has failed to perform one or more of his obligations under the lease. In New York, for example, the law allows a tenant singly to sue the landlord for failure to maintain the rent property in a safe manner. The tenant may, if the conditions are dangerous to life and health, ask the courts to serve as a receiver of rent monies and as a supervisor of repairs necessary to eliminate the unsafe conditions (Real Property Actions and Proceedings Law Sec. 755). Tenants living in a multiple dwelling also can force an uncooperative landlord to keep his building in good repair by collectively engaging in a rent strike (Real Property Actions and Proceedings Law Article 7-A). Again, the law requires the existence of conditions dangerous to life or health before a court can be permitted to collect rents for the sole purpose of paying for the repair of unsafe conditions. Although these laws greatly benefit tenants, they should be availed of cautiously and with the advice of competent counsel to be sure that all procedural requirements are complied with. Still, it is important to note that a landlord cannot manage his property carelessly and still demand rent from his tenants with impunity, despite the lease which provides the landlord with such "right."

Tenancies

Although the typical apartment lease runs for a set term as agreed to by the parties, there are basically four types of less-than-freehold estates. Since each type of tenancy carries with it its own legal quirks, it would be prudent to recognize the one under which you, as tenant, possess the land.

Signing a lease for two months, two years, or for any specified period of time, created an estate for years, an historical misnomer which might be better described as a *term tenancy*. This leasehold can come into existence only through an agreement between the landlord and tenant; an agreement which in most states must be reduced to writing if the term exceeds a year in length. At common law the major distinction between term tenancies of different lengths was the duration of the period in which a vacating tenant or landlord had to inform the other of the termination of the lease. Statutory law in most states now dictates that notice must be given which is equal to the period of the lease, except for leases for one year or more. Thus, in the case of a month-to-month tenancy, one party had to notify the other at least one month prior to his termination. Obviously such a requirement would place an undue burden upon parties to lengthier leases, so statutory law permits six months notice for termination of a year-to-year lease.

In some cases the parties to a lease agree to the rental, but do not establish a specific duration. The arrangement is known as a *periodic tenancy* which continues automatically from period to period until one party notifies the other within the prescribed time. That time is measured usually by the length of time covered in each rent payment. The major distinctions between a periodic tenancy and the third type of tenancy, a *tenancy at will*, is that in the latter the landlord and tenant must specifically agree to its creation and either can terminate at will. Otherwise, without expressed understanding, the payment of rent on any orderly, measurable period of time will lead to a periodic tenancy as an operation of law.

The fourth type is *tenancy at sufferance*. This situation occurs when a tenant who was originally in lawful possession of the premises under a prior lease does not vacate the leasehold at the end of the term. The landlord now has an option. If he wishes to continue letting the premises to the tenant and the tenant presents him with the rent payment, he can accept the offer and in effect reestablish the original lease. Thus, a tenant must be cautious not to commit himself unknowingly to another year term by holding over one month on the previous one-year lease and paying one month's rent. In such a situation, all provisions of the earlier lease are carried over and both parties become bound. One usual exception to this holdover rule applies to a seasonal lease where the landlord has no election to establish a period tenancy because the tenant holds over. The landlord, however, need not accept the rent and can consider the tenancy terminated. Still, to remove the holdover tenant, in most states, the landlord must inform the tenant of his intentions. Remember, however, that the landlord does not have this option where he expressly permits you to remain on the property, or for some other unforeseeable reason, you are unable to leave. Although you are still liable for rent prorated to the length of hold-over period, you are not binding yourself to another lease unless otherwise agreed to.

Covenants

A tenant might often hear the phrase, "covenants which run with the land." Covenants are the basic duties and obligations of the parties to the lease. Since they arise from the execution of the lease and actually delimit the scope of the landlord-tenant relationship, they become as much a part of the land as the landscaping. Should either party decide to pass his rights on, the subsequent taker is as readily bound by the terms of the lease as were the original parties. Because most leases now include "the parties, their heirs, executors, administrators, successors and *assigns*" for practical purposes all convenants "run with the land."

Covenants are the contractual elements of the lease, and as such, can be both expressed within the provisions of the lease or implied as a matter of law. In either case, the parties or their assignees or grantees are bound to honor them in order not to become liable for breach of a covenant. Unlike contract law, however, breach of a covenant does not necessarily allow repudiation of the lease by the wronged party.

For example, if a landlord merely disturbs the tenant in his enjoyment of the leasehold, without evicting him, the tenant cannot treat the disturbance as grounds for rescinding the lease. Instead, he is limited to a nuisance action against the landlord in tort law. In fact, if the nuisance orginates from a third source, without landlord interference, then the landlord is not liable under any law. Even though the tenant might be driven from the leasehold, his only recourse is against the third party creating the problem.

Since the covenants are the bearers of danger, it might be wise to familiarize yourself with landlord duties implied by law or firmly expressed in statute. A later comparison between a landlord's duties imposed by law and his obligations as they appear in his choicely worded lease will alert you to your rights— before you sign them away.

Covenant of Quiet Enjoyment

The landlord hereby covenants that the tenant, upon payment of the rent and upon performance of all the covenants and conditions herein contained, shall and may peaceably and quietly have, hold and enjoy the demised premises.

It is readily apparent that no tenant wishes to be disturbed in the enjoyment of his leasehold. The law recognized early that a landlord should not be in a position to be able to affect the agreement through acts intending to interfere with the tenancy. To safeguard the tenant's rights, the law therefore implies in each lease a covenant of quiet enjoyment.

In reality, the covenant is broader in scope than it may first appear to be, for not only does it protect the tenant against wrongful acts of his immediate landlord, it also extends to any successors to the landlord's interests. The landlord breaches the covenant at the outset if, in fact, he does not possess good and full title. If later, a third party appears and claims superior title, the landlord has violated his covenant to the tenant.

To invoke a cause of action for breach of the covenant of quiet enjoyment, the tenant must be forced to quit the premises. A nuisance so minor that it does not force the tenant from the leasehold may breach an expressed agreement between the parties leading to tort damages, but it does not give rise to an action under the implied covenant.

So, what are the tenant's remedies? The extent of the tenant's recourse against the landlord is usually contingent upon the degree of eviction. Generally the tenant may react as follows:

(a) Upon actual eviction. This action is an unequivocal invasion of the tenant's right to possession. In his defense the tenant may either treat the lease as terminated, thereby ending his duty to pay rent or, at his option, commence an action to regain possession.

(b) Upon partial actual eviction. This situation occurs when a third party, with superior title, forces the tenant from only a portion of the premises. For all practical purposes, the tenant's position is left unchanged, if the party asserting superior title wishes to continue leasing the disputed portion. Rent simply is apportioned between the holders of title. If the tenant is permanently deprived of part of the leasehold, he

JULIUS BLUMBERG, INC., PUBLISHER
62 WHITE STREET, NEW YORK, N. Y. 10013

LEASE AGREEMENT

This Lease is entered into on   19   between

who owns the building known as

and

who wants to rent Apt.   in that Building.

In this Lease,

will be called Landlord and

will be called Tenant. The words "Tenant's Guest" shall mean any person who uses or is in the Apartment.

APARTMENT

Landlord agrees that Tenant can use Apartment   (the word "Apartment" also means the Equipment
in it), from   to

TERM; USE

to live in with his family and relatives.

RENT AND PAYMENT

The rent shall be   per month and shall be paid on the first day of each month, except that
Tenant shall pay the first month's rent when this Lease is signed unless Tenant now lives in the Apartment.
Rent shall be paid by check or cash delivered to Landlord at

or at such other address as Landlord shall notify Tenant to use.

SERVICES BY LANDLORD

1. Landlord shall furnish the following to Tenant:*

*Cross out if not furnished

a. elevator service,

b. hot and cold water in reasonable amounts,

c. heat, as required by law,

d. air conditioning (Tenant to clean and change filters in units in the Apartment),

e. electricity,

f. repairs of the Apartment unless the damage was caused by Tenant or Tenant's Guest.

If any services are reduced or discontinued because of matters beyond the control of Landlord, Tenant may not withhold or reduce rent.

OBLIGATIONS AND UNDERTAKINGS BY TENANT

2. Tenant agrees that:

a. Tenant will pay the rent without any deductions, even if permitted by law.

b. Tenant waives the right it has under the law to cancel this Lease and collect damages if Landlord does not deliver possession of the Apartment to Tenant on the date the term of this Lease is supposed to start. However, Tenant does not have to pay rent until the date it does get possession.

c. Tenant will take good care of the Apartment.

d. Tenant will make all repairs to the Apartment required because of something Tenant or Tenant's Guest did or failed to do.

e. Tenant will comply with all laws, rules or regulations affecting the Apartment, including rules or regulations of insurance agencies.

f. If a claim is made against Landlord because of something Tenant or Tenant's Guest did or failed to do, Tenant will pay to Landlord any money which a court rules that Landlord must pay, as well as any legal fees or costs which Landlord must pay because of the claim.

g. Tenant will not, without Landlord's written approval:

1. install any panelling, flooring, "built-in" decorations, partitions or railings or do any painting or wall-papering;

2. drill into or attach anything to the floors, walls or ceilings of the Apartment;

3. put in any locks or chain-guards or change any lock-cylinders on the doors of the Apartment;

4. bring into the Apartment any dishwashing, clotheswashing or drying machines or any heating, ventilating, dehumidifying or air conditioning units or water-filled furniture;

5. keep any animal in the Apartment;

6. do or permit anything to be done in the Apartment which will cause an increase in the cost of fire insurance for Landlord;

7. put in any shades, blinds, screens, window guards, or signs or other things (other than curtains) in or outside of the windows of the Apartment; or

8. permit the accumulation of refuse in the Apartment.

REMOVAL
AT END
OF TERM

h. Tenant will remove all of its property at the end of this Lease and shall pay for any damage to the Apartment or Building caused by moving its property in or out of the Apartment. If Tenant leaves any of its property in the Apartment, Landlord may dispose of it and charge Tenant for the costs of disposal or keep it as abandoned property. At the end of this Lease, Tenant will leave the Apartment in as good condition as it was when the Lease started, subject to reasonable wear and tear and fire damage.

RULES OF
BUILDING

i. Tenant will comply with such reasonable rules as Landlord may adopt (on notice to Tenant) for the safety, care and cleanliness of the Building and the comfort, quiet and convenience of other tenants.

NO LIABILITY

j. Landlord shall not be liable for injury or damage to Tenant or Tenant's Guests or their property unless it results from something Landlord or Landlord's agents, servants or employees did or failed to do.

INSPECTION
BY
LANDLORD

k. Landlord and its agents and employees may inspect the Apartment at any reasonable time, may have prospective purchasers of the Building and, during the last 6 months of the Lease, prospective tenants, view the Apartment between 9 A.M. and 8 P.M. Landlord may authorize workmen to enter at reasonable times in order to make repairs, improvements or decorations in the Apartment or Building; if Tenant is not there, Landlord may enter by a master key or if Tenant has changed the lock or done something else to prevent entry Landlord may enter by force.

TENANT
TAKES
"AS IS"

l. Tenant shall take the Apartment in its present condition, except that Landlord shall do the work indicated in Article 5 of this Lease.

NO
ASSIGNMENT
OR
SUBLETTING

m. Tenant shall not assign this Lease or enter into a sublease unless it is allowed by a law of the State of New York. If Tenant makes an assignment or sublease, with or without the consent of Landlord, Landlord may collect rent from the new tenant and deduct it from any money Tenant owes under this Lease. If Landlord collects rent from the new tenant is does not mean that Landlord consents to the assignment or sublease. Tenant shall remain liable under this Lease after a sublease or assignment, unless released by Landlord or unless otherwise provided by law.

SUB-
ORDINATION

n. This Lease shall be subject and subordinate to the lien of all mortgages which now or in the future affect the Building. This means that the holder of a mortgage can, if it so elects, end this Lease upon a sale of the Building in a foreclosure of the mortgage.

RELEASE OF
LANDLORD

o. Landlord shall have no further liability under this Lease on the date it sells or leases the Building, but shall remain liable for things which happened before that date.

DEFAULT

p. If Tenant does not comply with the terms of this Lease, Landlord may give a notice to Tenant demanding that Tenant must correct the default. If Tenant does not correct the default within 5 days after the date the notice is mailed (or within such longer period of time as may be reasonably required, if Tenant begins to correct the default in the 5-day period and thereafter continues to act diligently) then Landlord may give a second notice that this Lease shall end on the date set forth in the second notice. The date set forth in the second notice must be not less than 5 days nor more than 10 days after the date the second notice is mailed. On the date set forth in the second notice this Lease shall end and Tenant shall deliver possession of the Apartment to Landlord, but Tenant shall remain liable under this Lease.

TENANT
LIABLE FOR
DAMAGES

q. If this Lease has been ended as provided above, then Landlord may re-enter and take possession of the Apartment by any lawful means, and remove Tenant and Tenant's Guests and their property, by dispossess proceedings, or otherwise, without being liable in any way. Landlord may re-rent the Apartment and any rent received by Landlord shall be used first to pay Landlord's expenses in getting possession and re-renting the Apartment, including, without being limited to, reasonable legal fees and costs, fees of brokers, advertising costs and the cost of cleaning, repairing and decorating the Apartment, and second to pay any amounts Tenant owes under this Lease. Landlord has no duty to re-rent the Apartment. Tenant shall pay to Landlord on the first day of each month any amounts Tenant owes under this Lease, less, if Landlord re-rents the Apartment, any amounts received from the new tenant and not used by Landlord to pay the expenses referred to above.

3. Landlord and Tenant agree as follows:

FIRE OR
OTHER
DAMAGES

a. If there is a fire or other casualty in the Building and Landlord advises Tenant within 10 days thereafter that it has decided not to repair the damage, this Lease shall end as of the date of the fire and any rent paid by Tenant for a period after that date shall be refunded to Tenant. If Landlord does repair the damage, it shall be done as soon as practical and if the Apartment cannot be used, no rent shall be payable from the date of the damage until the date it can be used. Tenant hereby gives up the right to end the Lease when the Apartment is unusable, except in a case where there is less than 6 months left in the term of this Lease. Each party hereby gives up any right of recovery against the other party for any loss in connection with any fire damage.

CONDEMNATION

b. If the Building or the Apartment is taken by a governmental agency or other body having the right to take property, this Lease shall end on the date of the taking and Tenant shall have no claim for the value of this Lease. Any rent paid by Tenant for a period after the date of the taking shall be refunded to Tenant.

c. Tenant has paid to Landlord $ as a security deposit which will be deposited in

a banking institution

located at   in an interest bearing account.
If Tenant is in default under this Lease, Landlord may use the security deposit, with the interest it earns, to pay amounts owed by Tenant under this Lease, including damages if this Lease is ended. The security deposit, with interest, less a fee for expenses equal to 1% per year of the amount of the security deposit, will be paid to Tenant within 15 days after this Lease ends.

d. Landlord and Tenant each waive trial by a jury in any matter which comes up between them under this Lease or because of this Lease (except for a personal injury or property damage claim). In a proceeding to get possession of the Apartment, Tenant shall not have the right to make a counterclaim.

e. Any notice by Landlord or Tenant to the other, or any consent by Landlord, must be in writing and must be personally delivered to Tenant or mailed by registered or certified mail (return receipt requested) in a stamped envelope addressed (i) to Tenant at the Building and (ii) to Landlord at

or to such other address as Landlord shall specify by notice to Tenant.

f. The provisions of this Lease shall run in favor of and be for the benefit of Landlord and Tenant and anybody who succeeds to their respective interests in this Lease.

4. Landlord agrees that:

If Tenant pays the rent and is not in default under this Lease, Tenant shall and may peaceably and quietly have, hold and enjoy the Apartment for the term of this Lease, subject to present and future mortgages as stated above.

5. Work to be done by Landlord:

The parties have entered into this **Lease** on the date first mentioned above.

LANDLORD:

TENANT:

WITNESS:

----

still is liable for rent, but at a reduced amount, to compensate him for his loss.

(c) Upon constructive eviction. Sometimes, the landlord's actions which lead to eviction are negative, rather than affirmative. For example, his failure to supply heat or water to an apartment, thereby rendering the premise uninhabitable, will breach the covenant of quiet enjoyment. If after notification of substantial interference, the landlord does not act, the tenant can abandon the premises and terminate his obligations.

(d) Upon partial constructive eviction. Again, if the landlord has failed to perform his duties, but only as to a portion of the leasehold, the tenant can adjust his rent accordingly, if he has abandoned the unfit portion.

As for damages from a breach of the covenant, the tenant can request and recover all damages he incurs as a result of the eviction. This sum is inclusive of the value of the remaining, unexpired term. If the landlord's intentional act or failure of title occurs at the outset and prevents the tenant from taking his rightful possession, then damages include the full value of the leasehold as well as any expenses shouldered by the tenant in order to assume possession.

Sometimes the covenant of quiet enjoyment is an expressed provision of the lease. Although this would appear to strengthen the tenant's rights if the clause does not cover all ramifications of the implied covenant, the landlord can be absolved from certain wrongful acts. In particular, if the provision makes no mention of landlord's warranty of good title, the tenant would be precluded from obtaining relief where a third party ousts him because of superior title.

Covenant to Pay Rent

In return for giving up possession of his land, the landlord collects rent from the lessee. Rent is the tenant's payment for use of the leasehold and does not arise from the promise to pay, but rather from the possession of the land.

Why then, do leases contain rent provisions, if the tenant is bound to make payment without it? By expressly committing himself, the tenant covenants to continue to pay rent for the entire length of the term at an agreed price. What was without the lease privity of estate now becomes privity of contract, and the tenant can no longer pack up, move on and not be liable for rent that accrues for the remainder of the term.

However, the tenant also benefits. Although he cannot terminate the lease at will, he need not fear capricious actions by the landlord. Not only is the term fixed so that the length of the tenancy is assured, but the amount of rent is set and the landlord cannot whimsically increase it during the term.

Expressed Covenants to Repair

Although the law imposes certain duties to repair on the landlord in the absence of a clause in the lease, normally all leases of premises will expressly delegate duties between the parties. The most common phrasing requires the tenant to make all repairs necessary to keep the leasehold tenantable and return it to the landlord in as good condition as received.

The tenant should be alert not to sign a lease which requires a greater duty. Some covenants state that the tenant will maintain the premises in *good* repair which could be construed as a duty on the tenant to put the premises in good repair if it is not already. This extra burden could prove costly and should be avoided.

By consenting to make tenantable repairs, what must the tenant do? Tenantable repairs is a phrase originating at common law. In the absence of an expressed covenant, the tenant must make all reasonable repairs which will leave the property in the same condition as when he took possession. At no time is he liable for major repairs to the structure. Neither is he liable for normal wear and tear and in some states, such as New York, a tenant may terminate a lease if the premises become untenantable through ordinary wear and tear.

If the tenant does not agree expressly to tenantable repairs, but only to keep premises in repair (remember not *good* repair), then he becomes liable for major repairs and reconstruction. Many states, however, have legislated against this unfair result by both relieving the tenant of the obligation and permitting him to move out. Otherwise, under an expressed covenant to repair, the tenant is liable for all repairs, including reconstruction, regardless of their cause.

If the landlord expressly covenants to make repairs, then he is in breach if he fails to repair, after having knowledge of the defect. The tenant has a duty to notify the landlord. Thereafter, the tenant can proceed with all minor repairs and in some states deduct the cost from the rent; in some states he can demand recompense. If the extent of the repairs needed is major, the tenant has an option to either bear the immediate cost and sue for reimbursement or sue for damages based on the reduced value of the premises.

Of course, as we stated earlier, the law has made substantial and significant inroads into the landlord's right to collect rent. Basically, the landlord's right is absolute; however, should he neglect the leasehold, and, as a result, it falls into disrepair, certain laws allow tenants to seek relief by asking the local courts to step in and assume control over the expenditure of rents in order to make sure that dangerous conditions are eliminated.

Implied Covenants to Repair

We mentioned at the outset of this chapter that the law in certain instances steps in to relieve the tenant of his requirement to pay rent to the landlord and forces the landlord to keep his property safe for its inhabitants. Although the particular statutes we are discussing are applicable only in New York State, other states and municipalities have seen fit to protect tenants from unscrupulous landlords by passing similar laws and ordinances. If you are having problems obtaining needed repairs to your own apartment or the building in which your apartment is located, you should consult an attorney to determine whether you can take legal action in your jurisdiction under similar statutes to force your landlord to act.

We have used the term "withholding of rent" in the opening of this chapter, but this term is actually a misnomer. Under a Sec. 755 proceeding or an Article 7-A proceeding, the tenant is not altogether escaping his rent obli-

gations. In fact, he must continue to pay rent when due under the terms of his lease, but payment is made to the court or court-appointed administrator, rather than to the landlord or his agent.

The reason for directing payment to someone operating under the authority of the courts is to assure that monies are channeled into repair of the leasehold. Before a tenant can approach the courts for relief under these statutes, a condition or conditions must exist or be likely to develop which are "dangerous to life, health, or safety." If the landlord cannot disprove these allegations or show that the tenant has created these conditions directly or indirectly, the court will collect the rent and dispense funds only to pay repairmen, janitors or utilities, depending upon the problem. Once the dangerous condition is remedied, the court will give the landlord any rents it holds in excess of the cost of repair or maintenance; but, as long as you have obtained your objective, there is nothing wrong with the landlord receiving the balance of rents paid to the court.

Until recently, these two proceedings, RPAPL Sec. 755 and Article 7-A, were the only ways a tenant could use the leverage of non-payment of his rent to force a landlord to live up to his end of the bargain. Rent withholding and the rent strike were placed on the books in order to offer tenants relief from an imminent danger. The New York State Legislature has now gone one step further. In 1975, Sec. 235-b of the Real Property Law was passed which stated that every landlord impliedly warranted that his building was,

> . . . fit for human habitation and *further uses reasonably intended by the parties* and that the occupants of such premises shall not be subjected to any conditions which would be dangerous, hazardous or detrimental to their life, health or safety. (Italics added.)

Although the imminent-danger clause of action is reiterated, the law also provides a rule of reason policy that both parties must get what they bargained for. The law, establishing what is referred to as the warranty of habitability, has enabled tenants to collect where landlords have not repaired stoves, ceilings and air conditioners, eliminated unwelcomed odors or toned down noisy neighbors. The courts have interpreted the new statute as a defense against non-payment of rent, and, upon proving the amount of damages involved, have allowed an appropriate abatement of rent. From now on, if the landlord does not maintain a habitable leasehold, the tenant has grounds for an adjustment of rent, regardless of contrary provisions in the lease.

Covenants on Personal Liability

Becoming legally trapped by a clause requiring you to bear the cost of repairs to the leasehold is certainly aggravating. But with today's jury awards in personal liability suits, nothing could be as odious or as financially onerous to the tenant as a clause relieving the landlord of all liability and casting it upon the tenant.

As a general rule, the tenant, as holder of the premises, is liable to third parties who are injured while rightfully on the premises. The distinguishing factor revolves upon the nature of the defect. If the defect is patent, one which the tenant could observe upon reasonable inspection of the premises, then the landlord is relieved of any obligation should injury result. On the other hand, the law does not hold the tenant liable for injury arising from defects which he could not readily observe and of which the landlord does not inform him. The landlord never warrants that the premises are free of latent defects and thus incurs no liability through privity of contract. His duty is fully discharged simply by informing the tenant of those defects of which he has knowledge. Still, should the landlord knowingly or negligently conceal a dangerous condition, he is liable in either fraud or negligence

to the tenant and for injuries or damages which proximately result.

The rental of a fully furnished residential premise imposes a greater duty upon the landlord. Although his liability continues for a willful or negligent failure to notify the tenant, he also is liable for patent as well as hidden dangers. In such a situation the law imposes an implied warranty by the landlord that the premises are in good repair. If the premises are not as implied, the landlord breaches the warranty and is liable for injury as a result.

In addition to the above instances where the landlord is liable for breach of warranty, certain circumstances permit the tenant to sue the landlord directly. If the landlord, after being notified of a dangerous condition by the tenant, endeavors to repair, he obligates himself to correct the condition, with reasonable care. Failure to meet this duty can result in liability. Common areas in multiple dwellings can also lead to liability. Since the common areas, such as halls and passageways, are not part of the demised premises, the landlord retains possession and incurs liability if injury results.

One other liability exception which exists in some states places the onus on a landlord who leases for a short term a building which he knows will be used by the public. If he is aware of a dangerous condition or if it can be shown that he should have known of its existence, any member of the public who is injured as a result can hold the landlord liable. Thus a tenant who is in the practice of leasing out halls or arenas for public showings is sheltered from personal liability for injuries caused by defective conditions in the building.

Additional Covenants

Parties to a lease can limit and restrict the leasehold as they see fit. Covenants, enforceable as contract rights, can be drawn to meet the particular needs of the situation. For example, in apartment leases, covenants forbidding assignment of the lease or subletting are common. Many leases also describe the use to which the premises can be put. Whatever the case, the tenant should be aware that any right which he might have as a matter of law can be extinguished by a pro-landlord lease.

Hopefully, the reader now possesses comprehension of basic lease law. Still, the purpose is not to make anyone skilled in legal theory, but to offer practical knowledge sufficient to alert the reader to possible legal entanglements. To this end, let us dissect specific lease provisions, so as to pinpoint those that should be avoided.

Typical Lease Provisions

Now that we have covered the basic knowledge concerning what is a lease and how it works, it is time to sift through the provisions of a typical lease and examine those clauses or phrases which can curtail tenants' rights and increase liabilities. These provisions are ones which are standard for leases used in states which have not yet adopted "plain English" laws.

As with most legal documents, the parties involved are identified in the initial provision. Few legal complications arise from this provision. However, some of the identification provisions are quite extensive. These provisions may limit the purpose for which the leasehold can be used and the number of occupants allowed to reside in it. The problems are few as long as the lessee does not bind himself to reside in a leasehold in which he intitially had intended to operate some kind of enterprise—for example, a laundromat. In other words, the intended use of the premises should be stated clearly. The tenant should also be certain that the length of the tenancy

and the terms of payment of the rent meet his satisfaction. Once the parties are named, the following 14 explanations cover some provisions which will likely confront the prospective tenant.

(1) Rent is a foregone conclusion. By holding the leasehold, the tenant has an obligation to pay rent. One advantage of the lease, as has been mentioned, is that the terms and amount of rent have been already determined. Lease forms contain the clause: "rent and any 'additional rent' . . . as the Landlord may designate from time to time hereafter." Regardless of the prospective tenant's bargaining position, he should demand that this clause be eliminated. When the tenant agrees to this clause, the landlord enjoys the freedom of hiking up the rent almost at whim. The tenant has lost his advantage in having the rent expressed definitively in the lease. The tenant must be cautious not to bind himself to a future occurrence which may be to his disfavor.

(2) Generally all leases require that the tenant "take good care of the premises and fixtures." This clause can be distinguished from a convenant to maintain the premises in *good* repair, which places a greater burden on the tenant. Under this clause, the tenant agrees only to maintain the premises in its current condition. Generally, the provision continues by holding the tenant responsible for the cost of repairs resulting from the tenant's misuse or neglect. Such a contingency seems equitable, but the tenant should read inquisitively and ascertain that he has not committed himself to repairs other than those needed as a result of his own fault. Unless he (or a party through him) is at fault, the tenant's promise to repair should be limited to those of keeping the premises tenantable.

(3) In the chapter on realty, an explanation of *appurtenances* and *personalty* is presented. Most leases make reference to appurtenances, fixtures and personalty. For our purposes the legal distinction is irrelevant. However, the tenant should not that most leases contain a clause which gives the landlord title to any improvements which the tenant makes to the premises. "All alterations or improvements made by the tenant shall be made only with the prior written consent of the landlord and at the sole expense of the tenant and shall become the property of the landlord and be surrendered with the apartment at the end of the term." What does this mean? First, the tenant must petition for approval; secondly, if granted, his improvement becomes the landlord's property. Thus, if the tenant affixes or builds anything, such as security door locks, a bedloft, curtain rods, shelving, etc., he forsakes title in them in favor of the landlord.

(4) It was mentioned above that the tenant should never agree to future provisions, such as rent increases. Although most rules and regulations which landlords adopt are inconsequential, seldom obeyed, and never enforced, the landlord does have grounds for evicting a tenant who does not comply with them, if the tenant is on notice of the restrictions at the onset and agrees to each specifically. Problems arise where the tenant also agrees to obey "such further reasonable Rules and Regulations as the Landlord may from time to time make or adopt. . . ." The tenant's duty may be limited to following "*reasonable* rules and regulations." However, the tenant should be aware that these provisions can be used as leverage to evict the tenant. If the landlord wishes to remove the tenant, a newly adopted rule or regulation, whether meritorious or whimsical, may create a violation and leave the tenant on the street.

(5) Inevitably, the landlord will attempt to hold the tenant liable for rent in the event of the partial or total destruction of the premises. Before the enactment of statutes to the contrary, the landlord would only be reiterating the common-law rule concerning premises by stating in the lease that "if the building shall be damaged by fire or other cause without the fault or neglect of the tenant . . . the damages shall be repaired as soon as reasonably convenient by and at the expense of the landlord, and no claim for compensation shall be made by reason of inconvenience or annoyance arising from the necessity of repairing any portion of the building." However, the renting of an apartment bears different consequences. The distinction turns on whether or not the subject matter of the leasehold includes an apartment, loft, or a building and the land on which it sits. In the latter instance, the destruction of the building does not terminate the leasehold or the tenant's obligation to pay rent. Many states, such as New York, have enacted statutes to remedy this apparently inequitable result. Thus, if the premises become untenantable due to an act of nature, the tenancy is ended upon the tenant's surrender. The landlord can preclude this right of the tenant by a provision in the lease which supercedes the statute.

If the tenant has no interest whatsoever in the land, as is the case with a strict apartment lease, the law changes and terminates the lease upon total destruction of the premises rented. However in many cases, this law is circumvented by a clause to the contrary. Thus if the lease states "if the building shall be damaged by fire or other cause without the fault or neglect of the Tenant, . . . the damages shall be repaired as soon as reasonably convenient by and at the expense of the landlord, and no claim for compensation shall be made by reason of inconvenience or annoyance . . ." then the tenant finds the lease still in effect; but during the time the building is untenantable, the rent is abated. The tenant must find suitable and temporary housing until the original leasehold is repaired, at which time, the rent obligation commences anew. Of course, the landlord agrees to repair "as soon as reasonably convenient," but the tenant should realize that complications could arise from such a nebulous provision.

(6) Whenever possible, people attempt to disclaim all liability, and a landlord is no different. Most disclaimer provisions refer to both personal and property damages and to all sources of possible injury (e.g., steam, electricity, gas, water, rain, ice or snow) and generally (". . . or arising from any other cause or happening whatsoever . . ."). The actual liability of the landlord has been discussed previously. The prospective tenant should understand that many leases exceed reasonable limits of disclaimers. Although some landlords accept liability resulting from personal injury or property damage caused by their own or their agent's negligence, others attempt to have the tenant indemnify them for all claims arising from the leasehold. Clauses such as "the Landlord shall not be liable for *any injury* to person or loss or damage to property . . ." are common. The important point for the tenant to realize, however, is that these all-inclusive provisions are not tenable, if taken to court. Unfortunately, this method of dealing with the problem can become expensive, so that complete avoidance of these provisions is recommended.

(7) After a hard day's work, the tenant returns home only to find the landlord in the apartment. The landlord is using the tenant's apartment as a model in order to rent a similar unit to a prospective lessee. Outraged at the invasion, the tenant demands that the parties leave only to be reminded of his lease which states that "the Landlord

shall be permitted to enter the apartment during reasonable hours to make such repairs . . . and to inspect or exhibit the apartment to prospective lessees or purchasers of the building. . . . If the Tenant shall not be personally present to open and permit an entry into the apartment, at any time, when for any reason an entry shall be in the judgment of the Landlord or the Landlord's agent necessary or permissible hereunder, the Landlord or the Landlord's agent may enter same by pass key or may forcibly enter the same without incurring any liability or responsibility . . ." As with the landlord's disclaimer of liability, this sweeping grant of authority to enter the apartment will normally be frowned upon by the courts. Some states, such as New York, charge the landlord with triple damages for forcible entry. However, the force must be unusual or violent and not merely the breaking of the lock. Without this provision, of course, the landlord would have no right, except in emergency situations, to invade the leasehold. His invasion would be tantamount to trespass. The tenant should know that intrusions such as the one described are not breaches of the covenant of quiet enjoyment and therefore, do not constitute eviction, constructive or actual. If the lease has been executed and the landlord exploits this provision, remember that his rights under the clause are limited. He must act reasonably and cannot use the provision as a weapon to harrass the tenant.

(8) Several references are made to tenant's failure under the lease and the landlord's rights to terminate the leasehold and reenter the premises with or without notice. The legal entanglements that could ensue in the event that the tenant does breach the lease are manifold, complicated and beyond the scope of this book. In almost all of these situations, state or municipal laws define what procedure the landlord must follow in

order to regain possession. He cannot restrict that procedure by having the tenant waive his rights. Usually these laws require a notice to the tenant demanding compliance. Until the landlord does so, the tenant legally can have the action dismissed in court. Thereafter, a formal dispossess proceeding must be instituted which conforms to all rules and laws of procedure. The tenant must be served with all appropriate papers notifying him of the proceeding. In any event, where legal action has been commenced by the landlord, the tenant should not feel bound by the terms of the lease. The tenant has rights. An attorney should be consulted who can inform him of these rights and advocate his position.

(9) The tenant should always be careful not to contract to pay any of the fees of the landlord's attorney under any condition. What legal costs the landlord incurs are his financial burden and should not be assumed by the tenant. For this reason, be wary and request deletion of any clause which reads that ". . . in such event, the sum or sums so paid by the Landlord together with all interests, costs, damages, and reasonable attorney's fees shall be considered additional rent . . ." One further note—usually, additional financial obligations which might arise from covenants in a lease are labeled as "additional rent." If the tenant recalls the explanation of the independence of the covenant for rent, the reason becomes clear. If the tenant must agree to bear the landlord's financial liability, he should do so separately from his duty to pay rent.

(10) Most consumers would not buy an article without examining it, and the same holds true for letting an apartment. The tenant should always inspect the premises, note defects and make arrangements with the landlord to cure those defects. The problem is that the lease contains a provision, agreed to between the parties: "No representation or promises with respect to the apartment have been made by the Landlord . . . The assumption of the occupancy by the Tenant shall be conclusive evidence that the apartment and the building of which it is part were in good and satisfactory condition at such time." The answer to the problem is simply to include in the lease all agreements to repair or cure defects in the apartment. In this manner, the landlord will be unable to deny later his promises.

(11) "In the event the apartment is not ready for occupancy at the set time herein for commencement of the term . . . this lease shall remain in full force and effect . . . the Landlord shall not be liable for the failure to give possession on said date. . . ." As mentioned earlier, all leases contain an implied covenant to give possession at the time set for the beginning of the term. Once the tenant is unable to take possession, regardless of the cause, he is no longer bound by the lease and can sue the landlord for breach of the covenant. By the clause above, the tenant waives this implied covenant and continues to be obligated by the terms of the lease even though occupancy is delayed.

(12) One clause to which serious consideration should be given is a renewal option at the same rental value for whatever term is agreeable to the parties. If the lease already contains a renewal clause, the tenant should consider whether he is agreeable to the terms it sets out before signing the lease. If no renewal provision exists, he should discuss with the landlord the possibility of including one.

(13) Most leases contain hidden clauses against *subletting* and *assignments*. An assignment is an extension of the original lease which transfers the entirety of the

tenant's interest in all or part of the premises; a sublease is a new landlord-tenant relationship carved out of part of the term of the original leasehold. In either instance, the original tenant remains liable to the landlord for all convenants agreed to in the lease. The assignor-tenant is relieved, however, for liability for breach of implied convenants after the assignment. The assignee (new tenant) becomes obligated to the original landlord under all covenants in the lease, whereas the sublessee is only responsible to his landlord, the original tenant, for covenants contained in the sublease. The sample sublease form presented here incorporates all of the covenants of the original lease; room is left for amendments. Parties to either should realize that form prevails over label and, so what is in fact an assignment, cannot be made a sublease simply by naming it such. Where no restrictions exist, the tenant can either assign or sublet as he pleases. However, where he is forbidden to do either, his sublet or assignment is voidable by the landlord. Whether the landlord can re-enter and terminate the leasehold if the tenant breaches a covenant against either act, is contingent upon reservation of the right in the lease. Otherwise, the landlord is limited to suing for damages for breach of the covenant. If the tenant anticipates executing either an assignment or sublease, he should be cautious not to agree to a prohibition of such in the lease. Additionally, he should know that a restriction on subletting does not prohibit assigning and vice versa.

As the result of a 1975 New York law, inappropriately alluded to as the right-to-sublet-law, many New York tenants feel they have an absolute right to sublet their apartments, regardless of a prohibition in the lease. All the law permits, contrary to popular belief, is the right to request a clause in your lease authorizing subletting.

You can ask, but if your landlord denies your request you cannot rent your place out to a subtenant. All is not lost, however, since you may be able to get out of your lease altogether if your landlord unreasonably refuses to add such a provision to your lease. In those instances where your main goal is to get out from under the monthly rent burdens, you actually come out ahead by breaking the lease, since you have no further obligation to the landlord. Remember you still remain fully liable should your subtenant or assignee fail to comply with all terms of the lease. However, where you wish to retain your apartment, your only choice is to concede and to sign a lease without a "right to sublet" clause.

(14) Most leases require the tenant to secure his promise to perform according to the covenants of the lease by depositing money with the landlord. This provision is a valid demand on the landlord's part and can be for any sum to which the parties agree.

Many states place restrictions on the landlord's use of the money. In New York, for example, statutory law states that such money advanced as a security deposit on a contract for the lease of real property must be placed in an interest-bearing account, with the depositor or tenant retaining full possession of the money. The landlord becomes trustee of the account which cannot be commingled with his personal assets. For the tenant's concern, he should remember that the security deposit may be retained by the landlord only to the extent of the damages—the remainder must be returned. In other words, if the deposit was $300.00 and damage to the leasehold sustained by the landlord totals $100.00, the landlord could not claim that he was entitled to the entire sum because the tenant breached the lease.

Sample Leases

The first lease printed here covering the renting of an apartment is not typical of most, since it has been revised to comply with the plain language law (see chapter 1) of New York. The office lease, on the other hand, contains provisions similar to those we have just discussed. You should remember, however, that each lease is peculiar unto itself at times. For example, a furnished apartment lease covers not only the space but the personalty inside. In effect, the tenant is renting every chair, lamp and utensil with the apartment. Thus, he might be wise to be more cautious and take an inventory describing the condition of valuable items, so that he is not later charged with their damage. Whatever the lease, however, where confusion prevails beforehand or disputes flare up after the signing, the tenant should consult an attorney for advice on handling the matter confronting him.

A 254—Form of Office Lease Approved by the Committee on Real Property Law of The Association of the Bar of the City of New York.

PRINTED BY JULIUS BLUMBERG, INC., LAW BLANK PUBLISHERS 80 EXCHANGE PLACE AT BROADWAY, NEW YORK

NOTE: THIS LEASE PROVIDES, IN ARTICLE 6, FOR THE FURNISHING BY THE LANDLORD TO THE TENANT OF ELECTRICITY AND AIR CONDITIONING. IF THE TENANT IS TO OBTAIN ITS OWN ELECTRICITY BY SEPARATE METER, SUBDIVISION (e) SHOULD BE DELETED FROM ARTICLE 6; IF THE LANDLORD IS NOT TO SUPPLY AIR CONDITIONING, SUBDIVISION (f) SHOULD BE DELETED THEREFROM.

Lease, made the   day of   19

between

whose address is

(hereinafter called Landlord)

and

whose address is

(hereinafter called Tenant)

DESCRIPTION WITNESSETH: Landlord hereby leases to Tenant and Tenant hereby hires from Landlord, the space as presently constituted (hereinafter called the Premises) known as

on the   floor in the building known as

in

New York (hereinafter called the Building),

TERM   FOR A TERM to commence on   19
             and end at 12 o'clock noon on   19
or on such earlier date as this Lease may terminate as hereinafter provided, except that, if any such date falls on a Sunday or a holiday, then this Lease shall end at 12 o'clock noon on the business day next preceding the
RENTAL   aforementioned date, AT THE ANNUAL RENTAL RATE OF $

payable in equal monthly instalments, in advance, on the first day of each calendar month during the term. Landlord acknowledges receipt from Tenant of the sum of $ by check, for rent to and including the   day of   19   .

If Landlord is unable to give possession of the Premises on the date of commencement of the term of this Lease by reason of the holding over of any tenant or occupant, or because construction, repairs or improvements are not completed, rent shall abate for the period that possession by Tenant is delayed. If such delay shall continue for more than 45 days, then Tenant may, within 10 days after the expiration of said 45 day period, give Landlord a notice of election to terminate this Lease. Unless possession of the Premises shall sooner be made available to Tenant, this Lease shall terminate on the 10th day after the giving of said notice and Landlord shall return to Tenant the consideration paid. Landlord shall have no obligation to Tenant for failure to give possession except as above provided.

The parties further agree as follows:

PURPOSE   1. Tenant shall use and occupy the Premises as

and for no other purpose. Landlord represents that the Premises may lawfully be used for said purpose.

COVENANT TO PAY RENT   2. Tenant shall pay rent and additional rent to Landlord at Landlord's said address or at such other place as Landlord may designate in writing, without demand and without counterclaim, deduction or set-off.

CARE AND REPAIR OF PREMISES   3. Tenant shall commit no act of waste and shall take good care of the Premises and the fixtures and appurtenances therein, and shall, in the use and occupancy of the Premises, conform to all laws, orders and regulations of the Federal, State and Municipal governments, or any of their departments, and regulations of the New York Board of Fire Underwriters, applicable to the Premises; Landlord shall make all necessary repairs to the Premises, except where the repair has been made necessary by misuse or neglect by Tenant or Tenant's agents, servants, visitors or licensees. All improvements made by Tenant to the Premises which are so attached to the Premises that they cannot be removed without material injury to the Premises, shall become the property of Landlord upon installation. Not later than the last day of the term Tenant shall, at Tenant's expense, remove all of Tenant's personal property and those improvements made by Tenant which have not become the property of Landlord, including trade fixtures, cabinet work, movable paneling, partitions and the like, repair all injury done by or in connection with the installation or removal of said property and improvements, and surrender the Premises in as good condition as they were at the beginning of the term, reasonable wear, and damage by fire, the elements, casualty, or other cause not due to the misuse or neglect by Tenant or Tenant's agents, servants, visitors or licensees, excepted. All property of Tenant remaining on the Premises after the last day of the term of this Lease shall conclusively be deemed abandoned and may be removed by Landlord, and Tenant shall reimburse Landlord for the cost of such removal. Landlord may have any such property stored at Tenant's risk and expense.

NEGATIVE COVENANTS   4. Tenant shall not, without Landlord's written consent: (a) make any alterations, additions or improvements in, to or about the Premises; (b) do or suffer anything to be done on the Premises which will increase the rate of fire insurance on the Building; (c) permit the accumulation of waste or refuse matter; (d) abandon the Premises or suffer the Premises to become vacant **NO ASSIGNMENT** or deserted; or (e) assign, mortgage, pledge or **NO SUBLETTING** encumber this Lease, in whole or in part, or underlet the Premises or any part thereof. Covenant (e) above shall be binding upon the legal representatives of Tenant, and upon every person to whom Tenant's interest under this Lease passes by operation of law, but shall not apply to assignment or subletting to the parent or subsidiary of a corporate Tenant or to consolidation or merger of such Tenant.

RULES AND REGULATIONS   5. Tenant shall observe and comply with the rules and regulations hereinafter set forth, which are made part hereof, and with such further reasonable rules and regulations as Landlord may prescribe, on written notice to Tenant, for the safety, care and cleanliness of the Building and the comfort, quiet and convenience of other occupants of the Building.

SERVICES   6. Landlord shall furnish the following services: (a) passenger elevator service on business days, except Saturdays, from 8:30 A.M. to 6:00 P.M., it being agreed that at all other times, there shall be one eleva-**ELEVATOR, HEAT, WATER, CLEANING** tor subject to call; (b) heat when and as required by law, on business days; (c) hot and cold water for lavatory purposes without charge, but if a further supply of water is required by Tenant, Tenant shall, at Tenant's expense, install (and shall thereafter maintain at Tenant's expense) a water meter to register such consumption, and Tenant shall pay as additional rent, when and as bills are rendered, for water consumed, at the cost to Landlord, and for sewer rents and all other rents and charges based upon such consumption of water; (d) cleaning services customary in the Building from time to time, if the Premises are used exclusively as offices; (e) subject to the **ELECTRICITY AND AIR CONDITIONING** provisions of Article 7, electricity for usual office requirements; and (f) air cooling, during the appropriate season, on business days, except Saturdays, from 8:30 A.M. to 6:00 P.M.

ELECTRIC LOAD   7. Tenant shall not use any electrical equipment which in Landlord's reasonable opinion will overload the wiring installations or interfere with the reasonable use thereof by Landlord or other tenants in the Building.

DAMAGE BY FIRE   8. If the Building is damaged by fire or any other cause to such extent that the cost of restoration, as reasonably estimated by Landlord, will equal or exceed 30% of the replacement value of the Building (exclusive of foundations) just prior to the occurrence of the damage, then Landlord may, no later than the 60th day following the damage, give Tenant a notice of election to terminate this Lease, or if said cost of restoration will equal or exceed 50% of said replacement value and if the Premises shall not be reasonably usable for the purposes for which they are leased hereunder, then Tenant may, no later than the 60th day following the damage, give Landlord a notice of election to terminate this Lease. In the event of either of said elections this Lease shall be deemed to terminate on the 3rd day after the giving of said notice, and Tenant shall surrender possession of the Premises within a reasonable time thereafter, and the rent and additional rent shall be apportioned as of the date of said surrender and any rent paid for any period beyond said date shall be repaid to Tenant. If the cost of restoration as estimated by Landlord shall amount to less than 30% of said replacement value of the Building, or if despite the cost Landlord does not elect to terminate this Lease, Landlord shall restore the Building and the Premises with reasonable promptness, subject to delays beyond Landlord's control and delays in the making of insurance adjustments by Landlord, and Tenant shall have no right to terminate this Lease except as herein provided. Landlord need not restore fixtures and improvements owned by Tenant.

In any case in which use of the Premises is affected by any damage to the Building, there shall be either an abatement or an equitable reduction in rent depending on the period for which and the extent to which the Premises are not reasonably usable for the purposes for which they are leased hereunder. The words "restoration" and "restore" as used in this Article shall include repairs. If the damage results from the fault of Tenant, or Tenant's agents, servants, visitors or licensees, Tenant shall not be entitled to any abatement or reduction of rent, except to the extent, if any, that Landlord receives the proceeds of rent insurance in lieu of such rent.

WAIVERS OF SUBROGATION   Notwithstanding the provisions of Article 3 hereof: In any event of loss or damage to the Building, the Premises and/or any contents, each party shall look first to any insurance in its favor before making any claim against the other party; and TO THE EXTENT POSSIBLE WITHOUT ADDITIONAL COST, EACH PARTY SHALL OBTAIN, FOR EACH POLICY OF SUCH INSURANCE, PROVISIONS PERMITTING WAIVER OF ANY CLAIM AGAINST THE OTHER PARTY FOR LOSS OR DAMAGE WITHIN THE SCOPE OF THE INSURANCE, and each party, to such extent permitted, for itself and its insurers waives all such insured claims against the other party.

EMINENT DOMAIN   9. If the Premises or any part thereof or any estate therein, or any other part of the Building materially affecting Tenant's use of the Premises, be taken by virtue of eminent domain, this Lease shall terminate on the date when title vests pursuant to such taking, the rent and additional rent shall be apportioned as of said date and any rent paid for any period beyond said date shall be repaid to Tenant. Tenant shall not be entitled to any part of the award or any payment in lieu thereof; but Tenant may file a claim for any taking of fixtures and improvements owned by Tenant, and for moving expenses.

DEFAULT REMEDIES   10. If Tenant defaults in the payment of rent or additional rent or defaults in the performance of any of the covenants or conditions hereof, Landlord may give to Tenant notice of such default and if Tenant does not cure any rent or additional rent default within 5 days, or other default within 10 days, after the giving of such notice (or, if such other default is of such nature that it cannot be completely cured within such 10 days, if Tenant does not commence such curing within such 10 days and thereafter proceed with reasonable diligence and in good faith to cure such default), then Landlord may terminate this Lease on not less than 3 days' notice to Tenant, and on the date specified in said notice the term of this Lease shall terminate, and Tenant shall then quit and surrender the Premises to Landlord, but Tenant shall remain liable as hereinafter provided. If this Lease shall have been so terminated by Landlord, Landlord may at any time thereafter resume possession of the Premises by any lawful means and remove Tenant or other occupants and their effects.

DEFICIENCY   In any case where Landlord has recovered possession of the Premises by reason of Tenant's default Landlord may at Landlord's option occupy the Premises or cause the Premises to be redecorated, altered, divided, consolidated with other adjoining premises, or otherwise changed or prepared for reletting, and may relet the Premises or any part thereof as agent of Tenant or otherwise, for a term or terms to expire prior to, at the same time as, or subsequent to, the original expiration date of this Lease, at Landlord's option, and receive the rent therefor, applying the same first to the payment of such expenses as Landlord may have incurred in connection with the recovery of possession, redecorating, altering, dividing, consolidating with other adjoining premises, or otherwise changing or preparing for reletting, and the reletting, including brokerage and reasonable attorneys' fees, and then to the payment of damages in amounts equal to the rent hereunder and to the cost and expense of performance of the other covenants of Tenant as herein provided; and Tenant agrees, whether or not Landlord has relet, to pay to Landlord damages equal to the rent and other sums herein agreed to be paid by Tenant, less the net proceeds of the reletting, if any, as ascertained from time to time, and the same shall be payable by Tenant on the several rent days above specified. In reletting the Premises as aforesaid, Landlord may grant rent concessions, and Tenant shall not be credited therewith. No such reletting shall constitute a surrender and acceptance or be deemed evidence thereof. If Landlord elects, pursuant hereto, actually to occupy and use the Premises or any part thereof during any part of the balance of the term as originally fixed or since extended, there shall be allowed against Tenant's obligation for rent or damages as herein defined, during the period of Landlord's occupancy, the

reasonable value of such occupancy, not to exceed in any event the rent herein reserved and such occupancy shall not be construed as a release of Tenant's liability hereunder.

Tenant hereby waives all right of redemption to which Tenant or any person claiming under Tenant might be entitled by any law now or hereafter in force.

Landlord's remedies hereunder are in addition to any remedy allowed by law.

NO WAIVER OR CHANGES   11. The failure of either party to insist on strict performance of any covenant or condition hereof, or to exercise any option herein contained, shall not be construed as a waiver of such covenant, condition or option in any other instance. This Lease cannot be changed or terminated orally.

LANDLORD'S RIGHT TO COLLECT RENT FROM ANY OCCUPANT   12. If (a) the Premises are underlet or occupied by anybody other than Tenant and Tenant is in default hereunder, or (b) this Lease is assigned by Tenant, then, Landlord may collect rent from the assignee, under-tenant or occupant, and apply the net amount collected to the rent herein reserved; but no such collection shall be deemed a waiver of the covenant herein against assignment and underletting, or the acceptance of such assignee, under-tenant or occupant as Tenant, or a release of Tenant from further performance of the covenants herein contained.

SUBORDINATION   13. This Lease shall be subject and subordinate to all underlying leases and to mortgages which may now or hereafter affect such leases or the real property of which the Premises form a part, and also to all renewals, modifications, consolidations and replacements of said underlying leases and said mortgages. Although no instrument or act on the part of Tenant shall be necessary to effectuate such subordination, Tenant will, nevertheless, execute and deliver such further instruments confirming such subordination of this Lease as may be desired by the holders of said mortgages or by any of the lessors under such underlying leases. Tenant hereby appoints Landlord attorney in fact, irrevocably, to execute and deliver any such instrument for Tenant. If any underlying lease to which this Lease is subject terminates, Tenant shall on timely request attorn to the owner of the reversion.

SECURITY DEPOSIT   14. Tenant shall deposit with Landlord on the signing of this Lease the sum of $ as security for the performance of Tenant's obligations under this Lease, including without limitation the surrender of possession of the Premises to Landlord as herein provided. If Landlord applies any part of said deposit to cure any default of Tenant, Tenant shall upon demand deposit with Landlord the amount so applied so that Landlord shall have the full deposit on hand at all times during the term of this Lease.

LANDLORD'S RIGHT TO CURE TENANT'S BREACH   15. If Tenant breaches any covenant or condition of this Lease, Landlord may, on reasonable notice to Tenant (except that no notice need be given in case of emergency), cure such breach at the expense of Tenant and the reasonable amount of all expenses, including attorneys' fees, incurred by Landlord in doing so (whether paid by Landlord or not) shall be deemed additional rent payable on demand.

MECHANIC'S LIEN   16. Tenant shall within 10 days after notice from Landlord discharge any mechanic's lien for materials or labor claimed to have been furnished to the Premises on Tenant's behalf.

NOTICES   17. Any notice by either party to the other shall be in writing and shall be deemed to be duly given only if delivered personally or mailed by registered or certified mail in a postpaid envelope addressed (a) if to Tenant, at the Building and (b) if to Landlord, at Landlord's address first above set forth, or at such other addresses as Tenant or Landlord, respectively, may designate in writing. Notice shall be deemed to have been duly given, if delivered personally, upon delivery thereof, and if mailed, upon the 3rd day after the mailing thereof.

LANDLORD'S RIGHT TO INSPECT AND REPAIR   18. Landlord may, but shall not be obligated to, enter the Premises at any reasonable time, on reasonable notice to Tenant (except that no notice need be given in case of emergency) for the purposes of inspection or the making of such repairs, replacements and additions in, to, on and about the Premises or the Building, as Landlord deems necessary or desirable. Tenant shall have no claim or cause of action against Landlord by reason thereof except as provided in Article 19 hereof.

INTERRUPTION OF SERVICES OR USE 19. Interruption or curtailment of any service maintained in the Building if caused by strikes, mechanical difficulties, or any causes beyond Landlord's control whether similar or dissimilar to those enumerated, shall not entitle Tenant to any claim against Landlord or to any abatement in rent, nor shall the same constitute constructive or partial eviction, unless Landlord fails to take such measures as may be reasonable in the circumstances to restore the service without undue delay. If the Premises are rendered untenantable in whole or in part, for a period of over 3 business days, by the making of repairs, replacements or additions, other than those made with Tenant's consent or caused by misuse or neglect by Tenant or Tenant's agents, servants, visitors or licensees, there shall be a proportionate abatement of rent during the period of such untenantability.

CONDITIONS OF LANDLORD'S LIABILITY 20. Tenant shall not be entitled to claim a constructive eviction from the Premises unless Tenant shall have first notified Landlord IN WRITING of the condition or conditions giving rise thereto, and, if the complaints be justified, unless Landlord shall have failed within a reasonable time after receipt of said notice to remedy such conditions.

LANDLORD'S RIGHT TO SHOW PREMISES 21. Landlord may show the Premises to prospective purchasers and mortgagees and, during the 4 months prior to termination of this Lease, to prospective tenants, during business hours upon reasonable notice to Tenant.

NO REPRESENTATIONS 22. Neither party has made any representations or promises, except as contained herein, or in some further writing signed by the party making such representation or promise.

QUIET ENJOYMENT 23. Landlord covenants that if and so long as Tenant pays the rent and additional rent and performs the covenants hereof, Tenant shall peaceably and quietly have, hold and enjoy the Premises for the term herein mentioned, subject to the provisions of this Lease.

TENANT'S ESTOPPEL 24. Tenant shall from time to time, upon not less than 10 days' prior written request by Landlord, execute, acknowledge and deliver to Landlord a written statement certifying that this Lease is unmodified and in full force and effect (or that the same is in full force and effect as modified, listing the instruments of modification), the dates to which the rent and other charges have been paid, and whether or not to the best of Tenant's knowledge Landlord is in default hereunder (and if so, specifying the nature of the default), it being intended that any such statement delivered pursuant to this Article may be relied upon by a prospective purchaser of Landlord's interest or mortgagee of Landlord's interest or assignee of any mortgage upon Landlord's interest in the Building.

WAIVER OF JURY TRIAL 25. To the extent such waiver is permitted by law the parties waive trial by jury in any action or proceeding brought in connection with this Lease or the Premises.

MARGINAL NOTATIONS 26. The marginal notations in this Lease are included for convenience only and shall not be taken into consideration in any construction or interpretation of this Lease or any of its provisions.

HEIRS, ASSIGNS 27. The provisions of this Lease shall apply to, bind and enure to the benefit of Landlord and Tenant, and their respective successors, legal representatives and assigns; it being understood that the term "Landlord" as used in this Lease means only the owner, or the mortgagee in possession, or the lessee for the time being of the Building, so that in the event of any sale or sales of the Building or of any lease thereof or if the mortgagee shall take possession of the Premises, the Landlord named herein shall be and hereby is entirely freed and relieved of all covenants and obligations of Landlord hereunder accruing thereafter, and it shall be deemed without further agreement that the purchaser, the lessee or the mortgagee in possession has assumed and agreed to carry out any and all covenants and obligations of Landlord hereunder.

IN WITNESS WHEREOF, the parties hereto have duly executed this Lease as of the day and year first above written.

In the presence of:

....

....
Landlord

....

....
Tenant

STATE OF NEW YORK, COUNTY OF   ss.:   STATE OF NEW YORK, COUNTY OF   ss.:

On the   day of   19   On the   day of   19
before me personally came   before me personally came

to me known, who being by me duly sworn, did depose and say   to me known, who being by me duly sworn, did depose and say
that   he resides at   that   he resides at

that   he is the   that   he is the
of   of
the corporation described in and which executed the foregoing   the corporation described in and which executed the foregoing
instrument; that   he knows the seal of said corporation; that   instrument; that   he knows the seal of said corporation; that it
the seal affixed to said instrument is such corporate seal; that it   the seal affixed to said instrument is such corporate seal; that it
was so affixed by order of the Board of Directors of said corpo-   was so affixed by order of the Board of Directors of said corporation; and that   he signed   name thereto by like order. ration; and that   he signed   name thereto by like order.

_____   _____

STATE OF NEW YORK, COUNTY OF   ss.:   STATE OF NEW YORK, COUNTY OF   ss.:

On the   day of   19   On the   day of   19
before me personally came   before me personally came

to me known and known to me to be the individual   described   to me known and known to me to be the individual   described
in and who executed the foregoing instrument, and duly acknowl-   in and who executed the foregoing instrument, and duly acknowledged to me that   he   executed the same.   edged to me that   he   executed the same.

_____   _____

RULES AND REGULATIONS REFERRED TO IN THE FOREGOING LEASE

1. The sidewalks, entrances, passages, courts, elevators, vestibules, stairways, corridors and public parts of the Building shall not be obstructed or encumbered by Tenant or used by Tenant for any purpose other than ingress and egress to and from the Premises. If the Premises are situated on the ground floor with direct access to the street, then Tenant shall, at Tenant's expense, keep the sidewalks and curbs directly in front of the Premises clean and free from ice, snow and refuse.

2. No awnings, air conditioning units or other projections shall be attached to the outside walls or windowsills of the Building or otherwise project from the Building, without the prior written consent of Landlord.

3. No sign or lettering shall be affixed by Tenant on any part of the outside of the Premises, or on any part of the inside of the Premises so as to be clearly visible from the outside of the Premises, without the prior written consent of Landlord. However, Tenant shall have the right to place its name on any door leading into the Premises, the size, color and style thereof to be subject to Landlord's approval, which approval shall not be unreasonably withheld. Landlord shall place Tenant's name on the directory in the lobby of the Building. Tenant shall not have the right to have additional names placed on the directory without Landlord's prior written consent, which consent shall not be unreasonably withheld.

4. The windows in the Premises shall not be covered or obstructed by Tenant, nor shall any bottles, parcels or other articles be placed on the windowsills or in the halls or in any other part of the Building, nor shall any article be thrown out of the doors or windows of the Premises.

5. Tenant shall not lay linoleum or other similar floor covering so that the same shall come in direct contact with the floor of the Premises, and if linoleum or other similar floor covering is desired to be used, an interlining of builder's deadening felt shall be first fixed to the floor by a paste or other material that may easily be removed with water, the use of cement or other similar adhesive material being expressly prohibited.

6. Tenant shall not make, or permit to be made, any unseemly or disturbing noises or interfere with other tenants or those having business with them.

7. No additional locks or bolts of any kind shall be placed upon any of the doors or windows by Tenant, and Tenant shall, upon the termina-tion of this tenancy, deliver to Landlord all keys to any space within the Building, either furnished to, or otherwise procured by, Tenant, and in the event of the loss of any keys so furnished, Tenant shall pay to Landlord the cost thereof.

8. The carrying in or out of freight, furniture or bulky matter of any description must take place during such hours as Landlord may from time to time reasonably determine. The installation and moving of such freight, furniture or bulky matter shall be made upon previous notice to the superintendent of the Building and the persons employed by Tenant for such work must be reasonably acceptable to Landlord. Tenant may, subject to the provisions of the immediately preceding sentence, move freight, furniture, bulky matter and other material into or out of the Premises on Saturday between the hours of 8:30 A.M. and 6:00 P.M. provided Tenant pays the additional costs, if any, incurred by Landlord for elevator operators, security guards and other expenses arising by reason of such move by Tenant and if, at least 2 days prior to such move, Landlord requests that Tenant deposit with Landlord, as security for Tenant's obligation to pay such additional costs, a sum which Landlord reasonably estimates to be the amount of such additional costs, then Tenant shall deposit such sum with Landlord as security for such costs.

9. Landlord reserves the right to prescribe the weight and position of all safes and other heavy equipment so as to distribute properly the weight thereof and to prevent any unsafe condition from arising. Business machines and other equipment shall be placed and maintained by Tenant at Tenant's expense in settings sufficient in Landlord's reasonable judgment to absorb and prevent unreasonable vibration, noise and annoyance.

10. Tenant shall not clean or permit the cleaning of any window in the Premises from the outside, except in strict conformity with §202 of the Labor Law and the rules of the Board of Standards and Appeals and any other body having jurisdiction thereof.

11. Landlord shall not be responsible to Tenant for the non-observance or violation of any of these Rules and Regulations by any other tenants.

ASSIGNMENT
OF
PROPRIETARY LEASE

T 396—Assignment of Proprietary Lease.

COPYRIGHT 1973 BY JULIUS BLUMBERG, INC., LAW BLANK PUBLISHERS
80 EXCHANGE PL. AT BROADWAY, N. Y. C. 10004

Know That

Assignor,

in consideration of the sum of

($) dollars,

paid by

Assignee,

and for other good and valuable consideration, does hereby assign unto the Assignee a certain proprietary lease dated
                            19   by and between
Lessor, and

Lessee,

covering apartment   in the building known as

To Have and To Hold the same unto the Assignee and Assignee's personal representatives and assigns, on and after   19   the effective date, for the balance of the term of the proprietary lease, and any renewals or extensions thereof, and subject to the covenants, conditions and limitations therein contained.

In order to induce the Lessor to consent to this assignment and Assignee to accept this assignment, the Assignor represents to Lessor and Assignee that:

a) Assignor has full right, title and authority to assign the shares and the proprietary lease appurtenant thereto,

b) Assignor has fully performed all the terms, covenants and conditions of the proprietary lease on Assignor's part to be performed to the effective date hereof,

c) Assignor has not done or suffered anything to be done which might impose any liability on the Lessor or Assignee, and

d) There are no claims, security interests or liens against the proprietary lease, or the shares in the Lessor corporation allocated to the apartment to which the proprietary lease is appurtenant, or to any fixtures and/or personal property installed by Assignor in the apartment.

The covenants and representations herein shall survive the delivery hereof, but any action based thereon must be instituted within one year from the effective date of this assignment.

Whenever the text hereof requires, the singular number as used herein shall include the plural and all genders.

IN WITNESS WHEREOF, the Assignor has executed this assignment on 19 .

....L. S.

....L. S.

State of
County of   } ss.:

On this   day of   19   before me

personally came

to me known and known to me to be the individual(s) described in and who executed the foregoing instrument, and duly acknowledged to me that   executed the same.

....

Form Lease of Apartment

Landlord hereby leases to Tenant the premises described above for a term of ___ years, beginning _____

and ending _____, at a rental rate of _____ per month, making a total rental amount payable under this

lease of _____ .

2. Tenant agrees to pay the rent as herein provided subject to the terms and conditions set forth herein.

3. Rent shall be payable in equal monthly installments to be paid in advance on the _____ day of each month, provided, that if Tenant is or shall become dependent upon any governmental agency for support, income supplementation, home relief, or other benefits, rent hereunder may, at the option of Tenant, be payable in equal semi-monthly installments to be paid in advance on the 2nd and 17th of each month.

4. Rent shall be paid in the following manner:

(Specify above if payments are to be made by mail, and if so, to what address; if payments are to be made to Landlord or his agent in person, state the place where and person to whom payments are to be made.)

5. Upon each payment of rent, Landlord agrees to issue a receipt stating clearly Tenant's name, a description of the premises, the amount of rent paid, and the period for which said rent is paid.

6. Tenant covenants that he shall not commit or permit a nuisance in the premises, that he shall not maliciously or by reason of gross negligence substantially damage the premises, and that he shall not engage in conduct such as to interfere substantially with the comfort and safety of Landlord or of other tenants or occupants of the same or another adjacent building or structure.

7. Landlord agrees that Tenant and Tenant's family shall have, hold, and enjoy the leased premises for the term set forth herein subject to the terms and conditions set forth herein.

8. Landlord covenants that the leased premises are safe, sound, and healthful and that said premises shall be kept in said condition at all times during the term of this lease and any extension, renewal, or continuation thereof. Landlord covenants that all essential services are now provided and shall be provided at all times during the term of this lease and any extension, renewal, or continuation thereof. "Essential services" hereunder are defined as heat, hot and cold running water, a properly functioning toilet, electricity, and if a gas stove is provided, gas. Landlord covenants that there exists in the leased premises no violation of any applicable housing code, law, or regulation, and that no such violation will be permitted to exist at any time during the term of this lease and any extension, renewal, or continuation thereof. Nothing in this lease shall be construed as an admission by Tenant concerning the condition of the leased premises at the time of Tenant's taking possession thereof or at any other time or as a waiver by Tenant of any right or remedy which he may have, now or at any future time, with respect to any condition in the leased premises, whether arising before or after the commencement of this lease.

9. In the event of any breach by Tenant of paragraphs "6" or "17" herein, Landlord may give Tenant five days' notice to cure said breach, setting forth in detail the manner in which said paragraph or paragraphs has or have been breached. If said breach is not cured within said five-day period, or reasonable steps to effectuate said cure are not commenced and diligently pursued within said five-day period and thereafter until said breach has been cured, Landlord may terminate this lease upon five days' additional notice to Tenant. Said termination shall be ineffective if Tenant cures said breach, or commences and diligently pursues reasonable steps to effectuate such cure, at any time prior to the expiration of said five-day notice of termination. Upon terminating this lease as provided herein, Landlord may commence summary proceedings against Tenant for his removal as provided by law.

10. In the event of any breach by Landlord of paragraphs "7" or "8" herein, Tenant may give Landlord ten days' notice to cure said breach, setting forth in detail the manner in which said paragraph or paragraphs has or have been breached. If said breach is not cured within said ten-day period, or reasonable steps to effectuate said cure are not commenced and diligently pursued within said ten-day period and thereafter until said breach has been cured, rent hereunder shall be fully abated from the time at which said ten days' notice expired until such time as Landlord has fully cured the breach set forth in the notice provided for in this paragraph. In no case shall any abatement of rent hereunder be effected where the condition set forth in the notice provided for herein was created by the intentional or negligent act of Tenant, but Landlord shall have the burden of proving that a rent abatement may not be effected for the foregoing reason.

11. In the event of any interruption, discontinuance, or termination of any essential service or services hereunder, the provisions of paragraph "10" herein shall apply; however, rent hereunder shall in such event be fully abated from the time that notice is given to Landlord until the time that the essential service or services is or are fully restored.

12. The remedies provided in paragraphs "9," "10," and "11" herein are not exclusive. Nothing in this lease shall be construed as a waiver by either party of such additional legal, equitable, or administrative remedies as are now, or may in the future be, available to him.

13. Tenant shall give prompt notice to Landlord of any dangerous, defective, unsafe or emergency condition in the leased premises, and said notice may be given by any suitable means, paragraph "22" herein notwithstanding. Landlord shall repair and correct said conditions immediately upon receiving notice thereof from Tenant.

14. Paragraphs "2," "6" and "17" herein shall comprise Tenant's substantial obligations under this lease.

15. Tenant shall pay for gas, electricity, and telephone service, if any, except to the extent otherwise set forth herein. Landlord covenants that consumption of electricity for the public halls and other common areas and uses and the consumption of gas for heat and hot water are recorded on separate meters, and that said electricity and gas are and will at all times be billed to and paid for by Landlord.

16. Tenant shall at reasonable times give access to Landlord or his agents for any reasonable and lawful purpose. Except in situations of compelling emergency, Landlord shall give Tenant at least 24 hours' notice of intention to seek access, the date and time at which access will be sought, and the reason therefor. Landlord covenants that Tenant shall have access at all times to the fuse-box or circuit-breakers which govern the flow of electricity to the leased premises.

17. Tenant shall not assign this lease or underlet the leased premises or any part thereof without Landlord's written consent, which consent Landlord agrees not to withhold unreasonably.

18. Landlord agrees to deliver possession of the leased premises at the beginning of the term provided for herein. In the event of the Landlord's failure to deliver possession at the beginning of said term, Tenant shall have the right to rescind this lease and to recover any consideration paid, which right shall not be deemed inconsistent with any right of action Tenant may have to recover damages.

19. Tenant agrees to make a security deposit with Landlord in the amount of one month's rent hereunder, to be used by Landlord at the termination of this lease for the cost of repairing damage, if any, to the premises caused by the intentional or negligent acts of Tenant, as well as for rent, if any, owed by Tenant. Landlord agrees, within ten days of receiving said security money, to deposit same in an interest-bearing account in a banking organization, which account shall earn interest at a rate which shall be the prevailing rate earned by other such deposits made with banking organizations in such area. Landlord agrees, within ten days of making such deposit, to notify Tenant of the name and address of the banking organization in which the deposit of security money has been made, and the amount of such deposit. Landlord shall be entitled to receive, as administration expenses, a sum equivalent to one per cent per annum upon the security money so deposited, which shall be in lieu of all other administrative and custodial expenses. The balance of the interest paid by the banking organization shall be the money of Tenant and shall be paid to Tenant on each anniversary of this lease or any extension, renewal, or continuation thereof. Landlord agrees to return said security deposit to Tenant upon Tenant's vacating the leased premises subject to the terms and conditions set forth herein.

20. In the event that Landlord conveys title to the leased premises he shall, at the time of delivery of the deed or within five days thereafter, (a) turn over the security deposit hereunder to his grantee and notify Tenant of such turning over and of the name and address of such grantee, or (b) return the security deposit hereunder to Tenant.

21. Landlord shall, within five days of any change in the preliminary information heretofore set forth herein, notify Tenant thereof.

22. Any notice required or authorized hereunder shall be given in writing, one copy of said notice mailed via U.S. certified mail, and one copy of said notice mailed via U.S. first class mail. Notice to Tenant shall be mailed to him at the leased premises. Notice to Landlord shall be mailed to him or to the registered managing agent at their respective addresses as heretofore set forth herein, or at such new address as to which Tenant has been duly notified.

23. This lease constitutes the entire agreement of the parties hereto. No changes shall be made herein except by writing, signed by each party, and dated. The failure to enforce any right or remedy hereunder and the payment or acceptance of rent hereunder shall not be deemed a waiver by either party of such right or remedy in the absence of a writing as provided for herein.

24. CAUTION TO THE PARTIES: This lease, when filled out and signed, is a binding legal obligation. Do not sign it if there are any blank spaces. Cross out all blanks before signing.

44

The Model Lease

The Protenant Lease: A Summary

In 1974 a Brooklyn Legal Services office published what may have been the first pro-tenant lease for use by individual tenants and tenant groups in New York City.* Although outdated, the lease serves as an example of a lease which clearly prevents a landlord from being unreasonable and which gives the tenant well-defined rights. From a tenant's viewpoint, it represents an improvement over the "standard form" prolandlord lease in at least three important respects.

First, the protenant lease omits the onerous "boilerplate" clauses which permeate the prolandlord lease. Among the *deleted* clauses are the following:

A waiver of the constitutional right to a jury trial;

A waiver of the right to countersue when the landlord sues for nonpayment of rent—for example, to counterclaim for money the tenant has spent on necessary repairs;

The notorious "no dog" clause;

A prohibition against subletting (under the protenant lease, the landlord may not unreasonably refuse to permit it);

A clause requiring the tenant to pay the landlord's legal expenses.

Second, the protenant lease provides needed information to the tenant and seeks to resolve, before they arise, many of the most common disputes between landlords and tenants:

The landlord must tell the tenant the name and phone number of a real person who is responsible for repairs. This is essential if the landlord is a corporation.

The landlord agrees to pay interest on the tenant's security deposit, and if he sells the building, either to return the security depo-sit or to turn it over to the new owner (¶¶ 19, 20).

The lease specifies how the rent shall be collected (¶4) and requires the landlord to issue receipts (¶5). Many small landlords refuse to issue receipts and have no regular procedure for payment of rent.

It is agreed that Welfare recipients may pay the monthly rent in two installments, corresponding to their receipt of assistance payments (¶3).

Third, the protenant lease redefines the rights and obligations of the parties so that their relationship conforms to widely held conceptions of fairness and equity:

The tenant promises that he will pay the rent and that he will not commit a "nuisance," willfully damage the apartment, or substantially disturb others in the building (¶6). The landlord has the right to enforce this promise by evicting a tenant who breaks it (¶9). (This differs from many pro-landlord leases which permit the landlord to evict a tenant for violations of nit-picking rules and regulations, such as that TVs shall not be played between 10 PM and 8 AM.)

The landlord agrees to keep the apartment in good condition, and to supply essential services such as heat and hot water (¶8). The tenant has the right to enforce this agreement by effectuating a rent abatement, after giving proper notice to the landlord, for the period during which repairs are needed or essential services are not provided (¶¶10, 11). (This differs from pro-landlord leases which, while they may say that the tenant is to receive heat and hot water, fail to provide any enforcement mechanism or means of compensating the tenant for the hardship suffered when such services are interrupted.)

The SBLS lease is discussed in detail in this article: Bentley, "An Alternative Residential Lease," *Columbia Law Review*, vol. 74, p. 836 (June 1974).

Cooperative Apartments and Condominiums

In a book of limited scope, it is not always easy to know where to place a certain subject. Cooperative apartments and condominiums are clearly not leaseholds; in fact, unlike the leaseholds, which do not constitute a form of ownership, but rather a possessory right, cooperatives and condominiums are forms of ownership. In that respect, they are like houses; yet, as you will see, some aspects of renting exist and the structures involved are usually part of a multiple-dwelling unit. Since cooperatives and condominiums are becoming a popular way of living, it would prove valuable to take a brief look at both.

Cooperatives

Cooperative apartment buildings are owned by tenant-controlled corporations. The tenants' control is exercised through their power to vote stock which they hold in the corporation. By voting their stock, tenants elect the board of directors and accept or reject issues affecting their corporation and hence their building.

In purchasing a cooperative apartment, a person is not buying the apartment itself, but a set amount of stock in the corporation and the right to enter into a proprietary lease with the corporation, either directly or by assignment from the previous tenant-stockholder. Although in essence the tenant-stockholder "owns" the apartment in which he lives, he does so under the terms of the proprietary lease. As a result, he may be as restricted by regulations of the corporation in what he can and cannot do with his cooperative as he may be by regulations of a landlord with an apartment. With respect to the common area, the tenant-stockholder has no direct control except to the extent he exercises his right to vote on issues involving the managment of the building.

The main feature of a cooperative, as with a condominium, is the tax advantages gained by the tenant-stockholder. To understand how these advantages flow to the tenant-stockholder, it is essential to know the cooperative structure. You must remember that title to the building is lodged in the name of the corporation. Generally, the corporation has mortgaged the building, either resulting from the initial purchase from the prior owner or resulting from a need to rehabilitate the building or to obtain a better interest rate on the financing arrangement. As with a homeowner, the corporation must make monthly mortgage payments consisting of a reduction in principle and current interest charges. Interest charges in the early years of the mortgage comprise a large portion of the monthly payment and are tax deductible. Also, the corporation must pay tax-deductible local real estate taxes on the assessed value of the building.

A tenant-stockholder pays the corporation a monthly maintenance charge, a portion of which is attributable to the mortgage and real estate tax payments. It is this portion of his monthly maintenance that is tax deductible on the tenant-stockholder's individual tax return. Moreover, most people also finance the cost of purchasing the stock, which represents their pro rata interest in the corporation. This financing follows the form of a standard mortgage with the mortgagee securing his interest by requiring as part of the mortgage commitment that the tenant-stockholder assign his stock to him. The interest paid on this mortgage is likewise tax deductible by the individual. The tenant-stockholder is now paying off two mortgages, one solely in his name and the other on a proportionate basis in the name of the corporation.

T 397—Consent to assignment of proprietary
lease: Cooperative apartment.

Dated   19

Apartment:

Address:

Number of shares:

IT IS HEREBY CERTIFIED that consent has been granted by the undersigned corporation to the assignment of the shares allocated to the above apartment and the proprietary lease appurtenant thereto to

Such consent has been given in writing by a majority of the now authorized number of directors of the corporation or by duly adopted resolution by its Board of Directors at a meeting duly held.

IT IS FURTHER CERTIFIED that all rent, maintenance or other charges due under the proprietary lease have been paid up to and including   19

....
Lessor

By ....

Title ....

Overall, then, the tenant-stockholder is paying for the following items:

1. Maintenance charge:
   (a) Interest on mortgage indebtedness;
   (b) Mortgage amortization;
   (c) Real estate taxes;
   (d) General building upkeep; and
   (e) Operating expenses.
2. Special assessments—one-time charges for a clearly identified purpose such as remodelling hallways or repairing or replacing a boiler.
3. Personal mortgage payments:
   (a) Interest on mortgage indebtedness; and
   (b) Mortgage amortization.

Before "purchasing a co-op," a buyer should be familiar with the documents he will be required to execute or obtain. Copies of certain of these are included here for your reference.

1. Contract for the sale of a cooperative apartment (see Chapter 3 on house purchase contracts).
2. Stock assignment—The assignment, as discussed earlier, can take two routes. The seller can either assign his stock to the buyer or assign it to the corporation which, in turn, assigns it to the new tenant-stockholder (See Chapter 10 on assignments).
3. Proprietary lease—This document is essentially no different from other leases discussed in this chapter. The lease will establish your stock ownership and your agreement to pay monthly maintenance to the corporation on the basis of your total stock ownership and the maintenance rate as determined by the board of directors. The lease also will list what you can and cannot do with or without the expressed permission of the corporation. One particular requirement will mandate that you obtain the consent of the corporation before selling your stock (and hence your apartment).
4. Consent of the corporation—Most proprietary leases will restrict transfer of ownership, unless the corporation expressly agrees to the sale. For their protection, the purchaser and seller should request a copy of the corporation's consent.
5. Mortgage papers—If the buyer is financing the purchase of stock, he will need to sign the same types of instruments described in Chapter 4.
6. Prospectus, corporate charter and by-laws—A buyer should obtain from the corporation or through the managing agent (and read carefully) these documents which will provide him with much needed data on the corporation and its operation.

In closing, it should be pointed out that many jurisdictions are in confusion as to the status of cooperatives. Although they have all the rudiments of real estate transactions, some courts view these dealings as sales and purchases of securities because of the transfer of stock. New York, for example, currently applies securities law to some issues involving cooperatives. As a result, it is difficult to ascertain in advance whether standard landlord-tenant law will carry the day in a dispute between the tenant-stockholder and the corporation or whether local securities law (blue-sky laws) will alter that decision. The best advice we can offer you is to consult an attorney if you find yourself in the midst of a problem with your cooperative.

Condominiums

Whereas cooperatives have been the rage in certain areas of the country, such as New York City, condominiums are the more acceptable form of ownership of multiple dwelling units in other locations, although all

T 395—Acceptance of assignment and assumption
of proprietary lease: Cooperative apartment.

Know That

the undersigned, Assignee named in a certain instrument of assignment dated   19

executed by

Assignor therein,

Lessor therein and owner of the

in order to induce

building at

to consent to the aforementioned assignment of a proprietary lease of apartment   in said building and the shares of
the Lessor to which said proprietary lease is appurtenant, and in consideration of such assignment and the consent of
the Lessor thereto, the undersigned HEREBY ASSUMES AND AGREES TO PERFORM AND COMPLY with all
the terms, covenants and conditions of the proprietary lease to be performed or complied with by Lessee on and after
19   the effective date of the assignment, as if the undersigned had originally executed
the proprietary lease as Lessee, and further agrees that at the request of the Lessor, the undersigned will surrender the
assigned proprietary lease to the Lessor and enter into a new proprietary lease of said apartment for the remainder of
the term thereof, in the same form and on the same terms, covenants and conditions as the assigned proprietary lease.

Whenever the text hereof requires, the singular number as used herein shall include the plural and all genders.

In Witness Whereof, Assignee has duly executed this acceptance and assumption instrument

on   19

....L. S.

....L. S.

⟶

State of
County of   } ss.:

On this   day of   19   before me
personally came

to me known and known to me to be the individual(s) described in and who executed the foregoing instrument, and
duly acknowledged to me that   executed the same.

----

states have specific statutes dealing with the subject.

Unlike a cooperative-apartment purchaser, the buyer of a condominium acquires full title to his unit, and thus he is not limited by rules and regulations of a proprietary lease. He holds by deed, not by lease. Instead of owning stock, a condominium purchaser owns his structure. In almost all respects, the sale and purchase of a condominium resemble the same transaction involving a house. In addition to title to the particular unit, an owner also receives an undivided interest in all common areas appurtenant to the condominium complex on the pro rata basis of the value of his unit to the total value of the complex. Despite this undivided interest in common areas, however, the condominium owner is not responsible for their maintenance, although he will be assessed the cost of their upkeep.

As you may remember, a tenant-stockholder is able to deduct from his taxes interest paid on financing commitments held by the corporation. This attractive tax feature also carries with it the obligation to satisfy the debt where one or more tenant-stockholders default. This is not true for condominiums. A condominium owner is liable only for the financing arrangement on his own unit and not for any blanket mortgage on the entire complex.

Since the documents covering the sale and purchase of a condominium are the same as those covering a house and are discussed in depth in Chapters 3 and 4, it makes sense here only to list the basic ones:

1. Contract for the sale of a condominium (see Chapter 3)
2. Warranty Deed (see Chapter 3)
3. Mortgage (see Chapter 4)
4. Mortgage Note (see Chapter 4)

In addition to these, it would also be advisable to obtain copies of the declaration of condominium, which will state the rights and liabilities of owners, and, if applicable, the articles of incorporation of an owners' association and its by-laws. Read all of these items carefully to be sure you are aware of any restrictions or prohibitions on the use of your unit which might be unacceptable to you. It is better to know in advance before your commitment is irrevocable.

W 123—Revised Contract of Sale of Cooperative Apartment.
Approved by The Cooperative Housing Lawyers Group.

COPYRIGHT 1973 BY JULIUS BLUMBERG, INC., LAW BLANK PUBLISHERS

CONSULT YOUR LAWYER BEFORE SIGNING THIS INSTRUMENT

CONTRACT OF SALE — COOPERATIVE APARTMENT

Agreement made as of the   day of   19

between

residing at

hereinafter called "Seller"

and

residing at

hereinafter called "Purchaser".

WITNESSETH:

SHARES 1. Seller agrees to sell and transfer and Purchaser agrees to buy (i)   shares (the "Shares") of

(the "Corporation") allocated to Apartment   (the "Apartment") in the cooperative apartment building located at

LEASE and (ii) the Seller's interest, as tenant, in the proprietary lease, as amended (the "Lease"), for the Apartment, which Lease is appurtenant to the Shares.

PERSONAL PROPERTY 2. (a) Subject to the rights of the landlord under the Lease and any holder of a mortgage to which the Lease is subordinate, this sale includes all of the Seller's right, title and interest, if any, in and to:

(i) the refrigerators, ranges, dishwashers, kitch-

Strike out inapplicable items en cabinets and counters, lighting and plumbing fixtures, air-conditioning equipment and other fixtures and articles of property attached to or appurtenant to the Apartment, except those listed in subparagraph (b) of this Paragraph 2;

(ii)

(b) Excluded from this sale are:
(i) furniture and furnishings, and
(ii)

The property referred to in Paragraph 2(a)(i) and 2(a)(ii) may not be purchased if title to the Shares and the Lease is not closed hereunder.

PRICE 3. The purchase price is $
payable as follows: $
by check, subject to collection, on the execution and delivery of this agreement; $ in cash, cashier's check or by unendorsed certified check of Purchaser drawn on a local bank or trust company, to the order of Seller, to be delivered at the closing.

WARRANTIES 4. Seller represents, warrants and covenants that: a) Seller is the sole owner of the Shares, the Lease and the property referred to in paragraph 2(a)(ii); the same are and will at closing be free and clear of liens, encumbrances and adverse interests, subject to the matters, if any, affecting the title to the real property of which the Apartment is a part; and Seller has the full right and power to sell and transfer the same; (b) the Shares were duly issued and fully paid for and are non-assessable; (c) the maintenance (rent) payable on the date hereof is at the rate of $ a month and at the date of closing will be fully paid to said date; (d) Seller has not received any

51

written notice of any intended assessment or increase in said maintenance (rent) not reflected in the figure set forth in sub-paragraph (c); (e) the Lease is and will at closing be in full force and effect; (f) Seller is not and will not become indebted for labor or material which might give rise to the filing of a notice of mechanic's lien against the building in which the Apartment is located; (g) there are and will at closing be no violations of record which the tenant would be obligated to remedy under the terms of the Lease; (h) Seller is not a Sponsor or a nominee of a Sponsor under any plan of cooperative organization affecting this Apartment.

The representations and warranties contained in this Paragraph 4 and in Paragraph 14 shall survive the closing but any action based thereon must be instituted within one year from the date of closing.

NO OTHER REPRESENTATIONS 5. Purchaser has examined and is satisfied with the certificate of incorporation, the by-laws of the Corporation and the form of the Lease, or has waived the examination thereof. Purchaser has inspected the Apartment, its fixtures, appliances and equipment and the personal property, if any, included in the sale, and knows the condition thereof, and agrees to accept the same "as is", i.e., in the condition they are in on the date hereof subject to normal wear and tear. Purchaser has examined or waived examination of the last audited financial statement of the Corporation, and has considered or waived consideration of all other matters pertaining to this agreement and to the purchase to be made hereunder, and does not rely on any representations made by any broker or by Seller or anyone acting or purporting to act on behalf of Seller as to any matters which might influence or affect the decision to execute this agreement or to buy the Shares, the Lease, or said personal property except those representations and warranties which are specifically set forth in this agreement.

REQUIRED APPROVAL 6. This sale is subject to the approval of the directors or shareholders of the Corporation as provided in the Lease or the corporate by-laws. Purchaser agrees to submit to Seller or to the Corporation's managing agent, within five (5) days after the execution and delivery hereof the names and addresses of persons to whom, or banks or corporations to which, reference may be had as to Purchaser's character and financial standing, and thereafter to attend [and to cause Purchaser's spouse to attend] one or more personal interviews, as requested by the Corporation, and submit to the Corporation or its managing agent such further references and information as are commonly asked for in such transactions. If any of the aforementioned references are submitted to Seller, Seller shall promptly redeliver same to the Corporation or its managing agent. Seller may, but shall not be required to take any steps in connection with the procurement of such approval. Seller shall promptly notify Purchaser of such approval or of the refusal thereof upon receipt of notice thereof. In the event of such refusal, this agreement shall thereby be deemed cancelled. If approval or refusal be not received by Seller or Purchaser at or before the closing, either may by notice given to the other on or before the date fixed in paragraph 10 for the closing, adjourn the closing for a period not to exceed thirty (30) days for the purpose of obtaining such approval, and if the party who has adjourned the closing is unable to obtain approval of this sale within said period of time, this agreement shall ipso facto be deemed cancelled. If this agreement is cancelled as provided in this Paragraph, all sums theretofore paid to Seller by Purchaser on account of the purchase price shall be returned without interest to Purchaser and both parties shall be relieved from all further liability hereunder.

REFERENCES

SALE AFTER APPROVAL; ASSUMPTION 7. If approval of this sale be granted, Seller agrees to transfer and assign to Purchaser the Lease, the Shares and the personal property, as in this agreement provided, and Purchaser agrees to pay the purchase price and to assume, with respect to obligations arising from and after the time of the closing, all of the terms, covenants and conditions of the Lease on the part of the lessee thereunder to be performed, and to be bound by the by-laws of the Corporation and the rules and regulations, if any, from time to time promulgated by the Corporation. To that end Purchaser shall execute and deliver to the Corporation at the closing an agreement containing such assumptions in the form requested or approved by the Corporation, and, if requested by the Corporation, a new proprietary lease for the balance of the lease term shall be executed by Purchaser and the Corporation and the Lease being assigned by Seller shall be surrendered for cancellation.

REMOVAL OF SELLER'S PROPERTY 8. Seller shall, prior to the closing, remove from the Apartment all the household furniture, furnishing and other personal property not included in this sale, and shall repair any damage caused by such removal, and shall deliver possession of the Apartment at the closing, broom-clean.

RISK OF LOSS, ETC. 9. (a) The risk of loss or damage to the Apartment, or to the property included in this sale in accordance with Paragraph 2, by fire or other cause, until the time of the closing, is assumed by Seller, but without any obligation on the part of Seller, except at Seller's option, to repair or replace any such loss or damage. Seller shall notify Purchaser of the occurrence of any such loss or damage within five (5) days after such occurrence or by the date of closing, whichever first occurs, and by such notice shall elect whether or not Seller will repair or replace the loss or damage and if Seller elects to do so, that he will complete the same within the sixty (60) day period hereinafter referred to. If Seller elects to make such repairs and/or replacements, then Seller's said notice shall set forth an adjourned date for the closing, which shall be not more than sixty (60) days after the date of the giving of Seller's notice. If Seller does not elect to make such repairs and/or replacements, or if Seller elects to make them and fails to complete the same on or before said adjourned closing date, Purchaser shall have the following options:

(i) to declare this agreement cancelled and receive a refund, without interest, from Seller of all sums theretofore paid on account of the purchase price; or

(ii) to complete the purchase in accordance with this agreement without reduction in the purchase price except as provided in the next sentence. If Seller carries hazard insurance covering such loss or damage, Seller shall turn over to Purchaser at the closing the net proceeds (after legal and other expenses of collection) actually collected by Seller under the provisions of such hazard insurance policies to the extent that they are attributable to loss of or damage to any property included in this sale; if Seller has not received such proceeds Seller shall assign (without recourse to Seller) Seller's right to any payment or additional payments from Seller's said insurance which are attributable to the loss of or damage to any property included in this sale, less any sums theretofore expended by him.

(b) If Seller does not elect to make such repairs and/or replacements, Purchaser may exercise the resulting option under (i) or (ii) of (a) only by notice given to Seller within five (5) business days after Purchaser's option arises. If Seller elects to make such repairs and/or replacements and fails to complete the same on or before the adjourned closing date, Purchaser may exercise the resulting options within five (5) business days after the adjourned closing date.

10. The closing documents referred to in Paragraph 11 shall be delivered, and payment of the balance of the purchase price shall be made, at the closing to be held on
19   at   M., at the office of

CLOSING DOCUMENTS

11. At the closing: (a) Seller shall deliver to Purchaser:

(i) Seller's certificate for the Shares, duly endorsed for transfer, or accompanied by a separate duly executed stock power, with necessary stock transfer stamps attached and in either case, with any guarantee of Seller's signature required by the Corporation;

(ii) Seller's duplicate original of the Lease and a duly executed assignment thereof to the Purchaser in the form requested or approved by the Corporation;

(iii) Certificate of the secretary of the Corporation or other evidence of the consent of the Corporation or its directors to the transfer of the Shares and Lease to Purchaser in accordance with the applicable provisions of the Lease or the corporate by-laws;

(iv) If requested, a statement by the managing agent that the maintenance and any special assessments then due and payable to the Corporation have been paid to the date of the closing;

(v) If requested, a bill of sale in customary form transferring the property referred to in Paragraph 2(a);

(vi) Keys to the outer doors of the Apartment.

(b) Purchaser shall deliver to Seller and the Corporation, together with the payment of the balance of the purchase price, the duly executed agreements and/or new lease referred to in Paragraph 7 hereof.

PROCESSING FEE

12. (a) Seller shall, at the closing, pay the processing fee, if any, charged by the managing agent for its services in connection with the approval of this sale and the transfer of the Shares and the Lease and the legal fee of the Corporation's attorney, if any, in connection with such transfer. Purchaser shall pay (i) the sales and transfer taxes, if any, on this sale, other than the transfer stamps provided for in Paragraph 11 (a)(i) and (ii) the cost of title search if required by the Corpora-

APPORTIONMENTS tion. (b) The parties shall at the closing apportion, as of midnight of the day preceding the date of actual closing, the rent under the Lease, and utility charges, if any, due the Corporation. Assessments will not be apportioned but will be payable by the party who is the Owner when the same become due and payable.

PRIOR LEASE TERMINATION

13. If prior to the closing the Corporation shall elect to cancel and terminate the Lease under any option or privilege reserved therein for any reason except Seller's default, this agreement shall thereupon become a nullity and Seller shall be deemed to be unable to convey the Lease and the Shares and Seller shall refund to Purchaser, without interest, all sums theretofore paid on account of the purchase price.

BROKER

14. Purchaser represents to Seller that Purchaser has not dealt with any brokers in con-

nection with this transaction other than

and Seller agrees to pay said broker a commission.

DEFAULTS, REMEDIES

15. If Purchaser defaults hereunder, Seller's sole remedy shall be to retain as liquidated damages the down payment mentioned in Paragraph 3, it being agreed that Seller's damages in case of Purchaser's default might be impossible to ascertain and that the down payment constitutes a fair and reasonable amount of damages in the circumstances. If Seller willfully defaults, Purchaser shall have such remedies as he is entitled to at law or in equity, including but not limited to specific performance because the Apartment and possession thereof cannot be duplicated.

ENTIRE AGREEMENT

16. All representations, understandings and agreements had between the parties with respect to the subject matter of this agreement are merged in this agreement which alone fully and completely expresses their agreement.

NO ASSIGNMENT BY PURCHASER

17. This agreement cannot be changed, discharged or terminated orally. Purchaser may not assign this agreement or any of his rights hereunder.

SELLER'S EXCULPATION

18. Notwithstanding any contrary provisions of this agreement, express or implied, or any contrary rule of law or custom, if Seller shall be unable to transfer the Lease and the Shares in accordance with this agreement and any conditions hereof, then the sole obligation and liability of Seller shall be to refund to Purchaser, without interest, all sums theretofore paid on account of the purchase price, and upon the making of such refund this agreement shall be deemed cancelled and shall wholly cease and terminate, and neither party shall have any further claim against the other by reason of this agreement. However, nothing contained in this paragraph shall be construed to relieve Seller from liability due to a misrepresentation or wilful default.

NOTICES

19. All notices or demands ("Notice") that must or may be given or made hereunder shall be in writing and sent by certified or registered mail, return receipt requested, to the address above set forth for the party to whom the Notice is given, or to such other address for such party as said party shall hereafter designate by Notice given to the other party pursuant to this paragraph. Each Notice shall be deemed given on the next business day following the date of mailing the same.

MARGIN HEADINGS

20. The margin headings are intended only for convenience in finding the subject matter and do not constitute part of the text of this agreement and shall not be considered in the interpretation of this agreement or any of its provisions.

21. A. The obligations of Purchaser hereunder are subject:

(a) to the issuance of a commitment letter by   a commercial bank, savings bank, savings and loan association or insurance company doing business in the State of New York to Purchaser, on or before   , 19   (a copy of which letter shall be furnished to Seller promptly after receipt thereof), pursuant to which the institution agrees to lend not less than $, at a rate of interest not to exceed   % per annum, for a term of at least   years solely upon the security of a pledge, security interest or assignment of, and/or mortgage on, the Shares and the Lease, in order to enable Purchaser to consummate the transaction provided herein;

(b) to the consent of the Corporation to the loan if such consent is required by the terms of the Lease or the by-laws of the Corporation and to the execution by the Corporation of an agreement, in form and substance satisfactory to the institution and the Corporation, for the protection of the institution's rights as a lender; and

(c) to the closing of the loan on or before the date fixed in Paragraph 10 for the closing.

B. Purchaser shall apply for the loan, shall furnish to the institution, within five (5) days of the date hereof, accurate and complete information on Purchaser and members of Purchaser's family, as required, shall advise Seller of the name and address of the institution to which such application has been made and the date upon which it was made and shall cause to be furnished to the Corporation, for its consideration, as soon as practicable, the agreement proposed to be made by the institution with the Corporation. Purchaser shall pay or reimburse Seller the fees charged by the Corporation and its counsel for reviewing and negotiating the aforesaid agreement.

C. Purchaser shall accept any commitment letter complying with the terms of subparagraph A(a) hereof, if issued, shall pay any application, appraisal, commitment or other fees in respect of the loan, and shall comply with the requirements of the commitment letter other than those relating to the Corporation.

D. Provided that Purchaser shall have fulfilled all of Purchaser's obligations under subparagraph B hereof, if the aforementioned commitment letter is not issued by the date provided for in subparagraph A(a) hereof, Purchaser shall have the right to terminate this agreement on Notice given not more than five (5) days thereafter, or if the other conditions provided for in subparagraph A   hereof are not met, Purchaser shall have the right to terminate this agreement on Notice to Seller, and in either such event all sums theretofore paid on account of the purchase price shall be returned without delay and without interest to Purchaser, and all parties hereto shall be relieved of and from any further liability hereunder.

IN WITNESS WHEREOF, the parties hereto have duly executed this agreement the day and year first above written.

....
Seller

....
Seller

....
Purchaser

....
Purchaser

CHAPTER 3

Land Purchase Contracts & Deeds

Introduction

Like landlord-tenant law, the law of conveyances and deeds has roots which run far back into the centuries and across the Atlantic to England. Fortunately, unlike landlord-tenant law, early common law does not hold such close reins. Statutory law in most states has liberalized the law, removing archaic technicalities that in the past impeded land conveyances without any practical purpose.

Of course, the major distinction between deeds and leases is that the former is a complete transferral of land rather than transferral of a limited estate. Because of this difference, the taker or grantee need not commit himself to oppressive covenants such as a lessee must do in order to obtain possession. Since the bargaining position between the grantor and grantee is more equal, one does not have to sign away his rights in order to realize his objective. This situation is a result of a more balanced land sale and purchase market.

Although fewer complications are encountered than with the conveyance of a less-than-freehold estate, the conveyance of title to property is a legal transaction and is bound by both common and statutory law. It would be helpful to understand your position as either grantor or grantee in the execution of a deed, and an explanation of the document, its legal history, its current statutory status, and its requirements will assist you in this regard.

Initially, a deed was not a necessary instrument to a transfer of title of land. As long as the grantor physically presented the land to the grantee, title passed and the exchange of a deed later on was a formality—a written description of the occurrence which defined the extent of the estate. The deed, however, was essential in order to create or transfer incorporeal rights in land such as easements (a right to use land without any right of possession) and estates which were to commence in the future or revert to the grantor at some later date. These less-than-freehold interests had to be granted and evidenced by a written deed since an actual physical delivery was an impossibility. As the law evolved, physical delivery known as *livery*, became extinct and was succeeded by *delivery of the deed* as an equally competent and less troublesome method of conveyance.

The law changing this tradition was the Statute of Uses which promoted what was previously known as a use, or an interest in land to commence in future, into an immediate legal estate in land. Any conveyance which fell within the purview of the statute vested the grantee with legal title at that time and eliminated the need for physical delivery on the date when the interest was to take effect. Since deeds, then, could convey all estates in land, their prominence increased as livery became outdated.

The Deed of Today

Evolving out of this overly technical ancestry, the modern deed may now be the instrument of conveyance for all land interests, regardless of whether they are incorporeal rights, complete title, or are to commence now or in the future. All ancient deed forms now operate as complete statutory deeds in transferring title between grantor and grantee, although differences still exist as to the extent of the grantor's warranties with respect to his own title to the property. Thus, title passes under a statutory warranty deed, quitclaim deed, deed of bargain and sale, deed of lease, or lease, coupled with release and surrender.

Even though title passes by any of these deeds, each has its own peculiarities. Since each still exists, at least in name, it would be worthwhile to discuss the purpose of the separate deeds.

The *warranty deed* offers the grantee the best protection of all the deeds. The covenants which it contains, similar to lease covenants, are lesser contractual agreements within the deed itself. As with a lease, a warranty deed creates both privity of estate and privity of contract between the parties and, in most instances, between successors-in-interests as well. Although the covenants extend as far as the promises made in each, they do not have any impact on the actual conveyance. In that sense the deed and the covenants are separate operative provisions. The statutory form of a warranty deed passes title to the property described "together with the appurtenances and all estate and rights of the party of the first part (grantor) in and to said premises." The sentence, for its purpose, is fine, but the purchaser of title would be well advised to ascertain the scope of the seller's interest in the land. Under the provision, the grantee-purchaser (and his assigns) takes only that interest which the seller possesses, no more, no less. In order to protect himself and have viable causes of action against the seller, if in fact he believes himself to be buying a full-fee interest, the purchaser must obtain the covenants which follow this initial statement. These constants will be discussed later on.

The *quitclaim deed*, on the other hand, provides the grantee with little protection against future problems. In essence, the grantor guarantees nothing except that, as between himself and the grantor, the grantee prevails. In other words, the seller of the property grants to the buyer only those rights on the land that the grantor possessed. Thus, if the grantor was not fully seized of the property, but had only a life estate, the grantee takes title of this lesser than estate in fee. At the end of the grantor's estate, i.e., at his death, the grantee is not protected from seizure of the land by the remainderman, who now has legal title to the property. Although a thorough title search should be executed before any property purchase, it is particularly important where a quitclaim deed is the instrument of conveyance. No one wants to be cast in a position of believing that he is seized of land in fee having paid consideration in anticipation of a fee and being dispossessed later on by a remainderman with paramount title. Solace is the grantee's only remedy in this situation. As the reader will note after examining the typical quitclaim deed, it is word-for-word the mirror of the full warranty deed, *without* the covenants.

Since no covenants are implied in the sale of land, the grantee must demand and receive covenants in the deed for any assurance of protection. This is of utmost importance since the purchaser of realty is not entitled as a matter of law to a warranty deed of title. In fact, once the contract of purchase is agreed to by both parties and no express commitment is made by the grantor to supply a full warranty deed, the grantee must settle for delivery of a quitclaim deed, unless defects in the grantor's title—not excepted to in the purchase agreement—become apparent. The grantee then has the option of continuing through with the sale or retracting before completion and possibly subjecting himself to a lawsuit.

A deed of *bargain and sale* is like a quitclaim deed and the remaining deeds to be discussed in that no covenants pass to the grantee along with title. The bargain and sale deed is merely a description of the land being sold and the consideration being paid for it. Before the Statute of Uses, the delivery of a bargain and sale deed usually created only a use interest in land which the statute converted into a legal estate. Today, the deed simply transfers to the grantee title in whatever land it purports to convey.

The remaining deeds are best left swathed in the cobwebs of history. Each provided a procedure for conveying title in specific situations. A *deed of release* was the method by which a landlord gave his tenant outright title. Since the tenant was already in possession, no livery needed to be made. The *deed of lease and release* was a method of evading English law which placed certain requirements on deeds of bargain and sale. As the name implies, the deed created, first, a term lease for years and, secondly, by release, a full legal estate in the tenant. Since modern deed law eliminates these technicalities, such devices have fallen into disuse.

A *surrender* is a deed only in the sense that it accelerates title to an estate that otherwise would not vest until a later date. Quitclaim deeds, for the most part, have taken the place of surrenders, since all that is necessary is a transfer of rights between the present and preceding estate holders. The only requirement which a surrender must meet is that the estate must be synonymous in size. Today the term is more commonly associated with landlord-tenant law.

Deed Requirements

Unlike a multi-page lease which explicitly defines the rights and liabilities of the parties, a deed by statute can be relatively free of verbiage. As long as a basic statutory prescription is met, the deed accomplishes its function of conveying realty between the grantor and grantee.

Statutes may vary to a minor extent, but certain essentials are required by the laws of most states. The following requisites may be found in all deeds: (a) a description of the premises with boundaries outlined, including all buildings and fixtures; (b) names and residences of parties to the conveyance; (c) date; (d) amount and type of consideration (absence of a recital of consideration will not invalidate a deed); (e) words of conveyance expressing intent (the "granting clause"); (f) encumbrances against the premises; (g) the habendum clause (the traditional name given to the second part of a deed) delimiting the estate which the grantee takes; (h) reservations of easements or profits by the grantor; (i) covenants warranting title on a warranty deed; (j) closing declarations, signatures and seal. (No seal is required in New York State.)

The description of the premises should be specific without being detailed. Modern technology and surveying equipment allow for an accurate description in metes and bounds. Older deeds frequently used cultural monuments or geographical features, such as rivers, streams or lakes, as boundaries or as boundary markers. In most cases, certain rules of constructions prevail in resolving conflicts created by ambiguities in either the intent of the parties or because of the boundary markers used. The most important concern should be to describe the premise so as to avoid any need for calling these rules into play. Thus, always measure as precisely as possible where distances are included; cultural monuments or geographical landmarks should never be used. They are susceptible to removal or change.

Relatively few problems arise as a result of the names of the parties. As long as identities can be ascertained, misspellings are unimportant. This law even extends to deeds which fail to include the name of the grantee. Although a deed is void by law in the absence of the grantor's name, delivery of a deed without the grantee's name can be valid. In this case, the grantee's name can be added by an agent, with or without written authority.

The *granting* and *habendum* clauses are similar but not identical. Where the former expresses the grantor's intent to grant or give the estate to another, the latter further defines the extent of the ownership in the land granted. In all cases, it may enlarge, explain, or qualify the estate so long as it is not totally contradictory. Generally, the habendum clause cannot lessen an estate created by the granting clause, although, under modern law, the only determination is whether the habendum clause restricts the estate to a less-than-fee one.

Both parties should always remain cognizant of the fact that a deed is not a contract. Consideration, even though expressed in the deed, is not essential for the deed to be valid. Consideration should be set out to protect creditors and the grantee, in the event that any question develops under the recording acts.

Signatures and seals are requirements which, in the case of the granting clauses, may be conditional, and in the case of the habendum clauses, may be eliminated in many states. Again, contingent upon the situs (position or site) of the property, statutes might mandate subscription of the parties' signatures at the end of the form. As for seals, most states have dispensed with the requirement, but where doubt exists, a seal should be impressed on the document.

Covenants of Warranty

A deed does not carry with it any implied covenants to protect the grantee from possible disturbances because of a failure title. To guarantee protection, the grantee must obtain an expressed warranty deed with expressed warranties as to title. As with leases, deed covenants are binding promises and are the grantee's only assurances against third party interference. Remember the deed alone does not offer this protection, because it is strictly a conveyance of land interests.

The covenants of seizen (right of possession) and right to convey are identical, for all practical purposes. Each is a warranty that the grantor is in a position to make the conveyance. Should the grantor not be in possession of the premises, buildings or fixtures, he is in breach of the deed at the time of conveyance and is liable for damages.

A full warranty deed also provides that no mortgages, liens or other encumbrances exist against the premises. In many cases, where parties are alerted to minor encumbrances, these can be excepted from the deed and do not effect the warranty. Similar to the two previous covenants, the convenant against encumbrances is breached at the time of conveyance.

The convenant for quiet enjoyment mirrors the same covenant under a lease, although in a deed, it must be explicit. The grantor is liable if the grantee is dispossessed by the grantor, by any successor-in-interest to him or by anyone holding superior title. The covenant does not extend to wrongful third parties who disturb the grantee's enjoyment and use of the land.

Another covenant which is broken only upon the eviction of the grantee, is the covenant of the warranty. The courts have stated that under this covenant the grantor promises to compensate the grantee for any damages or loss incurred upon the assertion of superior title by a third party. The covenant has also been interpreted to require that the grantor defend his title in such conflicts.

T 685   Standard N.Y.B.T.U. Form 8003—Warranty Deed
With Full Covenants—Ind. or Corp.   DATE CODE   JULIUS BLUMBERG, INC., LAW BLANK PUBLISHERS
80 EXCHANGE PL. AT BROADWAY, N. Y. C. 10004

CONSULT YOUR LAWYER BEFORE SIGNING THIS INSTRUMENT—THIS INSTRUMENT SHOULD BE USED BY LAWYERS ONLY.

THIS INDENTURE, made the   day of   , nineteen hundred and
BETWEEN

party of the first part, and

party of the second part,

WITNESSETH, that the party of the first part, in consideration of ten dollars and other valuable consideration paid by the party of the second part, does hereby grant and release unto the party of the second part, the heirs or successors and assigns of the party of the second part forever,

ALL that certain plot, piece or parcel of land, with the buildings and improvements thereon erected, situate, lying and being in the

TOGETHER with all right, title and interest, if any, of the party of the first part in and to any streets and roads abutting the above described premises to the center lines thereof; TOGETHER with the appurtenances and all the estate and rights of the party of the first part in and to said premises; TO HAVE AND TO HOLD the premises herein granted unto the party of the second part, the heirs or successors and assigns of the party of the second part forever.

AND the party of the first part, in compliance with Section 13 of the Lien Law, covenants that the party of the first part will receive the consideration for this conveyance and will hold the right to receive such consideration as a trust fund to be applied first for the purpose of paying the cost of the improvement and will apply the same first to the payment of the cost of the improvement before using any part of the total of the same for any other purpose.

AND the party of the first part covenants as follows: that said party of the first part is seized of the said premises in fee simple, and has good right to convey the same; that the party of the second part shall quietly enjoy the said premises; that the said premises are free from incumbrances, except as aforesaid; that the party of the first part will execute or procure any further necessary assurance of the title to said premises; and that said party of the first part will forever warrant the title to said premises.

The word "party" shall be construed as if it read "parties" whenever the sense of this indenture so requires.

IN WITNESS WHEREOF, the party of the first part has duly executed this deed the day and year first above written.

IN PRESENCE OF: ⟶

STATE OF NEW YORK, COUNTY OF   **ss:**

On the   day of   19   , before me personally came

to me known to be the individual   described in and who executed the foregoing instrument, and acknowledged that executed the same.

STATE OF NEW YORK, COUNTY OF   **ss:**

On the   day of   19   , before me personally came

to me known to be the individual   described in and who executed the foregoing instrument, and acknowledged that executed the same.

STATE OF NEW YORK, COUNTY OF   **ss:**

On the   day of   19   , before me personally came
to me known, who, being by me duly sworn, did depose and say that he resides at No.
                                      ;
that he is the
of
               , the corporation described in and which executed the foregoing instrument; that he knows the seal of said corporation; that the seal affixed to said instrument is such corporate seal; that it was so affixed by order of the board of directors of said corporation, and that he signed h name thereto by like order.

STATE OF NEW YORK, COUNTY OF   **ss:**

On the   day of   19   , before me personally came
the subscribing witness to the foregoing instrument, with whom I am personally acquainted, who, being by me duly sworn, did depose and say that he resides at No.
                                        ;
that he knows
                         to be the individual described in and who executed the foregoing instrument; that he, said subscribing witness, was present and saw execute the same; and that he, said witness, at the same time subscribed h name as witness thereto.

Warranty Deed
WITH FULL COVENANTS

TITLE NO.

            TO

SECTION

BLOCK

LOT

COUNTY OR TOWN

RECORD AND RETURN BY MAIL TO:

Zip No.

P 678—Warranty deed : lien clause, ind. or corp.

JULIUS BLUMBERG, INC., LAW BLANK PUBLISHERS
80 EXCHANGE PL. AT BROADWAY, N. Y. C. 10004

U.S. Internal
Revenue Stamps
Affixed

This Indenture *made* 19

Between

party of the first part, and

party of the second part,

Witnesseth *that the party of the first part, in consideration of*

Dollars ($)

lawful money of the United States,
paid by the party of the second part, does hereby grant and release unto the party of the second part,
the heirs or successors and assigns of the party of the second part forever, all

Together *with the appurtenances and all the estate and rights of the party of the first part in and to said premises,*

To have and to hold *the premises herein granted unto the party of the second part, the heirs or successors and assigns of the party of the second part forever.*

And *the party of the first part covenants as follows:*

First, *That the party of the second part shall quietly enjoy the said premises;*

Second, *That the party of the first part will forever* **Warrant** *the title to said premises.*

Third, *the party of the first part, in compliance with Section 13 of the Lien Law, covenants that the party of the first part will receive the consideration for this conveyance and will hold the right to receive such consideration as a trust fund to be applied first for the purpose of paying the cost of the improvement and will apply the same first to the payment of the cost of the improvement before using any part of the total of the same for any other purpose.*

The word "party" shall be construed as if it read "parties" whenever the sense of this indenture so requires.

In Witness Whereof, *the party of the first part has duly executed this deed the day and year first above written.*

In Presence of

.... { L. S. }

.... { L. S. }

.... { L. S. }

.... { L. S. }

STATE OF NEW YORK, COUNTY OF   ss.:
    On   19   , before me per-
sonally came   to me known,
who, being by me duly sworn, did depose and say that deponent
resides at No.
deponent is   of
                        the corporation described in and which
executed, the foregoing instrument; deponent knows the seal of
said corporation; that the seal affixed to said instrument is such
corporate seal; that it was so affixed by order of the Board of
Directors of said corporation; deponent signed deponent's name
thereto by like order.

STATE OF NEW YORK, COUNTY OF   ss.:
    On   19   , before me per-
sonally came

to me known to be the individual   described in, and who executed the foregoing instrument, and acknowledged that   he
executed the same.

The Modern Realty Transaction

Introduction

Although the deed is a necessary instrument in the conveyance of real property, today a seller or buyer will find himself executing legal documents in addition to the deed. The reason for this increase in legal papers is the interjection of the broker in the dealings between the parties. Although not a recent inclusion in real estate law, *brokerage contracts*, formalized *purchase options* and *purchase offers* are not very complicated and do not trace their roots back to ancient English real property law. Instead, contract law prevails, but with a few common-law and statutory peculiarities.

Without the tradition and concomitant entanglements attributable to real property law, there is no purpose in discussing the background of the contracts which initiate a realty transaction. Instead, we turn to various contracts in order to explain, and, where necessary, elaborate on specific provisions.

Contract Between Owner and Broker

The initial two paragraphs identify the parties and the subject matter. In most cases the seller employs the broker and, hence, must pay his fee; however, where the circumstances dictate, a buyer in search of land in a particular area may work through a broker to obtain speedier results. Whatever the case, be it buyer or seller-owner who is under contract to the broker, the party must watch for fees which may come due to the broker, even without a sale of the premises.

With that in mind, the third paragraph should be scrutinized. Subparagraph (a) states that no commissions shall be earned by the broker unless each of three requirements is satisfied:

(1) that the sale is complete and that it is completed on the owner's terms or terms to which he acquiesces;

(2) that the sale shall have been consummated through the broker who is party to the contract. The terms "negotiated and consummated," if read restrictively might even free the seller who initiates the transaction, arranges the details, and, in all senses, "negotiates" the sale, even though the broker obtains the finalizing assent by the purchaser. More realistically, the terms are read together. If the broker is involved on any step of the transaction, he will be due his commission; and

(3) that the deed and purchase price actually exchange hands.

Paragraphs (b) and (c) further delimit the conditions which must be met in order for the owner-seller to become liable. Under (b), the discovery of a last-minute encumbrance which cannot be promptly removed may defeat the sale, but does not bind the seller to payment of brokerage fees. Under (c) the seller incurs no obligation to pay, regardless of default by either party to the sale, unless the seller's default is willful. Additionally, the wording frees the seller from costly litigation against a defaulting purchaser in order to satisfy the broker's commission claim.

Collectively, these paragraphs relieve the seller of one of the hidden dangers to realty brokerage contracts. Unknown to most people, a broker in many states earns his commission upon the presentation of a ready, willing, and able buyer, whether or not the sale is consummated. As long as the buyer accepts the seller's conditions and stands in a position to complete the deal (i.e., has the cash or has opened the channels to obtain a loan), the seller as of that moment is obligated to the broker for commissions. The broker need not even require a down payment. If the broker balks at releasing this pre-established right, the seller should at least demand that the contract mandate the payment of a portion down, equal to or in excess of the brokerage fee. By so doing, the seller does not risk the possibility of expenses without a sale.

Paragraph (d) extends the seller's protected status. The right to terminate the agreement orally is self-explanatory. The major benefit offered by the paragraph is the unequivocal language that the agreement "in no event be deemed to be an exclusive listing . . . and the owner may hire and retain other and additional brokers to sell the premises . . ." Under an exclusive listing contract, the broker who is party to the contract becomes entitled to the commissions due upon the consummation of the contract. Thus, if the owner through his own efforts completes the sale, or if another broker finalizes the deal, the initial broker with the exclusive listing contract still collects his fee. This can be particularly expensive to the seller who has committed himself to the second broker. Instead of being indebted on one contract, the seller will find that he suddenly owes double commissions.

The remainder of the paragraph further limits the owner's liability. Should he decide to increase the asking price after the premises have been on the market for some time, he may do so at will without altering his contractual obligation with the broker. This provision is highly important in these times of inflation. Since buyers might have difficulties procuring mortgages and be legally able to back away from the deal after a significant period of time, the seller would not want to be locked into a fixed price as land values escalate.

Additionally, the owner should not bind himself to pay for expenses that the broker might accumulate in exorbitant efforts to sell the premises.

It should be noted here that the customary fee in New York and other jurisdictions is 6% of the total selling price of residential property. Brokerage fees for the sale of other types of realty, commercial property or raw land, are higher, generally around 10%.

The final paragraph recites an ultimate concern for the seller. The seller should never place himself in a position to be liable for commissions before the sale is completed. This paragraph ties the payment of the commissions to the delivery of the deed and the receipt of the full purchase price. The clause requires that the commissions be merited only upon compliance with all other provisions. Although the broker may balk at signing such a contract, it is ideal from the seller's perspective, and he should bargain to include as many of these provisions as possible.

Purchase Option

Any purchase option, whether for personal or real property, is purely a contractual agreement. All of the elements of a contract which were discussed earlier apply. Basically, an option allows a prospective buyer to consider the purchase over a period of time without fear of losing out to an intervening sale. The bilateral agreement consists of a promise by the seller not to sell to another buyer during that period, in return for the purchaser's promise to buy the premises for a preset amount and under the conditions of the option, if he so elects. In consideration for the option, the purchaser pays the seller a sum of money to which he relinquishes all rights.

As in all realty documents, the option should state the property covered by its terms. The boundaries should be clearly expressed as explained under the section on deeds. The first clause of importance which is unique to an option is the one by which the seller promises to apply the consideration for the option in reducing the already agreed-upon price. A purchaser should be steadfast in his insistence to include this provision in the option. Without it, the consideration is lost, whether or not the option is exercised. The provision dictates the manner in which the full purchase price is to be rendered. The purchaser should pay close attention. If he

Standard N.Y.B.T.U. Form 8001
Bargain & sale deed, without covenant against grantor's acts—Ind. or Corp.   DATE CODE   JULIUS BLUMBERG, INC., LAW BLANK PUBLISHERS
80 EXCHANGE PL. AT BROADWAY, N. Y. C. 10004

CONSULT YOUR LAWYER BEFORE SIGNING THIS INSTRUMENT—THIS INSTRUMENT SHOULD BE USED BY LAWYERS ONLY.

THIS INDENTURE, made the   day of   , nineteen hundred and

BETWEEN

party of the first part, and

party of the second part,

WITNESSETH, that the party of the first part, in consideration of ten dollars and other valuable consideration paid by the party of the second part, does hereby grant and release unto the party of the second part, the heirs or successors and assigns of the party of the second part forever,

ALL that certain plot, piece or parcel of land, with the buildings and improvements thereon erected, situate, lying and being in the

TOGETHER with all right, title and interest, if any, of the party of the first part in and to any streets and roads abutting the above described premises to the center lines thereof; TOGETHER with the appurtenances and all the estate and rights of the party of the first part in and to said premises; TO HAVE AND TO HOLD the premises herein granted unto the party of the second part, the heirs or successors and assigns of the party of the second part forever.

AND the party of the first part, in compliance with Section 13 of the Lien Law, covenants that the party of the first part will receive the consideration for this conveyance and will hold the right to receive such consideration as a trust fund to be applied first for the purpose of paying the cost of the improvement and will apply the same first to the payment of the cost of the improvement before using any part of the total of the same for any other purpose. The word "party" shall be construed as if it read "parties" whenever the sense of this indenture so requires.

IN WITNESS WHEREOF, the party of the first part has duly executed this deed the day and year first above written.

IN PRESENCE OF:

STATE OF NEW YORK, COUNTY OF   ss: | STATE OF NEW YORK, COUNTY OF   ss:

On the   day of   19   , before me
personally came

to me known to be the individual   described in and who
executed the foregoing instrument, and acknowledged that
        executed the same.

On the   day of   19   , before me
personally came

to me known to be the individual   described in and who
executed the foregoing instrument, and acknowledged that
        executed the same.

STATE OF NEW YORK, COUNTY OF   ss: | STATE OF NEW YORK, COUNTY OF   ss:

On the   day of   19   , before me
personally came
to me known, who, being by me duly sworn, did depose and
say that   he resides at No.
                                                            ;

that   he is the
of
                                , the corporation described
in and which executed the foregoing instrument; that   he
knows the seal of said corporation; that the seal affixed
to said instrument is such corporate seal; that it was so
affixed by order of the board of directors of said corporation, and that   he signed h   name thereto by like order.

On the   day of   19   , before me
personally came
the subscribing witness to the foregoing instrument, with
whom I am personally acquainted, who, being by me duly
sworn, did depose and say that   he resides at No.
                                                            ;

that   he knows

                                to be the individual
described in and who executed the foregoing instrument;
that   he, said subscribing witness, was present and saw
        execute the same; and that   he, said witness,
at the same time subscribed h   name as witness thereto.

𝔐ortgage

TITLE No. _____

SECTION

BLOCK

LOT

COUNTY OR TOWN

                    TO

RETURN BY MAIL TO:

Zip No.

intends to pay through installments over a period of time, he should prearrange the schedule before risking the option value. The seller, in such a situation, should consider the possibility of keeping the initial cash payment under thirty percent (30%) of the total selling price in order to qualify for an installment sale and enjoy tax benefits. Normally, however, the contents of this section, as with the contract for sale, include the different means by which the purchaser intends to convey the full price. Thus, the amount of down payment and the medium of exchange, i.e., check, cash, etc., the current mortgage and amount and manner of payment of the balance should all be defined clearly.

The third paragraph is not complicated although care should be taken by both parties to set a consideration and a time period commensurate with the realities of the transaction. The accompanying payment, along with the option price paid by the purchaser, can equal the down payment in order to simplify the transaction.

The remaining paragraphs contain sale contract provisions. These will be discussed below, but it should be stated now that no less concern should be given these provisions in an option than in a contract for sale. Depending on the option agreement, the purchaser is extending a sum of money which can be best protected by smoothing out difficulties now.

Offer to Purchase

Little explanation is needed to explain the purchase offer. As covered in the introduction, the offer is not elevated into a binding contract until accepted, but once signed by the seller, the offer acts as effectively as the contract for sale (to be discussed).

The document is sketchy. Although its brevity leaves little to be explained, it can create latent dangers. Since acceptance of the offer binds the parties, both should examine the instrument in order to ascertain whether all

matters are expressly covered. The purchaser should be sure that the premises on which he submits an offer are identical to those with which seller intends to part. The offer should describe not only the premises, but it should also detail the fixtures and appurtenances that accompany the property. As for the actual payment, the contract should not refer to "cash" as the medium of exchange for the balance, if the buyer intends to secure payment with a mortgage.

The remaining provisions will be discussed under the section on contract for sale. It is imperative that both parties are cognizant that the purchase offer, once it has been signed, binds them to its terms. Clauses that seem to be ambiguous and do not fully outline the duties of the parties should be negotiated to the satisfaction of the parties before acceptance.

Contract for the Sale of Property

Contracts for the sale of realty can take many forms, but an examination of each form will reveal that certain provisions are always included. Four different contracts have been included in the text in order to demonstrate this point and to apprise the reader of examples which may be encountered. The contract provisions will be dissected in order to illuminate wording which results in frequent problems.

The identity clause naming the parties initiates each contract. The clause is merely descriptive unless default occurs and not all parties are named. Then the trouble lies in the buyer's inability to sue for specific performance under the contract and to have the judgment operate against all those having an interest in the property. Both parties should be concerned that each has authority to execute the sale and conveyance. In particular, one should be altered to inquire into this authority when dealing with anyone who holds himself out as an agent of a primary party or as a corporate officer.

The clause immediately following describes the premises to be transferred. This topic has been covered under the discussion of deeds. It is sufficient to say that as long as the agreement makes the property readily identifiable and distinguishable, the purpose of the clause has been satisfied. Additionally, many sales contracts provide on the back of the document a map on which to plot the boundaries in metes and bounds or to list the block and lot number. Even though this information may seem technical at the time, it protects the parties if later discrepancies arise.

The improved contract for the sale of realty is more explicit than the others. Being a hybrid, suitable for New York City, it makes direct reference to interests and rights to abutting property. These rights and interests include *easements* (the right to make use of land belonging to someone else for some definite and limited purpose) and succession to awards resulting from the taking or damaging of the seller's fee. Since these interests are often capitalized in the value of the property and passed on to the purchaser, he should be cautious to succeed to these interests so as not to pay for a right which the seller retains.

The seller should also include in the contract all encumbrances of which the buyer has notice and to which he takes subject. Usually the contract provides for the seller to "convey said premises to the vendee in fee simple free and clear from all liens, rights of dower or other encumbrances (unless hereinafter specified)." Thus, to extricate himself from any conflict that might arise over whether the purchaser had notice of any particular encumbrance, lien or easement, the existence of each and acceptance by the purchaser should be noted in all cases.

We now turn to the means and manner of payment. Much of this has been explained in the discussion on the purchase option and need not be elaborated any further. Normally, the total payment is separated into: (1) the down payment at the signing of the contract;

(2) the amount of cash in currency or certified check to be delivered to the seller at the time of closing; (3) the amount, if any, of any mortgage or lien which the purchaser takes subject to or assumes (see chapter on mortgages); and (4) the amount of any note or bond secured by a purchase money mortgage. As has been impressed before, the payment schedule and medium should be stated as unequivocally as possible.

Before considering other sections, the purchaser should be aware of the recording statute at this time. Prior to purchase, a full title search should always be conducted and an acquaintance with the recordation of realty transactions and liens involving the property to be conveyed should be made by the purchaser. He should consider the importance of recording his interest in the property from the moment of the down payment. The recording of a memorandum or the executed contract prevents the seller from conveying the property to a third party. The purchaser's status as an equitable lienor is recorded, which secures his down payment against the property should the seller default. The complete consequences of the recording statutes are far beyond the scope of this book, but you should note that the recording act can be used to the purchaser's advantage even before the sale is consummated by delivery of the deed.

All of the contracts have special provisions dealing in detail with mortgages. (See chapter on mortgages.) Further discussion here would only confuse rather than inform. Moreover, because of the complexity of mortgages, the parties should seek legal advice.

We are next confronted with the clause describing the time and place of delivery of the deed and the type of deed. The purchaser should attach great importance to this provision. Normally, time is not of the essence in realty transactions, and the law does not impose a time requirement. If the purchaser or the seller requires the property or proceeds on a particular day, the contract should ex-

Contract for the Sale of Real Property

This AGREEMENT, made on the date hereinafter mentioned, between the party or parties herein designated as SELLER and the party or parties herein designated as PURCHASER WITNESSETH, as follows:

1. SELLER agrees to sell and convey and PURCHASER agrees to purchase premises as herein described under all terms and conditions stated herein.

2. SELLER shall convey said premises to PURCHASER by BARGAIN and SALE DEED in proper form for record, which deed shall include the covenant required by subdivision 5, section 13 of the Lien Law. The said deed shall be prepared, duly executed and acknowledged by SELLER and have transfer tax stamps in the proper amount affixed thereto, all at SELLER'S expense, so as to convey to PURCHASER the fee simple of said premises free and clear of all liens and encumbrances, except as herein stated.

3. SELLER shall convey said premises subject to all covenants, conditions, restrictions and easements of record and zoning laws. Subject also to any statement of facts which an inspection and/or an accurate survey of the premises may show provided the same does not render title unmarketable. Subject also to existing tenancies, if any, and to unpaid installments of street and improvement assessments payable after the date of transfer of title.

4. SELLER may pay and discharge any liens and encumbrances, specifically including SELLER'S mortgage on the premises, not provided for herein out of the moneys to be paid by PURCHASER on the transfer of title.

5. This agreement is contingent upon PURCHASER securing a mortgage loan. The PURCHASER agrees to make immediate application, through the office of the BROKER, for a mortgage loan in the amount of   on what is commonly known as a conventional   year direct reduction plan with interest per annum at the then prevailing rate. Either party hereto reserves the right to void this agreement by five days' written notice to the other party if the mortgage loan has not been arranged by   . Pending the disposition of said application, all moneys paid hereunder shall be held in the trust account of the SELLER'S ATTORNEY to be paid to the SELLER when mortgage contingency is met or waived, or returned to the PURCHASER if this agreement is voided as herein provided.

6. All rentals, taxes and interest shall be adjusted pro-rata to the day of transfer. If SELLER has already made or shall have made before the time of closing any payments in advance on account of insurance and/or taxes and water rents payable after closing to a mortgagee whose mortgage is to remain on the premises PURCHASER is to reimburse SELLER for the total of these payments, in cash at the time of closing.

7. If on the date of transfer of title, there is any fuel in the premises belonging to the SELLER, PURCHASER shall buy the same by paying the SELLER a sum equal to the market value thereof. Plumbing, heating and lighting fixtures, ranges, built-in bathroom and kitchen cabinets and built-in kitchen appliances, venetian blinds, shades, storm windows and screens, storm and screen doors, awnings, pumps, shrubbery and television aerials, if now in or on said premises, are represented to be owned by SELLER, free from all liens and encumbrances, and are included in the sale price together with the following items:

8. The buildings on the premises herein described are hereby sold "as is," without warranty as to condition, express or implied, and a conveyance thereof hereunder shall be made in their condition on the date of transfer of title, except that in case of any destruction within the meaning of the provisions of Section 5–1311 of the General Obligations Law of the State of New York entitled "Uniform Vendor and Purchaser Risk Act," said section shall apply to this Contract.

9. In the event SELLER is unable to convey title in accordance with the terms of this agreement, SELLER'S sole liability will be to refund the amount paid on account of the purchase price.

10. The PARTIES agree that
brought about this sale and SELLER agrees to pay an amount equal to 6% of the selling price as commission for Services to said BROKER.

11. The PURCHASER shall be entitled to possession of the premises and the rents, issues and profits, if any, thereof, immediately upon closing of title and delivery of deed.

12. This agreement is entered into upon knowledge of the parties as to the value of the land and whatever buildings are upon the same and not on any representations made as to character or quality.

13. PURCHASER represents that he has sufficient cash available (together with the mortgage referred to herein) to consummate this transaction.

14. This instrument contains all agreements of the parties hereto. There are no promises, agreements, terms, conditions, warranties, representations, or statements other than contained herein. There may be no modification or amendment of this agreement except in writing executed by the parties hereto. This contract, or any part thereof, shall not be assigned without prior written consent of the SELLER and BROKER herein.

Dated:

Seller:

Purchaser:

Price: $ Payable as follows:
         $ Deposit on signing this agreement.
         $ Additional deposit with BROKER (to be paid to SELLER by BROKER upon closing of title and delivery of deed).
         $ In cash or certified check upon the transfer of title.

Time and Place of Transfer: To be agreed upon mutually by PURCHASER and SELLER upon SELLER'S obtaining mortgage referred to in paragraph 5.

    IN WITNESS WHEREOF, the parties to these presents have hereunto set their hands and seals the day and year first above written.

_____   _____
PURCHASER   SELLER

_____   _____
PURCHASER   SELLER

Option for Purchase of Property

AGREEMENT made this   day of   19
between
hereinafter described as the SELLER, and
hereinafter described as the PURCHASER,

WITNESSETH, that for and in consideration of the sum of   Dollars ($),
paid by the PURCHASER, the receipt of which is hereby acknowledged by the SELLER, the
SELLER hereby gives and grants to the PURCHASER the exclusive option, right and privilege of
purchasing.

ALL THAT TRACT OR PARCEL OF LAND, with the buildings and improvements thereon,
situate in the
of   , County of
State of   , briefly described as follows:

for the sum of   Dollars ($), payable as follows: $ upon the execution and delivery of this option as hereinbefore provided, which amount SELLER agrees to apply
on the purchase price if PURCHASER elects to exercise the option; $ upon the
acceptance of this option by the PURCHASER as hereinafter provided; and the balance of the
purchase price, to wit, $, in the following manner:

Notice of election to purchase hereunder shall be given by the PURCHASER in writing by
registered mail, addressed to the SELLER, at
on or before   19   , which said notice shall be accompanied by the payment of
$ hereinbefore specified, and title shall close and the deed shall be delivered at the
office of
at   o'clock   .M. on
                    19   , following
the giving of such notice, or at such time and upon such other date as shall be mutually agreed
upon by the parties hereto.

SELLER shall convey said premises to PURCHASER in fee simple, free and clear of all liens,
rights of dower or other encumbrances (unless herein otherwise specified), by a good and sufficient deed of conveyance, in the usual form of a warranty deed, except that if SELLER conveys as
executor, trustee, administrator or guardian, or in any trust capacity, the usual deed given in such
cases shall be accepted. Said conveyance shall also be made subject to all restrictions, easements
and conditions of record, if any.

If PURCHASER gives a mortgage on the herein referred to premises, to secure to SELLER any
of the purchase money thereof, it shall be designated therein as being given for that purpose; it
shall be accompanied by the usual bond; both shall contain the usual statutory interest, insurance,
tax, assessment and receivership clauses, if SELLER requires. The mortgage recording tax,
recording fee for the mortgage and the revenue stamps on the bond accompanying the same, shall
be paid by the PURCHASER as part of the consideration of the said purchase.

PURCHASER is to have possession of the premises on the day of transfer of title, except

All rentals, insurance premiums, interest and all other matters affecting the property herein
referred to, not herein otherwise provided for, shall be adjusted pro rata to the day of the transfer
of title.

The transfer is to include, without further consideration and unless herein otherwise stated, all
fixtures and appurtenances now in said premises, including the heating plant and all appliances
connected therewith, ranges, service hot water heaters, gas and electric chandeliers and fixtures
(excepting portable lamps), bathroom fixtures attached, outside shades, screens, awnings and
storm doors.

IN WITNESS WHEREOF, this Agreement has been duly executed by the parties hereto as of
the date first above written.

_____
PURCHASER

_____
SELLER

pressly make time of the essence. If, at the closing, minor encumbrances lie against the property, the seller cannot postpone the delivery for a short time in order to discharge the liens. The seller is immediately in default, and the purchaser is relieved of performance. The clause can make time of the essence bilateral, which releases the seller, if the purchaser defaults by failing to tender the necessary cash payment or mortgage.

The purchaser should be wary of the type of deed. Since the purchaser is entitled only to a quitclaim deed (see discussion of deeds) unless the contract provides otherwise, he should be certain that reference is made to a full warranty deed. Without it, the purchaser does not have the assurances of title, etc., from the seller.

All of the contracts make expressed references to the inclusion of personal property, i.e., "heating, cooking and lighting fixtures, air-conditioning fixtures and units, ranges, refrigerators, radio and television antennas . . . mailboxes, weather vanes, flagpoles, pumps, shrubbery and outdoor statuary," in the sale. Both parties should be alerted to the provision on personal property and determine if it meets the needs of the situation. Case law has concluded that these terms are not deemed part of the sale of real property unless expressly provided for, yet the purchase price may reflect their value. A further distinction is made as to appurtenances and personal property. The former pass automatically with the conveyance of property, while the latter become the purchaser's possessions only if the sale contract so expresses.

The better practice is to request a bill of sale (see Chapter 8) from the seller for the personal property in conjunction with the contract of sale for the realty. This procedure protects the purchaser by giving him a warranty of title to the personalty which he does not receive under the realty contract. The seller should be cautious not to include items which he either does not own or has encumbered as the result of a chattel mortgage. In order to avoid later legal consequences, the seller should qualify the clause, passing only those items of personalty which he owns and earmarking in the contract those items subject to liens and mortgages.

In most cities, contracts make reference to the existence of municipal zoning laws, earlier structures and possible encroachments (see form). Although the first provision, which subjects the property to zoning regulations and ordinances of the city, town or village in which the premises are located, which are not violated by existing structures, in effect assures the purchaser that no current violations exist, this clause and the other remaining two do not justify rejection of the deed by the purchaser. Obviously, the seller should avoid this clause if possible, whereas the purchaser should avoid the latter two which release the seller from liability for former grants of authority to encroach upon the property and for his own encroachments upon public property.

Several clauses mention the burden of paying specific costs relating to the property. These clauses are of particular importance to the purchaser, since by obtaining the seller's acquiescence, he relieves himself of expenses for which he becomes liable upon ownership. The first are the installment assessments. Again the purchaser must realize that improvements to the property are usually capitalized in its value. Assessments are municipal charges for local public improvements which the owner can elect to pay over a period of time. Since the seller most likely increases the price of the property because of the improvement, the purchaser should be certain to hold the seller liable for the complete discharge of the cost by contracting that the unpaid assessments become liens against the property at the time of the delivery of the deed.

The other provisions require the pro rata distribution of profits and expenses arising

Contract Between Seller and Broker

KNOW ALL MEN BY THESE PRESENTS, that the undersigned, having a principal place of business at the address hereinbelow indicated, does hereby certify and agree:

1. That the undersigned is duly licensed as a real estate broker under the laws of the State of _____ .

2. That the undersigned is hereby employed as such real estate broker by _____, hereinafter called "Seller," in connection with the sale of premises known as _____.

3. That the terms and conditions of the contract of brokerage between the undersigned and the said Seller in connection with the premises above referred to are and have at all times been:

(a) That no commissions should be deemed earned on the part of the undersigned until:

1) a contract of sale has been executed by the Seller and the Purchaser upon the terms and conditions acceptable to the Seller in its sole and absolute judgment;

2) such contract of sale shall have been negotiated and consummated solely through the efforts of the undersigned as broker and;

3) the deed conveying title be delivered pursuant to the terms, covenants and conditions of the said contract of sale and the full purchase price be paid.

(b) That in the event the Seller shall fail to have a good title to said premises so as to be able to convey the same in accordance with the contract of sale, no commission shall be deemed earned on the part of the undersigned.

(c) If, after the Seller has entered into the contract of sale with the Purchaser, title does not close, whether due to the fault or default of the Seller or Purchaser or for any other reason whatsoever except Seller's wilful default in the performance of said contract of sale, no commission shall be deemed earned on the part of the undersigned, and in the event title does not close because of the Purchaser's default, the Seller shall not be obligated or required to resort to any legal remedy for the enforcement of the Purchaser's obligations under the said contract of sale and the Seller shall not be obligated to the broker for the payment of any commission.

(d) That, in any event, this Agreement may be terminated by the Seller at any time by either oral or written notice to the undersigned; that this hiring and the listing of the premises with the undersigned shall in no event be deemed to be an exclusive listing thereof with the undersigned, and the Seller may hire and retain other and additional brokers to sell the premises; that the premises may be withdrawn from sale by the Seller at any time, upon either oral or written notice, without liability of any kind on the part of the Seller to the undersigned, and that the purchase price at which the premises were listed with the undersigned may be changed at any time by the Seller without liability of any kind to the undersigned, and that the Seller shall in no event be liable or responsible to the undersigned for any expenses, fees or disbursements paid or incurred by the undersigned in connection with its endeavors to sell the premises.

(e) That the commission payable to the undersigned, if earned pursuant to the provisions hereof, shall be paid upon the delivery of the deed and the payment of the purchase price, and such commission shall be the sum of $ _____ at the rate prescribed by _____ .

That this contains all the terms of such employment and shall not be varied, changed or amended except by a written agreement signed by both the Seller and the broker.

IN WITNESS WHEREOF, the undersigned has caused this instrument to be duly executed this _____ day of _____, 19___.

_____
Broker

_____
Seller

Purchase Offer

TO THE OWNER OR PERSON EMPOWERED TO SELL THE PROPERTY DESCRIBED BELOW:

We agree to purchase the following property situated in the   of County of   , State of   , known as   , being a

For a more particular description of said premises reference is hereby made to the deed thereof. Together with all lighting, heating and plumbing fixtures, window shades, screen and storm doors and windows, if any, water heater, water meter and all fixtures and fittings appurtenant to or used in the operation of the premises and owned by you.

At the price of   ($) Dollars, payable as follows:
$ cash on or before   on passing of deed.

You are to deliver to me, or my attorney, at least five (5) days before closing, a forty-year abstract of title and ten-year search or tax receipts showing the property free and clear of all liens and encumbrances except as herein set forth, and except building and use restrictions, pole and wire easements of record, and subject to zoning ordinance and to any taxes for local improvements not now completed.

Transfer is to be completed at the office of on or before   or as soon thereafter as abstracts can be brought to date, at which time you are to convey to me by   deed, good title to the property free of all liens and encumbrances, except as hereinabove set forth, subject to rights of tenants, if any.

Interest, insurance premiums, rents, and taxes to be prorated and adjusted as of   , 19 .

City, State and County Taxes shall be adjusted and apportioned on a calendar year beginning Jan. 1, and ending Dec. 31.

Possession of premises shall be delivered on or before on passing of deed.

Upon any purchase money mortgage given we agree to pay the usual mortgage tax and recording fee and Revenue stamps on bond where required.

This offer may be assigned to an individual or corporation for the purpose of holding title thereto, except that the undersigned shall remain responsible for the faithful performance of the contract.

The risk of loss or damage to said premises by fire or other causes until the delivery of the deed is assumed by you.

We represent that is the broker in this transaction and that no other real estate broker or agent has been instrumental in bringing about this sale.

This offer, when accepted, shall constitute a binding contract of purchase and sale and it shall bind and inure to the benefit of the parties hereto and their respective executors, administrators, distributees, successors and assigns.

Dated _____

_____
Purchaser

_____
Seller

from the property. Specifically, one such clause refers to rents, mortgage interests, taxes, sewer rents and fuel costs, all of which are apportioned according to the percentage of time owned by each party. Another separate provision mandates the allocation of water costs based upon a last reading of the meter 30 days before the closing. All of these provisions accomplish the same purpose—to charge each party his equitable share.

Minor encumbrances against the property should not defeat the sale. The proper provision can solve any problem created by such encumbrances. Generally, the agreement creates liens against the property for costs attributable to the seller. Since liens can render the title unmarketable, the contract should allow for a reduction of the selling price by the amount of the cost in discharging of the liens. Such provision can protect the seller by not giving the purchaser opportunity to claim default on the seller's part and back out of the agreement, if time is of the essence. Additionally, the seller can further safeguard against default by allowing himself to use any portion of the purchase price to satisfy these and other minor encumbrances.

Another occurrence which all of the contracts provide for is the danger of destruction of the premises while the contract is executory. If strict attention is paid, it will be noticed that, in all but one instance, the seller is responsible for insuring the premises. Under common law, the majority of states placed the risk of loss for destruction or injury to the property on the purchaser. Because the purchaser held equitable title after execution of the contract, courts believed that it was his duty to procure insurance or suffer the loss. Thus purchasers began to contract for the seller to assume the obligation. The problem was that the usual provision, as can be noted on two of the contracts, only requires that the seller maintain fire insurance and thereby the purchaser risked loss resulting from any other catastrophe.

In attempts to solve the dilemma, many states adopted laws, such as New York's Uniform Vendor and Purchaser Risk Act, which supposedly spells out rights and liabilities. Similar to the earlier court decrees and unsophisticated contract attempts to cure the ill, the Act proved to be somewhat ineffective to the extent that it did not define liabilities in all situations. The result is that the Act solves some, but not all, problems. Since the Act is deemed part of contract, the safest course for both parties is to reduce to writing the rights and liabilities of each under all circumstances, covering all foreseeable happenings such as "fire or the elements or by any cause beyond either party's control or . . . by eminent domain." The provision should also state to whom the insurance proceeds are payable and at what time in the transaction one or both parties may cancel without repercussions. If the question of loss revolves around "materiality" or the degree of destruction necessary to trigger any clause in the provision, another clause should express some procedure such as arbitration to resolve the issue equitably and quickly.

The other provisions which appear in some of the contracts deserve comment. First, both parties should consent to a provision precluding oral changes or terminations. Any claims by either party that an oral agreement modified the contract would be dismissed, thus deterring fraudulent attempts to back out of the sale. Also the purchaser should be aware that under the law, the contract for sale is merged with the deed upon its delivery. Although a merger clause stating that the contract completely encompasses the agreement is not detrimental to the parties if they have fully investigated the ramifications of the sale, such provisions in the deed could be potentially harmful to the purchaser. By so agreeing, he no longer has any course of action under any covenant or the contract which is not expressed on the deed. The purchaser should demand a provision which reaffirms and adopts in the deed all earlier agreements.

Finally, the contract may make mention of brokerage fees for which the seller is liable. To safeguard his position the seller should clarify this provision so as not to become bound to pay a broker with whom the purchaser dealt. Since, more likely than not, the seller is under contract to his own broker, he should be cautious not to assume the cost of the purchaser's broker as well.

Real Estate Settlement Procedures Act

There is no question that the purchase of a home is the single largest investment most families ever make. Most people, realizing the expense involved, are careful not to get themselves in a position where they are unable to meet the monthly mortgage commitment for which they have contracted.

In the past, however, families have committed themselves solely on the bases of the amount of the down payment required by the lending institution and the monthly mortgage arrangement. These families have not taken into consideration that in buying residential property many other, and sometimes "hidden," costs can drive the final, all-inclusive purchase price beyond their means. It was not infrequent that these extra costs were discovered when it was too late to walk away from the deal. The purchasers had to ante up or face the consequences.

In an attempt to cure this problem, Congress passed in 1974 the Real Estate Settlement Procedures Act (RESPA), a federal law requiring full disclosure of all costs arising from the sale and purchase of a house. The onus of such disclosure is placed on the lender in the transaction, which generally will be a bank. Under the statute, the lender, within three days of the loan application, must make a reasonable estimate of the closing (settlement) costs which the purchaser and seller are likely to incur and provide these estimates to the parties in a format prescribed by the U.S. Department of Housing and Urban Development in the HUD Guide, which can be readily obtained from the lending institution. As the HUD Guide points out, the law does not establish specific fees or limit fees which settlement agents can charge. It does, however, put the buyer on notice of costs he must pay at the time of closing the deal.

What are these costs? In addition to the actual purchase price of a home, the purchaser will be called on to pay for the following services as well:

1. Broker's commissions—There may or may not be both buyer and seller broker's commissions. The seller will usually pay for this service, since it is he who engaged the broker. However, a buyer also may enlist the services of a broker to find a suitable house and thus will incur such an expense.

2. Attorney—Although a lawyer is not required, it is to your advantage to have someone on your side who knows what he is doing throughout the transaction. As a rule of thumb, an attorney will charge 1% of the purchase price up to a certain amount (say, $100,000) and ½% on the amount of the purchase price above such threshold. You may, however, be able to find someone who will offer his services for less, depending upon what you ask him to do (see title search discussion). Don't be afraid to shop around.

3. Title search—This consists of a review of all local public records to develop a history of the property and to ascertain whether any encumbrances (e.g., pre-existing mortgages, easements, unpaid taxes, judgments) render the title unmarketable. Your attorney may perform this function, although a title insurance company will do this where you are insuring your title through it.

4. Title insurance—There are two types of policies issued by title insurance companies—the title insurance policy and the

owner's policy. Most lending institutions will require that you secure a title insurance policy to protect their interests in the property. Remember, however, that this policy will safeguard only the lender should there be a pre-existing and superior claim to the property and hence a defect in the title. To protect you as the homeowner, you will need an owner's policy to complement the title policy. Since there is plenty of competition in this market, you again should shop around to obtain as low a rate as possible.

5. Lender's fees—A lending institution may pass on to a mortgagor specific costs attributable to the loan, such as an appraisal fee, credit report fee, its attorney's fee, the tax imposed on the recordation of the mortgage, and any cost for filing a notice of satisfaction of preceding mortgages or liens.

6. Fire insurance—Prior to releasing mortgage funds, the lender will require a mortgagor to obtain a fire insurance policy on the premises. Although the lender requires this for its own protection, such insurance will also protect you in the event of a disaster.

7. Taxes—Most taxes, such as state and local realty transfer taxes, are paid for by the seller. The buyer, however, may also face some tax charges in certain locations.

8. Incidental costs—Lenders will frequently require that the purchaser obtain a survey of the property and a termite or structural inspection of any building on the property.

9. Adjustments—At the closing the buyer will need to reimburse the seller for any prepaid costs, for example, water or fuel charges and school and property taxes. Likewise, if the seller has failed to pay these expenses, the purchase price will be adjusted in the buyer's favor.

Without going into greater detail, it should suffice to say that federal law provides for *advance* disclosure of all costs a buyer might incur in the purchase of a home. Home buyers should be aware of this statute and be ready to ask for a statement of estimated closing costs when such information is not given directly and freely.

LENDER:

GOOD FAITH ESTIMATE

THIS FORM IS NOT A LOAN COMMITMENT BY LENDER. It is required by HUD Regulations pursuant to the Real Estate Settlement Procedures Act.

This form does not cover all items you will be required to pay in cash at settlement, for example, deposit in escrow for real estate taxes and insurance. You may wish to inquire as to the amounts of such other items. You may be required to pay other additional amounts at settlement.

Description of Lender's requirements on selection of providers of settlement services for which borrower must pay all or a portion of the cost thereof:

Provider of Settlement Services: Name, Address & Tel. No.	Service provided. Refer to line number in Settlement Charges section	Does the provider have a business relationship with Lender (yes or no)

Lender's estimate set forth on the line item referred to are based upon the charges of the designated provider.

ESTIMATED SETTLEMENT CHARGES

(Line numbers correspond to numbers in Sec. L of the Uniform Settlement Statement)

800. ITEMS PAYABLE IN CONNECTION WITH LOAN

801.	Loan Origination Fee	$
802.	Loan Discount	
803.	Appraisal Fee	
804.	Credit Report	
805.	Lender's Inspection Fee	
806.	Mortgage Insurance Application Fee to	
807.	Assumtpion Fee	
808.		
809.		
810.		

900. ITEMS REQUIRED BY LENDER TO BE PAID IN ADVANCE

901.	Maximum interest	
902.	Maximum Insurance Premium	
904.		
905.		

1100. TITLE CHARGES

1101.	Settlement or closing fee	
1102.	Abstract or title search	
1103.	Title examination	
1104.	Title insurance binder	
1105.	Document preparation	
1106.	Notary fees	
1107.	Attorney's fees	
	(includes above items numbers;	
1108.	Title insurance	
	(includes above items numbers;	
1109.	Lender's coverage	
1110.	Owner's coverage	
1111.	Fee of attorney representing bank	
1112.		
1113.		

1200. GOVERNMENT RECORDING AND TRANSFER CHARGES

1201.	Recording fees: Deed $; Mortgage $	
1202.	City/county tax/stamps: Mortgage	
1203.	State tax/stamps: Mortgage	
1204.		
1205.		

1300. ADDITIONAL SETTLEMENT CHARGES

1301.	Survey	
1302.	Pest Inspection	
1303.		
1304.		
1305.		

I, the undersigned mortgage loan applicant, hereby acknowledge receipt of this Good Faith Estimate of the costs of settlement services and the Special Information Booklet.

Dated: 19

Mortgage Loan Applicant (Borrower):

SETTLEMENT COSTS WORK SHEET *(Use this worksheet to compare the charges of various lenders and providers of settlement services.)*	PROVIDER 1	PROVIDER 2	PROVIDER 3
800. ITEMS PAYABLE IN CONNECTION WITH LOAN			
801. Loan Origination Fee %			
802. Loan Discount %			
803. Appraisal Fee to			
804. Credit Report to			
805. Lender's Inspection Fee			
806. Mortgage Insurance Application Fee to			
807. Assumption Fee			
808.			
809.			
810.			
811.			
900. ITEMS REQUIRED BY LENDER TO BE PAID IN ADVANCE			
901. Interest from to @ $ /day			
902. Mortgage Insurance Premium for months to			
903. Hazard Insurance Premium for years to			
904. years to			
905.			
1000. 1000. RESERVES DEPOSITED WITH LENDER			
1001. Hazard insurance months @ $ per month			
1002. Mortgage insurance months @ $ per month			
1003. City property taxes months @ $ per month			
1004. County property taxes months @ $ per month			
1005. Annual assessments months @ $ per month			
1006. months @ $ per month			
1007. months @ $ per month			
1008. months @ $ per month			
1100. TITLE CHARGES			
1101. Settlement or closing fee to			
1102. Abstract or title search to			
1103. Title examination to			
1104. Title insurance binder to			
1105. Document preparation to			
1106. Notary fees to			
1107. Attorney's fees to			
(includes above items numbers:			
1108. Title insurance to			
(includes above items numbers:			
1109. Lender's coverage $			
1110. Owner's coverage $			
1111.			
1112.			
1113.			
1200. GOVERNMENT RECORDING AND TRANSFER CHARGES			
1201. Recording fees: Deed $; Mortgage $; Releases $			
1202. City/county tax/stamps: Deed $; Mortgage $			
1203. State tax/stamps: Deed $; Mortgage $			
1204.			
1205.			
1300. ADDITIONAL SETTLEMENT CHARGES			
1301. Survey to			
1302. Pest inspection to			
1303.			
1304.			
1305.			
1400. TOTAL SETTLEMENT CHARGES			

WAIVER OF THE RIGHT TO DELIVERY OF THE COMPLETED UNIFORM SETTLEMENT

STATEMENT NO LATER THAN AT SETTLEMENT

Identification of transaction:

Borrower(s)..

Address...

....

Seller(s)...

Address...

....

Property..

Date of Settlement...19...........

I, the undersigned, identified as Borrower(s) above, hereby waive my right under the Real Estate Settlement Procedures Act and the Rules and Regulations promulgated thereunder to have the completed Uniform Settlement Statement delivered or mailed to me at or before settlement, with the understanding, however, that it is to be delivered or mailed to me as soon as practical after settlement.

Dated...19........   Borrower(s):

....

....

An important objective of RESPA is to provide real estate buyers with information about the costs of settlement services so that they may make informed judgments in evaluating settlement services. This objective would be thwarted if, as a matter of routine, borrowers waived their rights to receive completed settlement statements at or before settlement.

In the unusual situation where a charge to be paid by borrower or seller can not be ascertained at settlement the Regulations [Sec. 3500.10(c)] provide a waiver procedure. This form of waiver is provided as a convenience and should be used with discretion and restraint.

FORM APPROVED OMB NO. 63-R-1501

A.

U.S. DEPARTMENT OF HOUSING AND URBAN DEVELOPMENT

SETTLEMENT STATEMENT

X 88 p. 1, Julius Blumberg, Inc., NYC 10013

B. TYPE OF LOAN
1. ☐ FHA   2. ☐ FMHA   3. ☐ CONV. UNINS.
4. ☐ VA   5. ☐ CONV. INS.

6. FILE NUMBER:	7. LOAN NUMBER:

8. MORTGAGE INSURANCE CASE NUMBER:

C. NOTE: This form is furnished to give you a statement of actual settlement costs. Amounts paid to and by the settlement agent are shown. Items marked *"(p.o.c.)"* were paid outside the closing; they are shown here for informational purposes and are not included in totals.

D. NAME OF BORROWER:	E. NAME OF SELLER:	F. NAME OF LENDER:

G. PROPERTY LOCATION:	H. SETTLEMENT AGENT:	PLACE OF SETTLEMENT
	I. SETTLEMENT DATE:	

J. SUMMARY OF BORROWER'S TRANSACTION		K. SUMMARY OF SELLER'S TRANSACTION	
100. GROSS AMOUNT DUE FROM BORROWER:		**400. GROSS AMOUNT DUE TO SELLER:**	
101. Contract sales price		401. Contract sales price	
102. Personal property		402. Personal property	
103. Settlement charges to borrower *(line 1400)*		403.	
104.		404.	
105.		405.	
Adjustments for items paid by seller in advance		*Adjustments for items paid by seller in advance*	
106. City/town taxes to		406. City/town taxes to	
107. County taxes to		407. County taxes to	
108. Assessments to		408. Assessments to	
109.		409.	
110.		410.	
111.		411.	
112.		412.	
120. GROSS AMOUNT DUE FROM BORROWER		**420. GROSS AMOUNT DUE TO SELLER**	
200. AMOUNTS PAID BY OR IN BEHALF OF BORROWER:		**500. REDUCTIONS IN AMOUNT DUE TO SELLER:**	
201. Deposit or earnest money		501. Excess deposit (see instructions)	
202. Principal amount of new loan(s)		502. Settlement charges to seller *(line 1400)*	
203. Existing loan(s) taken subject to		503. Existing loan(s) taken subject to	
204.		504. Payoff of first mortgage loan	
205.		505. Payoff of second mortgage loan	
206.		506.	
207.		507.	
208.		508.	
209.		509.	
Adjustments for items unpaid by seller:		*Adjustments for items unpaid by seller:*	
210. City/town taxes to		510. City/town taxes to	
211. County taxes to		511. County taxes to	
212. Assessments to		512. Assessments to	
213.		513.	
214.		514.	
215.		515.	
216.		516.	
217.		517.	
218.		518.	
219.		519.	
220. TOTAL PAID BY/FOR BORROWER		**520. TOTAL REDUCTION AMOUNT DUE SELLER**	
300. CASH AT SETTLEMENT FROM/TO BORROWER		**600. CASH AT SETTLEMENT TO/FROM SELLER**	
301. Gross amount due from borrower *(line 120)*		601. Gross amount due to seller *(line 420)*	
302. Less amounts paid by/for borrower *(line 220)*	( )	602. Less reductions in amt. due to seller *(line 520)*	( )
303. CASH (☐ FROM) (☐ TO) BORROWER		**603. CASH (☐ TO) (☐ FROM) SELLER**	

L. SETTLEMENT CHARGES

		PAID FROM BORROWER'S FUNDS AT SETTLEMENT	PAID FROM SELLER'S FUNDS AT SETTLEMENT
700.	**TOTAL SALES/BROKER'S COMMISSION** based on price $ @ % =		
	Division of Commission (line 700) as follows:		
701.	$ to		
702.	$ to		
703.	Commission paid at Settlement		
704.			
	800. ITEMS PAYABLE IN CONNECTION WITH LOAN		
801.	Loan Origination Fee %		
802.	Loan Discount %		
803.	Appraisal Fee to		
804.	Credit Report to		
805.	Lender's Inspection Fee		
806.	Mortgage Insurance Application Fee to		
807.	Assumption Fee		
808.			
809.			
810.			
811.			
	900. ITEMS REQUIRED BY LENDER TO BE PAID IN ADVANCE		
901.	Interest from to @ $ /day		
902.	Mortgage Insurance Premium for months to		
903.	Hazard Insurance Premium for years to		
904.	years to		
905.			
1000.	**1000. RESERVES DEPOSITED WITH LENDER**		
1001.	Hazard insurance months @ $ per month		
1002.	Mortgage insurance months @ $ per month		
1003.	City property taxes months @ $ per month		
1004.	County property taxes months @ $ per month		
1005.	Annual assessments months @ $ per month		
1006.	months @ $ per month		
1007.	months @ $ per month		
1008.	months @ $ per month		
	1100. TITLE CHARGES		
1101.	Settlement or closing fee to		
1102.	Abstract or title search to		
1103.	Title examination to		
1104.	Title insurance binder to		
1105.	Document preparation to		
1106.	Notary fees to		
1107.	Attorney's fees to		
	(includes above items numbers; *)*		
1108.	Title insurance to		
	(includes above items numbers; *)*		
1109.	Lender's coverage $		
1110.	Owner's coverage $		
1111.			
1112.			
1113.			
	1200. GOVERNMENT RECORDING AND TRANSFER CHARGES		
1201.	Recording fees: Deed $; Mortgage $; Releases $		
1202.	City/county tax/stamps: Deed $; Mortgage $		
1203.	State tax/stamps: Deed $; Mortgage $		
1204.			
1205.			
	1300. ADDITIONAL SETTLEMENT CHARGES		
1301.	Survey to		
1302.	Pest inspection to		
1303.			
1304.			
1305.			
1400.	**TOTAL SETTLEMENT CHARGES** *(enter on lines 103, Section J and 502, Section K)*		

We, the undersigned, identified as Borrower in section D hereof and Seller in section E hereof, hereby acknowledge receipt of this completed Uniform Settlement Statement (pages 1 & 2) on   19

Borrower: **Seller:**

_____   _____

_____   _____

CHAPTER 4

Realty Mortgages

Introduction

A mortgage is any conveyance of land which is intended by the parties at the time of making to be a security for the payment of money or the doing of some prescribed act. In essence, it is a security for a debt. The mortgagor has the right to possession and title in the land, while the mortgagee (e.g., a bank) has a lien upon the land (in some states such as New York, but not in all states).

The objective in this section is to familiarize the reader with commonly used mortgage documents. However, a few introductory notes are helpful in acquiring an understanding of the purpose and function of a mortgage and how it might affect the legal transaction to which the reader is a party.

Any transferable interest in real property may be mortgaged. The mortgage covers all real property described within the document, including fixtures on the property. The most common fixture that would be the object of a mortgage would be a house located on the property described in the mortgage. All accessions to mortgaged real property are subject to the mortgage. An *accession* is a legal principle by which the owner of property becomes entitled to all which the property produces, and to all that is added or united to it, either naturally or artificially (that is, by labor or skill of another), even where such

addition extends to a change of form or materials. The possessor of property becomes entitled to it as against the original owner.

Rights of the Parties

What are the rights of the parties involved in the transaction? The legal names of the parties are mortgagor and mortgagee. The mortgagor has, until foreclosure, the title and right to possession. He has a duty to maintain the property value and must not commit any affirmative acts of waste or other acts that would impair the value of the property. As stated earlier, the mortgagee merely has a lien. (Some states, like New York, follow this construction for mortgages which gives the mortgagee an equitable interest in the property, while the mortgagor holds legal title. However, one should consult the interpretation of his own locality in the event that his particular state has a different rule of construction whereby the mortgagor might be deemed to have equitable title and the mortgagee legal title until the debt is paid, at which time the legal title passes to the mortgagor.)

Let us pause here and define our basic terms—such as mortgagor, mortgagee, lien, and others. The *mortgagor* is one who, having all or some part of title to property, by written instrument, pledges that property for some particular purpose, such as security for debt. The classic example is where one purchases a home and borrows money from a bank to purchase the property. To secure the loan of the purchaser, the bank gets a mortgage on the property which is the security on the loan. In the event the purchaser defaults on a repayment installment of the loan, the bank holds the mortgage which allows it certain legal remedies and rights on the property. The bank in this example is the *mortgagee*. A mortgagee is simply the one who takes or receives a mortgage. A mortgagee does not have to be a bank. A *lien* is simply a claim on property for payment of some debt, obligation, or duty. In the above example, if the mortgagor breached the duty to repay the bank the money loaned to the purchaser, the bank could assert its lien (claim) on the property. A mortgage standing alone is void. It must serve a legal obligation. Without a legal obligation, there can be no mortgage.

Assuming and Taking Subject To

In the above example there is an implied assumption that the purchaser was buying property not subject to any previous mortgage. However, in many instances the buyer will be confronted with situations in which the property to be purchased is subject to a pre-existing mortgage previously executed by the seller. The purchaser must find out if the premises are to be sold merely *subject* to existing mortgages, or if the purchaser is required to *assume* the payment of existing mortgages. The purchaser usually should avoid the assumption of payment of existing mortgages. Simply stated, when a purchaser assumes this obligation, the purchaser becomes personally liable for the payment of the debt, and the seller of the property (original mortgagor) becomes a *surety*, as opposed to an *obligor* on the debt. (A surety promises

to pay money or to do any other act in event that his principal fails to do so.) In essence, what happens is that the purchaser has become primarily liable on the debt. Also, any material modification of the mortgage without the seller's consent will discharge him from responsibility.

If mortgaged property is transferred subject to the mortgage, the property becomes the primary source for the payment of the debt; the original mortgagor becomes a surety and continues to be liable on the note (debt). However, the difference is that if the mortgagee and the transferee modify the mortgage obligation, without the original mortgagor's consent, the original mortgagor (seller) is discharged from his suretyship, but only to the extent of the value of the land at the time of the mortgagee-transferee agreement.

The mortgage, subject to which the property is being sold, should be identified and described as fully as possible. This is accomplished by attaching copies of the bond (notes) and mortgage to the contract of sale. This allows the purchaser to examine the documents fully and removes the possibility of error. The purchaser should insist upon a summary of the terms of the mortgage. This will allow him the opportunity to determine the accuracy of the information given to him. The purchaser should know the rate of interest, the date of maturity, the name of holder and whether or not the mortgage contains any unusual provisions which might render it unjust.

So far, we have discussed what the mortgage document represents; who are the mortgagor and mortgagee; and what obligations result if a purchaser takes subject to or assumes a pre-existing mortgage. Hopefully, the reader has an understanding of the legal implications of a mortgage and of the roles of the particular parties to the mortgage.

Termination of the mortgage can happen in a few ways. Payment of the mortgage debt terminates the mortgage. The recording officer marks the record of a mortgage "discharged" when presented with a certificate signed and acknowledged by the mortgagee, specifying that the mortgage has been paid. A mortgage may also be terminated by acquisition by the same person of both the property described and the mortgage. If the mortgagor makes an appropriate offer of money in payment of the debt secured by the mortgage, and the offer is refused, the mortgage is terminated (but this does not terminate the underlying debt). A statute of limitation can also terminate a mortgage.

Foreclosure

When the mortgage debt is due and is unpaid, the mortgagee may either sue on the debt or foreclose the mortgage. The foreclosure action is the action brought by the mortgagee to foreclose the exercise of what is otherwise the equitable right of the mortgagor—to redeem the property from the mortgagee by offering payment. The foreclosure action may be brought upon any default on the payment of the debt which the mortgage secures. It is the sale which extinguishes all interests of persons included as party defendants in the foreclosure proceedings. In short, the foreclosure decree orders the sale of the mortgaged premises and the proceeds obtained from the sale are applied to satisfy the debt. The foreclosure sale is the actual sale of the mortgaged property. Its purpose is to obtain satisfaction of the mortgage debt out of the proceeds. The sale may be authorized by a decree of the court or by a power of sale contained in the mortgage.

Mortgages are extremely intricate legal instruments. It would be unfair to the reader to imply that he should undertake negotiation of a mortgage instrument without the aid of an attorney. This discussion of mortgages does not even scratch the surface of the subject.

But, a discussion of basic concepts of mortgage instruments will not hurt. Many people get involved in mortgage transactions and regret it later. The dream purchase today could be tomorrow's nightmare. This chapter should alert the reader to some of the problems that await a purchaser. Investment in property has many serious legal ramifications, and the extra expenditure on legal counsel would be well spent.

Acceleration of Payment in New York State

A clause that can trigger the acceleration of payment on the balance of the debt can place the mortgagor in a precarious predicament. These acceleration clauses, which the reader will notice in the individual mortgage documents that follow, are very powerful, and are binding.

An acceleration clause (or clauses) is part of a fair and legal contract which the parties had a right to enter into. It should not be regarded as a forfeiture or penalty clause. It merely accelerates the time when a legal obligation must be performed. The repayment of the debt is a legal obligation to be performed by the mortgagor. Acceleration of the time period in which it is to be fully repaid is simply an immediate demand for that legal obligation. The legal obligation has not been altered; only the time to perform has been changed. As in the case of the mortgage contracts contained in this section, acceleration clauses must be clear and certain and cannot be explained by inference. As long as the mortgagee has not acted in an unconscionable manner, he is entitled to the benefit of the acceleration clause.

An acceleration clause takes effect after a default in the payment of an installment of interest or principal occurs and must be evidenced by an unequivocal act of the mortgagee to serve as an election to declare

Standard N.Y.B.T.U. Form 8014 * First Mortgage
Individual or Corporation.

DATE CODE

JULIUS BLUMBERG, INC., LAW BLANK PUBLISHERS
80 EXCHANGE PL. AT BROADWAY, N. Y. C. 10004

CONSULT YOUR LAWYER BEFORE SIGNING THIS INSTRUMENT—THIS INSTRUMENT SHOULD BE USED BY LAWYERS ONLY.

THIS MORTGAGE, made the   day of   , nineteen hundred and

BETWEEN

, the mortgagor,

and

, the mortgagee,

WITNESSETH, that to secure the payment of an indebtedness in the sum of

dollars,

lawful money of the United States, to be paid

with interest thereon to be computed from the date hereof, at the rate of   per centum
per annum, and to be paid on the   day of   19   , next ensuing and
                thereafter,

according to a certain bond,
note or obligation bearing even date herewith, the mortgagor hereby mortgages to the mortgagee

ALL that certain plot, piece or parcel of land, with the buildings and improvements thereon erected, situate,
lying and being in the

TOGETHER with all right, title and interest of the mortgagor in and to the land lying in the streets and
roads in front of and adjoining said premises;

$\longrightarrow$

TOGETHER with all fixtures, chattels and articles of personal property now or hereafter attached to or used in connection with said premises, including but not limited to furnaces, boilers, oil burners, radiators and piping, coal stokers, plumbing and bathroom fixtures, refrigeration, air conditioning and sprinkler systems, wash-tubs, sinks, gas and electric fixtures, stoves, ranges, awnings, screens, window shades, elevators, motors, dynamos, refrigerators, kitchen cabinets, incinerators, plants and shrubbery and all other equipment and machinery, appliances, fittings, and fixtures of every kind in or used in the operation of the buildings standing on said premises, together with any and all replacements thereof and additions thereto;

TOGETHER with all awards heretofore and hereafter made to the 'mortgagor for taking by eminent domain the whole or any part of said premises or any easement therein, including any awards for changes of grade of streets, which said awards are hereby assigned to the mortgagee, who is hereby authorized to collect and receive the proceeds of such awards and to give proper receipts and acquittances therefor, and to apply the same toward the payment of the mortgage debt, notwithstanding the fact that the amount owing thereon may not then be due and payable; and the said mortgagor hereby agrees, upon request, to make, execute and deliver any and all assignments and other instruments sufficient for the purpose of assigning said awards to the mortgagee, free, clear and discharged of any encumbrances of any kind or nature whatsoever.

AND the mortgagor covenants with the mortgagee as follows:

1. That the mortgagor will pay the indebtedness as hereinbefore provided.

2. That the mortgagor will keep the buildings on the premises insured against loss by fire for the benefit of the mortgagee; that he will assign and deliver the policies to the mortgagee; and that he will reimburse the mortgagee for any premiums paid for insurance made by the mortgagee on the mortgagor's default in so insuring the buildings or in so assigning and delivering the policies.

3. That no building on the premises shall be altered, removed or demolished without the consent of the mortgagee.

4. That the whole of said principal sum and interest shall become due at the option of the mortgagee: after default in the payment of any instalment of principal or of interest for fifteen days; or after default in the payment of any tax, water rate, sewer rent or assessment for thirty days after notice and demand; or after default after notice and demand either in assigning and delivering the policies insuring the buildings against loss by fire or in reimbursing the mortgagee for premiums paid on such insurance, as hereinbefore provided; or after default upon request in furnishing a statement of the amount due on the mortgage and whether any offsets or defenses exist against the mortgage debt, as hereinafter provided. An assessment which has been made payable in instalments at the application of the mortgagor or lessee of the premises shall nevertheless, for the purpose of this paragraph, be deemed due and payable in its entirety on the day the first instalment becomes due or payable or a lien.

5. That the holder of this mortgage, in any action to foreclose it, shall be entitled to the appointment of a receiver.

6. That the mortgagor will pay all taxes, assessments, sewer rents or water rates, and in default thereof, the mortgagee may pay the same.

7. That the mortgagor within five days upon request in person or within ten days upon request by mail will furnish a written statement duly acknowledged of the amount due on this mortgage and whether any offsets or defenses exist against the mortgage debt.

8. That notice and demand or request may be in writing and may be served in person or by mail.

9. That the mortgagor warrants the title to the premises.

10. That the fire insurance policies required by paragraph No. 2 above shall contain the usual extended coverage endorsement; that in addition thereto the mortgagor, within thirty days after notice and demand, will keep the premises insured against war risk and any other hazard that may reasonably be required by the mortgagee. All of the provisions of paragraphs No. 2 and No. 4 above relating to fire insurance and the provisions of Section 254 of the Real Property Law construing the same shall apply to the additional insurance required by this paragraph.

11. That in case of a foreclosure sale, said premises, or so much thereof as may be affected by this mortgage, may be sold in one parcel.

12. That if any action or proceeding be commenced (except an action to foreclose this mortgage or to collect the debt secured thereby), to which action or proceeding the mortgagee is made a party, or in which it becomes necessary to defend or uphold the lien of this mortgage, all sums paid by the mortgagee for the expense of any litigation to prosecute or defend the rights and lien created by this mortgage (including reasonable counsel fees), shall be paid by the mortgagor, together with interest thereon at the rate of six per cent. per annum, and any such sum and the interest thereon shall be a lien on said premises, prior to any right, or title to, interest in or claim upon said premises attaching or accruing subsequent to the lien of this mortgage, and

shall be deemed to be secured by this mortgage. In any action or proceeding to foreclose this mortgage, or to recover or collect the debt secured thereby, the provisions of law respecting the recovering of costs, disbursements and allowances shall prevail unaffected by this covenant.

13.   That the mortgagor hereby assigns to the mortgagee the rents, issues and profits of the premises as further security for the payment of said indebtedness, and the mortgagor grants to the mortgagee the right to enter upon and to take possession of the premises for the purpose of collecting the same and to let the premises or any part thereof, and to apply the rents, issues and profits, after payment of all necessary charges and expenses, on account of said indebtedness. This assignment and grant shall continue in effect until this mortgage is paid. The mortgagee hereby waives the right to enter upon and to take possession of said premises for the purpose of collecting said rents, issues and profits, and the mortgagor shall be entitled to collect and receive said rents, issues and profits until default under any of the covenants, conditions or agreements contained in this mortgage, and agrees to use such rents, issues and profits in payment of principal and interest becoming due on this mortgage and in payment of taxes, assessments, sewer rents, water rates and carrying charges becoming due against said premises, but such right of the mortgagor may be revoked by the mortgagee upon any default, on five days' written notice. The mortgagor will not, without the written consent of the mortgagee, receive or collect rent from any tenant of said premises or any part thereof for a period of more than one month in advance, and in the event of any default under this mortgage will pay monthly in advance to the mortgagee, or to any receiver appointed to collect said rents, issues and profits, the fair and reasonable rental value for the use and occupation of said premises or of such part thereof as may be in the possession of the mortgagor, and upon default in any such payment will vacate and surrender the possession of said premises to the mortgagee or to such receiver, and in default thereof may be evicted by summary proceedings.

14.   That the whole of said principal sum and the interest shall become due at the option of the mortgagee: (a) after failure to exhibit to the mortgagee, within ten days after demand, receipts showing payment of all taxes, water rates, sewer rents and assessments; or (b) after the actual or threatened alteration, demolition or removal of any building on the premises without the written consent of the mortgagee; or (c) after the assignment of the rents of the premises or any part thereof without the written consent of the mortgagee; or (d) if the buildings on said premises are not maintained in reasonably good repair; or (e) after failure to comply with any requirement or order or notice of violation of law or ordinance issued by any governmental department claiming jurisdiction over the premises within three months from the issuance thereof; or (f) if on application of the mortgagee two or more fire insurance companies lawfully doing business in the State of New York refuse to issue policies insuring the buildings on the premises; or (g) in the event of the removal, demolition or destruction in whole or in part of any of the fixtures, chattels or articles of personal property covered hereby, unless the same are promptly replaced by similar fixtures, chattels and articles of personal property at least equal in quality and condition to those replaced, free from chattel mortgages or other encumbrances thereon and free from any reservation of title thereto; or (h) after thirty days' notice to the mortgagor, in the event of the passage of any law deducting from the value of land for the purposes of taxation any lien thereon, or changing in any way the taxation of mortgages or debts secured thereby for state or local purposes; or (i) if the mortgagor fails to keep, observe and perform any of the other covenants, conditions or agreements contained in this mortgage.

15.   That the mortgagor will, in compliance with Section 13 of the Lien Law, receive the advances secured hereby and will hold the right to receive such advances as a trust fund to be applied first for the purpose of paying the cost of the improvement and will apply the same first to the payment of the cost of the improvement before using any part of the total of the same for any other purpose.

Strike out this clause 16 if inapplicable.

16.   That the execution of this mortgage has been duly authorized by the board of directors of the mortgagor.

This mortgage may not be changed or terminated orally. The covenants contained in this mortgage shall run with the land and bind the mortgagor, the heirs, personal representatives, successors and assigns of the mortgagor and all subsequent owners, encumbrancers, tenants and subtenants of the premises, and shall enure to the benefit of the mortgagee, the personal representatives, successors and assigns of the mortgagee and all subsequent holders of this mortgage. The word "mortgagor" shall be construed as if it read "mortgagors" and the word "mortgagee" shall be construed as if it read "mortgagees" whenever the sense of this mortgage so requires.

IN WITNESS WHEREOF, this mortgage has been duly executed by the mortgagor.

IN PRESENCE OF:

STATE OF NEW YORK, COUNTY OF   **ss:**

On the   day of   19   , before me
personally came

to me known to be the individual   described in and who
executed the foregoing instrument, and acknowledged that
        executed the same.

STATE OF NEW YORK, COUNTY OF   **ss:**

On the   day of   19   , before me
personally came

to me known to be the individual   described in and who
executed the foregoing instrument, and acknowledged that
        executed the same.

STATE OF NEW YORK, COUNTY OF   **ss:**

On the   day of   19   , before me
personally came
to me known, who, being by me duly sworn, did depose and
say that   he resides at No.
                                                      ;

that   he is the
of
                                  , the corporation described
in and which executed the foregoing instrument; that   he
knows the seal of said corporation; that the seal affixed
to said instrument is such corporate seal; that it was so
affixed by order of the board of directors of said corporation, and that   he signed h   name thereto by like order.

STATE OF NEW YORK, COUNTY OF   **ss:**

On the   day of   19   , before me
personally came
the subscribing witness to the foregoing instrument, with
whom I am personally acquainted, who, being by me duly
sworn, did depose and say that   he resides at No.
                                                      ;

that   he knows

                                        to be the individual
described in and who executed the foregoing instrument;
that   he, said subscribing witness, was present and saw
            execute the same; and that   he, said witness,
at the same time subscribed h   name as witness thereto.

the full amount of real estate mortgage due. Although demand is unnecessary to enable the mortgagee to exercise his election to declare the full amount of the mortgage due, generally, a demand or notice to the mortgagor will suffice as the mortgagee's election to demand full payment.

The mortgagor should not be in despair if he is late on an installment payment of interest or principal. He might be in trouble, but the mortgagor has up to the time that the mortgagee makes an effective election to declare the entire principal due to tender the amount of that installment. It is not recommended that the mortgagor engage in this type of conduct, but if the situation occurs, always attempt to tender payment before an effective election is made. If the mortgagee has not made an effective election to declare the entire principal of mortgage due, the mortgagor has the right to pay installments past due with interest. In general, until an effective election is made by the mortgagee, the mortgagor has the right to pay and thus prevent acceleration.

There is no provision under Section 254 of the Real Property Law of New York that makes notice to the mortgagor a prerequisite to the mortgagee's election to deem the mortgage accelerated. However, a provision for written notice of default and election to accelerate the payment of principal is permissible in the mortgage contract, although not mandatory. This is an element that a mortgagor should attempt to insert in the contract.

Acceleration of payment of interest and principal does not result only from default on an installment payment due and owing. As evidenced by the mortgage contract illustrated in this chapter, the mortgagor's default in the performance of any covenant or agreement contained in a mortgage can operate as an acceleration, if the clause stipulates such. Another word of caution: The mortgagor should know what clauses in a mortgage contract have stipulated acceleration of payment.

The reader must remember that in any contractual transaction, it is prudent to ask questions first and sign later. Failure to do this will only lead to problems in the future, such as loss of a home.

T-139 Mortgage Loan Disclosure Statement

This form is included to give the reader an opportunity to see what a typical disclosure statement looks like. Since it is not particularly complicated, not much will be said about it. Notice the statement at the top of the form, which declares in bold print: "The statements herein contained are for disclosure only and do not in any way change, modify or vary the terms and conditions of any note, security instrument or other document relative to this loan."

This is a disclosure statement—not the mortgage loan instrument. Make sure (1) that when this form is filled out, it is understood that it is a disclosure statement of a mortgage loan and not an actual mortgage document, and (2) that any of the terms in the disclosure statement are not different from the terms of the mortgage loan. Even though that statement is placed at the top of the form, it is much wiser to make sure that the terms coincide with the terms and conditions of any note, security instrument, or other document relating to the loan. It is a very good practice not to execute conflicting documents, regardless of statements which direct the document that will control. It is a minor point, but one that can save problems later on.

A-283 Statutory Long Form Mortgage

Form #1 is a statutory long form mortgage with special clauses. It can be used by either an individual or corporation.

Page 1 sets forth the essential elements of the instrument. On this page the names of the mortgagee and mortgagor, the amount of the

T 139—Real Estate Loan Disclosure Statement: Truth In Lending Act:
Federal Reserve Regulation Z: 7-1-69.

MORTGAGE LOAN DISCLOSURE STATEMENT

The statements herein contained are for disclosure only and do not in any way change, modify or vary the terms and conditions of any note, security instrument or other document relative to this loan:

Borrower(s):

Lender:

Loan No.

Date .... 19 ......

street address (residence)

street address

city & state   zip   telephone   city & state   zip   telephone

IDENTIFICATION OF TRANSACTION

☐ Purchase money first lien mortgage loan (you may omit item A(5))

☐ Non-purchase money mortgage loan or loan transaction extending, modifying or refinancing an outstanding mortgage loan

A. **BASIC TERMS OF LOAN CONTRACT**

(1) Loan Proceeds .... $ ....

(2) Prepaid Finance Charge:

a) VA funding fee ....

b) ....

(3) Amount Financed   (1) minus (2) .... $ ....

(4) **FINANCE CHARGE:**

a) prepaid finance charge   item (2) ....

b) interest ....

c) FHA mortgage insurance premium ....

d) ....

(5) Total of Payments   (1) + (4) ....

(6) **ANNUAL PERCENTAGE RATE** .... %

B. **OTHER CHARGES:**

(1) Fees

a) title examination .... $ ....

b) title insurance ....

c) survey ....

d) legal, preparation of documents ..

e) appraisal ....

f) credit report ....

g) recording mortgage ....

h) recording deed ....

i) mortgage recording tax ....

j) ....

k) ....

(2) Escrow: **annual**   **monthly**

real estate tax .... $ .... $ ....

water & sewer rent ......

insurance premium ....

....

Total monthly payment .... $ ....

Escrow payment at closing .... $ ....

C. The **FINANCE CHARGE** begins to accrue on .... 19 ....

D. Terms of payment

(1) $ .... on .... 19 ...... , ... payments of $ .... each on same day of each succeeding month; and $ .... on .... 19 ...... BALLOON PAYMENT of $ .... is payable on .... 19 ...... and no provision is made for refinancing the same.

(2) Prepayment penalty charge: Prepayment penalty charge, as hereafter computed, shall be due and payable if the mortgage loan is prepaid:

(3) Default charge: If any payment is overdue in excess of 15 days borrower shall pay a default charge equal to .... cents for each dollar so overdue.

E. SECURITY INTEREST A mortgage lien upon real estate described in the mortgage to be made in connection with the underlying transaction shall secure the interest of the lender. The mortgage lien will cover after-acquired property. The real estate is located at ....

F. INSURANCE

(1) Property insurance in the minimum amount of $ .... is required under the terms of the loan, and may be obtained through any duly licensed agent or broker of borrower's choice, subject to lenders right to refuse to accept any insurer for reasonable cause.

*(2) CREDIT LIFE INSURANCE IS *NOT* REQUIRED. Cost of credit life insurance per month $ ....

☐ I desire credit life insurance

Party, covered ....

.... date   .... signature

☐ I do not desire credit life insurance

.... date   .... signature

Undersigned borrower(s) hereby acknowledges receipt of this disclosure statement prior to the consummation of the underlying transaction described herein.

Dated .... 19 ......

....
Borrower

....
Borrower

* If credit life insurance is required, strike out *not*, complete line F.(2) and enter amount in line A.(4)d) also.

90

debt, the manner and time of payment(s), the interest rate to be charged, and any other information that is relevant to payment (e.g., where the payments are to be made) can be located. The second half of page 1 is the description of the property to which the mortgage applies. This is a very important feature since the mortgage applies only to the property described on the face of the document. The mortgagee wants to make certain that the property is accurately described and defined as to location, boundaries, fixtures, and other property that is includable in the mortgage. Page 1 should be drawn up clearly, so that the mortgagor understands his obligation, the amount and time of payments, interest due thereon and a full description of the property that is subject to the mortgage.

Page 2 begins the formal clauses of the contract. The first three clauses, beginning with the word "TOGETHER" are read in conjunction with page 1, and in particular with the mortgaged property described on the front page. The contract reads, beginning midway on page 1, "according to an urban bond, note or obligation bearing even date herewith, the mortgagor hereby mortgages to the mortgagee, ALL described property." After the property has been described, the TOGETHER clauses are read in relation to the described property. The first TOGETHER clause is self-explanatory. The second TOGETHER clause gives the mortgagee rights in the fixtures and personal property on the premises, whether currently attached or to become affixed in the future. This is a standard clause which means that if the mortgagor gives a mortgage on the property where his house is located, and after execution of the mortgage, he puts an addition on his house, that addition would be subject to the terms of the mortgage. The third TOGETHER clause simply states that any awards (money) made to the owners of the mortgaged property by a governmental or other lawful authority, for any taking for

whatever reason, are automatically to be given to the mortgagee to be applied to the note due in reduction of the debt. The clause does not place the mortgagor at a disadvantage. The mortgagor also agrees to execute any instrument to effectuate the assignment of such awards to the mortgagee.

Beginning with "And the mortgagor covenants with the mortgagee as follows," the contract enters into specifics. Only those clauses which need some explanation or which could be detrimental to the mortgagor will be discussed. Clauses that are favorable to mortgagor will not be discussed. We do not mean by this that such clauses are unimportant. Each and every clause is important, but some do not require explanation.

Special Clauses

Clauses 2, 11, and *19*: These clauses simply state that the mortgagor is responsible for maintaining fire insurance policies which cover the mortgaged property. The mortgagor agrees to assign and deliver the policies to the mortgagee and the mortgagor is liable to the mortgagee for any premiums the mortgagee is required to pay by virtue of the fact that the mortgagor defaults on the premium payment. In essence, the mortgagee is only trying to protect himself from the risk of loss of the property which secures the underlying debt.

Clause 11 states that the mortgagee is only covered by the fire insurance policy to the extent of the mortgage debt. This rule is based on the theory that an insurance policy insuring property is a contract of indemnity; hence, the insured is not entitled to recover more than his loss. This is the law in New York and is generally accepted in most states. However, the reader should consult the state laws to ascertain whether his state has the same policy. When both interests—that of mortgagor and mortgagee—are covered in the mortgagor's policy (as is often the case), the

PTD. BY JULIUS BLUMBERG, INC., NYC 10013

Lender:

Borrower(s):

Loan No. ....

MORTGAGE LOAN DISCLOSURE STATEMENT

☐ Purchase money first lien mortgage loan [omit part A (5)]

☐ Non-purchase money mortgage loan or loan transaction extending, modifying or refinancing an outstanding mortgage loan.

Date...19.`........

A.

(1) Loan Proceeds .... $...............

(2) Prepaid Finance Charge:

    a) VA funding fee ....

    b) ....

    ....

(3) Amount Financed (1) minus (2) $...............

(4) **FINANCE CHARGE:**

    a) prepaid finan. chge. item (2) ....

    b) interest ....

    c) FHA mortgage insur. prem... ....

    d) ....

(5) Total of Payments (1) + (4) ....

B. ANNUAL PERCENTAGE RATE: ....%

C.   ADDITIONAL CHARGES

title examination .... $...............

title insurance ....

survey ....

legal, document prep. ....

appraisal ....

credit report ....

recording mortgage ....

recording deed ....

mortgage recording tax ....

....

....

Escrow

real estate tax ....

water & sewer rent ....

....

....

....

D.   TERMS OF PAYMENT

One irregular payment of $...............,
                  estimate

due on ....,
              approximation

and thereafter .... consecutive

equal payments of $..............., payable on the first day of each month/quarter and one final irregular payment of

$..............., due on ....,
                  approximation

for a Total of Payments of $...............
                  estimate

E. INSURANCE

Property insurance is required and may be obtained by the Borrower from any insurance company acceptable to Lender.

F. SECURITY

This loan is secured by a   mortgage on property located at more particularly described in the mortgage. In certain circumstances, Lender has a right to after-acquired property of the Borrower in connection with the security given for any loan from Lender to the Borrower. Proceeds of the sale of the property covered by this mortgage may be applied to the payment of any other obligation of the Borrower to Lender. Lender may, under applicable law, have a right to apply other property of the Borrower, including deposit balances in its possession, to the payment of the Borrower's obligations under the loan referred to in this Statement.

G. LATE PAYMENTS AND DEFAULT

If any installment, payment and/or deposit to be made pursuant to the note or the mortgage, referred to in this statement, is not made within 15 days after the date on which such installment, payment and/or deposit is to be made, the Borrower will pay to Lender upon demand an amount equal to   % of the total amount of such installment, payment and/or deposit not made within said 15 days to defray the expenses, including attorneys' fees, incurred by Lender in handling and processing such delinquent installment, payment and/or deposit. In the event of any default in the performance of any of the covenants in the mortgage, referred to in this Statement, by the Borrower, Lender may, at its option, perform the same, and the costs thereof, with interest at   %, per annum, shall be due immediately from the Borrower to Lender and shall be secured by the Mortgage. In any event where Lender shall make use of counsel, the Borrower shall, in addition to the payments described above, pay all reasonable counsel fees and expenses incurred by Lender.

H. DATE OF CLOSING

This statement is based upon an approximate closing date of   19   . The amounts of the above estimates and dates of the above approximations will vary depending upon the actual closing date. In no event will the dollar amounts be greater than those disclosed herein.

I. PREPAYMENT

....

....

....

....

....

ACKNOWLEDGMENT BY BORROWER

☐ The loan refered to in the above statement is for business or commercial purposes, not primarily for personal, family, household, or agricultural purposes, and Lender need not complete the above Mortgage Loan Disclosure Statement before agreeing to extend to me the credit requested.

☐ The loan to which the above Mortgage Loan Disclosure Statement relates is primarily for personal, family, household, or agricultural purposes, and I hereby acknowledge receipt of the above, fully completed, Mortgage Loan Disclosure Statement.

Dated .... 19........   ....
                                                 Borrower   Borrower

mortgagee is paid up to the amount of the mortgage debt which is reduced as of that moment. The mortgagor recovers the remainder up to the amount of the loss. Naturally, all the above could vary with different types of clauses in the particular insurance policies. This is meant to be just a quick view of the standard fire insurance coverage expected by a mortgagee. It is a standard clause—one that every mortgagee will insist upon. Section 254 of the Real Property Law, subdivision 4, states in statutory language what has been covered in Clauses 2, 11, and 19. The section is attached hereto if the reader is interested in reading the statutory language applicable to this particular clause (11 in the mortgage instrument).

Clause 19 is the third part of the trilogy of clauses relating to fire insurance coverage. It has a little more bite to it. It is highly unlikely that the mortgagor will be able to negotiate any of the terms of the clause, but it is important that the mortgagor understands the penalty for failing to fulfill his requirements. The main thrust of this clause is that the mortgagee has the option to demand payment in full for the debt secured by the mortgage, if the mortgagor defaults on keeping the buildings on the property insured as required by clauses 2 and 11. This is a serious penalty imposed upon the mortgagor and one of which the mortgagor should be aware. This provision, which will effectuate an acceleration of payment of the debt, will take effect if the mortgagor fails to assign and deliver to the mortgagee the policies of fire insurance or reimburse the mortgagee for premiums paid on such fire insurance (as provided in clause 2).

Clause 10 refers to a statute that is applicable if the mortgage is executed on property located within the state of New York. Section 13 of Lien Law states that a subsequently recorded mortgage will have priority over previously recorded mechanics' liens to the extent of advances of the mortgage made prior to the mechanics' lien, provided that the mortgage includes a provision that payments under it are subject to the trust fund provisions of Section 13 of the Lien Law. This clause is protection for the mortgagee against other parties (i.e., builders or other materialmen) who might have other liens against the property. The mortgagor does not have to concern himself with the mechanics of Section 13 of the Lien Law and should not worry about its application. It protects the mortgagee from third parties and does not affect the mortgagor.

Clauses 4, 14, 15, 16, and *17*: These are grouped together because they can be classified in one large category entitled acceleration clauses. They primarily concern themselves with the right of the mortgagee to demand payment of the debt. This acceleration is triggered by the mortgagor's failure to perform an obligation called for under the contract. Specifically, he has failed to perform an obligation arising out of one of these particular clauses. In that sense, the clauses are similar to the penalty imposed for failure to perform the duties they require. Each clause has a distinct breach which could result in the acceleration of payment. Of course, failure to make payment of the debt due gives the mortgagee the right to foreclose.

The mortgagor of property must be able to fulfill his duties or he is in serious danger. The mortgagee might require him to tender full payment of the balance of the debt due and owing. Another remedy afforded the mortgagee would be to foreclose on the mortgaged property. Neither situation is a desirable one and the mortgagor should realize that these potential problems will become unfortunate realities upon a failure to perform as required. It is imperative that the mortgagor has the ability to live up to the obligations called for under the mortgage agreement. Failure to perform these obligations could result in loss of property.

Clause 13 allows the mortgagee the

280—Statutory Form I.
Assignment of Mortgage without Covenant.
Individual or Corporation.

JULIUS BLUMBERG, INC., LAW BLANK PUBLISHERS
80 EXCHANGE PLACE, AT BROADWAY, NEW YORK

Know That

assignor,

in consideration of

Dollars,

paid by

assignee

hereby assigns unto the assignee,

a certain mortgage made by

given to secure payment of the sum of

Dollars and interest,

dated the   *day of*

recorded on the   *day of*   *19*   *in the office of the*

of the county of   *in liber*   *of mortgages,*

at page   *covering premises*

together with the bond or obligation described in said mortgage, and the moneys due and to grow due thereon, with the interest,

To have and to hold the same unto the assignee,

and to the successors,   legal representatives

and assigns of the assignee forever.

In Witness Whereof, the assignor has duly executed this assignment this

day of   nineteen hundred and

In presence of :

STATE OF
COUNTY OF   } ss.:

On the   day of   nineteen hundred and
before me came

to me known and known to me to be the individual   described in, and who executed, the foregoing instrument and acknowledged to me that   he   executed the same.

STATE OF   } ss.:
COUNTY OF

    On the   *day of*   *nineteen hundred and*
before me came   *the subscribing*
witness to the foregoing instrument, with whom I am personally acquainted, who, being by me duly
sworn, did depose and say that   he resides in

that   he knows

                                      to be the individual   described in, and who
executed the foregoing instrument; that   he, said subscribing witness, was present, and saw
execute the same; and that   he, said witness, at the same time subscribed h   name as witness thereto.

STATE OF   } ss.:
COUNTY OF

    On the   *day of*   *nineteen hundred and*
before me came   *to me known, who,*
being by me duly sworn, did depose and say that   he resides at No.

that   he is the   *of*

the corporation described in, and which executed, the foregoing instrument; that   he knows the seal
of said corporation; that the seal affixed to said instrument is such corporate seal; that it was so affixed
by order of the board of   *of said corporation; and that   he signed h*
name thereto by like order.

additional right to possession in the event of default on the part of the mortgagor in performing any of the terms, covenants or agreements. If the mortgagor is allowed to remain on the premises, the mortgagee is allowed to charge him rent; if he defaults on these payments, the mortgagee may dis-

possess him by summary proceedings. Foreclosure, once again, is a remedy afforded the mortgagee.

It is emphasized that if a mortgagor defaults on any of the obligations contained within a mortgage contract, he will find himself at the mercy of the mortgagee. It is not automatic that the mortgagee would bring an action to accelerate payment of the debt, nor is it automatic that the mortgagee would bring an action to foreclose or repossess on account of mortgagor's default of an obligation contained within the mortgage instrument. But it is very unlikely that the mortgagee would not proceed legally against the mortgagor. This is the purpose of the mortgage. It is a security instrument executed just for the purpose of providing remedies to the mortgagee in the event of some default on the part of the mortgagor. The mortgagee is interested in repayment of the debt. If the mortgagee cannot get the money, acquiring the property is probably just as good, if not better. In most instances, the property is worth more than the debt, and the mortgagee stands to benefit by acquiring title to the property.

Form 27—Mortgage Note, Individual or Corporation

The mortgage note is another document, which on its face does not have much content, but is capable of much impact. It serves as evidence of the actual underlying debt which created the mortgage. The parties to the contract have the same rights, liabilities and remedies that have been discussed before. Any obligations or duties provided on this form, or in any other form which is executed in conjunction, are enforceable. A reference on this form to the mortgage should probably be present. If none is made, ask that the mortgage be referred to specifically on this form. Despite its brevity, this note will cause the mortgagor many problems if he does not fulfill his obligations.

There is only one clause to be especially noted. It applies to all mortgage notes. It is the last clause on the document, which states: "This note may not be changed *orally*, but only by an agreement in *writing* and signed by the party against whom enforce-

ment of any waiver, change, modification or discharge is sought."

This clause is very important; perhaps an illustration of the legalities involved is appropriate: Peter Propertyholder is the mortgagor and XYZ Bank is the mortgagee. Peter's payments on the note (debt) are due monthly to the bank, and if he defaults, the bank has the option to accelerate payment of the debt to make him pay within 20 days. If he fails to make total payment within that time, the bank can foreclose on the property. This is a very serious and real consequence. Peter's best friend is the president of XYZ Bank. In fact, it is his signature in the capacity as president of the bank, that is alongside Peter's signature at the bottom of the mortgage note. The president is the highest ranking officer in the bank. One day, while playing tennis together, Peter informs him that money is scarce and that he is his signature, in the capacity as president of bank president then informs Peter that he can skip the next payment of his mortgage loan and make it up when things are going well. Peter believes him. He is Peter's best friend and president of XYZ Bank. So, Peter skips a payment. The bank brings an action against Peter to accelerate payments or foreclosure. He claims as a defense that his friend, president of XYZ Bank, had waived that right by authorizing him to skip a payment. He relied on the statement, and it is now going to work to his detriment. What was the result? Peter loses the case and along with it his property. Moral of the story: Any amendatory agreements, regardless of their content, in relation to the mortgage note, must be in writing and signed by the parties.

Form 124—Satisfaction of Mortgage

This instrument is the mortgagor's release from bondage. When this instrument has been executed between the mortgagor and mortgagee, the property is no longer encumbered by a mortgage. The mortgagor has clear title to the property (provided there are no other liens).

In essence, all this instrument states is that the mortgagee has fulfilled his obligations under the mortgage agreement, and, as of this date forward, the mortgage does not exist. This generally means that the debt for which the mortgage was security has been paid in full. Remember what was mentioned in the introduction. The mortgage instrument follows the note (debt). If there is no debt, no legal obligation, then there is no mortgage. This instrument is the proof and when the mortgagor has this document in his hands, signed by the mortgagee, he should go out and celebrate.

Appendix To Mortgages
New York Real Property Law, Article 8, §254, (2), (3), (4), (5), (6), (8).

Two. Covenant that whole sum shall become due. A covenant "that the whole of the said principal sum and interest shall become due at the option of the mortgagee: after default in the payment of any installment of principal or of interest for . . . . . . days; or after default in the payment of any tax, water rate or assessment for . . . . . . days after notice and demand; or after default after notice and demand either in assigning and delivering the policies insuring the buildings against loss by fire or in reimbursing the mortgagee for premiums paid on such insurance, as hereinbefore provided; or after default upon request in furnishing a statement of the amount due on the mortgage and whether any offsets or defenses exist against the mortgage debt as hereinafter provided," must be construed as meaning that should any default be made in the payment of any installment of principal or of any part thereof, or in the payment of the said interest, or any part thereof, on any day whereon the same is made payable, or should any tax, water rate or assessment, and/or any installment of any assessment which has been divided into annual installments pursuant to provision of law in such cases made and provided which now is or may be hereafter imposed upon the premises hereinafter described, become due or payable, and should the said installment of principal or interest remain unpaid and in arrear for the space of . . . . . days, or such tax, water rate or assessment or annual installment remain unpaid and in arrear for . . . . . days after written notice by the mortgagee or obligee, his executors, administrators, successors or assigns, that such tax or assessment and/or annual installment is unpaid and demand for the payment thereof, or should any default be made after notice and demand either in assigning and delivering the policies insuring the buildings against loss by fire or in reimbursing the mortgagee for premiums paid on such insurance, as hereinafter provided, or upon failure to furnish such statement of the amount due on the mortgage and whether any offsets or defenses exist against the mortgage debt, as hereinafter provided, after the expiration of . . . . . days in case the request is made personally, or after the expiration of . . . . . days after the mailing of such request in case the request is made by mail, then and from thenceforth, that is to say, after the lapse of either one of said periods, as the case may be, the aforesaid principal sum, with all arrearage of interest thereon, shall at the option of the said mortgagee or obligee, his executors, administrators, successors or assigns, become and be due and payable immediately thereafter, although the period above limited for the payment thereof may not then have expired, anything thereinbefore contained to the contrary thereof in any wise notwithstanding.

Three. Covenant to pay indebtedness. In default of payment, mortgagee to have power to sell. A covenant "that the mortgagor will pay the indebtedness, as hereinbefore pro-

JULIUS BLUMBERG, INC., LAW BLANK PUBLISHERS
80 EXCHANGE PLACE AT BROADWAY, NEW YORK

THIS IS A LEGAL INSTRUMENT AND SHOULD BE EXECUTED UNDER SUPERVISION OF AN ATTORNEY.

Know all Men by these Presents,

THAT

*

DO   HEREBY CERTIFY *that the following Mortgage*   IS PAID, *and do*   hereby consent *that the same be discharged of record.*

Mortgage dated the   day of   , 19   , made by

to

in the principal sum of $ and recorded on the   day of   19   ,
in Liber   of Section   of Mortgages, page   , in the office
of the   of the

which mortgage   has not been †   assigned of record.

Dated the   day of   , 19

IN PRESENCE OF:

* Insert residence, giving street and street number.
† Insert "further" when required.

→

STATE OF NEW YORK, COUNTY OF   ss:

On the   day of   19   , before me
personally came

to me known to be the individual   described in and who
executed the foregoing instrument, and acknowledged that
executed the same.

STATE OF NEW YORK, COUNTY OF   ss:

On the   day of   19   , before me
personally came

to me known to be the individual   described in and who
executed the foregoing instrument, and acknowledged that
exécuted the same.

STATE OF NEW YORK, COUNTY OF   ss:

On the   day of   19   , before me
personally came

the subscribing witness to the foregoing instrument, with whom
I am personally acquainted, who, being by me duly sworn, did
depose and say that   he resides at

that   he knows

to be the individual   described in and who executed the fore-
going instrument; that   he, said subscribing witness, was
present and saw   execute the same; and that   he,
said witness, at the same time subscribed h   name as wit-
ness thereto.

Section 321 of the Real Property Law expressly provides who must execute the certificate of discharge in specific cases and also provides, among other things, that (1) no certificate shall purport to discharge more than one mortgage, (except that mortgages affected by instruments of consolidation, spreader, modification or correction may be included in one certificate if the instruments are set forth in detail in separate paragraphs); (2) if the mortgage has been assigned, in whole or in part, the certificate shall set forth; (a) the date of each assignment in the chain of title of the person or persons signing the certificate, (b) the names of the assignor and assignee, (c) the interest assigned, and (d) if the assignment has been recorded, the book and page where it has been recorded or the serial number of such record, or (e) if the assignment is being recorded simultaneously with the certificate of discharge, the certificate of discharge shall so state, and (f) if the mortgage has not been assigned of record, the certificate shall so state; (3) if the mortgage is held by any fiduciary, including an executor or administrator, the certificate of discharge shall recite the name of the court and the venue of the proceedings in which his appointment was made or in which the order or decree vesting him with such title or authority was entered.

vided," must be construed as meaning that the mortgagor for himself, his heirs, executors and administrators or successors, doth covenant and agree to pay to the mortgagee, his executors, administrators, successors and assigns, the principal sum of money secured by said mortgage, and also the interest thereon as provided by said mortgage. And if default shall be made in the payment of the principal sum or the interest that may grow due thereon, or of any part thereof, or in the case of any other default, that then and from thenceforth it shall be lawful for the mortgagee, his executors, administrators or successors to enter into and upon all and singular the premises granted, or intended so to be, and to sell and dispose of the same, and all benefit and equity of redemption of the said mortgagor, his heirs, executors, administrators, successors or assigns therein, at public auction, and out of the money arising from such sale, to retain the principal and interest which shall then be due, together with the costs and charges of advertisment and sale of the said premises, rendering the overplus of the purchase-money, if any there shall be, unto the mortgagor. . . .

Four. Mortgagor to keep buildings insured. A covenant "that the mortgagor will keep the buildings on the premises insured against loss by fire for the benefit of the mortgagee; that he will assign and deliver the policies to the mortgagee; and that he will reimburse the mortgagee for any premiums paid for insurance made by the mortgagee on the mortgagor's default in so insuring the buildings or in so assigning and delivering the policies," shall be construed as meaning that the mortgagor, his heirs, successors and assigns will, during all the time until the money secured by the mortgage shall be fully paid and satisfied, keep the buildings erected on the premises insured against loss or damage by fire, to an amount to be approved by the mortgagee not exceeding in the aggregate one hundred per centum of their full insurable

value and in a company or companies to be approved by the mortgagee, and will assign and deliver the policy or policies of such insurance to the mortgagee, his executors, administrators, successors or assigns, which policy or policies shall have endorsed thereon the standard New York mortgagee clause in the name of the mortgagee, so and in such manner and form that he and they shall at all time and times, until the full payment of said moneys, have and hold the said policy or policies as a collateral and further security for the payment of said moneys, and in default of so doing, that the mortgagee or his executors, administrators, successors or assigns, may make such insurance from year to year, in an amount in the aggregate not exceeding one hundred per centum of the full insurable value of said buildings erected on the mortgaged premises for the purposes aforesaid, and pay the premium or premiums therefor, and that the mortgagor will pay to the mortgagee, his executors, administrators, successors or assigns, such premium or premiums so paid, with interest from the time of payment, on demand, and that the same shall be deemed to be secured by the mortgage, and shall be collectible thereupon and thereby in like manner as the principal moneys, and that should the mortgagee by reason of such insurance against loss by fire receive any sum or sums of money for damage by fire, and should the mortgagee retain such insurance money instead of paying it over to the mortgagor, the mortgagee's right to retain the same and his duty to apply it in payment of or on account of the sum secured by the mortgage and in satisfaction or reduction of the lien . . . Any excess of said insurance money over the amount so payable to the mortgagor shall be applied in reduction of the principal of the mortgage. Provided, however, that if and so long as there exists any default by the mortgagor in the performance of any of the terms or provisions of the mortgage on his part to be performed the mortgagee shall not be obligated to pay over any of said insurance money received by him. If the mortgagor shall fail to comply with any of the foregoing provisions within the time or times hereinabove limited, . . . or if the entire principal of the mortgage shall have become payable by reason of default or maturity, the mortgagee shall apply said insurance money in satisfaction or reduction of the principal of the mortgage; and any excess of said insurance money over the amount required to satisfy the mortgage shall be paid to the mortgagor. . . .

Five. Mortgagor to warrant title. A covenant "that the mortgagor warrants the title to the premises," must be construed as meaning that the mortgagor warrants that he has good title to said premises and has a right to mortgage the same and that the mortgagor shall and will make, execute, acknowledge and deliver in due form of law, all such further or other deeds or assurances as may at any time hereafter be reasonably desired or required for the more fully and effectually conveying the premises by the mortgage described. . . .

Six. Mortgagor to pay all taxes, assessments or water rates. A covenant "that the mortgagor will pay all taxes, assessments or water rates and in default thereof, the mortgagee may pay the same" must be construed as meaning that until the amount hereby secured is paid, the mortgagor will pay all taxes, assessments and water rates which may be assessed or become liens on said premises, and in default thereof the holder of this mortgage may pay the same, and the mortgagor will repay the same with interest, and the same shall be liens on said premises and secured by the mortgage.

Eight. Notice and demand. A covenant "that notice and demand or request may be made in writing and may be served in person or by mail" must be construed as meaning that every provision for notice and demand or request shall be deemd fulfilled by written notice and demand or request personally served on one or more of the persons who shall at the time hold the record title to the premises, or on their heirs or successors, or mailed by depositing it in any post-office station or letter-box. . . .

Standard N.Y.B.T.U. Form 8011
Mortgage Note. Individual or Corporation.

DATE CODE

JULIUS BLUMBERG, INC., LAW BLANK PUBLISHERS
80 EXCHANGE PL. AT BROADWAY, N. Y. C. 10004

CONSULT YOUR LAWYER BEFORE SIGNING THIS INSTRUMENT—THIS INSTRUMENT SHOULD BE USED BY LAWYERS ONLY.

MORTGAGE NOTE

$ New York,   19

FOR VALUE RECEIVED,

promise   to pay to

or order, at

or at such other place as may be designated in writing by the holder of this note, the principal sum of

dollars

with interest thereon to be computed from the date hereof, at the rate of   per centum
per annum and to be paid on the   day of   19   , next ensuing and
                              thereafter

IT IS HEREBY EXPRESSLY AGREED, that the said principal sum secured by this note shall become due at the option of the holder thereof on the happening of any default or event by which, under the terms of the mortgage securing this note, said principal sum may or shall become due and payable; also, that all of the covenants, conditions and agreements contained in said mortgage are hereby made part of this instrument.

Presentment for payment, notice of dishonor, protest and notice of protest are hereby waived.

This note is secured by a mortgage made by the maker to the payee of even date herewith, on property situate in the

This note may not be changed or terminated orally.

STATE OF NEW YORK, COUNTY OF   **ss:**

On the   day of   19   , before me
personally came

to me known to be the individual   described in and who
executed the foregoing instrument, and acknowledged that
executed the same.

STATE OF NEW YORK, COUNTY OF   **ss:**

On the   day of   19   , before me
personally came

to me known to be the individual   described in and who
executed the foregoing instrument, and acknowledged that
executed the same.

STATE OF NEW YORK, COUNTY OF   **ss:**

On the   day of   19   , before me
personally came
to me known, who, being by me duly sworn, did depose and
say that   he resides at No.

                                ;
that   he is the
of
                         , the corporation described
in and which executed the foregoing instrument; that   he
knows the seal of said corporation; that the seal affixed
to said instrument is such corporate seal; that it was so
affixed by order of the board of directors of said corporation, and that   he signed h   name thereto by like order.

STATE OF NEW YORK, COUNTY OF   **ss:**

On the   day of   19   , before me
personally came
the subscribing witness to the foregoing instrument, with
whom I am personally acquainted, who, being by me duly
sworn, did depose and say that   he resides at No.

                                  ;
that   he knows

                           to be the individual
described in and who executed the foregoing instrument;
that   he, said subscribing witness, was present and saw
                    execute the same; and that   he, said witness,
at the same time subscribed h   name as witness thereto.

Standard N.Y.B.T.U. Form 8025— Extension Agreement. DATE CODE JULIUS BLUMBERG. INC., LAW BLANK PUBLISHERS 80 EXCHANGE PLACE AT BROADWAY. NEW YORK

CONSULT YOUR LAWYER BEFORE SIGNING THIS INSTRUMENT—THIS INSTRUMENT SHOULD BE USED BY LAWYERS ONLY.

AGREEMENT, made the   day of   nineteen hundred and

BETWEEN

hereinafter designated as the party of the first part, and

hereinafter designated as the party of the second part,

WITNESSETH, that the party of the first part, the holder of the following mortgage   and of the bond or note   secured thereby:
Mortgage dated the   day of   , 19   , made by

to

In the principal sum of $ and recorded in (Liber) (Record Liber) (Reel)
            of section   of Mortgages, page   , in the office of the   of the

now a   lien upon the premises situate

and on which bond   or note   there is now due the sum of
                         dollars, with interest thereon, in consideration of one dollar paid by said party of the second part, and other valuable consideration, the receipt whereof is hereby acknowledged, does hereby extend the time of payment of the principal indebtedness secured by said bond or note   and mortgage   so that the same shall be due and payable

PROVIDED, the party of the second part meanwhile pay interest on the amount owing on said bond   or note
from the   day of   , 19   , at the rate of

per centum per annum on the   day of   , 19   , next ensuing and
                    thereafter,

and comply with all the other terms of said bond   or note   and mortgage as hereby modified.

AND the party of the second part, in consideration of the above extension, does hereby assume, covenant and agree to pay said principal sum and interest as above set forth and not before the maturity thereof as the same is hereby extended, and to comply with the other terms of said bond or note and mortgage as hereby modified.

AND the party of the second part further covenants with the party of the first part as follows:

1.   That the party of the second part will pay the indebtedness as hereinbefore provided.
2.   That the party of the second part will keep the buildings on the premises insured against loss by fire for the benefit of the party of the first part; that he will assign and deliver the policies to the party of the first part; and that he will reimburse the party of the first part for any premiums paid for insurance made by the party of the first part on default of the party of the second part in so insuring the buildings or in so assigning and delivering the policies.

3.   That no building on the premises shall be altered, removed or demolished without the consent of the party of the first part.

4.   That the whole of said principal sum and interest shall become due at the option of the party of the first part: after default in the payment of any instalment of principal or of interest for fifteen days; or after default in the payment of any tax, water rate, sewer rent or assessment for thirty days after notice and demand; or after default after notice and demand either in assigning and delivering the policies insuring the buildings against loss by fire or in reimbursing the party of the first part for premiums paid on such insurance, as hereinbefore provided; or after default upon request in furnishing a statement of the amount due on the mortgage and whether any offsets or defenses exist against the mortgage debt, as hereinafter provided. An assessment which has been made payable in instalments at the application of the party of the second part or lessee of the premises shall nevertheless, for the purpose of this paragraph, be deemed due and payable in its entirety on the day the first instalment becomes due or payable or a lien.

5.   That the holder of this mortgage, in any action to foreclose it, shall be entitled to the appointment of a receiver.

6.   That the party of the second part will pay all taxes, assessments, sewer rents or water rates, and in default thereof, the party of the first part may pay the same.

7.   That the party of the second part within five days upon request in person or within ten days upon request by mail will furnish a written statement duly acknowledged of the amount due on this mortgage and whether any offsets or defenses exist against the mortgage debt.

8.   That notice and demand or request may be in writing and may be served in person or by mail.

9.   That the party of the second part warrants the title to the premises.

10.   That the fire insurance policies required by paragraph No. 2 above shall contain the usual extended coverage endorsement; that in addition thereto the party of the second part, within thirty days after notice and demand, will keep the premises insured against war risk and any other hazard that may reasonably be required by the party of the first part. All of the provisions of paragraphs No. 2 and No. 4 above relating to fire insurance and the provisions of Section 254 of the Real Property Law construing the same shall apply to the additional insurance required by this paragraph.

11.   That in case of a foreclosure sale, said premises, or so much thereof as may be affected by said mortgage, may be sold in one parcel.

12.   That if any action or proceeding be commenced (except an action to foreclose said mortgage or to collect the debt secured thereby), to which action or proceeding the party of the first part is made a party, or in which it becomes necessary to defend or uphold the lien of said mortgage, all sums paid by the party of the first part for the expense of any litigation to prosecute or defend the rights and lien created by said mortgage (including reasonable counsel fees), shall be paid by the party of the second part, together with interest thereon at the rate of six per cent. per annum, and any such sum and the interest thereon shall be a lien on said premises, prior to any right, or title to, interest in or claim upon said premises attaching or accruing subsequent to the lien of said mortgage, and shall be deemed to be secured by said mortgage. In any action or proceeding to foreclose said mortgage, or to recover or collect the debt secured thereby, the provisions of law respecting the recovering of costs, disbursements and allowances shall prevail unaffected by this covenant.

13.   That the party of the second part hereby assigns to the party of the first part the rents, issues and profits of the premises as further security for the payment of said indebtedness, and the party of the second part grants to the party of the first part the right to enter upon the premises for the purpose of collecting the same and to let the premises or any part thereof, and to apply the rents, issues and profits, after payment of all necessary charges and expenses, on account of said indebtedness. This assignment and grant shall continue in effect until said mortgage is paid. The party of the first part hereby waives the right to enter upon said premises for the purpose of collecting said rents, issues and profits and the party of the second part shall be entitled to collect and receive said rents, issues and profits until default under any of the covenants, conditions or agreements contained in said mortgage, and agrees to use such rents, issues and profits in payment of principal and interest becoming due on said mortgage and in payment of taxes, assessments, sewer rents, water rates and carrying charges becoming due against said premises, but such right of the party of the second part may be revoked by the party of the first part upon any default, on five days' written notice. The party of the second part will not, without the written consent of the party of the first part, receive or collect rent from any tenant of said premises or any part thereof for a period of more than one month in advance, and in the event of any default under said mortgage will pay monthly in advance to the party of the first part, or to any receiver appointed to collect said rents, issues and profits, the fair and reasonable rental value for the use and occupation of said premises or of such part thereof as may be in the possession of the party of the second part, and upon default in any such payment will vacate and surrender the possession of said premises to the party of the first part or to such receiver, and in default thereof may be evicted by summary proceedings.

14.   That the whole of said principal sum and the interest shall become due at the option of the party of the first part: (a) after failure to exhibit to the party of the first part, within ten days after demand, receipts showing payment of all taxes, water rates, sewer rents and assessments; or (b) after the actual or threatened alteration, demolition or removal of any building on the premises without the written consent of the party of the first part; or (c) after the assignment of the rents of the premises or any part thereof without the written consent of the party of the first part; or (d) if the buildings on said premises are not maintained in reasonably good repair; or (e) after failure to comply with any requirement or order or notice of violation of law or ordinance issued by any governmental department claiming jurisdiction over the premises within three months from the issuance thereof; or (f) if on application of the party of the first part two or more fire insurance companies lawfully doing business in the State of New York refuse to issue policies insuring the buildings on the premises; or (g) in the event of the removal, demolition or destruction in whole or in part of any of the fixtures, chattels or articles of personal property covered hereby, unless the same are promptly replaced by similar fixtures, chattels and articles of personal property at least equal in quality and condition to those replaced, free from chattel mortgages or other encumbrances thereon and free from any reservation of title thereto; or (h) after thirty days' notice to the party of the second part, in the event of the passage of any law deducting from the value of land for the purposes of taxation any lien thereon, or changing in any way the taxation of mortgages or debts secured thereby for state or local purposes; or (i) if the party of the second part fails to keep, observe and perform any of the covenants, conditions or agreements contained in said mortgage or in this agreement.

15.   That the lien of said mortgage is hereby extended so as to cover all fixtures, chattels and articles of personal property now or hereafter attached to or used in connection with said premises, including but not limited to furnaces, boilers, oil burners, radiators and piping, coal stokers, plumbing and bathroom fixtures, refrigeration, air conditioning and sprinkler systems, wash-tubs, sinks, gas and electric fixtures, stoves, ranges, awnings, screens, window shades, elevators, motors, dynamos, refrigerators, kitchen cabinets, incinerators, plants and shrubbery and all other equipment and machinery, appliances, fittings, and fixtures of every kind in or used in the operation of the buildings standing on said premises, together with any and all replacements thereof and additions thereto.

16.   That the party of the second part does hereby assign to the party of the first part all awards heretofore and hereafter made to the party of the second part for taking by eminent domain the whole or any part of said premises or any easement therein, including any awards for changes of grade of streets, which said awards are hereby assigned to the party of the first part, who is hereby authorized to collect and receive the proceeds of such awards and to give proper receipts and acquittances therefor, and to apply the same toward the payment of the mortgage debt, notwithstanding the fact that the amount owing thereon may not then be due and payable; and the said party of the second part hereby agrees, upon request, to make, execute and deliver any and all assignments and other instruments sufficient for the purpose of assigning said awards to the party of the first part, free, clear and discharged of any encumbrances of any kind or nature whatsoever.

17.   That the party of the second part is now the owner of the premises upon which said mortgage is a valid lien for the amount above specified with interest thereon at the rate above set forth, and that there are no defenses or offsets to said mortgage or to the debt which it secures.

18.   That the principal and interest hereby agreed to be paid shall be a lien on the mortgaged premises and be secured by said bond or note and mortgage, and that when the terms and provisions contained in said bond or note and mortgage in any way conflict with the terms and provisions contained in this agreement, the terms and provisions herein contained shall prevail, and that as modified by this agreement the said bond or note and mortgage are hereby ratified and confirmed.

This agreement may not be changed or terminated orally. The covenants contained in this agreement shall run with the land and bind the party of the second part, the heirs, personal representatives, successors and assigns of the party of the second part and all subsequent owners, encumbrancers, tenants and sub-tenants of the premises, and shall enure to the benefit of the party of the first part, the personal representatives, successors and assigns of the party of the first part and all subsequent holders of this mortgage. The word "party" shall be construed as if it reads "parties" whenever the sense of this agreement so requires.

IN WITNESS WHEREOF, this agreement has been duly executed by the parties hereto the day and year first above written.

In PRESENCE OF :

STATE OF NEW YORK, COUNTY OF   ss:

On the   day of   19   , before me
personally came

to me known to be the individual   described in and who
executed the foregoing instrument, and acknowledged that
executed the same.

STATE OF NEW YORK, COUNTY OF   ss:

On the   day of   19   , before me
personally came

to me known to be the individual   described in and who
executed the foregoing instrument, and acknowledged that
executed the same.

STATE OF NEW YORK, COUNTY OF   ss:

On the   day of   19   , before me
personally came
to me known, who, being by me duly sworn, did depose and
say that   he resides at No.
                                                                        ;

that   he is the
of
                                              , the corporation described
in and which executed the foregoing instrument; that   he
knows the seal of said corporation; that the seal affixed
to said instrument is such corporate seal; that it was so
affixed by order of the board of directors of said corporation, and that   he signed h   name thereto by like order.

STATE OF NEW YORK, COUNTY OF   ss:

On the   day of   19   , before me
personally came
to me known, who, being by me duly sworn, did depose and
say that   he resides at No.
                                                                        ;

that   he is the
of
                                              , the corporation described
in and which executed the foregoing instrument; that   he
knows the seal of said corporation; that the seal affixed
to said instrument is such corporate seal; that it was so
affixed by order of the board of directors of said corporation, and that   he signed h   name thereto by like order.

CHAPTER 5

Partnership

Introduction

In this chapter only two contracts will be examined. One is an article of co-partnership and the other is a certificate of conducting business as partners. The latter is much less detailed and shorter in length. The contents of this chapter will be based totally on New York law, whether it be the Uniform Partnership Act or case law.

Obviously, the rules and principles which apply to partnerships within New York do not apply outside the state. However, whether for reasons dealing with local law or general partnership law, legal counsel should be sought.

Many friendships have ended because two friends became partners in some operation and, in the end, each claimed that the other owed him money. The situation is aggravated when other people (non-partners) also claim that both of these friends held themselves out to be partners and owe them money for debts incurred while operating this "partnership." Not only were friendships lost, but also a lot of money. The problems might have been avoided, if the parties had possessed some knowledge of the implications of their acts before the commencement of the venture. They might have proceeded anyway, but with a little more caution, had they known the consequences.

Formation

A partnership may be defined as an association of two or more competent persons to carry on a business as co-owners for profit. A partnership is not a corporation, although it does have some similar elements. For example, a partnership may hold title to property in the partnership's name and it may be sued and bring suit.

One of the key aspects of a partnership is that the debts of the partnership are the debts of the individual partners. In addition, one partner may be held liable for the partnership's entire indebtedness. These are a couple of reasons why some people are wary of entering into partnerships. Not only are they afraid of losing a good friendship, but their money also is at stake.

A partnership is a contract (agreement), and is governed by the general rules of contract law (and agency, which, when applicable, will be explained). Any person can enter into a partnership if he is capable of entering into a legal contract. However, if a party enters into a partnership with another party who lacks capacity, no liability extends to the incompetent party except to the extent of his contribution of capital to the partnership.

Thus, for example: X and Y form a partnership. X contributes $100.00 and Y contributes $100.00. X is 15 years old. The partnership incurs debts of $130.00 to **Z**. **Z** can collect out of the $100.00 contributed by **X**. However, if the partnership had incurred debts of $230.00, **X** would be liable for only $100.00. **Y** would be liable for the remaining $130.00.

How is a partnership formed? Two forms have been provided at the end of this chapter, but they are not absolutely necessary to the formation of a partnership. In fact, there is no particular set of formalities to be followed. One statutory requirement is that in certain situations a partnership agreement must conform with the Statute of Frauds. This means, for example, that a partnership agreement must be in writing where the purpose of the partnership cannot be performed within one year of its inception.

If there is no statute relating to partnership or its formation, it may be formed simply by the conduct of the parties, without a formal agreement. If two people represent themselves to the public as partners, and their conduct would lead a third party to believe that they are in fact partners, the law will imply a partnership, and both will be held liable under partnership law. If another person desires to enter into a pre-existing partnership, there must be consent, either expressed or implied, by the other partners.

What are the determining factors which establish the existence of a partnership if there is no express agreement? Certain types of evidence tend to prove the existence of a partnership, but they are by no means conclusive. Title to property in a partnership name and the designation of the entity as a partnership might be indicative of intent. If the parties agree to share in the profits of a business, this is considered *prima facie* evidence that they are partners in the business. On the other hand, if there is evidence that indicates the parties did not intend to share losses, this evidence supports the presumption that there was not a partnership.

One must be wary of his conduct with another person in his representations to the public. When one person, in conjunction with another, represents himself, either privately or publicly, to be a partner with that person, he is liable to third parties who extended credit to the actual or apparent partnership. If a person permits another to represent him as a partner, he will be liable to third persons who extend credit to the partnership (even though it does not actually exist). A person who consents to being held out publicly as a partner is liable to any third party who extends credit, regardless of whether the third party knows of the representation. If a person consents only to being privately held out, he is only liable to third persons if they in fact relied on that representation.

In any of these situations, the result can be disastrous, since a party is held liable for debts incurred by his partner. Under no circumstances should one allow himself (or his name) to be held out as a partner, unless he is one in fact.

General and Limited Partnerships

There are two fundamental forms of partnerships—the general and limited partnerships. Discussion throughout the chapter is geared to the general partnership situation; however, mention should be made about the characteristics of a limited partnership, in order to cover the scope of the subject.

In a general partnership, each partner devotes his time, money and efforts to the furtherance of the firm's business. As mentioned, subject to the terms of the agreement, each partner has complete authority to act within the scope of the partnership and is equally as completely liable for partnership obligations.

On the other hand, the limited partnership, which is created in accordance with state law, is comprised of partners who are both active and inactive. The latter or limited partners perform no managerial functions and their liability is limited to their monetary contribution.

A limited partner does become personally liable where his actions exceed statutory restrictions. This does not mean that the limited partner bears the risk of loss without possessing certain corresponding rights. Specifically, the limited partner has the right to a full appraisal of partnership affairs and activities and a right to an accounting. He likewise has the right to his allocable share of the profits and priority over all funds upon dissolution. However, these rights only apply between the limited and general partners and do not extend to actual business conducted with the public. In fact, the limited partner's name may not appear in the partnership name except for certain statutorily defined purposes. In essence, the limited partner is a silent partner.

Professional Partnerships

The professional partnership differs from the commercial partnership in two basic areas: (1) the chief assets in a professional partnership are the professional skills and earning power of the partners, and (2) the fact that in many situations the sale of the professional partnership is limited to another qualified professional.

In a commercial partnership the heirs have the option of liquidating the partnership, coming into the business as partners, selling their interest to an outsider or selling their interest to the surviving partners. In a professional partnership, the first two options are not generally available. The heirs cannot succeed to the partnership interest unless they are also qualified professionally. Furthermore, it would be unusual in the majority of professional partnerships for the surviving partners to consider closing the practice and to retire after the death of a partner.

Therefore, it is imperative that a value is established for an individual's interest in this type of partnership and that some purchase and sale arrangement is agreed upon in writing (buy-sell agreements are covered in more depth in another chapter). The following are the factors commonly considered in valuing professional partnership interests:

(a) The value of the capital account. The capital account includes the value of the buildings, fixtures, equipment, inventory, accounts receivable and cash accounts less the liabilities of the partnership.

(b) The value of the work-in-process. Work-in-process is work that has not been completed or billed to a customer.

(c) The value of goodwill. The likelihood is that present patients or clients will return to the partnership to do business in the future. The courts, typically, will not place a value on goodwill to a professional partnership interest in the absence of an agreement among the partners to that effect. The rule of thumb is that goodwill dies with the dissolution of the partnership, in the absence of a contrary agreement.

There are many methods of determining the value of a professional partnership (discussed in greater detail in the chapter dealing with buy-sell agreements). There does not appear to be an agreed-upon or unanimous formula. However, the following are some of the methods utilized quite frequently:

(1) Agreed dollar value

(2) Book value

(3) Fair market value plus a multiple of past earnings

(4) Capitalization of average yearly net earnings

(5) Book value plus value of goodwill

Business Certificate for Partners

The undersigned do hereby certify that they are conducting or transacting business as members of a partnership under the name or designation of

at

in the County of _____ , State of New York, and do further certify that the full names of all the persons conducting or transacting such partnership including the full names of all the partners with the residence address of each such person, and the age of any who may be infants, are as follows:

NAME Specify which are infants and state ages.   RESIDENCE

....

....

....

....

....

....

WE DO FURTHER CERTIFY that we are the successors in interest to

the person or persons heretofore using such name or names to carry on or conduct or transact business.

In Witness Whereof, We have this _____ day of _____ 19 ___ made and signed this certificate.

....

....

....

....

....

....

State of New York, County of _____   ss.:   INDIVIDUAL ACKNOWLEDGMENT

On this _____ day of _____ 19 ___ , before me personally appeared

to me known and known to me to be the individual   described in, and who executed the foregoing certificate, and   he   thereupon   duly acknowledged to me that   he   executed the same.

(6) Valuation fixed by appraisers.

Once a price is determined, the partners must determine the manner in which the purchase payments are made. The payment can be made in one sum, or spread out over a period of time. There is no question that the payments should be guaranteed in some fashion regardless of how the payments are to be made—lump sum or installment.

Rights

Assuming that a partnership has been formed, what are the rights and liabilities between partners and third parties? What is partnership property? What is an individual partner's property? In other words, what happens once Joe and Lou open that motorcycle shop as a partnership?

Partnership capital is the property or money contributed by each of the partners, intended to be used for carrying on the firm's business. Partnership property generally consists of everything the firm owns. Property acquired with partnership funds is usually partnership property. The term "generally" is used, since, if the partners have a different intent, their intent will govern. Common-sense factors are considered by the court in determining the intention of the parties and need not be discussed.

The rights of partners in partnership property are straightforward. Each partner has a specific partnership property right which is termed a *tenancy in partnership*. This ownership entitles each partner to an equal right to possess the property with his co-partners; a partner needs the consent of the co-partners to use it for any other reason. Upon the death of a partner, his interest passes and vests in the remaining partners.

A partner has an interest in the firm. He has an interest in his share of the profits and any surplus of the partnership which is treated as personal property. Assignment of this interest, which is allowable since it is a personalty, does not dissolve the partnership.

All partners are deemed to have equal rights in the running of the partnership business regardless of their individual percentage of profits. The simple rule is that one man is entitled to one vote. Profits made in the course of the partnership belong to the firm, and one partner will not be allowed to profit personally at the expense of the firm. If a partner makes payments or incurs liabilities in the furtherance of business, the partnership must indemnify that partner for those expenditures. This would also apply if the partner makes a capital outlay to preserve the property of the partnership. Along the same lines, if a partner pays a partnership debt, he is entitled to contribution from the other partners for their proportionate shares. Each and every partner has a right to inspect the partnership books which are to be kept at the partnership's place of business.

Authority to Act

As a general rule, a partner may not sue or be sued by the partnership, because he is personally liable for all debts and obligations of the partnership, and the effect of the suit would be a suit against himself.

Each and every partner, when dealing with third parties, is considered an agent of the partnership, if his course of conduct is in the furtherance of the partnership business. This theory is based upon the law of agency. The acts of the partners bind the partnership as long as their acts are within the scope of the partnership. Liability may be in contract, tort, or breach of trust.

Authorization is the term that is used to determine if a particular partner was acting within his authority. If authority was granted

JULIUS BLUMBERG, INC., LAW BLANK PUBLISHERS
80 EXCHANGE PLACE AT BROADWAY, NEW YORK

Articles of Agreement,

Made the   *day of*   *one thousand nine hundred and*

BETWEEN

WITNESSETH: *The said parties above named have agreed to become co-partners and by these presents form a partnership under the trade name and style of*

for the purpose of buying, selling, vending and manufacturing

and all other goods, wares and merchandise belonging to the said business and to occupy the following premises:

their co-partnership to commence on the   *day of*   *19*
and to continue

and to that end and purpose the said

to be used and employed in common between them for the support and management of the said business, to their mutual benefit and advantage. AND it is agreed by and between the parties to these presents, that at all times during the continuance of their co-partnership, they and each of them will give their attendance, and do their and each of their best endeavors, and to the utmost of their skill and power, exert themselves for their joint interest, profit, benefit and advantage, and truly employ, buy, sell and merchandise with their joint stock, and the increase thereof, in the business aforesaid. AND ALSO, that they shall and will at all times during the said co-partnership, bear, pay and discharge equally between them, all rents and other expenses that may be required for the support and management of the said business; and that all gains, profit and increase, that shall come, grow or arise from or by means of their said business shall be divided between them, as follows:

and all loss that shall happen to their said joint business by ill-commodities, bad debts or otherwise shall be borne and paid between them, as follows:

AND it is agreed by and between the said parties, that there shall be had and kept at all times during the continuance of their co-partnership, perfect, just, and true books of account, wherein each of the said co-partners shall enter and set down, as well all money by them or either of them received, paid, laid out and expended in and about the said business, as also all goods, wares, commodities and merchandise, by them or either of them, bought or sold, by reason or on account of the said business, and all other matters and things whatsoever, to the said business and the management thereof in anywise belonging; which said book shall be used in common between the said co-partners, so that either of them may have access thereto, without any interruption or hindrance of the other. AND ALSO, the said co-partners, once in

or oftener if necessary, shall make, yield and render, each to the other, a true, just and perfect inventory and account of all profits and increase by them or either of them, made, and of all losses by them or either of them, sustained; and also all payments, receipts, disbursements and all other things by them made, received, disbursed, acted, done, or suffered in this said co-partnership and business; and the same account so made, shall and will clear, adjust, pay and deliver, each to the other, at the time, their just share of the profits so made as aforesaid.

AND the said parties hereby mutually covenant and agree, to and with each other, that during the continuance of the said co-partnership,   of them shall nor will endorse any note, or otherwise become surety for any person or persons whomsoever, nor will sell, assign, transfer, mortgage or otherwise dispose of the business of the co-partnership, nor each of   share, title and interest therein without the written consent of the parties hereto. And at the end or other sooner termination of their co-partnership the said co-partners each to the other, shall and will make a true, just and final account of all things relating to their said business, and in all things truly adjust the same; and all and every the stock and stocks, as well as the gains and increase thereof, which shall appear to be remaining, either in money, goods, wares, fixtures, debts or otherwise, shall be divided between them as follows:

after the payment of the co-partnership liabilities; and should said co-partners be unable to ascertain the value of any of the assets belonging to the co-partnership at the termination of their co-partnership, the said assets shall then be sold either at private or public sale to be agreed upon by the parties hereto and a division of the proceeds of said sale shall be made as herein provided.

IT IS FURTHER AGREED that during the continuance of the co-partnership herein, all notes, drafts or money received for and in behalf of the said co-partnership by the parties hereto shall be deposited in a bank to be agreed upon by the parties hereto and the moneys credited to said co-partnership shall only be withdrawn by check signed by who shall also receive said notes, drafts or moneys or other orders for payment of moneys of the said co-partnership for the purpose of making said deposits.

IT IS FURTHER AGREED *that during the continuance of said co-partnership the parties hereto shall mutually agree in writing, upon a weekly allowance, to be paid to each of the parties hereto for services to be rendered, and said allowance shall be charged as an item of expense of the co-partnership business, or if otherwise agreed upon in writing may be charged against their personal interest in said business.*

IN THE EVENT *of the death of a party hereto, the surviving co-partner shall within a period of weeks, make and give, to the legal representative of the deceased co-partner, a true, just and final account of all things relating to the co-partnership business, and within a period of months, in all things truly adjust the same with the legal representative of the deceased co-partner. The surviving co-partner shall have the privilege of purchasing the interest of the deceased co-partner from his legal representative, upon a true and proper valuation of the interest of the deceased co-partner; and until the purchase of said interest by the surviving co-partner , or a division as herein agreed upon, the legal representative of the deceased co-partner during reasonable business hours shall have access to the books of the co-partnership and examine same personally or with the aid of other persons and make copies thereof or any portion thereof without any interruption or hindrance, and the said legal representative of said deceased co-partner shall have equal and joint control of the said co-partnership with the surviving partner or partners.*

This instrument may not be changed orally.

IN WITNESS WHEREOF, *the parties hereto have hereunto set their hands and seals the day and year first above mentioned.*

In presence of:

STATE OF

            of   } *ss.:*

County of

                        On the   *day of*   *in the year*
one thousand nine hundred and   *before me personally came*

to me known, and known to me to be the individual described in, and who executed the foregoing instrument, and *acknowledged to me that he executed the same.*

him in the Article of Partnership, then the partnership will be bound by his act. If the partner was not authorized to do the particular act by the agreement, then a majority vote of the partners is needed to ratify his actions.

The partnership agreement governs the partnership. However, if the agreement fails to provide certain authorizations, then a unanimous vote is required to authorize a partner to perform certain acts which will effectively bind the partnership. The situations requiring this measure are matters involving arbitration, assignment for benefit of creditors, confession of judgment, and the disposition of the goodwill of the firm.

If a partner does not have actual authority, he may be deemed to have apparent authority. Generally, a person is not responsible for the acts of another who assumes to represent him. However, partners are not assuming to represent the other partners when business is conducted. That is the purpose of the partnership, and each partner actually does represent the partnership. So, when a partner holds himself out to a third party as having authority and that party reasonably believes that the authority exists, the partner has the apparent authority to act, even though the partnership agreement has not granted it to him, and the partners have not actually consented to his act. This theory is grounded in agency law to provide protection for innocent third parties in dealing with partners. Example: **X** and **Y** are partners in the **XY Co. XY Co.** owns an apartment building in which **Z** has leased an apartment. The rent is due on the fifth of the month. **Z** sees **X** on the fifth of the month and explains that he will not be able to pay for two weeks due to some illness in the family and a shortage of funds. **X** tells **Z** that late payment is permissible and not to worry about it. **XY Co.** will accept the rent late. Even though **X** might not have had the actual authority to extend the due date of the rental payment, he had the apparent authority, and the partnership will be bound by his extension. **Z** relied on **X**'s apparent authority to extend the payment date and would have a valid defense for non-payment.

Liabilities

The partnership is liable for any wrongful act by a partner if committed while the partner was conducting business within the scope of the partnership or with the other partner's consent. Where a partner, acting within the scope of business, defrauds a third party, the partnership will be held liable. If a partner defrauds the partnership in alliance with a third party, the partnership is not liable to the third party. Whenever a partner acts outside the scope of the partnership, it will not be held liable. If a partner breaches a trust, such as misapplication of money from a third person given to him within the scope of his apparent (or actual) authority, the partnership is liable.

One of the major reasons why there are so many small, closed corporations instead of partnerships is that the liability of partners is rather far-reaching. Partners are liable on contracts executed by the firm in the scope of business and on any other contracts expressly authorized by the partnership. Partners are also liable for torts committed by the other partners (or employees), if committed within the course and scope of the firm's business. Again, in general, partners are jointly liable for civil liability and jointly and severally liable in tort actions.

This is the key point to note. Each partner is personally and individually liable for the entire amount of all partnership obligations, whether resulting from contract or tort; and to relate to an earlier part of this chapter, if one partner pays more than his share, he is then entitled to indemnification from the partnership and may also get a *pro rata* contribution from the partners if the partnership is unable to pay. Personal liability should make one think carefully with whom he desires to form a partnership. If liabilities are incurred and the partnership cannot pay, the creditor has the right to satisfy the debt from a partner's personal assets.

An incoming (new) partner to the firm is liable for all pre-existing debts incurred by the partnership before he enters. It is as if he had been one of the partners at the time the obligations were incurred. His liability, however, is limited only to the partnership property; he is not held personally liable, although he may become personally liable, if he promises to pay the existing debts that extend beyond his interest in the partnership property. A partner who is leaving the firm is liable on all debts incurred by the firm up to the time of departure. Partners are not responsible for criminal acts performed by another partner, even if committed within the scope of partnership business, unless the other partners participated in the commission of the crime.

Dissolution

Under no circumstances should a partnership be dissolved without the consultation of an attorney. Dissolution of a partnership can be a complex process, but does not necesarily involve a court proceeding. In most instances, the partnership is dissolved effectively without court interference. However, the "wrapping up" of partnership business does involve settling all matters that relate to the partnership, and an attorney should be consulted in order to assure each and every partner that all matters relating to the partnership have been terminated properly.

Unless the partnership agreement provides to the contrary, a partnership necessarily must dissolve and terminate upon the death of any one partner. The actual practice of dissolution and the final cleaning up of business affairs is one fraught with legal complexities and financial entanglements. In order to avoid

incurring further liabilities, surviving partners would be best advised to seek legal counsel. Still, a person should be aware of the ramifications of his continuing business activities after dissolution is in order.

Dissolution occurs from a change in the relationship of the partners, whether it be through election or death. Any partner withdrawing from the agreed purpose of the firm's existence forces termination of the partnership, since all parties' original positions are altered if only to a minor extent. The law similarly mandates dissolution in the event of partnership bankruptcy, illegality of business activities or incapacity or misconduct of a partner.

Upon dissolution, the surviving partners are obliged to wind up partnership affairs. Generally, this duty entails the finishing of incomplete business transactions, the collection of unpaid accounts, the payment of business debts, the liquidation of partnership assets and distribution to all involved parties, partners or representatives, of net amounts owed as a result of capital contributions or respective shares in profits and surplus. In fulfilling these obligations, the surviving partners become liquidating trustees and are liable for indiscretions or breaches of their fiduciary responsibilities. They must make a full accounting and disclosure of partnership assets and liabilities and distribute accordingly.

Dissolution and "winding up," then, are different concepts. Once dissolution is called for, the authority of all partners to act is terminated except that necessary to wind up the business. Thus, the partners can conclude old business, but any new business places sole liability upon the acting partners. Yet even though dissolution gives each partner the right to have the partnership liquidated and to receive his share in cash, the remaining partners can carry on in certain situations. If a partner is expelled in accordance with the agreement, if the dissolution contravenes the agreement or if the agreement provides for continuation, then after satisfying the withdrawing partner's share in the business, the remaining partners may proceed with partnership activities. Still in order to avoid unnecessary personal liability, a partner should consult an attorney, so that all prior business is properly terminated.

Articles of Co-Partnership

This is a model of a formal partnership agreement. If two parties enter into this signed agreement, a formal partnership exists. The Articles of Co-Partnership is a good model, since it defines the scope of the partnership and details basic rights and duties of the partners.

On page 1 of the agreement, the parties are identified, and a partnership is in formation. The partnership name is indicated, and the nature of business is declared. This is very important, since, as previously pointed out, action by one partner conducted outside the scope of the partnership business does not hold the partnership liable.

It is on the first page of the agreement that the parties should definitely outline the scope and nature of the business to be undertaken. This page is the most important one and has to be constructed carefully by the parties. The language does not have to be lengthy or complicated. In fact, the opposite effect is desired. Simple and straightforward language which accurately describes what business is to be conducted by the partnership is advantageous. If well constructed, this agreement might prevent future problems.

The latter part of the first page deals with duties and obligations touched upon in this chapter. The language is not particularly obstruse and should be readily understood. In essence, it states that the partners will work in furtherance of partnership business and that their primary objective is to promote the best interests of the firm. They agree to share profits, losses and expenses incurred in the course of conducting partnership business.

The top of page 2 allows for the parties to divide profits at various percentage rates, in the event they do not want to share them equally. In addition, the clause following allows the parties to distribute losses at variable percentage levels, if they desire. *Note: The rule of one man, one vote, still applies, regardless of the fact that profits and losses are allocated in various percentages.*

Clause (A) simply states that the books of the partnership's records will be kept in order to record the transactions of the partnership business. Each and every partner has the right to inspect the books at any time. Clause (A) allows a partner to determine the specific time and place where the books may be examined regularly.

Clause (B) states that the parties are prohibited from engaging in certain transactions, such as assignments, transfers, mortgages, etc.—basically it prohibits a partner from tampering with partnership property. For these transactions to be authorized, the consent of the partners is required. The language of the clause is straightforward and self-explanatory.

The second part of Clause (B) provides a method of distribution in the event of the dissolution of the partnership. The parties can determine the division of the assets that the partnership retains after dissolution. However, as stated previously, this is a very intricate procedure, and an attorney should be consulted. If there is enough left in the kitty to permit a distribution, there is enough to pay for an attorney who will distribute it properly.

Clause (C) designates the bank of the partnership account. The important element of this clause is the designation of the partner(s) whose signature must appear on any negotiable instrument negotiated by the partnership. The party who is authorized to sign the partnership's negotiable instruments could be considered the treasurer. If the partnership consists of only two parties, a requirement for both parties' signatures would be wise.

Clause (D) limits the expense account of each partner. Each partner relishes the thought of having an unlimited expense account, but this tends to be abused. Reasonable expenses should be estimated and allocated appropriately. Remember, as a partner, a person is spending his own money.

Clause (E) is concerned with the procedure of final accounting when a partner dies. Since this is another form of dissolution (partial), an attorney is recommended.

The partnership form entitled "Business Certificate for Partners" is a short form of an agreement of partnership. All rules of partnership law are applicable to persons signing this agreement, just as if they had signed a lengthier one. The short form does not spell out the rights and obligations of the parties in detail, but many of them still apply.

CHAPTER 6

Wills

This is the only chapter dealing with a non-contractual legal instrument—a will. Although the book concentrates primarily on contracts, a will is a very important legal instrument that merits our attention to some degree. Most people regard a contract as an instrument that, among other formalities, requires a signature. A will falls in this genre since it generally not only requires the testator's signature, but usually the signature of at least two or three witnesses in order for the document to be valid and enforceable. As such, many people regard a will as a contract, if only a contract with themselves, their heirs and their property.

Before the importance of the testamentary instrument can be fully appreciated, it is important to understand what happens if an individual dies without a will, more commonly referred to as "dying intestate." The law of intestacy governs the disposition of the assets of those persons who die without a valid will. Through statutes and case law, each state, in effect, draws the decedent's will for him according to what seems equitable for the greatest number of its citizens. Although the laws differ among the states, they follow a general pattern. (See Appendix A at the end of this chapter.)

Disadvantages of Intestacy

The laws relating to intestacy are designed to achieve equity for the population as a whole. Obviously, distribution of property under this type of legislation is quite impersonal and inflexible. Who gets what is determined by law. No preference is highlighted in the law of intestacy. Unfortunately, in many cases, forced liquidation of the estate assets is the final result. An individual's estate can be left shattered by the laws of the state in which he lived and paid taxes.

There is a particularly onerous disadvantage to the decedent's spouse. Many people are under the mistaken impression that a surviving spouse inherits everything automatically when the other spouse dies. This is not the case in most situations. If the wife survives, ordinarily she will be entitled to no more than from one-third to one-half of the decendent's estate. Her share is usually dependent upon the number of children the decedent had. Not only has the surviving spouse lost the ability to enjoy the entire estate but the decedent's estate will probably not be able to take full advantage of the marital deduction (discussed later). This situation is even more unfitting if the couple was childless. Under the laws of many states, the decedent's assets are then divided among the surviving spouse and the decedent's parents, brothers, sisters and even possibly nephews and nieces. It should be noted that property owned by the spouses in joint tenancy with right of survivorship, life insurance proceeds with the spouse as beneficiary and any other property that is deemed to have passed by law to the spouse will, in any event (whether or not there is a will), pass to the surviving spouse.

Not only is the surviving spouse's interest under the laws of intestacy restricted quantitatively, but, in many states, there also are qualitative limitations upon the interest received. Thus, according to the provisions of a number of intestacy statutes, the surviving spouse receives only a life estate in the real estate owned by the decedent. A life estate is that interest which entitles a person to the use and benefit of property during his lifetime. The remainderman succeeds to the property until the life tenant's death. The owner of the life estate does not own property absolutely, and cannot sell or dispose of it; he possesses only the right to use it, or to receive the benefits from it, while he lives. The widow's dower interest is quite frequently only such a life estate, often in only one-third of the realty. She can legally dispose of her life interest, but for all practical purposes such an interest is not readily marketable, for who wants a right of use which might end tomorrow? And any sale the owners of the full legal title might attempt would have to be made subject to the widow's life estate, which is an unattractive offer to a prospective purchaser who realizes that the property cannot be useful or beneficial to him for perhaps a number of years. The life estate virtually strangles the property and keeps its owners from its full value and use. In most instances, the life estate is not likely to be of any real benefit to the widow unless it happens to be substantial income-producing property. In smaller estates, the widow will find her life estate in a portion of realty left by her husband as much of a burden as it is a blessing.

There are also disadvantages to the children of the decedent who dies intestate. As the statutes of intestacy (summarized in Appendix A) indicate, children of an intestate parent share equally in his property. Under these statutes, special circumstances and needs of individual offspring are not taken into consideration. An obvious yet real example would be the child who is suffering from a mental disorder or some type of physical handicap. The law does not take this fact into account in determining the distribution of the estate of a person who dies intestate. An additional problem is that each child receives his individual share outright (assuming he has reached the age of majority). This distribution is made despite the child's ability to manage his financial affairs in a reasonable and prudent manner. If a child is a minor, a guardian is required to manage the distribution until the child reaches the age of majority, at which point a complete distribution must be made to the child.

The laws of intestacy require outright distribution of the property and, as a result, certain assets' values may be reduced. A good example is real estate, most often the most valuable asset in an individual's estate. If the decedent is survived by a wife and children and owns real estate at death, it may be necessary to distribute the real property in fractional shares. If the children are minors, there may be complications regarding the future sale or lease of the property.

In the absence of a will, the law selects the estate representative—the administrator. Generally, where a married man dies intestate, his widow, unless she cannot act due to disability, will be appointed to administer the estate. The possibility of estate shrinkage in this instance will be increased substantially simply because the widow is probably not familiar with her duties in connection with the conservation and management of the estate pending distribution to the heirs. Although the role of women in society has changed immensely in recent years, most married women are still concerned primarily with the day-to-day duties of maintaining a home and bringing up the children, and financial matters concerning business and the management of the estate assets have been left to the husband.

If the decedent owns a business interest,

such as a close corporation, without specific statutory authorization to continue the business, it must be sold, often at a loss. Even if the business interest may be retained, the family members may find themselves cast into the position of unwilling co-owners of the business. If minors are involved the situation is aggravated.

Administrators are often restricted to specified types of investments. Other restrictions upon the representative's freedom of action exemplify the extremely conservative nature of the statutes governing fiduciaries. Protection of the estate is often achieved at the expense of, or at least as a hindrance to, sound management and effective administration. Some states have enacted liberal enabling statutes which recognize this problem; as a result the granting of adequate powers to the estate representative has been forthcoming in many states. However, a properly drawn will providing the representative (executor) with adequate powers to do his job is the ideal solution to this problem. Why rely on the state and its statutes when you are far more capable to make this very important choice concerning the management of your estate?

The cost of administering an intestate estate may be greater than if there is a will. In most jurisdictions, the administrator must furnish a bond to guarantee the faithful performance of his duties, while a will provision may authorize the executor to serve without bond. Since the administrator is limited regarding the scope of his powers in the absence of enabling legislation, judicial authority must be obtained in order to act regarding the estate, such as where claims against the estate are to be compromised or a lease of estate property is proposed. The cost of such proceedings are paid out of estate assets. Intestacy may well result in larger estate taxes. Under most intestacy statues, the surviving spouse receives a fixed percentage of estate assets, and the flexibility afforded by the full or partial use of tax-saving devices, such as the marital deduc-

tion, is lost. In addition, the property which a wife receives from her husband is subject to tax again in her estate when it passes to the children.

There is no doubt that a will benefits the testator and his heirs. Not only will it obviate confusion in the distribution of the estate assets, but it will also save a substantial amount of money in the overall settlement of the estate.

Advantages of a Will

In reviewing the disadvantages of dying intestate, it would appear that drafting a will would be the best solution for avoiding potential estate problems. That assumption or conclusion is correct. Let's list specifically the advantages of having a will, from the perspective of the estate owner.

A. You can select the relatives and friends to whom you want your property to go and the amount they are to receive. You can leave some property to your church, school, or other charity.

B. An executor, either corporate or individual, experienced in estate management, can be named to administer the estate and carry out your objectives.

C. You may dispense with the necessity of surety bonds for a trustee or executor, if you choose. This is advisable where a corporate trustee or executor is named.

D. You can save administration costs and time by giving the executor broad powers so that it is not necessary to petition the court for every action the executor desires to take, thereby providing for an orderly distribution of the estate.

E. You can name a guardian and successor guardians for minor children. This is particularly important where there is no surviving parent.

F. Trusts may be created for the benefit of

minor children, in which they will not only be relieved of management responsibilities, but expensive and complex guardianship accountings can be avoided.

G. Trusts may be created to provide income from certain property for named beneficiaries, making the property in trust available for the beneficiary when needed. Or you can have income accumulated, and thereby conserved, during periods when it is not needed.

H. Spendthrift trusts may be created, in most states, to guard against dissipation of trust money by the beneficiary.

I. You can designate the trustee of any trusts created, rather than leaving this designation to a court, and you can provide for successor trustees in the event that those named in the will cannot serve.

J. If married and possessing a sizable estate, you can save federal and possibly state death taxes in both estates by providing for the maximum allowable marital deduction, and leaving to your wife property which is in excess of the allowable marital deduction in a non-qualified trust that will not be taxed in her estate upon her death.

K. You may make your own provision for distribution of your property in the event of common disaster. Where a marital deduction is involved, a special provision may save thousands of dollars in estate taxes.

L. You can exercise in your will any power of appointment given you over property remaining from a previous will or trust of another.

M. Provision can be made for continuation or disposal of your business interests, or for confirmation of any agreement for the sale of your business interest at time of death. Where other plans are not feasible, an executor can be given powers to continue your business for the benefit of the estate, or to liquidate the business if it seems more advisable.

N. You may dispose of any property held jointly in the event you survive the other joint tenant or in the event of simultaneous deaths.

O. You can designate the persons or property to which federal and state death taxes should be charged. You can remove the burden of death taxes from life insurance beneficiaries.

P. A will may be an aid as evidence in establishing your domicile to avoid difficulties in probate and the possibility of death taxes being imposed by more than one state on the same property.

Q. You may provide for the maintenance or disposal of insurance policies on the lives of others.

Realizing the advantages of a will is a step in the right direction. It is important to understand the reasons why a will is beneficial to you and your family especially when compared to pitfalls that beset an estate owner dying intestate. However, understanding the importance of executing a properly drafted will is only part of the process under which your estate will be distributed. The real art in determining the proper distribution of your estate is in deciding the optimum "plan of attack." This is referred to as "estate planning." Estate planning is simply a process in which you decide the method of arranging your property in order to distribute it to the people you wish to enjoy it, at the least amount of cost to you and your heirs. You want to provide sufficiently for the present and future needs of the family unit. The reason why estate planning has become an important concern of the public in recent years is that most people are so preoccupied with building an estate that they give little thought to passing on their property in a manner that will achieve maximum conservation of estate assets, and hence maximum benefit to the heirs. As a result, many familes have realized the onerous burden of extremely large and depleting estate taxes. With the public becoming more aware of taxes, it stands to reason that estate taxes become as well publicized as income taxes. People are aware that estate planning can save thousands of dollars. Therefore, it is appropriate that we cover certain aspects of estate planning in this chapter dealing with wills.

We will review some of the commonly used planning techniques which may reduce taxes. The Tax Reform Act of 1976 has handcuffed estate planners in their quest for large tax-savings but certain techniques remain.

Marital Deduction

The estate marital deduction permits an individual to leave property to a surviving spouse free of the estate tax. The maximum tax-free amount is the greater of: (1) $250,000, or (2) 50% of the adjusted gross estate (gross estate minus expenses and debts). If the surviving spouse receives less than the maximum allowable (such as in intestacy), the deduction is limited to what he or she actually receives.

The primary concern of most husbands is the security of their wives and children. However, if the wife already has a substantial estate of her own, it may be unwise to make maximum use of the marital deduction. The tax savings at the husband's death may be more than offset by the huge additional estate tax liability when the wife dies later with no marital deduction available (unless she has remarried and predeceases her second husband). Also, it may not be wise to use the $250,000 marital deduction in a smaller estate. An example will illustrate the point:

Husband's Estate

	$250,000 marital deduction	50% marital deduction
Gross estate	$400,000	$400,000
Deductions	(40,000)	(40,000)
Adjusted gross estate	360,000	360,000
Marital deduction	(250,000)	(180,000)
Taxable estate	$110,000	$180,000
Tentative tax	26,800	47,800
Credit (1981)	(47,000)	(47,000)
Tax at H's death	$-0-	$800

Wife's Estate

	$250,000 marital deduction	50% marital deduction
Marital share	$250,000	$180,000
Deductions	(25,000)	(18,000)
Taxable estate	225,000	162,000
Tentative tax	62,800	42,640
Credit (1981)	(47,000)	(47,000)
Tax at W's death	$15,800	-0-
Total tax (two deaths)	$15,800	$800

By using the $250,000 maximum marital deduction, the husband saves $800 but it costs his wife's estate $15,800. Needless to say, proper analysis and planning could have avoided the extra amount of tax payable.

Gift Tax Marital Deduction

The gift tax marital deduction used to be 50% of marital gifts. It still applies for gifts over $200,000. But for the first $100,000 of marital gifts, there is a 100% deduction. No deduction is allowed for the next $100,000, and then the 50% rule is effective thereafter. When lifetime marital gifts are less than $20,000, a reduction in the estate tax marital deduction is required. This is because the individual has paid tax on less than 50% of the total marital gifts. The following formula may be helpful in calculating the reduction in the estate tax marital deduction:

$X = A - (B - c/2)$, where

A = regular maximum estate tax marital deduction,

B = gift tax marital deduction allowed,

C = total lifetime gifts, and

X = reduced estate tax marital deduction available.

Let's assume a decedent made a $100,000 marital gift during life for which he received a $97,000 gift tax marital deduction (after subtracting the $3,000 exclusion). His adjusted gross estate is $900,000. The formula would be:

$X = \$450,000 - (\$97,000 - \$50,000)$

$X = \$450,000 - \$47,000$

$X = \$403,000$

When lifetime marital gifts equal or exceed $200,000, the regular maximum estate marital deduction applies.

Marital Deduction in Community Property States

This deduction is $250,000 reduced by the decedent's interest in net community prop-erty. Thus, small estates in community states can now escape the estate tax just as in common-law states.

Where a deceased spouse in a community state dies owning both separate and community property, the marital deduction available for the separate property must be reduced pro rata by the I.R.C. Sec.'s 2053–2054 deductions for debts, expenses, etc., allocable to the separate property. An example should illustrate this point:

Assume the value of a decedent's gross estate is $400,000, of which $300,000 represents separate property and $100,000 represents the one-half interest in community property. The total Sec.'s 2053–2054 deductions are $40,000. The adjusted gross estate for marital purposes is calculated as follows:

Value of Gross Estate		$400,000
Community Property	$100,000	
Allocation of 2053–2054 deductions ($40,000x $300,000/$400,000)	$30,000	$130,000
Adjusted Gross Estate		$270,000
50% of A.G.E.		$135,000

A further calculation is necessary to see if the prorated $250,000 minimum marital deduction exceeds 50% of the adjusted gross estate, since the decedent's estate is entitled to the larger of these two. The formula for this computation is:

$$X = \$250,000 - \left(A - (B - \frac{(C - A)(B)}{C})\right)$$

where C = gross estate,

A = community property included in gross estate,

B = total Sec.'s 2053–2054 deductions, and

X = reduced marital deduction

By calculating the figures, the reduced minimum marital deduction is $172,500; since that exceeds 50% of the adjusted gross estate (as reduced), the decedent's estate could utilize the larger $172,500 figure.

Lifetime Gifts

The Tax Reform Act of 1976 unified the gift and estate taxes so that all transfers (lifetime and death) are now cumulated (and taxed according to the same rate schedule). When lifetime gifts are added back into the tax base at death, the tax base will shift into a higher tax bracket. While the estate gets a credit for gift taxes paid during life, these taxes were paid in a lower bracket than the estate is going to be taxed in.

Lifetime gifts are still an effective tax-minimizing device. Any appreciation in the property which occurs after the gift is not subject to the estate tax (after the expiration of three years). The amount cumulated at death is based only upon the value of the property at the time it was transferred.

In addition, there are certain gift tax exclusions and deductions which reduce the amount that is cumulated into the tax base at death. These specific deductions are:

1. The gift tax marital deduction (previously discussed)
2. The gift tax charitable deduction
3. The $3,000 annual exclusion
4. Gift-splitting between husband and wife

We have already discussed and illustrated the gift tax marital deduction exclusion. Any charitable gift made, for which a gift tax charitable deduction is allowed, is not taxed at death. An example should illustrate the final two exclusions. Mr. Benoit wishes to gift $50,000 to his daughter, and his wife, Sara, splits the gift with him.

Gross Gift		$50,000
Less: gift attributable		
to Sara	$25,000	
Bill's annual		
exclusion	$3,000	$28,000
Taxable gift of Bill		$22,000

Bill has reduced the $50,000 down to $22,000; Sara also has made a gift of $22,000 that will be cumulated into her tax base at death. Each can utilize part of his or her respective unified gift tax credit to eliminate any gift tax liability currently.

Another use of lifetime gifts that may be beneficial to you is the transferring of income-producing property to a third party, such as your child, who is in a lower income tax bracket than you. The income is taxed to the donee rather than the donor who is undoubtedly in a higher tax bracket. This is a very effective tool for reducing not only estate taxes but also income taxes.

Trusts

An express trust is a fiduciary relationship by which an owner of property, known as the grantor or settlor, conveys legal title in trust to a trustee for the benefit of a third person, the beneficiary, who holds equitable title to the property.

An *inter vivos*, or living trust, is simply one which is created to take effect during the lifetime of the grantor or settlor. This is to be distinguished from the testamentary trust which does not become operative until death. The trust instrument is a very good financial tool and used quite frequently in estate planning. Where, perhaps, the donor has a lack of confidence in the beneficiary's ability as a financial manager, an *inter vivos* trust may be the answer. Such an instrument is extremely appropriate where the donor's holdings are significant, he is advanced in years and desires to be relieved of the cares of management. Additionally, the costs of probate are avoided in the settlement of the estate. There can also be tax savings depending upon the revocable or irrevocable nature of the trust instrument.

The *revocable inter vivos* trust is a trust under which the grantor retains the right to revoke the agreement during his lifetime and recover the property for himself, or the right to change or terminate the trust. No gift is made except to the extent the trust property or income is distributed to beneficiaries.

This trust is quite flexible because the donor maintains continued control over the assets of the trust. Because of a change of financial circumstances or for any other reason, the grantor may revest himself the absolute ownership of all or part of the property. He is always protected as to his future financial needs. Through this instrument, the grantor can test how a contemplated irrevocable trust or a testamentary disposition will work while, at the same time, establishing a financial program for a beneficiary which can be modified to fit changing circumstances. But this type of instrument in which the grantor retains complete control has no inherent tax advantages.

The *irrevocable inter vivos* trust is a trust that the grantor does not reserve the right to revoke or terminate at his pleasure. The most attractive feature of the irrevocable *inter vivos* trust is that the donor can achieve almost all of the tax and other advantages of an outright gift without surrendering complete control over the property. By the terms of the trust, the grantor may direct future administration and disposition of the trust property and, like the revocable trust, is free of property management duties. Likewise, probate costs are avoided. In order to achieve tax savings, however, the grantor must completely divest himself of all control over the property. As a result, a certain degree of flexibility is lost.

An irrevocable *short-term* reversionary trust is an irrevocable trust created generally for a term of at least 10 years, at the end of which term the trust terminates and the property comprising the trust reverts to the grant-

or. The grantor has the option to postpone such reversion and, thus, prolong the trust's existence. The short-term reversionary trust is primarily an income-tax savings device. If the ten-year minimum term is observed, a grantor in a high-income tax bracket can shift tax liability for income on trust property to either the trust itself or to a beneficiary in a lower bracket, such as a child or grandchild. At the same time, the property is not relinquished forever.

A *testamentary* trust does not take effect until the death of the grantor which distinguishes it from an *inter vivos* trust which becomes effective during the lifetime of the grantor. A testamentary trust is contained within a will. Some of the practical and tax advantages of the irrevocable *inter vivos* trust are also applicable to the testamentary trust. Through this instrument, the estate owner can vest income-producing property in trustees who are knowledgeable in property management and investment matters, and can exercise such business judgment for the benefit of the trust beneficiaries who may be immature, inexperienced or improvident in financial matters. It is also useful where the estate owner wishes one beneficiary to have the beneficial use of income for life, and desires to control the ultimate disposition of property comprising the trust principal.

A *nonmarital* trust is utilized to manage property not qualifiying for the marital deduction. With regard to property qualifying for marital deduction, because of the substantial control which must be given to the surviving spouse (even if the property is placed in a marital trust), the value of such property will be included in the survivor's estate unless the survivor relinquishes control of the property via *inter vivos* gift. The property placed in the nonmarital trust may be shielded from estate tax in the survivor's estate since the survivor does not have sufficient control over the property. Under this type of arrangement, decedent's property which does not qualify for the marital deduction is placed in a non-marital trust, with the income usually payable to the spouse for life, and with limited rights, by the survivor, to invade corpus under certain circumstances.

The *sprinkling* or *spray* trust may be *inter vivos* or testamentary. The trustee has the power to determine which member or members of a definite class of beneficiaries shall receive income and principal payments from the trust, and in what proportions, usually according to need. Its principal value as an instrumentality in estate planning is its flexibility. Recognizing that circumstances change with passing years, the trustee is given considerable discretion with regard to disbursements of trust income and principal. It results in substantial income tax savings.

A *life insurance* trust is an express trust whose principal is composed either wholly or partly of life insurance contracts or proceeds. It may be *inter vivos* or testamentary, revocable or irrevocable, funded or unfunded. The *unfunded* life insurance trust is a trust in which the trustee is the beneficiary of life insurance proceeds, the terms of the trust covering the investment, administration and distribution of the proceeds. The insured usually pays premiums from his own funds so that the trustee has no substantial duties prior to the insured's death. The *funded* life insurance trust is a trust which the grantor assigns life insurance policies on his or another's life to a trustee and also transfers to the trustee other property (usually income-producing) from which the trustee can maintain the insurance from this other property, either from the earnings or corpus. Unfortunately, this arrangement may cause unforeseen income taxation to the grantor. Under I.R.C. Section 677 (a)(3), income of a funded trust will be taxable to the grantor to the extent that such income is used to pay premiums on a policy insuring the grantor or his spouse.

Life Insurance and Annuities

In the smaller estates, life insurance is the most valuable instrumentality available, and it usually constitutes the bulk of such estates. However, regardless of the size of the estate, life insurance is a highly desirable instrumentality because of its pliability. Its primary function is to create estate liquidity with funds that come into existence at the insured's death. Insurance has many other uses and much can be done through insurance settlement options. Annuities are also very useful tools which can relieve the estate owner of the burdens of custody, management and investment of property and, at the later ages, provide higher installments of income than would otherwise be available.

Joint Interests in Property

The major advantage of placing property in certain types of joint ownership is that probate is avoided. Title to the property will pass to the survivor (in a joint tenancy or tenancy by the entirety) without the necessity of administration.

The identifying characteristic of a *joint tenancy*, as an interest in property, is the right of survivorship. At the death of one joint owner, the property passes automatically and completely to the surviving joint owner or owners.

A *tenancy in common* differs from a joint tenancy in the right of survivorship, which joint tenants have, and tenants in common do not. When a tenant in common dies, his interest in the property passes to his estate and his heirs or devisees, and not to the surviving owner(s).

A *tenancy by the entirety* is a joint estate with right of survivorship between a husband and wife. It exists only where a husband and wife own property in their joint names, with full ownership passing to the survivor at death.

For estate tax purposes, 100% of the value of jointly owned property is to be included in the gross estate of a deceased joint tenant, except to the extent that the surviving joint tenant can establish independent contribution to the acquisition of such property [I.R.C. Sec. 2040(a)]. However, certain "qualified joint interests" created after December 31, 1976 between husband and wife are subject to special treatment [I.R.C. Sec. 2040(b)]. Under a *qualified joint interest*, only 50% of the value of a qualified joint interest between husband and wife is included in the estate of the first spouse to die. A qualified joint interest refers to property held by the decedent and his spouse as joint tenants or as tenants by the entirety. The interest must have been created by the decedent, the decedent's spouse or both, and the interest must have constituted a gift for gift-tax purposes. Where a joint tenancy is involved, the decedent and his spouse must be the only joint tenants.

Conclusion

This chapter is simply an introduction to wills and estate planning. The important consideration should be the optimum manner in which you distribute your assets from a cost point of view. It is important to consider to whom you are distributing your assets, but as important is how you distribute them. Your will and estate plan should be reviewed regularly (minimum every two years) with your financial advisors—attorney, accountant and insurance agent. Many people have lost most of what they have worked to attain because they have not periodically reviewed their wills and estate plans.

APPENDIX A: Estate Administration Timetable

Preliminary

Alert and knowledgeable administration of an estate requires prompt consideration of the property, investments and business interests of the decedent. The holdings and commitments of a tycoon or wheeler-dealer will call for the quick tempo. Those of the elderly widow will be more orderly and subdued. The business operations of a deceased sole owner need a steward.

Attention must be given to matters such as the following as promptly as possible:

Secure the residence and private offices of the decedent.

Review insurance coverage for real estate, tangible property and liability exposure including ownership designations, payment of premiums and expiring terms.

Check permissible usage and insurance coverage of decedent's automobiles.

Impending maturity of investments such as certificates of deposit, bonds or debentures, time deposits or other evidences of indebtedness.

Tender offers for the purchase of securities.

Securities held on margin.

Review outstanding leases including rights to renew or extend term, options or rights thereunder or desirability to end term.

Review outstanding contractual obligations to take appropriate steps to protect rights of the estate.

Protection of the rights and limiting the liabilities of the estate may justify immediate application for preliminary letters testamentary or letters of temporary administration.

After appointment of the fiduciary consider petition for continuance of business of which decedent was a sole owner.

Tax factors must be reviewed. These will vary in great measure with the time of death, fiscal tax periods and the activities of the decedent. Questions to be considered are:

What tax (income, gift, sales, employer taxes, etc.) have accrued?

What is the status of preparation of the returns? Are extensions of time necessary or desirable? Ascertain what foreign death taxes may be due because of real estate situated in or corporations incorporated in other states or countries and prepare and file appropriate forms when due.

Consider election to accrue interest on discount-type savings bonds on decedent's final returns or on fiduciary returns (IRC 454a).

Early consideration of choice of first taxable year for estate for fiduciary income tax returns (fiscal or calendar).

Within 30 Days

Administration Generally

Probate will or obtain letters of administration.

Set off exempt property pursuant to local statute.

Marshall assets:

If necessary, order may be obtained to open safe deposit box for will, deed to burial plot or insurance policy; after appointment, open safe deposit box and obtain release from State Tax Commission (STC).

Obtain from STC tax waiver notices for securities and bank accounts and insurance over certain amounts varying from state to state.

For bank accounts, obtain date of death valuation letters from banks.

For loans and mortgages, obtain statement of principal balance outstanding with interest to date of death from lenders.

Obtain securities from brokerage accounts, especially if in nominee name.

Review will concerning: fiduciary's powers, especially regarding employing agents such as investment advisors and accountants, principal and income allocations, and investment restrictions.

Prepare inventory of assets and schedule of cash requirements.

Pay funeral expenses, utilities and rent.

Consider waiver of commissions by fiduciary.

Death Taxes

File with District Director within 30 days of issuance of letters notice of fiduciary relationship.

Income Taxes and Other Taxes

Subchapter S Corporation—File consent to Subchapter S election by Executor or Administrator within 30 days of issuance of letters but in no event later than 60 days following end of tax year of corporation in which estate became a stockholder (trust cannot be a stockholder) (IRC 1372).

Within 3 Months

Administration Generally

Consider publication of notice to creditors to present claims within 3 months of date of first publication. If no publication, consult local statute regarding distribution of assets after a certain period of time.

Arrange for appraisals of real estate and tangibles.

Obtain consents to transfer valuable tangibles from IRS and STC.

Consider distribution of specific legacies.

Pay general bequests as contemplated under local statute.

Ascertain from company or union whether employee death benefits are payable and information as to plan's qualification and what decedent contributed to plan.

Obtain from life insurance companies federal forms 712 (on decedent's life) and 938 (on life of another owned by decedent).

File Blue Cross, major medical and Medicare claims.

Within 6 Months

Administration Generally

If estate will not be formally administered, proceed under local statute to collect from debtors not more than $3,000, (including wages from decedent's employer), and under local statute for voluntary administration of an estate of personal property of not more than $3,000.

Consider surviving spouse's right of election—must be served and filed within 6 months (under most state statutes) of issuance of letters, unless time extended.

Renunciation of an intestate share—must be filed within 6 months (under most state statutes) of issuance of letters, unless time extended.

Challenge of charitable gifts must be made within 6 months (under most state statutes) of issuance of letters, unless time extended.

Death Taxes

Must consult local statutes for time period allowed for payment of estate/inheritance taxes.

Within 9 Months

Administration Generally

Submit "Flower Bonds" for redemption (U.S. Treasury bonds redeemable at par for payment of estate tax).

Consider Section 303 redemption—generally must be completed within 48 months of death.

Prepare post mortem estate and fiduciary income tax plan (whether allowable deductions will be taken for estate tax purposes or on income tax returns and timing of distributions and payment of administration expenses, etc.).

Pay balance of debts.

If required, obtain releases of lien on real property to be sold from IRS (4422) and STC unless tenancy by the entirety.

Death Taxes

Prepare federal estate tax return (return and payment due 9 months after death).

Consider request on or before date tax due for extension of time to pay federal estate tax (IRC 6161a) (Form 4768).

If estate contains closely held business and qualifies under the statute, consider filing for an extension on or before due date of return notice of election to pay federal estate tax. (IRC 6166).

If impossible or impracticable to file a reasonably complete federal estate tax return by the due date, apply in advance of the due date for a 6-month extension (Reg. 20.6081—1).

Consider applying for discharge of executor or administrator from personal liability for federal estate tax within 9 months of due date of return (IRC 2204).

After 9 Months

Administration Generally

Renunciation of testamentary disposition—must be filed within a certain time frame of probate of will, unless time extended (consult local statute).

Apply for Social Security and Veterans Administration death benefits before 2 years after death.

Ascertain if a report is to be filed with local Probate Court for estate not fully distributed within 2 or 3 years of issuance of letters—necessity for report depends on size of estate and county or department practice.

If distributions in kind to residuary legatees are contemplated, consider obtaining from legatees hold harmless letter or indemnity agreement to protect fiduciary from liability for loss in value prior to distribution.

Prepare fiduciary's final account for judicial settlement or informal settlement by receipt and release containing indemnity agreement, refunding bond and waiver of citation of judicial accounting.

Death Taxes

Review state estate tax estimate.

Apply for refund of any overpayment of federal estate tax before 3 years from due date of return or 2 years from time tax was due or paid, whichever is latest (Form 843).

Submit to IRS evidence of payment of state death taxes before 4 years from date 706 filed.

Report to IRS newly discovered asset unless more than 3 years after due date of 706 or later filing, but, if omitted asset exceeds 25% of re-

ported gross estate, time limitation on assessment extended to 6 years (IRC 6501(e) 2).

Income Taxes and Other Taxes

Apply for employer identification number for trust under will (estate uses decedent's social security number for 706 and 1041).

If needed, apply for extension of time to file federal fiduciary income tax return before due date of return (Form 2758). Generally, extension will be limited to 60 days, unless estate elects to pay tax in equal installments on or before 15th day of 4th, 7th, 10th and 13th months after close of tax year, in which case extension will be until due date of second installment.

If needed, apply for an extension of time to pay federal fiduciary income tax on or before payment date—generally not to exceed 6 months at 6% (Form 1127).

Consider requesting prompt assessment of income taxes of decedent and estate to reduce period from 3 years after return was filed to 18 months after request (IRC 6501 (d)).

APPENDIX B: Glossary of Common Legal Terms

Ademption by Extinction: The failure of a specific testamentary bequest due to the absence of the specific property in the estate at the testator's death.

Ademption by Satisfaction: The failure of a general or demonstrative testamentary bequest due to the testator's having transferred property to the beneficiary during his lifetime with the intent to satisfy the testamentary provision.

Administrator—Executor: An administrator is a man appointed by the court to settle an estate. An executor is a man named by the estate owner in his will as the one to settle that estate. The administrator is always named by the court, the executor by the deceased in his will.

An administrator may be appointed (1) when the deceased left no will, (2) where the deceased left a will but failed to name an executor, (3) where the executor in the will failed to qualify or refused to serve, and (4) where the executor in the will, after having qualified, failed to settle the estate, as in the case of his death.

Administratrix—Executrix: A woman appointed by the court (administratrix), or named in the will (executrix), to settle the estate.

Advancement: Money or property given by a parent to his or her child, other descendant, or heir (depending upon the statute's wording), or expended by the former for the latter's benefit, by way of anticipation of the share which the child, for example, will inherit in the parent's estate and intended to be deducted therefrom.

After-born Child: A child born after the execution of a parent's will.

Attestation: The attestation clause is the paragraph appended to the will indicating that certain persons by their signatures thereto have heard the testator declare the instrument to be his or her will and have witnessed his or her signing of the will.

Bequest: A bequest, though strictly a gift by will of personal property as distinguished from a gift of real estate, is often used to cover a gift of either personal property or land, or both. "To bequeath" generally means to dispose of property of any kind by will. (See also: **Devise** and **Legacy**.)

Bequests are classified, generally speaking, as specific or general. A specific bequest is a gift of a particular specified class or kind of property as, for example, a gift of the testator's diamond ring to a named individual or a gift of designated stock in a corporation. A general bequest is one which may be satisfied from the general assets of the estate as, for example, a bequest of a sum of money without reference to any particular fund from which it is to be paid or a bequest of a certain number of shares of stock where the testator owns a large number of such shares. Since a specific bequest designates a particular item of the estate which is to be given, if that item is not in existence at the time of the testator's death, the gift fails.

Codicil: A supplement or addition to an existing will, to effect some revision, change, or modification of that will. A codicil must meet the same requirements regarding execution and validity as a will.

Collateral Relations: A phrase used primarily in the law of intestacy to designate uncles and aunts, cousins, etc., those relatives not in a direct ascending or descending line, like grandparents or grandchildren, the latter which are designated as lineal relations.

Curtesy: A common law, the estate by which a man was entitled to a life estate in all lands owned by his wife during marriage, provided lawful issue was born of the union. As with dower, modern-day statutes have, in many cases, repealed or modified common-law curtesy interests.

Descent and Distribution: Descent refers to the passing of real estate to the heirs of one who dies without a will. Distribution refers to the passing of personal property to the heirs of one who dies without a will. The laws of descent relate to real property; those of distribution relate to personal property. When a person receives either real estate or personal property under a will, he or she takes it not by descent or distribution but by the will. Modern-day usage has substituted *intestacy* to designate the legal effect of dying without a will.

Devise: Traditionally, a devise is a bequest of real estate under a will as distinguished from a bequest of personal property. The trend among the states is to make "devise" a generic term which is sufficient to pass any property in the probate estate. (See also: **Bequest** and **Legacy**.)

Donee: The recipient of a gift. In the law of wills, the term is used to refer to one who is the recipient of a power of appointment.

Donor: A person who makes a gift. In the law of wills, the term refers to the person who grants a power of appointment to another.

Dower: The provision which the law makes for a widow out of the real estate owned by her husband. At common law the widow was entitled to receive a one-third life interest in all the lands which her husband owned during their marriage. The amount to which the widow is entitled has been changed by statute in many states, and the term "dower" has been replaced by "statutory interest" in some jurisdictions.

Executor—Executrix: See: **Administrator** and **Administratrix**.

Family Allowance: Allowance of money from the estate to family for support during administration.

Guardian: A person named to represent the interests of minor children, whether named in a will or appointed by a court.

Heir: Technically, those persons designated by law to succeed to the estate of an intestate (also designated as *next of kin*).

Holographic Will: One entirely in the handwriting of the testator. In many states, such a will is not recognized unless it is published, declared and witnessed as required by statute for other written wills.

Homestead Exemption: Statutes exempting the homestead and, often, specified chattels from the debts of a deceased head-of-household, notwithstanding provisions of a will or the intestate laws.

Intestacy Statutes: Statutes designating the persons to whom an *intestate's* property is to be distributed, and the share each is to take.

Intestate: Without a will. A person who leaves no will is an intestate. A person who dies without a will dies intestate.

Joint Will: The same instrument is made the will of two or more persons and is jointly signed by them. When it is joint and mutual it contains reciprocal provisions; see **Mutual Wills**, this *Glossary*.

Lapse: The failure of a testamentary bequest due to the death of the devisee or legatee during the life of the testator.

Last Will and Testament: The usual term referring to a will. The phrase is an outgrowth of the old English law under which a "will" was a disposition of real estate and a "testament" was a disposition of personal property. The two terms originally meant different things. The difference is no longer recognized, however. Nothing is added by coupling "testament" with "will," the latter being sufficiently inclusive.

Legacy: A legacy is a bequest of personal property by will. It would perhaps be proper to use the term "bequest" to include any disposition by will, the term "devise" to cover gifts of real estate, and the term "legacy" to cover gifts of personal property. However, both at law and in common practice, the terms are not used with any great respect for this distinction and often appear more or less interchangeably.

Mutual Wills: The separate wills of two or more persons, with reciprocal provisions in favor of the other person contained in each will; may be treated as a contract under state law.

Noncupative Will: An oral will, declared or dictated by the testator in his or her last sickness before a sufficient number of witnesses, and afterwards reduced to writing.

Posthumous Child: A child born after the death of its father.

Power of Appointment: A power or authority conferred by one person by deed (i.e., during life) or will upon another to select and nominate the person or persons who are to receive and enjoy property or the income therefrom after the death of the testator or the death of the person upon whom the power is conferred, or after the termination of a certain period of time. For example, a testator might bequeath property to a trust to pay the income to his widow for her life and giving her a power to appoint the principal of the trust to whomsoever she desires. The person conferring the power is called the donor; the person given the power is called the donee or the holder of the power. The ultimate recipient of the property is called the appointee.

Pretermitted Heir: A child or other descendant omitted from testator's will. Where a testator fails to make provision for a child, either living at execution of the will, or born thereafter, statutes often provide that such child, or the issue of a deceased child, take an intestate share in testator's estate.

Probate: The process of proving the validity of the will in court and executing its provisions under the guidance of the court. When a person dies, his or her will must be filed before the proper officer of the proper court, giving this court jurisdiction in the matter of enforcing the document. This is called "filing the will for probate." When the will has been filed, it is said to be "admitted to probate." The process of "probating" the will involves recognition by the court of the executor named in the will (or appointment of an administrator if none has been named), the filing of the proper reports and papers as required by law, determination of validity of the will if it is contested, and distribution and final settlement of the estate under the supervision of the court.

Residuary Estate: The remaining part of testator's estate, after payment of debts and bequests. Wills usually contain a clause disposing of the residue of the estate which the testator has not otherwise bequeathed or devised.

Testamentary: The disposition of property by will. A testamentary document is an instrument disposing of property at death, either a will in fact or in the nature of a will.

Testamentary Trust: A trust of certain property passing under a will and created by the terms of the will.

Testator—Testatrix: The person who makes a will. If a man, he is a testator. If a woman, she is a testatrix. The term will-maker is descriptive, but not generally used. The term willor is never used. The term testator, one who makes a testament, is the proper designation.

APPENDIX C: The Laws of Intestacy For Each State

ALABAMA

Spouse and Child(ren)[1]:

Real Estate: Life estate in 1/3 to widow (dower);[2] life estate in all realty to widower (curtesy); balance to the children[3] equally, or their issue *per stirpes*.

Personalty: Widow shares equally with children[3] (or their issue *per stirpes*), the widow taking a child's share, but not less than 1/5,[2] 1/2 to widower; 1/2 to children, or their issue *per stirpes*.

No Spouse, but with Child(ren):

Real Estate and Personalty: All to the children[3] equally or their issue *per stirpes*.

Spouse and no Child(ren):

Real Estate: Life estate in 1/2 to widow (dower);[2] life estate in all realty to widower (curtesy); balance to parents. If only one parent survives, the surviving parent takes 1/2 of the balance; the other 1/2 of the balance passes to brothers and sisters[4] equally, or their issue *per stirpes*. If no brothers and sisters or issue, the surviving parent takes the entire balance; if no parent survives, the balance to brothers and sisters, or their issue *per stirpes*. If no parents, brothers and sisters or their issue, all to the spouse.

Personalty: All to the widow;[2] 1/2 to the widower, with the other 1/2 distributed in accordance with the rules applicable to real estate.

No Spouse or Child(ren), but with Parents:

Real Estate and Personalty: All to the parents equally. If only one parent survives, the surviving parent takes 1/2; the other 1/2 passes to brothers and sisters[4] equally, or their issue *per stirpes*. If no brothers and sisters or their issue, all to the surviving parent.

No Spouse, Child(ren), or Parents:

Real Estate and Personalty: All to brothers and sisters[4] equally, or their issue *per stirpes*. If none, to the next of kin.[4] If no next of kin, to the next of kin of predeceased spouse.

[1] Including adopted and posthumous children.
[2] The value of the widow's separate estate reduces her dower in realty and her intestate share of personalty. If the value of her separate estate exceeds her dower plus her share of personalty, she takes nothing. In this calculation, the value of her dower equals seven years' rent of the dower lands. Real and personal property not going to the widow descends to heirs next entitled. Life insurance proceeds are considered as part of a widow's separate estate [*Beck* v. *Karr*, 209 Ala. 199, 95 So. 881].
[3] Advancements to child or other descendants deducted from intestate share.
[4] Kindred of the half blood inherit equally with those of the whole blood in the same degree; however, as to ancestral property, half bloods, unrelated by blood to the ancestor, do not inherit.

ALASKA

Spouse and Child(ren)[1]:

Real Estate and Personalty: If all of the children are children of the surviving spouse, the spouse takes the first $50,000 plus 1/2 of the balance of the estate. If some of the children are not children of the surviving spouse, the spouse takes 1/2 of the estate. In either case, the children share equally, the issue of any deceased child sharing *per stirpes*.

No Spouse, but with Child(ren):

Real Estate and Personalty: All to the children[2] equally, or their issue *per stirpes*.

Spouse and No Child(ren):

Real Estate and Personalty: If no parent of the decedent is alive, the entire estate passes to the spouse. Otherwise, the spouse takes 1/2 of the estate, and the other 1/2 passes to the parent, or parents equally.

No Spouse or Child(ren), but with Parents:

Real Estate and Personalty: All to the parents equally, or the survivor.

No Spouse, Child(ren), or Parents:

Real Estate and Personalty: All to brothers and sisters[3] equally, or their issue *per stirpes*. If none, all to the next of kin[3] in equal degree.

[1] Including adopted children.
[2] Advancements to child or issue deducted from intestate share.
[3] Kindred of the half blood inherit equally with those of the whole blood in the same degree.

ARIZONA

Spouse and Child(ren) [1]: If the children are all children of the surviving spouse, the surviving spouse takes the decedent's separate property and his or her one-half of community property. If some of the children are not children of the surviving spouse, the surviving spouse takes ½ of the decedent's separate property but no part of the decedent's one-half of community property. In either case, the children take the balance of the estate equally, the issue of a deceased child sharing *per stirpes*.

No Spouse, but with Child(ren):
Real Estate and Personalty: All to the children [2] equally, or their issue *per stirpes*.

Spouse and No Child(ren): All of the decedent's estate passes to the spouse.

No Spouse or Child(ren), but with Parents: All of the decedent's estate passes to his or her parent, or parents equally.

No Spouse, Child(ren), or Parents:
Real Estate and Personalty: All to brothers and sisters equally, or their issue *per stirpes*. If none, ½ each to maternal and paternal kindred and their descendants *per stirpes*.

---

[1] Including adopted children, and posthumous children and other posthumous descendants.
[2] Advancements to child deducted from intestate share.

ARKANSAS

Spouse and Child(ren) [1]:
Real Estate: Life estate in ⅓ to spouse; [2] balance to the children [3] equally, or their issue *per stirpes*.
Personalty: ⅓ to the spouse; [2] ⅔ to the children [3] equally, or their issue *per stirpes*.

No Spouse, but with Child(ren):
Real Estate and Personalty: All to the children [3] equally, or their issue *per stirpes*.

Spouse and No Child(ren):
Real Estate and Personalty: ½ to the spouse; [2] ½ to the parents equally, or the survivor. If neither parent survives, this ½ passes to brothers and sisters [1] equally, or their issue *per stirpes*. If no brothers and sisters, to grandparents, uncles and aunts and their descendants [4] in equal parts. If none, all to the spouse.

No Spouse or Child(ren), but with Parents:
Real Estate and Personalty: All to the parents equally, or the survivor.

No Spouse, Child(ren), or Parents:
Real Estate and Personalty: All to brothers and sisters [4] equally, or their issue *per stirpes*. If none, to grandparents, uncles and aunts and their descendants [4] in equal parts.

---

[1] Including adopted and posthumous children.
[2] Regarding ancestral real estate, widow takes a life estate in ½; the widower a life estate in ⅓.
[3] Advancements to child deducted from intestate share.
[4] Kindred of the half blood inherit equally with those of the whole blood in the same degree; however, as to ancestral property, half bloods, unrelated by blood to the ancestor, do not inherit.

CALIFORNIA

Spouse and One Child [1]:
Separate Realty and Personalty: ½ to the spouse; ½ to the child or its issue. [2]
Community Property: All to the spouse.

Spouse and Children:
Separate Realty and Personalty: ⅓ to the spouse; ⅔ to the children equally, or their issue *per stirpes*.
Community Property: All to the spouse.

No Spouse, but with Child(ren):
Real Estate and Personalty: All to the children equally, or their issue *per stirpes*.

Spouse and No Child(ren):
Separate Realty and Personalty: ½ to the spouse, ½ to the parents equally or the survivor. If neither parent survives, to brothers and sisters [3] equally, or their issue *per stirpes*. If none, all to the spouse.
Community Property: All to the spouse.

No Spouse or Child(ren), but with Parents:
Real Estate and Personalty: All to the parents equally, or the survivor.

No Spouse, Child(ren), or Parents:
Real Estate and Personalty: All to brothers and sisters [3] equally, or their issue, *per stirpes*. If none to the next of kin [3] in equal degree, with exceptions.

---

[1] Including adopted children.

136

[2] Advancements to child *or other heirs* deducted from intestate share.

[3] Kindred of the half blood inherit equally with those of the whole blood in the same degree; however, as to ancestral property, half bloods, unrelated by blood to the ancestor, do not inherit.

COLORADO

Spouse and Child(ren)[1]: If all of the children are children of the surviving spouse, the surviving spouse takes the first $25,000 plus ½ of the balance of the estate. If some of the children are not children of the surviving spouse, the surviving spouse takes ½ of the estate. In either case, the children take what remains equally, the issue of a deceased child sharing *per stirpes*.

No Spouse, but with Child(ren):

Real Estate and Personalty: All to the children[2] equally or their issue *per stirpes*.

Spouse and No Child(ren):

Real Estate and Personalty: All to the spouse.

No Spouse or Child(ren), but with Parents:

Real Estate and Personalty: All to the parents equally, or the survivor.

No Spouse, Child(ren), or Parents:

Real Estate and Personalty: All to brothers and sisters[3] equally, or their issue, *per stirpes*. If none, to the grandfather, grandmother, uncles, aunts, and their descendants,[3] in equal shares, *per stirpes*.

---

[1] Including adopted children, posthumous children and other posthumous descendants.

[2] Advancements to child deducted from intestate share.

[3] Collateral kindred of the half blood take a full share, except if there are also collaterals of the whole blood of the same class, in which case, half bloods take a one-half share.

CONNECTICUT

Spouse and Child(ren)[1]:

Real Estate and Personalty: The first $50,000 to the surviving spouse plus one-half of the balance; the children *share* the one-half of the balance equally, or their issue *per stirpes*. If one or more of the children are children only of decedent, the spouse takes one-half and the other half is shared by decedent's children equally.

No Spouse, but with Child(ren):

Real Estate and Personalty: All to the children[2] equally, or their issue *per stirpes*.

Spouse and No Child(ren):

Real Estate and Personalty: First $50,000 plus ¾ of the balance to the spouse: the other ¼ to the parents equally, or the survivor. If neither parent survives, all to the spouse.

No Spouse or Child(ren), but with Parents:

Real Estate and Personalty: All to the parents equally, or the survivor.

No Spouse, Child(ren), or Parents:

Real Estate and Personalty: All to brothers and sisters[3] equally, or their issue *per stirpes*. If none, then to the next of kin[3] in equal degree.

---

[1] Including adopted children.

[2] Advancements to child or other descendants deducted from intestate share.

[3] Collateral kindred of the whole blood take in preference to those of the half blood.

DELAWARE

Spouse and Child(ren)[1]: If all of the children are children of the surviving spouse, the surviving spouse takes the first $50,000, plus ½ of the balance of the personal estate, plus a life estate in the real estate. If some of the children are not children of the surviving spouse, the surviving spouse takes ½ the personal estate plus a life estate in the real estate. The children and the issue of a deceased child take *per stirpes*.

No Spouse, but with Child(ren):

Real Estate and Personalty: All to the children[2] equally, or their issue *per stirpes*.

Spouse and No Child(ren): If the decedent is survived by parents, the surviving spouse takes the first $50,000 of the personal estate plus ½ of the balance of the personal estate plus a life estate in the real estate, and the parents take the balance equally. If the decedent is not survived by parents, the surviving spouse takes the entire estate.

No Spouse or Child(ren), but with Parents:

Real Estate and Personalty: All to the parents equally, or the survivor.

No Spouse, Child(ren), or Parents:

Real Estate and Personalty: All to brothers and

sisters,[3] or their issue *per stirpes*. If none, then to the next of kin[3] in equal degree.

---

[1]Including adopted and posthumous children.
[2]Advancements to child or issue deducted from intestate share.
[3]Kindred of the half blood share equally with those of the whole blood in the same degree.

DISTRICT OF COLUMBIA

Spouse and Child(ren)[1]:
Real Estate: Life estate in ⅓ to spouse; the balance to the children[2] equally, or their issue *per stirpes*.

Spouse and Child(ren)[1]:
Real Estate: Life estate in ⅓ to spouse; the balance to the children[2] equally, or their issue *per stirpes*.

Personality: ⅓ to spouse; ⅔ to children[2] or their issue *per stirpes*.

No Spouse, but with Child(ren):
Real Estate and Personality: All to the children[2] equally, or their issue *per stirpes*.

Spouse and No Child(ren):
Real Estate: Life estate in ⅓ to spouse; the balance to the parents equally, or the survivor. If neither parent survives, the balance passes to brothers and sisters[3] equally, or their issue *per stirpes*. If none, to collateral kindred[3] in equal degree. If none, to grandparents equally.

Personalty: ½ to spouse; ½ in same manner as balance of real estate.

If the decedent is not survived by children, parents, grandchildren, brothers or sisters or their descendants, the surviving spouse takes the entire estate.

No Spouse or Child(ren), but with Parents:
Real Estate and Personalty: All to the parents equally, or the survivor.

No Spouse, Child(ren) or Parents:
Real Estate and Personalty: All to brothers and sisters[3] equally, or their issue *per stirpes*. If none, to collateral kindred[3] in equal degree. If none, to grandparents equally.

---

[1]Including adopted children, posthumous children and other posthumous descendants.
[2]Advancements to child or other descendants deducted from intestate share.
[3]Kindred of the half blood share equally with those of the whole blood in the same degree.

FLORIDA

Spouse and Child(ren)[1]:
Real Estate and Personalty: If all the children are children of the surviving spouse, the first $20,000 worth of property plus ½ the balance of the estate passes to the spouse. If some of the children are not children of the surviving spouse, the surviving spouse takes ½ of the estate. What remains passes to the children equally or to their issue *per stirpes*.

No Spouse, but with Child(ren):
Real Estate and Personalty: All to the children equally, or their issue, *per stirpes*.

Spouse and No Child(ren):
Real Estate and Personalty: All to the spouse.

No Spouse or Child(ren), but with Parents:
Real Estate and Personalty: All to the parents equally or the survivor.

No Spouse, Child(ren), or Parents:
Real Estate and Personalty: All to brothers and sisters[2] equally, or their issue, *per stirpes*. If none, ½ each to paternal and maternal kindred[2] and their descendants, *per stirpes*.

---

[1]Including adopted children.
[2]Where collateral kindred of the whole and half blood survive, those of the half blood take only half shares.

GEORGIA

Spouse and Child(ren)[1]:
Real Estate and Personalty: Spouse and each child[2] (or its issue *per stirpes*), take equal shares; the spouse takes a child's share, but widow[3] entitled to at least ⅕.

No Spouse, but with Child(ren):
Real Estate and Personalty: All to the children[2] equally or their issue, *per stirpes*.

Spouse and No Child(ren):
Real Estate and Personalty: All to the spouse.[3]

No Spouse or Child(ren), but with Parents:
Real Estate and Personalty: All to parents and brothers and sisters[4] equally, or their issue *per stirpes*.

No Spouse, Child(ren), or Parents:
Real Estate and Personalty: All to parents and brothers[4] equally, or their issue *per stirpes*. If none, all to nephews and nieces equally, or their issue, *per stirpes*. If none, to the paternal and maternal next of kin.

[1] Including adopted and posthumous children.

[2] Advancements to child deducted from intestate share.

[3] A widow, in lieu of her intestate share to real property, may elect to receive dower—a life estate in 1/3 of the realty.

[4] Brothers and sisters of the half blood, and their issue, inherit equally with those of the whole blood, and their issue.

HAWAII*

Spouse and Child(ren)[1]:

Real Estate and Personalty: 1/2 to the surviving spouse; 1/2 to the children[2] equally.

No Spouse, but with Child(ren)[3]:

Real Estate and Personalty: All to the children[2] equally, or their issue *per stirpes*.

Spouse and No Child(ren):

Real Estate and Personalty: If there is also no surviving parent of the decedent, the surviving spouse takes the entire estate. If there are surviving parents, 1/2 to the surviving spouse; 1/2 to decedent's parents equally, or to the survivor.

No Spouse or Child(ren), but with Parents:

Real Estate and Personalty: All to the parents equally, or the survivor.

No Spouse, Child(ren), or Parents:

Real Estate and Personalty: All to brothers and sisters equally,[4] or their issue, *per stirpes*. If none, to grandparents in equal shares, or to the surviving grandparent. If no grandparents survive, to the uncles and aunts[4] equally.

*Governs descent and distribution of estates of decedents dying after 6–30–77.

[1] Including adopted and posthumous children.

[2] Advancements to child deducted from intestate share.

[3] If decedent is survived by several children, or one child and the issue of one or more other children, and a surviving child dies unmarried during minority, his intestate share is distributed in equal shares, to other children of the same parent *per stirpes*.

[4] Kindred of the half blood inherit equally with those of the whole blood in the same degree; however as to ancestral property, half bloods, unrelated by blood to the ancestor, do not inherit.

IDAHO

Spouse and One Child:

Separate Realty and Personalty: If surviving issue is also issue of surviving spouse, first $50,000 plus 1/2 of balance to the spouse; remainder to the child; if surviving issue is not also issue of surviving spouse, 1/2 to spouse and 1/2 to child.

Community Property: All to the spouse. [1]

Quasi-Community Property: Surviving spouse receives 1/2, and also the remaining 1/2 if not otherwise disposed of by decedent.[2]

Spouse and Children:

Separate Realty and Personalty: If surviving issue is also issue of surviving spouse, first $50,000 plus 1/2 of balance to spouse, remainder to children; if any of surviving issue is not also issue of suviving spouse, 1/2 to spouse and 1/2 to children equally.

Community Property: All to the spouse.

Quasi Community Property: See "Quasi-Community Property" above.

No Spouse, but with Child(ren):

Real Estate and Personalty: Everything to child or children.

Spouse and No Child(ren):

Separate Realty and Personalty: First $50,00 plus 1/2 of balance to the spouse: remainder to decedent's parents equally, or the survivor. If neither parent survives, all to the spouse.

Community Property: All to the spouse.

Quasi-Community Property: See "Quasi-Community Property" above.

No Spouse or Child(ren), but with Parents:

Real Estate and Personalty: Everything to parents equally, or to suviving parent.

No Spouse, Child(ren), or Parents:

Real Estate and Personalty: To brothers and sisters, or their issue.

[1] Decedent's share of community property not otherwise disposed of by will passes in this order: (1) to surviving spouse; (2) if none, to decedent's children; (3) if none, to parents or parent; (4) if none, to brothers and sisters of their issue; (5) if none, to grandparents or their issue.

Any person who fails to survive the decedent by 120 hours is deemed to have predeceased the decedent for purposes of homestead allowance, exempt property and intestate succession, and the decedent's heirs are determined accordingly (IC §15–2–104).

[2] Quasi-community property is property acquired by decedent while a nonresident of Idaho, which property would have been community property had decedent been a resident of Idaho, and the property acquired in exchange for such property.

ILLINOIS

Spouse and Child(ren)[1]:

Real Estate and Personalty: ⅓ to the surviving spouse, ⅓ to the children[3] equally, or their issue *per stirpes*.

No Spouse, but with Child(ren):

Real Estate and Personalty: All to the children[2] equally, or their issue *per stirpes*.

Spouse and No Child(ren):

Real Estate and Personalty: All to the surviving spouse.

No Spouse or Child(ren), but with Parents:

Real Estate and Personalty: To the parents, brothers, and sisters equally. If only one parent survives, he receives a double share. The issue of deceased brothers and sisters[3] take *per stirpes*.

No Spouse, Child(ren), or Parents:

Real Estate and Personalty: All to brothers and sisters[3] equally, or their issue *per stirpes*. If none, ½ each to maternal and paternal grandparents equally, or the survivor; if none surviving, to their issue *per stirpes*.

---

[1] Including adopted and posthumous children.
[2] Advancements to child or other descendants deducted from intestate share.
[3] Kindred of the half blood inherit equally with those of the whole blood.

INDIANA

Spouse and One Child[1]:

Real Estate and Personalty: ½ to the spouse;[2] ½ to the child[3] or its issue.

Spouse and Children:

Real Estate and Personalty: ⅓ to the spouse;[2] ⅔ to the children[3] equally, or their issue *per stirpes*.

No Spouse, but with Child(ren):

Real Estate and Personalty: All to the children equally, or their issue *per stirpes*.

Spouse and No Child(ren):

Real Estate and Personalty: ¾ to the spouse; ¼ to the parents equally, or the survivor. If neither parent survives, all to the spouse.

No Spouse or Child(ren), but with Parents:

Real Estate and Personalty: To the parents, brothers and sisters equally, but each surviving

parent takes at least ¼. The issue of deceased brothers and sisters[4] take *per stirpes*.

No Spouse, Child(ren), or Parents:

Real Estate and Personalty: All to brothers and sisters[4] equally, or their issue *per stirpes*. If none, then to the surviving grandparents equally. If none to uncles and aunts *per stirpes*.

---

[1] Includes adopted children, and posthumous children and other descendants.
[2] If decedent left a child or children of a former marriage, or descendants of such child or children, and no child by the marriage with the surviving spouse, the spouse takes a ⅓ life estate in realty; the spouse takes her statutory share of the personal property.
[3] Advancements to child *or other heirs* deducted from intestate share.
[4] Kindred of the half blood inherit equally with kindred of the whole blood.

IOWA

Spouse and Child(ren)[1]:

Real Estate: ⅓ to spouse;[2] ⅔ to children[3] equally, or their issue *per stirpes*.

Personalty: All property exempt from execution in hands of decedent as head of family at death, and ⅓ of remainder not necessary for payment of debts and charges to spouse;[2] balance to children[3] equally, or their issue *per stirpes*.

No Spouse, but with Child(ren)[1]:

Real Estate and Personalty: All to the children[3] equally, or their issue *per stirpes*.

Spouse and No Child(ren):

Real Estate: ⅓ to spouse;[4] ⅔ to parents equally, or the survivor. If neither parent survives, this ⅔ goes to the parents' heirs,[5] *per stirpes*. If none, all to the spouse or spouse's heirs.

Personalty: All property exempt from execution in hands of decedent as head of family at death, and ⅓ of remainder not necessary for payment of debts and charges to spouse;[4] balance to parents equally, or the survivor. If neither parent survives, this ⅔ goes to the parents' heirs,[5] *per stirpes*, or their issue *per stirpes*. If none, all to the spouse.

No Spouse or Child(ren), but with Parents:

Real Estate and Personalty: All to the parents equally, or the survivor.

No Spouse, Child(ren), or Parents:

Real Estate and Personalty: All to brothers and

sisters equally, or their issue *per stirpes*. If none, then to heirs of spouse of intestate.

---

[1] Including adopted children, posthumous children, and other posthumous heirs.

[2] Spouse entitled to $25,000 minimum of combined personal and real property.

[3] Advancements to child *or other heirs* deducted from intestate share.

[4] But spouse is entitled to a minimum of $25,000 in value from all non-exempt real and personal property and any remaining homestead interest plus ½ net value of estate over $25,000 and value of exempt personal property.

[5] e.g., decedent's brothers and sisters.

KANSAS

Spouse and Child(ren)[1]:

Real Estate and Personalty: ½ to the spouse; ½ to the children[2] equally, or their issue *per stirpes*.

No Spouse, but with Child(ren):

Real Estate and Personalty: All to the children[2] equally, or their issue *per stirpes*.

Spouse and No Child(ren):

Real Estate and Personalty: All to the spouse.

No Spouse or Child(ren), but with Parents:

Real Estate and Personalty: All to the parents equally, or the survivor.

No Spouse, Child(ren), or Parents:

Real Estate and Personalty: All to parents, heirs[3], *per stirpes*. If one parent died without heirs, all to heirs of the other parent.

---

[1] Including adopted and posthumous children.

[2] Advancements to children, *or other heirs*, deducted from intestate share. Children of the half blood inherit equally with children of the whole blood from the common parent [*Genschorck v. Blumer*, 136 Kan. 228, 14 P.2d 722 (1932)]

[3] e.g., decedent's brothers and sisters.

KENTUCKY

Spouse and Child(ren)[1]:

Real Estate and Personalty: ½ to the spouse;[2] ½ to the children[3] equally, or their issue *per stirpes*.

No Spouse, but with Child(ren):

Real Estate and Personalty: All to the children[3] equally, or their issue *per stirpes*.

Spouse and No Child(ren):

Real Estate and Personalty: ½ to the spouse; ½ to the parents equally, or the survivor. If neither parent survives, this ½ passes to decedent's brothers and sisters[4] or their issue *per stirpes*. If none, all to the spouse[5] equally.

No Spouse or Child(ren), but with Parents:

Real Estate and Personalty: All to the parents equally, or the survivor.

No Spouse, Child(ren), or Parents:

Real Estate and Personalty: ½ each to maternal and paternal kindred. First to grandmother and grandfather equally,[4] or the survivor. If none, then to uncles and aunts,[4] and their issue *per stirpes*. The order of succession is continued among lineal ancestors.

---

[1] Including adopted and posthumous children.

[2] In addition to ½ fee interest in real property, spouse has a life estate in ⅓ of the realty.
$3,500 of personalty first set aside for minor children and spouse.

[3] Advancements to child or other descendants deducted from intestate share.
$3,500 of personalty first set aside for spouse and minor children.

[4] Collateral kindred of the half blood inherit only half shares.

[5] When the intestate dies without issue, owning real estate which is the gift of either parent, the parent making such gift inherits the whole of such estate.

LOUISIANA

Spouse and Child(ren)[1]:

Separate Property: All to the children[2] equally, or their issue *per stirpes*.

Community Property: One half passes outright to the spouse. In addition, the spouse has a usufruct interest during his or her life in the portion of community property that is inherited by issue of the decedent and surviving spouse. The usufruct ceases in the event the surviving spouse remarries, unless it has been confirmed for life or any other designated period by the decedent's will.

No Spouse, but with Child(ren):

All Property: To the children[2] equally, or their issue *per stirpes*.

Spouse and No Child(ren):

Separate Property: ¼ to each parent; ½ to the brothers and sisters, or their issue *per stirpes*. If only one parent survives, the brothers and sisters[3] equally, or their issue *per stirpes*, receive ¾. Where neither parent survives, the brothers and sisters[3] equally, or their issue *per stirpes*, take all the separate property. If none, all to the surviving parent or parents. In event decedent leaves no parent, brother, sister, nephew, or niece, the separate property passes to his more remote kindred; if no kindred, to the spouse.

Community Property: ¾ to the spouse; ¼ to the parents equally, or the survivor. If neither parent survives, all to the spouse.

No Spouse or Child(ren), but with Parents:

All Property: ¼ to each parent; ½ to the brothers and sisters, or their issue *per stirpes*. If only one parent survives, the brothers and sisters or their issue *per stirpes* take ¾. If decedent leaves no brother or sister or issue, all passes to the surviving parent or parents.

No Spouse, Child(ren), or Parents:

All Property: All to brothers and sisters[4] equally or their issue *per stirpes*. If none, to more remote kindred.

---

[1] Including adopted and posthumous children.

[2] Advancements to children or grandchildren deducted from intestate share.

If decedent dies "rich" leaving the surviving spouse in "necessitous circumstances," the survivor may take a *marital portion* of the intestate's separate property. This equals ¼ outright where decedent left no children, or a usufruct in a child's share (but not less than ¼) if there are children.

[3] Brothers and sisters of the half blood take half shares. As to ancestral property, half-brothers or half-sisters, unrelated by blood to the ancestor, do not inherit.

MAINE

Spouse and Child(ren)[1]:

Real Estate and Personalty: ⅓ to the spouse;[2] ⅔ to the children[3] equally, or their issue *per stirpes*.

No Spouse, but with Child(ren):

Real Estate and Personalty: All to the children[3] equally, or their issue *per stirpes*.

Spouse and No Child(ren):

Real Estate and Personalty: First $10,000 and ⅔ of excess realty and ½ excess personalty to spouse; balance of realty and personalty to parents in equal shares. If only one parent, ½ of balance to

parent, and ½ to brothers and sisters[4] equally; or their issue *per stirpes*. If no brothers and sisters, all of balance to surviving parent. If no parent, all of balance to brothers and sisters, or their issue *per stirpes*.

No Spouse or Child(ren), but with Parents:

Real Estate and Personalty: All to the parents. If only one parent, ½ to parent and ½ to brothers and sisters[4] equally or their issue *per stirpes*. If no brothers and sisters, all to surviving parent.

No Spouse, Child(ren), or Parents:

Real Estate and Personalty: All to brothers and sisters[4] equally, or their issue *per stirpes*. If none, to next of kin[4] in equal degree.

---

[1] Including adopted children.

[2] Special rules apply where intestate and his surviving widow were not living together at his death.

[3] Advancements to child or grandchild deducted from intestate share.

[4] Kindred of the half blood inherit equally with those of the whole blood in the same degree.

MARYLAND

Spouse and Child(ren)[1]:

Real Estate and Personalty: ⅓ to the spouse; ⅔ to the children[2] equally, or their issue *per stirpes*.

No Spouse, but with Child(ren):

Real Estate and Personalty: All to the children[2] equally, or their issue *per stirpes*.

Spouse and No Child(ren):

Real Estate and Personalty: ½ to the spouse, ½ to the parents equally, or the survivor. If neither parent survives, first $4,000 and ½ the balance to the spouse; other ½ of balance to brothers and sisters[4] equally, or their issue *per stirpes*. If none, all to the spouse.

No Spouse or Child(ren), but with Parents:

Real Estate and Personalty: All to the parents equally, or the survivor.

No Spouse, Child(ren), or Parents:

Real Estate and Personalty: All to brothers and sisters[3] equally, or their issue *per stirpes*. If none, to the collateral kindred[3] in equal degree.

---

[1] Including adopted and posthumous children.

[2] Advancements to child or other descendants deducted from intestate share.

[3] Collateral kindred of the half blood share equally with those of the whole blood in the same degree.

MASSACHUSETTS

Spouse and Child(ren)[1]:

Real Estate and Personalty: ½ to the spouse;[2] ½ to the children[3] equally, or their issue *per stirpes*.

Spouse and No Child(ren):

Real Estate and Personalty: First $50,000 and ½ the balance to the spouse;[2] the other ½ of balance passes to the parents equally, or the survivor. If neither parent survives, this ½ of balance passes to brothers and sisters[4] equally, or their issue *per stirpes*. If none, to the next of kin[4] in equal degree. If none, all to the spouse.[5]

No Spouse, but with Child(ren):

Real Estate and Personalty: All to the children[3] equally, or their issue *per stirpes*.

No Spouse or Child(ren), but with Parents:

Real Estate and Personalty: All to the parents equally, or the survivor.

No Spouse, Child(ren), or Parents:

Real Estate and Personalty: All to brothers and sisters[4] equally, or their issue *per stirpes*. If none, to the next of kin in equal degree.

---

[1] Including adopted and posthumous children.

[2] The spouse, in lieu of his or her intestate share, may elect a ⅓ life estate in realty ("dower" and "curtesy").

[3] Advancements to child or other descendants deducted from intestate share.

[4] Kindred of the half blood inherit equally with those of the whole blood in the same degree.

[5] If the entire estate is less than $50,000 the spouse takes it all, even though there are kindred but no issue.

MICHIGAN

Spouse and One Child[1]:

Real Estate: ⅓ to the spouse;[2] ⅔ to the child[3] or its issue.

Personalty: ½ to the spouse;[2] ½ to the child[3] or its issue.

Spouse and Child(ren):

Real Estate and Personalty: ⅓ to the spouse;[2] to the children equally, or their issue *per stirpes*.

No Spouse, but with Child(ren):

Real Estate and Personalty: All to the children[3] equally, or their issue *per stirpes*.

Spouse and No Child(ren):

Real Estate: ½ to the spouse;[2] ½ to the parents equally, or the survivor.[4] If neither parent survives, this ½ passes to the brothers and sisters[5]

equally, or their children *per stirpes*. If none, this ½ passes to the spouse.

Personalty: ½ to widower; ½ passes as does the balance over the widow's share noted next. First $3,000 and ½ of balance to widow; other ½ of balance to parents equally, or the survivor. If neither parent survives, this ½ of balance passes to brothers and sisters[5] equally, or their issue *per stirpes*. If none, all to the widow.

No Spouse or Child(ren), but with Parents:

Real Estate and Personalty: All to the parents equally, or the survivor.[4]

No Spouse, Child(ren), or Parents:

Real Estate and Personalty: All to brothers and sisters equally, or their children *per stirpes*. If none, to the next of kin[5] in equal degree.

---

[1] Including adopted and posthumous children.

[2] In place of her intestate share in real property, a widow may elect dower—a life estate of ⅓ of the realty.

[3] Advancements to child or other descendants deducted from intestate share.

[4] However, if an unmarried intestate dies while a minor, that portion of his estate derived by inheritance from a parent, descends to his brothers and sisters equally or their issue *per stirpes*.

[5] Kindred of the half blood inherit equally with those of the whole blood in the same degree; however, as to ancestral property, half bloods, unrelated by blood to the ancestor, do not inherit.

MINNESOTA

Spouse and One Child[1]:

Real Estate and Personalty: ½ to the spouse;[2] ½ to the child[3] or its issue.

Spouse and Child(ren):

Real Estate and Personalty: ⅓ to the spouse;[2] ⅔ to the children[3] equally, or their issue *per stirpes*.

No Spouse, but with Child(ren):

Real Estate and Personalty: All to the children[3] equally, or their issue *per stirpes*.

Spouse and No Child(ren):

Real Estate and Personalty: All to the spouse.[4]

No Spouse or Child(ren), but with Parents:

Real Estate and Personalty: All to the parents equally, or the survivor.

No Spouse, Child(ren), or Parents:

Real Estate and Personalty: All to brothers and

sisters[5] equally, or their issue *per stirpes*. If none, to the next of kin[5] in equal degree.

---

[1] Including adopted and posthumous children.

[2] The spouse takes a life interest in the homestead, free of creditors, with the remainder interest to the children equally, or their issue *per stirpes*.

[3] Advancements to child or other descendant deducted from intestate share.

[4] The spouse takes a fee interest in the homestead.

[5] Kindred of the half blood inherit equally with those of the whole blood in the same degree; however, as to ancestral property, half bloods, unrelated by blood to the ancestor, do not inherit.

MISSISSIPPI

Spouse and Child(ren)[1]:

Real Estate and Personalty: Spouse and each child[2] (or its issue *per stirpes*), take equal shares; the spouse takes a child's share.

No Spouse, but with Child(ren):

Real Estate and Personalty: All to children,[2] or their issue *per stirpes*.

Spouse and No Child(ren):

Real Estate and Personalty: All to the spouse.

No Spouse or Child(ren), but with Parents:

Real Estate and Personalty: All to the parents and brothers and sisters equally, the issue of deceased brothers and sisters[3] taking *per stirpes*. If no brothers and sisters or issue, all to the parents equally or the survivor.

No Spouse, Child(ren), or Parents:

Real Estate and Personalty: All to brothers and sisters[3] equally, or their issue *per stirpes*. If none, to grandparents and uncles and aunts equally. If none, to the next of kin[3] in equal degree.

---

[1] Including adopted children.

[2] Including children of a former marriage. Advancements to child or other descendants deducted from intestate share.

[3] Kindred of the whole blood, in equal degree, are preferred to kindred of the half blood in the same degree.

MISSOURI

Spouse and Child(ren)[1]:

Real Estate and Personalty: ½ to spouse;[2] ½ to the children[3] equally, or their issue *per stirpes*.

No Spouse, but with Child(ren):

Real Estate and Personalty: All to the children[3] equally, or their issue *per stirpes*.

Spouse and No Child(ren):

Real Estate and Personalty: ½ to spouse[2]; ½ to parents, and brothers and sisters equally, the issue of deceased brothers and sisters taking *per stirpes*.

No Spouse or Child(ren), but with Parents:

Real Estate and Personalty: All to the parents and brothers and sisters[4] equally, the issue of deceased brothers and sisters taking *per stirpes*. If no brothers and sisters or their issue, all to parents, or the survivor.

No Spouse, Child(ren), or Parents:

Real Estate and Personalty: All to brothers and sisters[4] equally, or their issue *per stirpes*. If none, to grandparents,[4] uncles[4] and aunts[4] or their issue *per stirpes*.

---

[1] Including adopted children, and posthumous children and descendants.

[2] Spouse also takes a homestead allowance equal to the lesser of ½ the estate or $7,500.

[3] Advancements to child or grandchild deducted from intestate share.

[4] Regarding ascending and collateral kindred of decedent, those of the half blood inherit only half as much as those of the whole blood; however if all collaterals are half bloods, they take whole portions, and ascendants double portions.

MONTANA

Spouse and One Child[1]:

Real Estate and Personalty: If the child is not a child of the surviving spouse,[2] the surviving spouse takes ½, the child[3] takes the other half, or its issue shares *per stirpes*. If a child of the surviving spouse, the surving spouse takes all.

Spouse and Child(ren):

Real Estate and Personalty: If all of the children are children of the surviving spouse, the surviving spouse takes all. If more than one of the children is not a child of the surviving spouse, the surviving spouse takes ⅓, and the children take the balance, equally, the issue of deceased children sharing *per stirpes*.

No Spouse, but with Child(ren):

Real Estate and Personalty: All to the children[3] equally, or their issue *per stirpes*.

Spouse and No Child(ren):

Real Estate and Personalty: All to the spouse.

No Spouse or Child(ren), but with Parents:

Real Estate and Personalty: All to the parents equally, or the survivor.[4]

No Spouse, Child(ren), or Parents:

Real Estate and Personalty: All to the brothers and sisters[5] equally, or their issue *per stirpes*. If none, to the next of kin[5] in equal degree.

---

[1] Including adopted and posthumous children.

[2] Apparently, a widow receives a 1/3 life estate (dower) in lands owned by the husband during the marriage, *in addition to* her statutory share. The widow also has a life estate in the homestead.

[3] Advancements to child, or other descendants, deducted from intestate share.

[4] However, if an unmarried intestate dies while a minor, that portion of his estate derived by inheritance from a parent, descends to his brothers and sisters *per stirpes*.

[5] Kindred of the half blood inherit equally with those of the whole blood in the same degree; however, as to ancestral property, half bloods, unrelated by blood to the ancestor, do not inherit.

NEBRASKA

Spouse and Child(ren)[1]:

Real Estate and Personalty: If all of the children are children of the surviving spouse, the spouse takes the first $35,000 plus 1/2 of the balance of the estate. If some of the children are not children of the surviving spouse, the spouse takes 1/2 of the estate. In either case, the children share equally, the issue of any deceased child sharing *per stirpes*.

No Spouse, but with Child(ren):

Real Estate and Personalty: All to the children equally, or their issue *per stirpes*.

Spouse and No Child(ren):

Real Estate and Personalty: If no parent of the decedent is alive, the entire estate passes to the spouse. If either of the parents of the decedent survives, the spouse takes the first $35,000 plus 1/2 of the balance of the estate, and the parents or the survivor take the balance.

No Spouse or Child(ren), but with Parents:

Real Estate and Personalty: All to parents equally, or the survivor.

No Spouse, Child(ren), or Parents:

Real Estate and Personalty: All to brothers and sisters[3] equally, or their children *per stirpes*. If

none, 1/2 each to paternal and maternal kindred or their decendants *per stirpes*.

---

[1] Including adopted and posthumous children.

[2] Advancements to children or other descendants deducted from intestate share.

[3] Kindred of the half blood inherit equally with those of the whole blood in the same degree.

NEVADA

Spouse and One Child[1]:

Separate Realty and Personalty: 1/2 to the spouse; 1/2 to the child[2] or its issue.

Community Property: All to the spouse.

Spouse and Child(ren):

Separate Realty and Personalty: 1/3 to the spouse; 2/3 to the children[2] equally, or their issue *per stirpes*.

Community Property: All to the spouse.

No Spouse, but with Child(ren):

Real Estate and Personalty: All to the children[2] equally, or their issue *per stirpes*.

Spouse and No Child(ren):

Separate Realty and Personalty: 1/2 to the spouse, 1/2 to the parents equally, or the survivor. If neither parent survives, this 1/2 goes to brothers and sisters[3] equally, or their children *per stirpes*. If none, all to the spouse.

Community Property: All to the spouse.

No Spouse or Child(ren), but with Parents:

Real Estate and Personalty: All to the parents equally, or the survivor.

No Spouse, Child(ren), or Parents:

Real Estate and Personalty: All to brothers and sisters[3] equally, or their issue *per stirpes*. If none, to the next of kin[3] in equal degree.

---

[1] Including adopted and posthumous children.

[2] Advancements to child *or any heir* deducted from intestate share.

[3] Kindred of the half blood inherit equally with kindred of the whole blood in the same degree; however, as to ancestral property, half bloods, unrelated by blood to the ancestor, do not inherit.

NEW HAMPSHIRE

Spouse and Child(ren)[1]:

Real Estate and Personalty: If all of the children[2] are children of the surviving spouse, the spouse takes the first $50,000 plus ½ the balance of the estate. If some of the children are not children of the surviving spouse, the spouse takes ½ of the estate. In either case, the children share equally, the issue of any deceased child sharing *per stirpes*.

No spouse, but with Child(ren):

Real Estate and Personalty: All to the children[3] equally, or their issue *per stirpes*.

Spouse and No Child(ren):

Real Estate and Personalty: First $50,000 plus ½ of the balance to the spouse; the other ½ to the parents equally, or to the survivor.[3] If neither parent survives, all to the spouse.

No Spouse or Child(ren), but with Parents:

Real Estate and Personalty: All to the parents equally, or the survivor.[5]

No Spouse, Child(ren), or Parents:

Real Estate and Personalty: All to brothers and sisters equally, or their issue *per stirpes*. If none, ½ to paternal and maternal kindred or their descendants *per stirpes*.

---

[1] Including adopted and posthumous children.

[2] Advancements to child *or any heir* deducted from intestate share.

[3] However, if an unmarried intestate dies while a minor, that portion of his estate derived by inheritance from a parent descends to his brothers and sisters equally, or their issue *per stirpes*.

NEW JERSEY

Spouse and Child(ren)[1]:

Real Estate: The spouse takes a life estate in ½; the balance passes to the children equally, or issue *per stirpes*.

Personalty: ⅓ to the spouse; ⅔ to the children equally, or their issue *per stirpes*.

No Spouse, but with Child(ren):

Real Estate and Personalty: All to the children equally or their issue *per stirpes*.

Spouse and No Child(ren):

Real Estate and Personalty: All to the spouse..

No Spouse or Child(ren), but with Parents:

Real Estate and Personalty: All to the parents, brothers and sisters[2] equally. Issue of deceased brothers and sisters take *per stirpes*.

No Spouse, Child(ren), or Parents:

Real Estate and Personalty: All to brothers and

sisters,[2] or their issue *per stirpes*. If none, to the next of kin[2] in equal degree.

---

[1] Including adopted and posthumous children.

[2] Kindred of the half blood inherit equally with those of the whole blood.

NOTE: If a person who is entitled to a share of an intestate's estate received an advancement during the intestate's life, the value of the advancement at the time it was made is subtracted from the share to which the person would otherwise be entitled.

NEW MEXICO

Spouse and Child(ren)[1]:

Separate Realty and Personalty: ¼ to the spouse; ¾ to the children[2] equally, or their issue *per stirpes*.

Community Property: All to the spouse.

No Spouse, but with Child(ren):

Real Estate and Personalty: All to the children equally, or their issue *per stirpes*.

Spouse and No Child(ren):

Separate Realty and Personalty: All to the spouse.

Community Property: All to the spouse.

No Spouse or Child(ren), but with Parents:

Real Estate and Personalty: All to the parents equally, or the survivor.

No Spouse, Child(ren), or Parents:

Real Estate and Personalty: All to brothers and sisters[3] equally, or their issue *per stirpes*. If none, ½ each to maternal and paternal grandparents, or their issue.[3]

---

[1] Including adopted and posthumous children.

[2] Advancements to child *or any heir* deducted from intestate share.

[3] Kindred of the half blood inherit equally with those of the whole blood in the same degree.

NEW YORK

Spouse and One Child:

Real Estate and Personalty: First $2,000 plus ½ of the balance of the estate to the spouse;[2] other remaining balance to the child[3] or its issue.

Spouse and Child(ren)[1]:

Real Estate and Personalty: First $2,000 plus ⅓ of balance of the estate to the spouse; remaining balance to the children[3] equally, or their issue *per stirpes*.

No Spouse, but with Child(ren):

Real Estate and Personalty: All to the children equally, or their issue *per stirpes*.

Spouse and No Child(ren):

Real Estate and Personalty: The spouse takes the first $25,000 plus ½ the balance. The other ½ of the balance to the parents equally, or the survivor. If neither parent survives, all to the spouse.

No Spouse or Child(ren), but with Parents:

Real Estate and Personalty: All to the parents equally, or the survivor.

No Spouse, Child(ren), or Parents:

Real Estate and Personalty: All to brothers and sisters[4] or their issue *per stirpes*. If none, to grandparents equally, or their issue *per capita*. If none, to the next of kin[4] in equal degree.

---

[1] Including adopted children, and posthumous children or other posthumous heirs.

[2] The widow, in lieu of her intestate share may elect to receive dower—a life estate in ⅓ of the realty—provided the couple was married before September 1, 1930.

[3] Advancements to child *or other heirs* deducted from intestate share.

[4] Kindred of the half blood inherit equally with those of the whole blood in the same degree.

NORTH CAROLINA

Spouse and One Child:

Real Estate and Personalty: ½ to the spouse; ½ to the child[2] or its issue.

Spouse and Child(ren):

Real Estate and Personalty: ⅓ to the spouse; ⅔ to the children[2] equally, or their issue.

No Spouse, but with Child(ren):

Real Estate and Personalty: All to the children equally,[2] or their issue.

Spouse and No Child(ren):

Real Estate: ½ to the spouse; ½ to the parents equally, or the survivor. If neither parent survives, all to the spouse.

Personalty: First $10,000 and ½ of the balance to the spouse; the other ½ of the balance to parents in the same manner as real estate.

No Spouse or Child(ren), but with Parents:

Real Estate and Personalty: All to the parents equally, or the survivor.

No Spouse, Child(ren), or Parents:

Real Estate and Personalty: All to brothers and sisters[3] equally, or their issue *per stirpes*. If none, ½ each to maternal and paternal grandparents, or their issue.[3]

---

[1] Including adopted children, and posthumous children and other descendants.

[2] Advancements to child *or any heir* deducted from intestate share.

If one child has died leaving children of his own, they take their parent's share. But where two or more children have so died their children divide *per capita* the parents' combined shares.

[3] Collateral relations of the half blood inherit equally with those of the whole blood.

NORTH DAKOTA

Spouse and Child(ren)[1]:

Real Estate and Personalty: If all the children are children of the surviving spouse, the spouse takes the first $50,000 plus ½ of the balance of the estate. If some of the children are not children of the surviving spouse, the spouse takes ½ of the estate. In either case, the children share equally, the issue of any deceased child sharing *per stirpes*.

No Spouse, but with Child(ren):

Real Estate and Personalty: All to the children[2] equally, or their issue *per stirpes*.

Spouse and No Child(ren):

Real Estate and Personalty: If there is no surviving parent, the spouse takes all. If there is a surviving parent or parents, the spouse takes the first $50,000 plus ½ of the balance of the estate; and the parents or the survivor take the balance.

No Spouse or Child(ren), but with Parents:

Real Estate and Personalty: All to the parents equally, or the survivor.

No Spouse, Child(ren), or Parents:

Real Estate and Personalty: All to the brothers and sisters[3] equally, or their issue *per stirpes*. If none, ½ each to maternal and paternal grandparents or their issue *per stirpes*.

---

[1] Including adopted and posthumous children.

[2] Advancements to child or other descendants deducted from intestate share.

[3] Kindred of the half blood inherit equally with those of the whole blood in the same degree.

OHIO

Spouse and One Child: The spouse receives the first $30,000 if he or she is the natural or adoptive parent of the child, the first $10,000 otherwise, plus in either case ½ of the balance of the intestate estate. The balance passes to the child or the child's lineal descendants *per stirpes*.

Spouse and Child(ren)[1]**:** The spouse receives the first $30,000 if he or she is the natural or adoptive parent of the child, the first $10,000 otherwise, plus in either case ⅓ of the balance of the intestate estate. The balance passes to the children[2] equally, or to the lineal descendants of any deceased child *per stirpes*.

No Spouse, but with Child(ren):

Real Estate and Personalty: All to the children equally, or their issue *per stirpes*.

Spouse and No Child(ren): If no issue of children, all to the spouse.

No Spouse or Child(ren), but with Parents:

Real Estate and Personalty: All to the parents equally, or the survivor.

No Spouse, Child(ren), or Parents:

Real Estate and Personalty: All to brothers and sisters equally, or their issue *per stirpes*. If none, ½ to maternal grandparents equally or the survivor. If none, this ½ to their issue *per stirpes*. Other ½ to paternal grandparents equally, or the survivor. If none, to their issue *per stirpes*. If no surviving grandparents, or descendants, then to next of kin in equal degree.

---

[1] Including adopted and posthumous children.

[2] Advancements to children *or other heirs* deducted from intestate share.

OKLAHOMA

Spouse and One Child[1]**:**

Real Estate and Personalty: ½ to the spouse;[2] ½ to the child[3] or its issue.

Spouse and Children:

Real Estate and Personalty: ⅓ to the spouse;[2] ⅔ to the children[3] equally, or their issue *per stirpes*.

No Spouse, but with Child(ren):

Real Estate and Personalty: All to the children[3] equally, or their issue *per stirpes*.

Spouse and No Child(ren):

Real Estate and Personalty: ½ to the spouse;[4] ½ to the parents equally, or the survivor. If none, this ½ passes to brothers and sisters[5] equally, or their children *per stirpes*. If none, all to the spouse.

No Spouse or Child(ren), but with Parents:

Real Estate and Personalty: All to the parents equally, or the survivor.[6]

No Spouse, Child(ren), or Parents:

Real Estate and Personalty: All to brothers and sisters[5] equally, or the survivor *per stirpes*. If none, to the next of kin[5] in equal degree.

---

[1] Including adopted and posthumous children.

[2] However, if the decedent was married more than once, regarding property not acquired during the marriage with decedent, the surviving spouse takes only a child's share.

[3] Advancements to child or other descendants deducted from intestate share.

[4] Regarding real and personal property acquired by the joint industry of the decedent and his spouse during marriage, *all* such property goes to the survivor.

[5] Kindred of the half blood inherit equally with those of the whole blood in the same degree; however, as to ancestral property, half bloods, unrelated by blood to the ancestor, do not inherit.

[6] If the decedent is a minor, and his parents are not living together, the estate passes to the parent having had the care of the minor. If the decedent minor dies unmarried, that portion of his estate derived by inheritance from a parent, descends to his brothers and sisters equally, or their issue *per stirpes*.

OREGON

Spouse and Child(ren)[1]**:** The spouse takes a ½ interest in the net intestate estate, and the balance of the net intestate estate passes to the children equally, or to their issue *per stirpes*.

No Spouse, but with Child(ren):

Real Estate and Personalty: All to the children[2] equally, or their issue *per stirpes*.

Spouse and No Child(ren):

Real Estate and Personalty: All to the spouse.

No Spouse or Child(ren), but with Parents:

Real Estate and Personalty: All to the parents equally, or the survivor.[3]

No Spouse, Child(ren), or Parents:

Real Estate and Personalty: All to brothers and

sisters[4] equally, or their issue *per stirpes*. If none, to the next of kin in equal degree.

---

[1] Including adopted and posthumous children.

[2] Advancements to child or other descendants deducted from intestate share.

[3] If the decedent dies a minor without spouse or children, any real estate which descended to the intestate child from an ancestor passes to the heirs of his ancestor as if the child pre-deceased the ancestor.

[4] Kindred of the half blood inherit equally with those of the whole blood in the same degree.

PENNSYLVANIA

Spouse and One Child[1]:
Real Estate and Personalty: ½ to the spouse; ½ to the child[2] or its issue.

Spouse and Children:
Real Estate and Personalty: ⅓ to the spouse; ⅔ to the children[2] equally, or their issue *per stirpes*.

No Spouse, but with Child(ren):
Real Estate and Personalty: All to the children[2] equally, or their issue *per stirpes*.

Spouse and No Child(ren):
Real Estate and Personalty: First $20,000 and ½ of the balance to the spouse; other ½ of balance to the parents equally, or the survivor. If none, this ½ of balance passes to brothers and sisters equally[3], or their issue *per stirpes*. If none, ½ each to maternal and paternal grandparents equally, or the survivor. If none, this ½ of balance to uncles and aunts[3] or their issue. If none, all to the spouse.

No Spouse or Child(ren), but with Parents:
Real Estate and Personalty: All to the parents equally, or the survivor.

No Spouse, Child(ren), or Parents:
Real Estate and Personalty: All to brothers and sisters[3] equally, or their issue *per stirpes*. If none, ½ each to maternal and paternal grandparents equally, or the survivor. If none, to uncles or aunts[3] and their issue.

---

[1] Including adopted children, posthumous children and other posthumous heirs.

[2] Advancements to any person are deducted from the person's share.

[3] Kindred of the half blood share equally with those of the whole blood in the same degree.

RHODE ISLAND

Spouse and Child(ren)[1]:
Real Estate: Life estate to widower; ⅓ life estate to widow; balance to children[2] equally, or their issue *per stirpes*.
Personalty: ½ to spouse; ½ to children[2] equally, or their issue *per stirpes*.

No Spouse, but with Child(ren):
Real Estate and Personalty: All to the children[2] equally, or their issue *per stirpes*.

Spouse and No Child(ren):
Real Estate: Life estate to spouse. The court, in its discretion, may award $25,000 in fee to the spouse; balance to the parents equally, or the survivor. If none, the balance passes to brothers and sisters equally, or the survivor. If none, ½ each to maternal and paternal grandparents equally, or their issue *per stirpes*. If none, to more remote kindred. If none, all to the spouse.
Personalty: First $50,000 and ½ of the balance to the spouse; other ½ of balance to the parents equally, or the survivor. If none, his ½ of balance to brothers and sisters equally, or their issue *per stirpes*. If none, ½ each to maternal and paternal grandparents equally. If none, to more remote kindred. If none, all to the spouse.

No Spouse or Child(ren), but with Parents:
Real Estate and Personalty: All to the parents equally, or the survivor.

No Spouse, Child(ren), or Parents:
Real Estate and Personalty: All to brothers and sisters equally, or their issue *per stirpes*. If none, ½ each to maternal and paternal grandparents equally. If none, to more remote kindred.

---

[1] Including adopted and posthumous children.

[2] Advancements to child or grandchild deducted from intestate share.

SOUTH CAROLINA

Spouse and One Child[1]:
Real Estate and Personalty: ½ to the spouse;[2] ½ to the child[3] or its issue.

Spouse and Children:
Real Estate and Personalty: ⅓ to the spouse; ⅔ to the children[3] equally, or their issue *per stirpes*.

No Spouse, but with Child(ren):
Real Estate and Personalty: All to the children[3] equally, or their issue *per stirpes*.

Spouse and No Child(ren):

Real Estate and Personalty: ½ to the spouse; ½ to parents and brothers and sisters in equal shares, the issue of deceased brothers and sisters taking *per stirpes*. If no parents, ½ to brothers and sisters,[4] *per stirpes*. If no brothers and sisters, to the parents equally, or the survivor. If neither parents nor brothers or sisters survive, ½ to grandparents equally, or the survivor. If none, all to the spouse.

No Spouse or Child(ren), but with Parents:

Real Estate and Personalty: If no brothers and sisters, all to the parents equally or to the survivor.

No Spouse, Child(ren), or Parents:

Real Estate and Personalty: All to brothers and sisters[4] *per stirpes*. If none, to grandparents equally, or the survivor. If none, to uncles and aunts equally, or their issue. If none, to the next of kin in equal degree.

_____

[1] Including adopted children. Stepchildren take only in the absence of next of kin.

[2] A widow, in lieu of her intestate share, may elect dower—a ⅓ life estate in realty, or ⅙ absolute.

[3] Advancements to child or its issue deducted from intestate share.

[4] Brothers and sisters of the half blood take only in the absence of surviving parents and brothers and sisters of the half blood. In such event, the ½ passes to the half bloods and issue of brothers and sisters of the whole blood equally. In the absence of the latter, the half bloods take this ½.

SOUTH DAKOTA

Spouse and One Child[1]:

Real Estate and Personalty: ½ to the spouse; ½ to the child[2] or its issue.

Spouse and Children:

Real Estate and Personalty: ⅓ to the spouse; ⅔ to the children[2] equally, or their issue *per stirpes*.

No Spouse, but with Child(ren):

Real Estate and Personalty: All to the children[2] equally, or their issue *per stirpes*.

Spouse and No Child(ren):

Real Estate and Personalty: First $100,000 and ½ of the balance to the spouse; other ½ of balance to the parents equally, or the survivor. If none, this ½ of balance to brothers and sisters[3] equally, or their issue *per stirpes*. If none, all to the spouse.

No Spouse or Child(ren), but with Parents:

Real Estate and Personalty: All to the parents equally, or the survivor.

No Spouse, Child(ren), or Parents:

Real Estate and Personalty: All to brothers and sisters equally, or their issue *per stirpes*. If none, to the next of kin[3] in equal degree.

_____

[1] Including adopted and posthumous children.

[2] Advancements to child or other descendant deducted from intestate share.

[3] Kindred of the half blood share equally with those of the whole blood in the same degree; however, as to ancestral property, half bloods, unrelated by blood to the ancestor do not inherit.

TENNESSEE

Spouse and Child(ren)[1]:

Real Estate and Personalty: ⅓ or a child's share, whichever is greater, to the spouse; balance to the children, or their issue *per stirpes*.

No Spouse, but with Child(ren):

Real Estate and Personalty: All to the children[2] equally, or their issue *per stirpes*.

Spouse and No Child(ren):

Real Estate and Personalty: All to the spouse.

No Spouse or Child(ren), but with Parents:

Real Estate and Personalty: All to the parents equally, or to the survivor.

No Spouse, Child(ren), or Parents:

Real Estate and Personalty: All to brothers and sisters equally, or their issue *per stirpes*. If none, ½ to maternal and paternal grandparents equally, or the survivor; if none surviving, to their issue *per stirpes*.

_____

[1] Including adopted and posthumous children.

[2] Advancements to child deducted from intestate share.

[3] Kindred of the half blood inherit equally with those of the whole blood.

TEXAS

Spouse and Child(ren)[1]:

Separate Realty: Life estate in ⅓ to the spouse; balance to the children[2] equally, or their issue *per stirpes*.

Separate Personalty: ⅓ to spouse; ⅔ to the children[2] equally, or their issue *per stirpes*.

Community Property: ½ to spouse; ½ to the children[2] equally, or their issue *per stirpes*.

No Spouse, but with Child(ren):

Real Estate and Personalty: All to the children[2] equally, or their issue *per stirpes*.

Spouse and No Child(ren):

Separate Realty: ½ to the spouse; ½ to the parents equally. If only one surviving parent and brothers and sisters[3], the parent takes ¼ with the other ¼ divided equally among the brothers and sisters, or their issue *per stirpes*. If no brothers and sisters or issue, the surviving parent takes the entire ½. If no parents, the brothers and sisters, or their issue *per stirpes*, take this half. If no parents, brothers, sisters, or their issue survive, this ½ is divided equally among maternal and paternal kindred[3] (grandparents and their descendants). If none, all to the spouse.

Separate Personalty: All to the spouse.

Community Property: All to the spouse.

No Spouse or Child(ren), but with Parents:

Real Estate and Personalty: All to the parents equally. If only one surviving parent, the survivor takes ½; the other ½ passes to brothers and sisters[3] equally, or their issue *per stirpes*. If no brothers or sisters or their issue, all to the surviving parent.

No Spouse, Child(ren), or Parents:

Real Estate and Personalty: All to brothers or sisters[3] equally, or their issue *per stirpes*. If none, ½ each to maternal and paternal kindred[3] (grandparents and their decendents).

---

[1] Including adopted children, and posthumous children and other descendants.

[2] Advancements to child *or any heir* deducted from intestate share.

[3] Where collateral kindred of the whole and half blood survive, those of the half blood take half shares. If only half bloods survive, they take whole portions.

UTAH

Spouse and Child(ren)[1]:

Real Estate and Personalty: If all the children[2] are children of the surviving spouse, the spouse takes the first $50,000 plus ½ of the balance of the estate. If some of the children are not children of the surviving spouse, the spouse takes ½ of the estate. In either case, the children share equally, the issue of any deceased child sharing *per stirpes*.

No Spouse, but with Child(ren):

Real Estate and Personalty: All to the children[2] equally, or their issue *per stirpes*.

Spouse and No Child(ren):

Real Estate and Personalty: First $100,000 and ½ the balance to the spouse; other ½ of balance to the parents equally, or the survivor. If neither parent survives, all to the spouse.

No Spouse or Child(ren), but with Parents:

Real Estate and Personalty: All to the parents equally, or the survivor.

No Spouse, Child(ren), or Parents:

Real Estate and Personalty: All to brothers and sisters[3] equally, or their issue *per stirpes*. If none, ½ each to maternal and paternal grandparents or their descendants *per stirpes*. If none, to the next of kin[3] in equal degree.

---

[1] Including adopted and posthumous children.

[2] Advancements to child or other descendant deducted from intestate share.

[3] Kindred of the half blood inherit equally with those of the whole blood in the same degree.

VERMONT

Spouse and One Child[1]:

Real Estate: ½ to the spouse; ½ to the child[2] or its issue.

Personalty: ⅓ to the spouse; ⅔ to the children[2] equally, or their issue *per stirpes*.

Spouse and Children:

Real Estate and Personalty: ⅓ to the spouse; ⅔ to the children[2] equally, or their issue *per stirpes*.

No Spouse, but with Child(ren):

Real Estate and Personalty: All to the children equally, or their issue *per stirpes*.

Spouse and No Child(ren):

Real Estate and Personalty: First $25,000 and ½ of the balance to the spouse;[3] other ½ of the balance to the parents equally, or the survivor. If neither parent survives, this ½ balance goes to brothers and sisters[4] equally, or their issue *per stirpes*. If none, this ½ of balance goes to the next of kin[4] in equal degree. If none, all to the spouse.

No Spouse or Child(ren), but with Parents:

Real Estate and Personalty: All to the parents equally, or the survivor.

No Spouse, Child(ren), or Parents:

Real Estate and Personality: All to brothers and sisters[3] equally, or their issue *per stirpes*. If none, to the next of kin[3] in equal degree.

---

[1] Including adopted children.

[2] Advancements to child or other descendants deducted from intestate share.

[3] In the alternative, spouse may elect to take a ⅓ dower interest in decedent's real property.

[4] Kindred of the half blood inherit equally with those of the whole blood in the same degree.

VIRGINIA

Spouse and Child(ren)[1]:

Real Estate: Life estate in ⅓ to the spouse; balance to the children[2] equally, or their issue *per stirpes*.

Personality: ⅓ to the spouse; ⅔ to the children[2] equally, or their issue *per stirpes*.

No Spouse, but with Child(ren):

Real Estate and Personality: All to the children[2] equally, or their issue *per stirpes*.

Spouse and No Child(ren):

Real Estate and Personality: All to the spouse.[3]

No Spouse or Child(ren), but with Parents:

Real Estate and Personality: All to the parents equally, or the survivor.[3]

No Spouse, Child(ren), or Parents:

Real Estate and Personality: All to brothers and sisters[4] equally, or their issue *per stirpes*. If none, ½ each to paternal and maternal kindred. First to grandmothers and grandfathers equally, or the survivor. If none, to uncles and aunts[4] and their descendants. If no paternal (maternal) kindred, then all to maternal (paternal) kindred.[4]

---

[1] Including adopted children, posthumous children or other heirs, and children born as a result of artificial insemination.

[2] Advancements to child or other descendants deducted from intestate share.

[3] If an unmarried intestate dies without issue, owning real property derived by inheritance or gift from a parent, such property passes to kindred of that parent. If no such kindred, to kindred of other parent.

[4] Collateral kindred of the half blood inherit only half shares if kindred of the whole blood survive; if only collaterals of the half blood survive, lineal ancestors, if any, take double portions.

WASHINGTON

Spouse and Child(ren)[1]:

Community Property: All to the spouse.

Separate Property: ½ to the children equally, or to their issue *per stirpes*.

No Spouse, but with Child(ren):

Real Estate and Personality: All to the children[2] equally, or their issue *per stirpes*.

Spouse and No Child(ren):

Separate Property: ¾ to spouse; ¼ to parent or parents, or their issue.[3]

Community Property: All to the spouse.

No Spouse or Child(ren), but with Parents:

Real Estate and Personality: All to the parents equally, or the survivor.[4]

No Spouse, Child(ren), or Parents:

Real Estate and Personality: All to brothers and sisters[3] equally, or their children *per stirpes*. If none, then to grandparents[5] or their issue.

---

[1] Including adopted and posthumous children.

[2] Advancements to child or other descendants deducted from intestate share.

[3] Kindred of the half blood inherit equally with those of the whole blood in the same degree.

[4] However, if an unmarried intestate dies while a minor, that portion of his estate derived by inheritance from a parent descends to his brothers and sisters equally, or their issue *per stirpes*.

[5] If both maternal and paternal grandparents or a survivor are alive, ½ each to the maternal and paternal kindred.

WEST VIRGINIA

Spouse and Child(ren)[1]:

Real Estate: Life estate in ⅓ to spouse; balance to the children[2] equally, or their issue *per stirpes*.

Personality: ⅓ to the spouse; ⅔ to the children equally, or their issue *per stirpes*.

No Spouse, but with Child(ren):

Real Estate and Personality: All to the children equally, or their issue *per stirpes*.

Spouse and No Child(ren):

Real Estate and Personality: All to the spouse.

No Spouse or Child(ren), but with Parents:

Real Estate and Personality: All to the parents equally, or the survivor.

No Spouse, Child(ren), or Parents:

Real Estate and Personality: All to brothers and

sisters equally, or their issue *per stirpes*. If none, ½ each to paternal and maternal kindred. First to grandmothers and grandfathers equally, or the survivor. If none, to uncles and aunts and their descendants *per stirpes*. If no paternal (maternal) kindred, then to maternal (paternal) kindred.

---

[1] Including adopted and posthumous children.
[2] Advancements to child *or any heir* deducted from intestate share.
[2] Collateral kindred of the half blood take only half as much as those of the whole blood. If only half bloods survive, lineal ancestors, if any, take double portions.

WISCONSIN

Spouse and One Child [1]:
Real and personal property: If the child is the surviving spouse's child as well, the spouse takes the first $25,000 plus ½ of the balance of the estate. If the child is not the surviving spouse's child, the spouse takes ½ of the estate. In either case, the child takes the balance, or his issue shares *per stirpes*.

Spouse and Children:
Real and personal property: If all of the children are children of the surviving spouse, the spouse takes the first $25,000 plus ⅓ of the balance of the estate. If some of the children are not children of the surviving spouse, the spouse takes ⅓ of the estate. In either case, the children share equally, the issue of any deceased child sharing *per stirpes*.

No Spouse, but with Child(ren):
Real Estate and Personalty: All to the children [2] equally, on their issue *per stirpes*.

Spouse and No Child(ren):
Real Estate and Personalty: All to the spouse.

No Spouse or Child(ren), but with Parents:
Real Estate and Personalty: All to the parents equally, or the survivor. [3]

No Spouse, Child(ren), or Parents:
Real Estate and Personalty: All to brothers and sisters [4] equally, or their issue *per stirpes*. If none,

all to the grandparents, or the survivor. If none, all to the next of kin in equal degree.

---

[1] Including adopted and posthumous children.
[2] Advancements to child or other heirs deducted from intestate share.
[3] However, if an unmarried intestate dies while a minor, that portion of his estate derived by inheritance from a parent descends to his brothers and sisters equally, or their issue *per stirpes*.
[4] Kindred of the half blood inherit equally with those of the whole blood in the same degree.

WYOMING

Spouse and Child(ren) [1]:
Real Estate and Personalty: ½ to the spouse; [2] ½ to the children [3] equally, or their issue *per stirpes*.

No Spouse but with Child(ren):
Real Estate and Personalty: All to the children [3] equally, or their issue *per stirpes*.

Spouse and No Child(ren):
Real Estate and Personalty: First $20,000 and ¾ of the balance to the spouse; [2] the other ¼ of the balance to the parents equally, or the survivor. If neither parent survives, this ¼ of balance to brothers and sisters [4] equally, or their issue *per stirpes*. If none, all to the spouse.

No Spouse or Child(ren), but with Parents:
Real Estate and Personalty: All to the parents, brothers, and sisters [4] equally, the issue of any deceased brother or sister sharing *per stirpes*.

No Spouse, Child(ren), or Parents:
Real Estate and Personalty: All to brothers and sisters [4] equally, or their issue *per stirpes*. If none, to the grandfather, grandmother, uncles and aunts [4] or their issue *per stirpes*.

---

[1] Including adopted and posthumous children.
[2] The homestead passes separately to the spouse.
[3] Advancements to child deducted from intestate share.
[4] Collateral kindred of the half blood take only a half share if collaterals of the whole blood survive.

CHAPTER 7

Business Continuation Agreements

Introduction

One of the main purposes of a Buy and Sell Agreement is to assure uninterrupted and harmonious—and thus profitable—continuation of the business upon the death of one of its part-owners. Another is to provide a ready market for the deceased's interest in the business, thus removing the uncertainty of his estate obtaining a fair price therefor. A third is to avoid lengthy, expensive litigation with respect to valuation, particularly for tax purposes.

The advantages of such an arrangement should receive thorough consideration whenever plans are made for the efficient disposition of a business interest upon the death of its owner. The importance of perfecting such plans during his lifetime needs no emphasis.

Agreements of this sort are particularly suited to small business-partnerships and close corporations. Such agreements have been recommended by the Small Business Administration of the United States Department of Commerce.

As a rule, neither the firm nor its individual owners are in a position to purchase a deceased part-owner's interest out of liquid funds available upon his death. Hence, the need for life insurance. It provides the necessary cash at the very time when it is needed—at death—regardless of when such need may arise.

The Agreement

Buy and Sell Agreements are based on the mutual promises of the parties. Their validity and enforceability generally have been sustained by the courts as executory contracts supported by adequate consideration. They are not in the nature of a testamentary disposition by the seller, even though actual transfer of his interest in the business will take effect only upon his death. In the absence of fraud, or unless the agreement be deemed a sham, the fact that the value at death of his business interest may be more or less than the agreed price will not cause the agreement to become unenforceable.

If the Buy and Sell Agreement covers stock to be purchased by the issuing corporation upon the death of a stockholder, particular consideration should be given to applicable state law. Today no state prohibits such a purchase altogether. In most jurisdictions, the matter is now covered by statute (Appendix A to this chapter). As a rule, subject to contrary provisions in its own charter or bylaws, a corporation may purchase its own stock out of surplus, or under such circumstances as will not impair the rights of its creditors or non-consenting stockholders. The life insurance proceeds payable at death would normally create the necessary surplus, assuming the corporation is solvent, from which the redemption may be made.

What's in the Agreement?

Explore with your attorney the following general outline.

1. The names of all the parties to the agreement.
2. A clear statement of purpose.
3. A provision binding the estate of the deceased to sell his interest.
4. The purchase price of the interest, or a formula for reaching it.
5. A provision as to the manner in which the purchase price shall be paid to the estate, and the manner of transfer of the deceased's interest.
6. Provision for revocation, alteration or termination of the agreement—other than by fulfillment of the purpose for which the agreement was set—e.g., bankruptcy, termination of the business during lifetime, common disaster.
7. Provisions for buy-out in the event of long-term disability.
8. A list of the insurance policies purchased.
9. An election permitting the corporation the option to redeem stock if the tax basis results are superior. The surviving stockholder would be able to contribute the proceeds received on the deceased to the company if necessary. (For closely held corporation.)

The Value of a Buy and Sell Agreement

Close Corporation Stock

It is incumbent upon the principal shareholders of a close corporation to consider a plan which will provide the most advantageous method (from a business, legal and economic standpoint) of liquidating their respective interests in the company at their deaths (and, perhaps, at retirement).

The following business factors illustrate the value of a buy-sell agreement:

1. The inadvisability of a decedent's heirs retaining an interest in a close corporation which, in the usual case, will not produce sufficient dividend income for them, due to its "double taxation."
2. If the family should subsequently find it necessary to liquidate their interest, they would, in all probability, have no market for the stock other than the surviving shareholders, who could then purchase the decedent's interest at what could amount to a distress-sale price.
3. The surviving shareholders, on the other hand, in the absence of a planned disposition of the stock at the death of one, might be faced with potentially dissident outside shareholders—i.e., the heirs of a deceased shareholder or even the heirs' vendees.

Cross Purchase (Assuming life insurance is used as funding vehicle)

1. Purchaser	Surviving stockholder.
2. Seller	Estate of deceased stockholder.
3. The Plan	Stockholders agree among themselves that survivors will purchase stock of deceased at an agreed-upon price.
4. Claims of Creditors	Corporate creditors cannot reach proceeds of non-corporate assets.
5. Tax Basis of Seller	Stock receives no stepped-up basis at death.
6. Estate Tax Effects to Stockholder	If estate is bound to sell to stockholders, agreed price will control for Federal Estate purposes.

7. Basis of Decendent's Stock to Remaining Stockholder — Purchasing stockholders receive stepped-up basis for shares purchased from decedent's estate. Subsequent lifetime sale does not result in as much taxable gain to them.

8. Proceeds—Taxability — Full life insurance proceeds received by surviving stockholders tax-free.

9. Effect on Value of Corporate Stock — Equity to all parties is achieved, net worth of corporation unaffected by receipt of insurance proceeds by stockholders.

10. Family Corporation—Effect — No problems of constructive ownership and attribution under Sec. 318 when stock is purchased by other than the corporation.

11. Change in Plan to Stock Redemption — No transfer for value problem, therefore, if in doubt, start with cross-purchase.

Stock Redemption (Assuming life insurance is used as funding vehicle)

1. Purchaser — The corporation.

2. Seller — Estate of deceased stockholder.

3. The Plan — Corporation contracts with stockholders that upon death of any of them the stock will be purchased by the corporation at an agreed upon price.

4. Claims of Creditors — Corporate creditors can can usually claim against proceeds and cash values of corporate-owned life insurance.

5. Tax Basis of Seller
6. Estate Tax Effects to Stockholder
7. Basis of Decendent's Stock to Remaining Stockholder — Stock receives no stepped-up basis at death. If estate is bound to sell, agreed price will control for Federal Estate Tax. Surviving stockholders do not receive stepped-up basis since corporation is purchaser. Value of their stock is enhanced but not their basis. Their lifetime sale of their stock after a redemption results in more taxable gain to them.

8. Proceeds—Taxability — Full life insurance proceeds received by corporation tax-free.

9. Effect on Value of Corporate Stock — Difference between cash value and proceeds is gain to corporation on balance sheet, therefore increases value of stock.

10. Family Corporation—Effect — When stock owned by related persons and where beneficiary of an estate owns stock, redemption may result in unfavorable tax results to the estate through Sec. 318 rules of attribution and constructive ownership.

11. Change in Plan to Cross-Purchase — Transfer for value problem, i.e., proceeds in excess of premiums are taxable income.

In many buy-sell situations a cross-purchase agreement is indicated in preference to a redemption agreement because:

1. The purchase is to take place among family members whose relationship would cause a distribution in redemption of stock to be treated as a dividend, under I.R.C. Sec. 318 attribution rules, or

2. The corporation has an accumulated earnings problem, and it is feared either the additional accumulation to pay premiums or the payment in redemption of stock, or both, would result in imposition of the penalty tax on unreasonably accumulated earnings, under I.R.C. Sec. 531, or

3. The shareholders wish to have a different distribution of ownership after the purchase of a deceased shareholder's stock than would result from a stock redemption, or

4. A shareholder feels that, should he survive his co-owner, he might wish to sell his stock during his lifetime with the least possible capital gains tax.

5. Due to the "carryover basis provisions" under the *Tax Reform Act of 1976* this approach may reduce potential capital gains upon a sale of the stock after the death of a shareholder. The survivors will receive an addition to cost basis equal to the amount of the purchase price, under I.R.C. Sec. 1023 (a) (1).

Partnership

In the absence of a properly drafted partnership agreement, it is axiomatic that, upon the death of a partner, legally the partnership is dissolved. This means that the business must either be:

1. Liquidated, or
2. Reorganized.

In the alternative, the surviving partner becomes a liquidating trustee. As such, it is his duty to:

a. Collect all outstanding debts of the partnership;
b. Pay off all outstanding accounts which the business owes;

c. Account to the estate of the deceased partner.

During this period of liquidation, the surviving partner may not draw his usual share of profits, nor continue any salary to his partner's estate, nor carry on the business as a going concern except at his sole risk.

In the second alternative, that of reorganization, one of four situations must occur with respect to the future of the business:

a. The surviving partner may sell out his interest in the business to the heirs of the deceased partner;
b. The surviving partner may form a new partnership with the deceased partner's heirs;
c. If the deceased partner's heirs sell their interest to an outsider, the surviving partner may form a new partnership with that outsider;
d. Or, finally, he may purchase the interest of the deceased partner from the heirs.

As a practical matter the first three means listed above do not provide a satisfactory plan of reorganization. There are many questions which illustrate the impracticability of selling the surviving partner's interest to the decedent's heirs or of forming a new partnership with the decedent's family or an outsider.

Would the heirs of the decedent be willing to purchase the survivor's interest? At what price?

Would the surviving partner be willing to have his ex-partner's widow in the business?

Should a complete stranger be brought into the business?

From the Surviving Partner's Point of View

1. The buy and sell agreement, financed by life insurance, provides the legal framework

for the smooth, uninterrupted transition of the business.

2. It facilitates the execution of the plans with the availability of funds, as guaranteed by the life insurance policy.

The best, and most businesslike, solution is for the surviving partner to purchase the interest of the deceased from his heirs. In order to effectuate the solution to the problem, it is suggested that a legally binding agreement be entered into between the partners.

The agreement, in writing, should provide that:

1. The surviving partner take over the business, paying the deceased partner's heirs a price which, by its terms, has been established as fair.
2. The heirs be obliged to sell for this price.
3. The partners (or the partnership) maintain life insurance sufficient to provide the cash to buy the business interest from the estate.

The purchase of the deceased partner's interest by the surviving partner with insurance proceeds works in favor of everyone.

From the Family of the Deceased Partner's Point of View

1. It eliminates bargaining with the survivors of the business, or the alternative liquidation proceedings.
2. It assures the payment in cash for the value of the partner's interest in the business. As such, it becomes an indispensable part of his estate planning.
3. It establishes the value of the deceased partner's interest for federal estate tax purposes.

Funding

This contract will only be as good as the funds available for the purchase price at the date performance is demanded, i.e., at the death or retirement of one of the principals. It is generally conceded that the only method of assuring that the funds will be available when performance is called for is to insure the lives of the participating principals so that, at death, an instantaneous cash fund is generated. Of course, the shareholders could enter into, and possibly consummate, such an arrangement without the use of life insurance; but, if this were the case, there would always be doubt about their ability to raise the purchase price. This problem would be acute if the death of a principal ensued within a short time after the execution of an unfunded buy-sell agreement.

Therefore, cash value insurance is recommended as the funding vehicle; moreover, it is considered advisable to arrange for the insurance before the buy-sell agreement is actually executed, in order to permit the insertion of the appropriate provisions should it develop that one or more participants are uninsurable. To make certain that the survivors will have the funds on hand at the death of a stockholder, they agree to purchase and maintain a specified amount of insurance on each other.

Valuation of the Business Interest

A buy-sell agreement will fix the value of the business interest for federal estate tax purposes, binding the Internal Revenue Service, if the following conditions are met: (1) the decedent's estate must be obligated to sell the business interest; (2) the transaction is at arm's length; i.e., fair when set; and (3) the owner is precluded from disposing of his interest during his lifetime.

Some of the available formulas for determining the value are:

1. Book Value—Net Assets Minus Net Liabilities: In order to achieve an equitable result, goodwill must be included; the assets and liabilities must also be adequately valued by accounting for actual appreciation or depreciation.

2. Agreed Dollar Value: The parties themselves agree on value based on the many factors involved. Under this approach, it is imperative for periodic re-evaluation of the business.

3. Capitalization of Average Yearly Net Earnings: An average yearly net earnings figure for a specified number of prior years is capitalized by a percentage rate of return demanded by a potential investor in this type of business:

For example:

Average net earnings
for last three years   .... $ 59,900
Rate of return
demanded 8%
Value = $59,900 ÷ .08 .... $748,750

4. Value Based on Estimated Future Earnings: This method assumes that future earnings will approximate past earnings over a predetermined number of years; therefore, the average net earnings for this previous period of years is multiplied by the number of years chosen.

For example:

Average net earnings for
last three years   .... $ 59,900
Number of years factor 10
Value = $59,900 × 10   .... $599,000

5. Income Tax Method: This method is frequently used by the Internal Revenue Service.* (Rev. Rul. 68–609)

For example:

Allow fair return (8%) of tangible net worth for last 5 years (capital + surplus).

Ascertain net earnings in excess of 8% of the average tangible net worth, and capitalize on a 5 years purchase basis to arrive at value of goodwill. Add this figure to tangible net worth to get overall value including goodwill.

Average value of tangible net worth for last five years $304,700

Average net earnings for last five years $59,900

8% of average tangible net worth 24,400

Excess $35,500

Value of good will (5 × 35,500) ... $177,500

Total value including good will $482,200

*Based on three years.
Average of Formulas
   3. $748,750
   4. 599,000
   5. 482,200
   6. 643,300
   $2,473,250 ÷ 4 = $618,212

6. The Year's Purchase Method: This formula is similar to the Income Tax Method but uses net worth of the present taxable year instead of the averaging device.

For example:

Present Net Worth (Book Value) ...	$416,300
Average Earnings	$ 78,800
8% of Present Net Worth	33,300
Excess	$ 45,400
Value of good will (5 × 45,400)	$227,000
Total Value.....................	$643,300

How Much Does It Really Cost to Buy Your Business on an Installment Basis?

Assume the surviving partner is in a 50% tax bracket. His partner has died. He has agreed to purchase his partner's interest (worth $500,000) over a ten-year period (interest at 6%).

Year	Principal Payment	Pre-Tax Earnings Required	Interest Cost (Net After Taxes)	Total Earnings Required
1	$ 50,000	$ 100,000	$15,000	$ 115,000
2	$ 50,000	$ 100,000	$13,500	$ 113,500
3	$ 50,000	$ 100,000	$12,000	$ 112,000
4	$ 50,000	$ 100,000	$10,500	$ 110,500
5	$ 50,000	$ 100,000	$ 9,000	$ 109,000
6	$ 50,000	$ 100,000	$ 7,500	$ 107,500
7	$ 50,000	$ 100,000	$ 6,000	$ 106,000
8	$ 50,000	$ 100,000	$ 4,500	$ 104,500
9	$ 50,000	$ 100,000	$ 3,000	$ 103,000
10	$ 50,000	$ 100,000	$ 1,500	$ 101,500
TOTALS	$500,000	$1,000,000	$82,500	$1,082,500

APPENDIX A: Authority of a Corporation to Purchase Its Own Stock

Alabama—Ala. Code. Bus. Corp. Act, Tit. 10, § 21(57) (1959)

Alaska—Alaska Stat., Tit. 10, § 10.05.012 (1962)

Arizona—*Copper Belle Mining Co.* v. *Costello*, 11 Ariz. 334, 95 P. 94 (1908)

Arkansas—Ark. Stat. Ann., Bus. Corp. Act, Tit. 64, Ch. 1, § 64–105(E) (1966)

California—Cal. Corp. Code Ann., Tit. 1, §§1706–1707–1708 (Deering, 1962)

Colorado—Colo. Rev. Stat. Ann., Ch. 31, § 31–28–2 (1960 Perm. Supp.)

Connecticut—Conn. Gen. Stat. Rev., Tit. 33, § 33–358 (1958)

Delaware—Del. Code Ann., Tit. 8. § 160 (1953)

District of Columbia—D.C. Code Ann., Tit. 29, § 29–904a (1961)

Florida—Fla. Stat. Ann., Tit. 34, Ch. 608, § 608.13(9)(b) (1956)

Georgia—Ga. Code Ann., Rev. Tit. 22, § 22–1828(d) (1966)

Hawaii—Hawaii Rev. Laws, Tit. 23, Ch. 172, § 172–25 (1955)

Idaho—Idaho Code Ann., Tit. 30, § 30–149 (1948). See *LaVoy Supply Company* v. *Young*, 84 Idaho 120, 369 P. 2d 45, 49 (1962), which implies that a corporation has power to repurchase its own capital stock if it is solvent.

Illinois—Ill. Ann. Stat., Bus. Corp. Act, Ch. 32, § 157.6 (Smith-Hurd 1954)

Indiana—Ind. Ann. Stat., Tit. 25, § 25–202(b)(8) (Burn's 1960)

Iowa—Iowa Code Ann., Bus. Corp. Act, Tit. 19, Ch. 496A, § 496A.5 (1962)

Kansas—Kan. Stat. Ann., Ch. 17, § 17–3004 (1964)

Kentucky—Ky. Rev. Stat. Ann., Tit. 23, Ch. 271, § 271.135 (Baldwin's 1963)

Louisiana—La. Rev. Stat. Ann., Bus. Corp. Act, Tit. 12, § 12:23 (West's 1950)

Maine—Me. Rev. Stat. Ann., Tit. 13, § 202 (1964). See *Bates Street Shirt Co.* v. *Waite*, 130 Me. 352, 156 A.293, 302 (1931)

Maryland—Md. Ann. Code, Art. 23, § 32 (1966)

Massachusetts—Ann. Laws Mass., Ch. 156B, § 9(m) (1959)

Michigan—Mich. Stat. Ann., Tit. 21, § 21.10h (1963)

Minnesota—Minn. Stat. Ann., Bus. Corp. Act, Ch. 301, § 301.22(6) (1947)

Mississippi—Miss. Code Ann., Tit. 21, Ch. 4, § 5309–05 (1957)

Missouri—Mo. Ann. Stat., Ch. 351, § 351.390 (Vernon's 1966)

Montana—Mont. Rev. Codes Ann., Tit. 15, § 15–801(9) (1947)

Nebraska—Neb. Rev. Stat., Bus. Corp. Act, Art. 20, § 21–2005 (1965 Supp.)

Nevada—Nev. Rev. Stat., Tit. 7, Ch. 78, § 78.070(3) (1963)

New Hampshire—N.H. Rev. Stat. Ann., Ch. 294, Bus. Corp. Act, § 294:28 (1966)

New Jersey—N.J. Stat. Ann., Tit. 14, §§14:8–3.1 and 14:11–5 (1939). See *Berger* v. *U.S. Steel Corp.*, 63 N.J. Eq. 809, 53 A.68 (1902).

New Mexico—N.M. Stat. Ann., Ch. 51, § 51–3–18 (1953). New Mexico corporation laws are based on those of New Jersey. See *Cartwright* v. *Albuquerque City Hotel*, 36 N.M. 189, 11 P. 2d 261 (1932)

New York—N.Y. Bus. Corp. Law, § 202(14), and §§513–514 (McKinney's 1963)

North Carolina—N.C. Gen. Stat., Bus. Corp. Act, Ch. 55, § 55–52 (1965)

North Dakota—N.D. Cent. Code, Bus. Corp. Act, § 10–19–05 (1960)

Ohio—Ohio Rev. Code Ann., Tit. 17, § 1701.35 (Page's 1964)

Oklahoma—Okla. Stat. Ann., Bus. Corp. Act, Tit. 18, § 1.136 (1953)

Oregon—Ore. Rev. Stat., Tit. 7, § 57.035 (1965)

Pennsylvania—Pa. Stat. Ann., Bus. Corp. Act, Tit. 15, § 2852–701 (Purdon's 1958)

Rhode Island—R.I. Gen. Laws Ann., § 7–2–10(g) (1956)

South Carolina—S.C. Code, Tit. 12, § 12–15.17 (1962)

South Dakota—S.D. Bus. Corp. Act, Laws 1965, Ch. 22, § 5

Tennessee—Tenn. Code Ann., § 48–117(9) (1964)

Texas—Tex. Bus. Corp. Act, Art. 2.03 (Vernon's 1956)

Utah—Utah Code Ann., Bus. Corp. Act, Ch. 10, § 16–10–5 (1962)

Vermont—Vt. Stat. Ann., Tit. 11, § 103 (1958)

Virginia—Va. Code Ann., Tit. 13.1, § 13.1–4 (1964)

Washington—Wash. Rev. Code Ann., Bus. Corp. Act, Tit. 23A, § 23A.08.030 (1966)

West Virginia—W. Va. Code Ann., Ch. 31, § 31–1–39 (1966)

Wisconsin—Wis. Stat. Ann., Bus. Corp. Act, Ch. 180, § 180.385 (1957)

Wyoming—Wyo. Stat. Ann., Tit. 17, § 17–36.5 (1965)

APPENDIX B

SPECIMEN STOCK RETIREMENT AGREEMENT—
CORPORATION AND THREE OR MORE STOCKHOLDERS
(ENTITY PLAN)

THIS AGREEMENT is made by and between _____, a corporation organized under the laws of the State of _____, with its principal place of business at _____, hereinafter referred to as the corporation, and _____, _____ and _____, all the stockholders thereof, hereinafter referred to as stockholders.

The purpose of this agreement is to provide (a) for the continued close control of the corporation and for the harmonious operation thereof, upon the death of a stockholder, (b) for the purchase of the shares in the corporation of a deceased stockholder by the corporation at a price fairly established, and (c) funds for such purchase.

In consideration of the mutual agreements as hereinafter set forth, the corporation and each stockholder hereby agrees as follows:

Article 1

The number of shares now owned by each stockholder is as follows:

Names	*Shares*
_____	_____
_____	_____
_____	_____

Article 2

No stockholder during his lifetime shall sell, assign, encumber or otherwise dispose of all or any part of his shares in the corporation, except with the written consent of the corporation.

Article 3

Upon the death of each stockholder, his estate shall sell, and the corporation shall buy, all the shares in the corporation then owned by such decedent at the price and in the manner hereinafter set forth.

Article 4

On the signing of this agreement and semi-annually thereafter, the value of each share of stock, including good will, shall be determined by the stockholders and the corporation and set forth in Schedule A, attached hereto.

The value last previously determined and set forth in Schedule A shall control, except that if more than one year has elapsed since the date of the last determination of value, the value of each share of stock shall be determined, as of the date of death of a stockholder by the corporation and the executors or administrators of the deceased stockholder's estate.

If the corporation and the executors or administrators of the deceased stockholder's estate are unable to agree upon such value within _____ days after such executors or administrators have qualified to administer the estate of the deceased stockholder, then such value shall be settled by arbitration in accordance with the Commercial Arbitration Rules then in effect of the American Arbitration Association, to the extent consistent with the laws of the State of _____, and judgment upon the award rendered by the arbitrator(s) may be entered in any court having jurisdiction thereof. Arbitration shall be held in the City of _____, State of _____.

The corporation's books shall show, as an asset, the cash value, including the cash value of dividend additions and deposits, if any, less the amount of any policy loan with accrued interest, if any, of all life insurance policies on the life of each stockholder, subject to the terms of this agreement. The amount payable as death proceeds of such policies on a deceased stockholder's life, in excess of the cash values thereof, as set forth in the sentence immediately preceding, just prior to his death, shall not be taken into account in determining the value of each share of such deceased stockholder's stock.

The value of each share of stock, as determined above, shall be the purchase price for each share of stock in the event of a stockholder's death.

Article 5

The corporation, as applicant, beneficiary and owner, has purchased, or will purchase, insurance on the life of each of its stockholders with The Mutual Life Insurance Company of New York, as follows:

Amount of Policy	Policy No.	Insured
$25,000	000	A
$25,000	111	B
$25,000	222	C

The corporation shall pay premiums when due on each policy owned by it, subject to the terms of this agreement. In the event the corporation fails to pay a premium, any stockholder shall have the right to pay such premium and if a stockholder shall pay such premium, he shall have the right to be reimbursed therefor by the corporation, and there shall be no right of termination with respect to such non-payment by the corporation, as provided in Article 9.

All rights, options, benefits and privileges conferred by each policy or allowed by the insurance company shall be reserved to the corporation and the corporation shall notify the insured, in writing, at the time of the exercise of any such rights, options, benefits and privileges in connection with a policy on the insured's life. Such life insurance policies, and any additional policies which may hereafter be listed in Schedule B, attached hereto, over the signatures of all the parties to this agreement shall be subject to the provisions hereof.

Article 6

On the death of each stockholder, the corporation shall promptly collect the proceeds of insurance on the deceased stockholder's life and promptly apply so much of such proceeds as is necessary to pay to the executors or administrators of the deceased stockholder's estate the purchase price, as established in Article 4, in cash. If such proceeds exceed the purchase price, the excess shall be retained by the corporation.

If such proceeds are insufficient to pay the full purchase price in cash, the corporation shall apply the full amount of such proceeds on account of the purchase price and pay the balance in cash or in _____ equal consecutive monthly payments, with the first payment due _____ months after the date of the stockholder's death, with interest at the rate of _____% per year running from the date of the stockholder's death. Such deferred payments shall be evidenced by a negotiable promissory note payable to the executors or administrators of the deceased stockholder's estate, and such note shall provide (a) for the immediate acceleration of the remaining unpaid balance, with interest thereon, upon default in any payment, and (b) the right of prepayment, in whole or in part, at any time.

Article 7

Upon payment of the purchase price, whether in cash or by promissory note and cash, the executors or administrators of the estate of the deceased stockholder shall execute and deliver all instruments necessary to effectuate the transfer of such deceased stockholder's shares to the corporation, as of the date of death of the deceased stockholder. Such transfer of the deceased stockholder's shares shall be made free and clear of all taxes, debts, claims, judgments, liens or encumbrances.

Article 8

Each stock certificate subject to this agreement, shall have endorsed thereon:
"The sale or transfer of this certificate is subject to the terms and conditions of a Stock Retirement Agreement dated _____ , a copy of which is on file with the Secretary of the corporation."

Article 9

This agreement may be terminated, altered or amended by a writing signed by all stockholders and the corporation. Also, it shall terminate (a) in the event of bankruptcy or dissolution of the corporation, (b) at the option of any stockholder, if the corporation, by an officer other than such stockholder, violates any provision of this agreement or in connection with any policy or policies of life insurance, subject to the terms of this agreement, fails to pay a premium within the grace period (and if such premium has not otherwise been paid as provided for in Article 5) or assigns, surrenders, borrows against, changes the beneficiary or makes the proceeds thereof payable other than in a lump sum, without the written consent of all living stockholders, or (c) if all stockholders die within a period of thirty (30) days.

Article 10

Within thirty (30) days after termination of this agreement, each stockholder shall have the right to purchase any policy or policies owned by the corporation on his life, subject to the terms of this agreement, upon paying the corporation an amount equal to the cash value, including the cash value of dividend additions or deposits, if any, of such policy as of the date such right is exercised, less the amount of any policy loan with accrued interest, which may then exist against such policy. Upon such payment the corporation shall execute the instruments necessary to transfer such policy or policies to the insured.

There shall be no obligation on the corporation or the insured to pay any premiums which become due on any policy or policies subject to the right of purchase following the termination of this agreement. However, any premium so paid by the insured shall be taken into account and credited to the insured in the event he shall exercise such right of purchase.

Article 11

The Mutual Life Insurance Company of New York shall not be a party to this agreement, nor shall it be bound to inquire into, nor shall it be chargeable with notice of, any provision hereof.

Notwithstanding any provision in this agreement to the contrary, the signature of the corporation, by any executive officer thereof, shall be full and sufficient authority to The Mutual Life Insurance Company of New York to take or permit any action in connection therewith. Payment or performance by The Mutual Life Insurance Company of New York, in accordance with the terms of its policies, shall completely discharge said Company from all claims, suits, or demands of all persons whatsoever.

Article 12

This agreement shall be binding on each stockholder, his heirs, executors, administrators and assigns, and upon the corporation and its successors.

Article 13

This agreement shall be subject to, and governed by, the laws of the State of _____.

IN WITNESS WHEREOF, the parties hereto have executed this agreement this _____ day of _____, 19____.

_____ (L.S.)
_____ (L.S.)
_____ (L.S.)

(Corporate Seal)
Attest:

_____
(Corporation)

_____ By _____
(Secretary)   (Title)

Schedule A

The value of the stock of _____ Corporation as of _____, for the purposes of this agreement, shall be $_____ per share.
Dated: _____, 19____.

_____ (L.S.)
_____ (L.S.)
_____ (L.S.)

(Corporate Seal)
Attest:

_____
(Corporation)

_____ By _____
(Secretary)   (Title)

Schedule B

Amount of Policy	Policy No.	Insured	Owner	Signature of Owner
_____	_____	_____	_____	_____
_____	_____	_____	_____	_____
_____	_____	_____	_____	_____

THIS AGREEMENT is made by and between _____, and _____, hereinafter referred to as stockholders, who are all the stockholders of _____, a corporation organized under the laws of the State of _____, with its principal place of business at _____, hereinafter referred to as the corporation.

The purpose of this agreement is to provide (a) for the purchase of the shares in the corporation of a deceased stockholder by the surviving stockholders or stockholder at a price fairly established, and (b) funds for such purchase.

In consideration of the mutual agreements as hereinafter set forth, each stockholder hereby agrees as follows:

Article 1

The number of shares now owned by each stockholder is as follows:

Names	Shares

Article 2

No stockholder during his lifetime shall sell, assign, encumber or otherwise dispose of all, or any part, of his shares in the corporation, except with the written consent of all stockholders.

Article 3

Upon the death of each stockholder, his estate shall sell all of such decedent's shares then owned, and each surviving stockholder shall purchase a proportion of such decedent's shares, at the price and in the manner hereinafter set forth. The number of shares to be purchased by each surviving stockholder shall be in the same ratio that the number of shares owned by him bears to the total shares owned by all the stockholders, excluding the shares then owned by the deceased stockholder.

Article 4

On the signing of this agreement and semi-annually thereafter, the value of each share of stock, including good will, shall be determined by the stockholders and set forth in Schedule A, attached hereto.

The value last previously determined and set forth in Schedule A shall control, except that if more than one year has elapsed since the date of the last determination of value, the value of each share of stock shall be determined, as of the date of death of a stockholder, by the surviving stockholders or stockholder and the executors or administrators of the deceased stockholder's estate.

If the surviving stockholders or stockholder and the executors or administrators of the deceased stockholder's estate are unable to agree upon such value within _____ days after such executors or administrators have qualified to administer the estate of the deceased stockholder, then such value shall be settled by arbitration in accordance with the Commercial Arbitration Rules then in effect of the American Arbitration Association, to the extent consistent with the laws of the State of _____, and judgment upon the award rendered by the arbitrator(s) may be entered in any court having jurisdiction thereof. Arbitration shall be held in the City of _____, State of _____.

The value of each share of stock, as determined above, shall be the purchase price for each share of stock in the event of a stockholder's death.

Article 5

Each stockholder has purchased, or will purchase, insurance on the life of the other stockholders from The Mutual Life Insurance Company of New York, as follows:

Amount of Policy	Policy No.	Insured	Applicant, Owner, Beneficiary and Premium Payor
$25,000	000	A	B
$25,000	111	A	C
$25,000	222	B	A
$25,000	333	B	C
$25,000	444	C	A
$25,000	555	C	B

Each stockholder shall pay premiums when due on each policy owned by him, subject to the terms of this agreement. In the event a stockholder fails to pay a premium, any other stockholder shall have the right to pay such premium and to be reimbursed therefor by the owner, and if such other stockholder shall pay such premium, there shall be no right of termination with respect to such non-payment by the owner, as provided for in Article 9.

All rights, options, benefits and privileges conferred by each policy or allowed by the insurance company shall be reserved to the stockholder indicated above as owner, if living, if not, to such stockholder's executors or administrators. Such owner shall notify the insured, in writing, at the time of the exercise of any such rights, options, benefits and privileges in connection with a policy on the insured's life. Such life insurance policies, and any additional policies which may hereafter be listed in Schedule B, attached hereto, over the signatures of all the parties to this agreement, shall be subject to the provisions hereof.

Article 6

Upon the death of a stockholder, each surviving stockholder shall promptly collect the proceeds of insurance on the deceased stockholder's life which is payable to him, and promptly apply so much of such proceeds as is necessary to pay the executors or administrators of the deceased stockholder's estate the purchase price, in cash, for the proportionate number of shares of the decedent's stock that each surviving stockholder is obligated to purchase in accordance with the terms of this agreement. If such proceeds exceed such purchase price, the excess shall be retained by the surviving stockholder who was the beneficiary and owner of the particular policy.

If such proceeds are insufficient to pay the full purchase price in cash, each surviving stockholder shall apply the full amount of such proceeds on account of the purchase price for the shares he is obligated to purchase and pay the balance in cash or in _____ equal consecutive monthly payments, with the first payment due _____ months after the date of the stockholder's death, with interest at the rate of _____% per year running from the date of the stockholder's death. Such deferred payments shall be evidenced by a negotiable promissory note payable to the executors or administrators of the deceased stockholder's estate, and such note shall provide (a) for the immediate acceleration of the remaining unpaid balance, with interest thereon, upon default in any payment, and (b) the right of prepayment, in whole or in part, at any time.

Article 7

Upon payment of the purchase price, whether in cash or by promissory note and cash, the executors or administrators of the estate of the deceased stockholder shall execute and deliver all instruments necessary to transfer such deceased stockholder's shares to the surviving stockholders or stockholder, as of the date of the deceased stockholder's death, in the proportion necessary to effectuate the terms of purchase set forth in this agreement. Such transfer of the deceased stockholder's shares shall be made free and clear of all taxes, debts, claims, judgments, liens or encumbrances, except that all such shares acquired by the surviving stockholders shall remain subject to the obligations assumed under this agreement.

Article 8

Each stock certificate subject to this agreement shall have endorsed thereon:
"The sale or transfer of this certificate is subject to the terms and conditions of a Stock Purchase Agreement dated _____, a copy of which is on file with the Secretary of the corporation."

Article 9

This agreement may be terminated, altered or amended by a writing signed by all of the stockholders. Also, it shall terminate (a) in the event of bankruptcy or dissolution of the corporation, (b) at the option of any stockholder, if any other living stockholder violates any provision of this agreement or in connection with any policy or policies of life insurance, subject to the terms of this agreement, fails to pay a premium within the grace period (and if such premium has not otherwise been paid as provided for in Article 5) or assigns, surrenders, borrows against, changes the beneficiary or makes the proceeds thereof payable other than in a lump sum, without the written consent of all living stockholders, or (c) if all stockholders die within a period of thirty (30) days.

Article 10

Each stockholder shall have the right to purchase any policy or policies on his life, subject to the terms of this agreement, from the (a) estate of a deceased stockholder within thirty (30) days after an executor or administrator has qualified to administer such estate, or (b) other stockholder or stockholders within thirty (30) days of termination of this agreement.

Such rights of purchase may be exercised by paying the policy-owner, within the time specified, an amount equal to the cash value, including the cash value of dividend additions or deposits, if any, of such policy as of the date such right is exercised, less the amount of any policy loan with accrued interest, which may then exist against such policy. Upon such payment the owner or the executors or administrators of any deceased owner shall execute the instruments necessary to transfer such policy or policies to the insured.

There shall be no obligation on an insured or on the estate of a deceased stockholder to pay any premiums which become due on any policy or policies subject to this right of purchase following the death of such deceased stockholder or termination of this agreement. However, any premium so paid by the insured shall be taken into account.

Article 11

This agreement shall be binding on each stockholder, his heirs, executors, administrators and assigns.

Article 12

This agreement shall be subject to, and governed by, the laws of the State of
_____.

IN WITNESS WHEREOF, the parties hereto have executed this agreement this _____
day of _____, 19____.

_____ (L.S.)
_____ (L.S.)
_____ (L.S.)

Schedule A

The value of the stock of _____ Corporation as of
_____, for the purposes of this agreement, shall be $_____ per share.
Dated: _____, 19____.

_____ (L.S.)
_____ (L.S.)
_____ (L.S.)

Schedule B

Amount of Policy	*Policy No.*	*Insured*	*Signature of Owner*
_____	_____	_____	_____
_____	_____	_____	_____
_____	_____	_____	_____

APPENDIX C: Partnerships

SPECIMEN BUY AND SELL AGREEMENT—TWO PARTNERS
(CROSS-PURCHASE)

THIS AGREEMENT is made by and between _____ and
_____ engaged in the business of _____, as co-partners,
under the name of _____, in the City of _____, State of
_____.

The purpose of this agreement is to provide (a) for the purchase of the interest in the partnership of a deceased partner by the surviving partner at a price fairly established, and (b) funds for such purchase.

In consideration of the mutual agreements, as hereinafter set forth, each partner hereby agrees as follows:

Article 1

Neither partner shall during his lifetime sell, assign, encumber or otherwise dispose of his interest in the partnership, in whole or in part, without the written consent of the other partner.[1]

Article 2

Upon the death of either partner, the surviving partner shall purchase, and the estate of the deceased partner shall sell, the interest in the partnership then owned by the decedent at the price and in the manner hereinafter set forth.

Article 3

On the signing of this agreement and semi-annually thereafter, the value of the respective interest of each partner in the partnership, including good will [and a specified amount for un-realized receivables],[2] shall be determined by the partners and set forth in Schedule A, attached hereto.

The values last previously determined and set forth in Schedule A shall control, except that if more than one year has elapsed since the date of the last determination of values, the value of the respective interest of each partner in the partnership shall be determined, as of the date of death of a partner, by the surviving partner and the executors or administrators of the deceased partner's estate.

If the surviving partner and the executors or administrators of deceased partner's estate are unable to agree upon such value within _____ days after such executors or administrators have qualified to administer the estate of the deceased partner, then such value shall be settled by arbitration in accordance with the Commercial Arbitration Rules then in effect of the American Arbitration Association, to the extent consistent with the laws of the State of _____, and judgment upon the award rendered by the arbitrator(s) may be entered in any court having jurisdiction thereof. Arbitration shall be held in the City of _____, State of _____.[3]

The value of each partner's interest, as determined above, shall be the purchase price for such interest in the event of a partner's death.

Article 4

Each partner has purchased or will purchase insurance on the life of the other partner from The Mutual Life Insurance Company of New York, as follows:

Amount of Policy	Policy No.	Insured	Applicant, Owner, Beneficiary and Premium Payor
$50,000	000	B	A
$50,000	111	A	B

Each partner shall pay premiums when due on each policy owned by him, subject to the terms of this agreement. In the event a partner fails to pay a premium, the insured shall have the right either (a) to terminate the agreement, as provided for in Article 7, or (b) to pay such premium and to be reimbursed therefor by the owner, and if the insured shall pay such premium, there shall be no right to terminate the agreement with respect to such non-payment by the owner, as provided for in Article 7.

All rights, options, benefits and privileges conferred by each policy or allowed by the insurance company shall be reserved to the insured's partner, if living, if not, to such partner's executors or administrators. Such partner shall notify the insured, in writing, at the time of the exercise of any such rights, options, benefits and privileges in connection with a policy on the insured's life. Such life insurance policies, and any additional policies which may hereafter be listed in Schedule B, attached hereto, over the signatures of the parties to this agreement, shall be subject to the provisions hereof.

Article 5

Upon the death of either partner, the surviving partner shall promptly collect the proceeds of the insurance on the deceased partner's life and promptly apply so much of such proceeds as is necessary to pay to the executors or administrators of the deceased partner's estate the purchase price as established in Article 3, in cash. If such proceeds exceed the purchase price, the excess shall be retained by the surviving partner.

If such proceeds are insufficient to pay the full purchase price in cash, the surviving partner shall apply the full amount of such proceeds on account of the purchase price and pay the balance in cash or in _____ equal consecutive monthly payments, with the first payment due _____ months after the date of the partner's death, with interest at the rate of _____%[3a] per year running from the date of the partner's death. Such deferred payments shall be evidenced by a negotiable promissory note[4] payable to the executors or administrators of the deceased partner's estate, and such note shall provide (a) for the immediate acceleration of the remaining unpaid balance, with interest thereon, upon default in any payment, and (b) a right of prepayment, in whole or in part, at any time.

Article 6

Upon payment of the purchase price, whether in cash or by promissory note and cash, the executors or administrators of the estate of the deceased partner shall execute and deliver all instruments necessary to vest the partnership interest of the deceased partner in the surviving partner, as of the date of the deceased partner's death,[5] free and clear of all taxes, debts, claims, judgments, liens or encumbrances other than those which are partnership obligations. The surviving partner shall be entitled to all profits of the business and suffer all losses arising between the date of the deceased partner's death and the date of transfer of the interest of the deceased partner to the survivor, and upon such transfer the surviving partner shall execute and deliver to the executors or administrators of the deceased partner's estate an agreement indemnifying the estate of the decedent against all claims and obligations of the partnership.

Article 7

This agreement may be terminated, altered or amended by a writing signed by both partners. Also, it shall terminate (a) in the event of dissolution of the partnership, other than by death, (b) at the option of one partner, if the other partner violates any provision of this agreement, or in connection with any policy or policies of life insurance, subject to the terms of this agreement, fails to pay a premium within the grace period (and if such premium has not otherwise been paid as provided for in Article 4) or assigns, surrenders, borrows against, changes the beneficiary or makes the proceeds thereof payable other than in a lump sum, without the written consent of the partner whose life is insured, or (c) if both partners die within a period of thirty (30) days and the purchase and sale of the interest in the partnership of the partner first to die has not been consummated.

Article 8

A partner, within thirty (30) days after (a) an executor or administrator has qualified to administer the estate of a deceased partner, or (b) termination of this agreement, shall have the right to purchase any policy or policies owned by the other partner on his life, subject to the terms of this agreement, upon paying the policy-owner an amount equal to the cash value, including the cash value of dividend additions or deposits, if any, of such policy as of the date such right is exercised, less the amount of any policy loan with accrued interest, which may then exist against such policy. Upon such payment the owner or the executors or administrators of any deceased owner shall execute the instruments necessary to transfer such policy or policies to the insured.

There shall be no obligation on either the insured or the estate of a deceased partner to pay any premiums which become due on any policy or policies subject to this right of purchase following the death of the deceased partner or termination of this agreement. However, any premium so paid by the insured shall be taken into account and credited to the insured in the event he shall exercise such right of purchase.

Article 9

This agreement shall be binding on the partners, their heirs, executors, administrators and assigns.

Article 10

This agreement shall be subject to, and governed by, the laws of the State of _____.

IN WITNESS WHEREOF, the parties hereto have executed this agreement this _____ day of _____, 19____.

_____ (L.S.)

_____ (L.S.)

Schedule A

The value of the respective interest of each partner as of _____, as determined in accordance with the terms of this agreement, shall be:

	Unrealized Receivables[6]	Total Value		Signatures
Partner A	$____	$____		_____ (L.S.)
				Partner A
Partner B	$____	$____		_____ (L.S.)
				Partner B

Dated _____, 19____.

Schedule B

Amount of Policy	Policy No.	Insured	Signature of Owner
_____	_____	_____	_____
_____	_____	_____	_____
_____	_____	_____	_____

---

[1] Sometimes the parties wish to include a provision permitting disposal of a partner's interest during lifetime after first offering such interest to the other partner, who may purchase it within a specified time. If such a provision is included, other changes in the agreement must be considered, such as the purchase price for such interest, the terms of payment, etc.

[2] If no value is to be placed on unrealized receivables, the bracketed material should be omitted. Reg. §1.751–1(c)(3) provides that any arm's length agreement between the buyer and seller or between the partnership and a distributee partner will generally establish the amount or value of unrealized receivables.

[3] If the attorney feels that he would prefer to use some method other than arbitration, in the event the parties cannot agree as to the valuation, he may want to consider drafting some type of formula clause. The firm's accountant can be of help here.

[3a] If interest rate per annum is less than 4% simple interest, see IRC§483, dealing with imputed interest.

[4] The parties may wish to include at this point a provision obligating the surviving partner to furnish collateral to secure the promissory note.

[5] A sale as of date of death may not always be desirable for Federal income tax purposes. If this date will cause a bunching of income in the deceased partner's estate because it closes the partnership taxable year as to the decedent, it may be desirable to have the sale effective as of a different date.

[6] See Footnote 2.

APPENDIX D

THIS AGREEMENT is made by and between _____, a partnership, doing business as such under the firm name of _____, in the City of _____, State of _____, hereinafter referred to as the partnership, and _____, _____, and _____, hereinafter referred to as partners.

The purpose of this agreement is to provide (a) for the partnership's continued existence by the surviving partners without interruption upon the death of a partner, (b) for payment by the partnership in liquidation of the interest of a deceased partner in the partnership at a value fairly established, and (c) funds to implement such liquidation.

In consideration of the mutual agreements as hereinafter set forth, the partnership and each partner hereby agree as follows:

Article 1

No partner shall during his lifetime, sell, assign, encumber or otherwise dispose of his interest in the partnership, in whole or in part, except with the written consent of all the other partners.

Article 2

Upon the death of each partner, the partnership shall (a) be continued by the surviving partners, and (b) make payment to the executors or administrators of the estate of such deceased partner in full satisfaction of the interest in the partnership then owned by such decedent. Such payment shall be equal to the value, and made in the manner, hereinafter set forth.

Article 3

On the signing of this agreement and semi-annually thereafter, the value of the respective interests of each partner in the partnership [including specified amounts for good will] [and for unrealized receivables], shall be determined by the partners and set forth in Schedule A, attached hereto.

The values last previously determined and set forth in Schedule A shall control, except that if more than one year has elapsed since the date of the last determination of values, the value of the respective interest of each partner in the partnership shall be determined, as of the date of death of a partner, by the surviving partners and the executors or administrators of the deceased partner's estate.

If the surviving partners and the executors or administrators of the deceased partner's estate are unable to agree upon such value within _____ days after such executors or administrators have qualified to administer the estate of the deceased partner, then such value shall be settled by arbitration in accordance with the Commercial Arbitration Rules then in effect of the American Arbitration Association, to the extent consistent with the laws of the State of _____, and judgment upon the award rendered by the arbitrator(s) may be entered in any court having jurisdiction thereof. Arbitration shall be held in the City of _____, State of _____.

The partnership books shall show the cash value, including the cash value of dividend additions and deposits, if any, less the amount of any policy loan with accrued interest, if any, of all life insurance policies on the life of each partner, subject to the terms of this agreement, as an asset. The amount payable as death proceeds of policies on the deceased partner's life, in excess of the cash values thereof, as set forth in the sentence immediately preceding, just prior to his death, shall not be taken into account in determining the value of such deceased partner's interest in the partnership.

The value of each partner's interest, as determined above, shall be the amount to be paid in full satisfaction of such interest in the event of a partner's death.

Article 4

The amount payable as death proceeds of the policies on the deceased partner's life, in excess of the cash values thereof, including the cash value of dividend additions and deposits, if any, less the amount of any policy loan with accrued interest, if any, shall be credited as a distributive share on the partnership books to the account of the surviving partners in the ratios that the value of each surviving partner's interest in the partnership bears to the value of the total interest in the partnership of all partners other than the deceased partner.

Article 5

The partnership, as applicant, beneficiary and owner, has purchased, or will purchase, insurance on the life of each partner from The Mutual Life Insurance Company of New York, as follows:

Amount of Policy	Policy No.	Insured
$25,000	000	A
$25,000	111	B
$25,000	222	C

The partnership shall pay premiums when due on each policy owned by it, subject to the terms of this agreement. In the event the partnership fails to pay a premium, any partner shall have the right to pay such premium and to be reimbursed therefor by the partnership, and if a partner shall pay such premium, there shall be no right of termination with respect to such non-payment by the partnership, as provided for in Article 8.

All rights, options, benefits and privileges, conferred by each policy or allowed by the insurance company, shall be reserved to the partnership. The partnership shall notify the insured, in writing, at the time of the exercise of any such rights, options, benefits and privileges in connection with a policy on the insured's life. The partnership may deal with such policies on the signature of any one partner other than the partner whose life is insured. Such life insurance policies, and any additional policies which may hereafter be listed in Schedule B attached hereto, over the signatures of all parties to this agreement, shall be subject to the provisions hereof.

Article 6

Upon the death of each partner, the partnership shall promptly collect the proceeds of the insurance on the deceased partner's life and promptly apply so much of such proceeds as is necessary to pay the executors or administrators of the deceased partner's estate the amount, as established in Article 3, in cash. If such proceeds exceed such amount, the excess shall be retained by the partnership.

If such proceeds are insufficient to pay in full the amount, as established in Article 3, in cash, the partnership shall apply the full amount of such proceeds on account and pay the balance in cash or in _____ equal consecutive monthly payments, with the first payment due _____ months after the date of the partner's death, with interest at the rate of _____% per year running from the date of the partner's death. Such deferred payments shall be evidenced by a negotiable promissory note payable to the executors or administrators of the deceased partner's estate, and such note shall provide (a) for the immediate acceleration of the remaining unpaid balance, with interest thereon, upon default in any payment, and (b) a right of prepayment, in whole or in part, at any time.

Article 7

Upon payment of the amount as established in Article 3, whether in cash or by promissory note and cash, (a) such deceased partner's interest in the partnership shall terminate as of the date of the deceased partner's death, (b) the executors or administrators of the deceased partner's estate shall execute and deliver all instruments necessary to evidence the termination of such deceased partner's interest in the partnership, free and clear of all taxes, debts, claims, judgments, liens or encumbrances other than those which are partnership obligations, and (c) the surviving partners shall execute and deliver to the executors or administrators of the deceased partner's estate an agreement indemnifying the estate of the decedent against all claims and obligations of the partnership.

The surviving partners shall be entitled to all the profits of the business and suffer all the losses after the date of the deceased partner's death.

Article 8

This agreement may be terminated, altered or amended by a writing signed by all parties. Also, it shall terminate (a) in the event of dissolution of the partnership, other than by death, (b) at the option of one partner, if any other partner or partners, on behalf of the partnership, violates any provision of this agreement, or in connection with any policy or policies of life insurance, subject to the terms of this agreement, fails to pay a premium within the grace period (and if such premium has not otherwise been paid as provided for in Article 5) or assigns, surrenders, borrows against, changes the beneficiary or makes the proceeds thereof payable other than in a lump sum, without the written consent of all partners, or (c) if all partners die within a period of thirty (30) days.

Article 9

Within thirty (30) days after termination of this agreement, each partner shall have the right to purchase any policy or policies owned by the partnership on his life, subject to the terms of this agreement, upon paying the partnership an amount equal to the cash value, including the cash value of dividend additions or deposits, if any, of such policy as of the date such right is exercised, less the amount of any policy loan with accrued interest, which may then exist against such policy. Upon such payment the partnership shall execute the instruments necessary to transfer such policy or policies to the insured.

There shall be no obligation on the partnership or the insured to pay any premiums which become due on any policy or policies subject to the right of purchase following the termination of this agreement. However, any premium so paid by the insured shall be taken into account and credited to the insured in the event he shall exercise such right of purchase.

Article 10

This agreement shall be binding on the partnership or its successors and each partner, his heirs, executors, administrators and assigns.

Article 11

This agreement shall be subject to, and governed by, the laws of the State of
_____.

IN WITNESS WHEREOF, the parties hereto have executed this agreement this _____
day of _____, 19____.

_____ (L.S.)

_____ (L.S.)

_____ (L.S.)

_____

Partnership

By _____ (L.S.)

Partner

Schedule A

The value of the respective interest of each partner as of _____, as determined in accordance with the terms of this agreement, shall be:

	Good Will	Unrealized Receivables	Remaining Partnership Interest	Total Value
Partner A	$_____	$_____	$_____	$_____
Partner B	$_____	$_____	$_____	$_____
Partner C	$_____	$_____	$_____	$_____

Dated: _____, 19____.

_____ (L.S.)

Partner A

_____ (L.S.)

Partner B

_____ (L.S.)

Partner C

_____

Partnership

By _____ (L.S.)

Partner

Schedule B

Amount of Policy	Policy No.	Insured	Owner	Signature of Partners
_____	_____	_____	_____	_____
_____	_____	_____	_____	_____
_____	_____	_____	_____	_____

CHAPTER 8

The Sales Contract

Introduction

After all of our discussion about contracts, many people might be surprised to find out that when the contract deals with the sale of goods, which is best described as anything other than realty and intangibles, the rules of the game change. For the most part, the offer to sell, coupled with the acceptance, cemented by valuable consideration and the transferral of goods from the seller to the buyer, is a contract; but states have enacted statutes which regulate such transactions differently. The reason for this variation is that the everyday store purchase or wholesale or supply situation requires uniformity between states.

For the uniform statute to be triggered, certain requirements must be met. First, the item sold must be considered goods as stated above, and second, the contracting parties must consist of a consumer and a merchant or two merchants in the chain of producer-retailer. "Goods" is defined in the UCC as anything other than real estate (although goods linked to real estate, such as growing crops or movable fixtures, fall within the statute's purview) and intangibles such as services.

Formation

One of the first divergents from contract law occurs in the formation of the agreement. Under common law contract rules, certainty of terms was a requisite, and if a term to the contract was left undetermined, the contract would necessarily fail. The sales laws grant greater latitude. Whereas, before the contents of the contract had to include the names of the parties, identify the subject matter and quote the price and time of delivery, sales contracts need not satisfy price and time as long as both fall within the congenial limits of reasonableness. By permitting the going market price to control where no price is agreed on, sales contracts do not fail for lack of certainty and the market place does not shut down. Basically, the test to determine whether a binding sales contract exists between the parties is not whether all the common law formalities of contracts have been adhered to, but rather is a two-fold test of (1) did the parties intend to contract and (2) does a basis exist for granting a remedy? If both of these contingencies are met, then the law creates a binding sales contract between the parties. As mentioned before, price need not be prearranged but can be set by the marketplace at the time of delivery or by a reasonable conclusion. Also, whereas common law contracts must be definite as to the subject matter, be it toothpicks or Tiffany lamps, sales contracts need not be so specific as to detail every characteristic of the item, such as quality or color. However, where these characteristics are bargained for and agreed upon, then, as will be seen, the terms of the contract must be met. Overall, as long as the two criteria listed above are satisfied, a contract is formed and the economy flows smoothly.

Offer and Acceptance

If you will recall the discussion in the introduction to contracts, perhaps the two basic elements of a contract, much like the subject and predicate of a sentence, are the *offer* and *acceptance*. The uniform sales statute in New York, known as the Uniform Commercial Code, or UCC, has had an impact on these two elements. First of all, the UCC has eliminated the common law distinction between *unilateral* and *bilateral* contracts and treats both equally. As always, the parties can agree otherwise, thus permitting acceptance by the offeree's performance or promise, but where the latter conditions are not stipulated in the offer, the two concepts are merged. At common law, a unilateral contract was consummated upon the offeree's performance. If X promised to pay Y $100 to climb to the top of the Eiffel Tower, Y, merely by reaching the top, completes performance and is entitled to X's $100. This result is so even though Y never communicated his intention to act or returned a promise to act. Since all that X bargained for was Y's performance, his reaching the summit binds X to his promise to pay.

This seems all well and good and certainly just, but the next logical question is for how long does X's promise remain alive. Can Y fail to communicate his plans to X, procrastinate for a fortnight, and then one evening, after mustering sufficient courage at the local bistro, stumble down to the Tower, heave himself to the top and claim his due? The answer, more likely than not, is no, judging from a standpoint of reasonableness. Under common law doctrines, an offer was only irrevocable if the offeree, in this case Y, paid consideration for the opportunity to delay his acceptance. Current law does not require the exchange of consideration if the offeror expresses in writing that his offer is irrevocable. The same rule applies if the *executory contract* is for the sale of goods, but is limited to offers from merchants and for a three-month period, unless a shorter duration is stated. If, on the other hand, the typical consumer extends an offer for goods, then the UCC resorts to common law rules, and the offer is irrevocable only if he receives consideration in exchange.

So much for offer, how does the UCC alter the element of acceptance? In general, the UCC changes the concept of acceptance in two ways. The first occurs in the situation where the offeree in his acceptance modifies the terms of the original offer. The common law answer was to declare the modified acceptance a counter offer. No contract was formed and the offeror had the opportunity to refuse the new terms or accept as modified. In order to free market dealings with goods, the UCC eliminated this problem, which could result in a tennis-like volley of counter offers without a contract being formed. As between the merchant and non-merchant situations were differentiated. In the case of one party being a non-merchant, the newly varied acceptance acted as an acceptance accompanied by an offer to the initial offeror on the modified or additional terms. The offeror could accept or reject these new terms as he pleased, but the contract was formed. If the parties were both merchants, then the return of an altered acceptance would act not only as an acceptance for the unchanged part of the offer, but would act as an acceptance for the altered terms as well. However, this law does not permit the offeree total leeway in modifying a contract offer and holding the offeror to different terms. The modified or additional terms became part of the contract, but only if the offer did not restrict acceptance to its original terms and the changes were not a *material* change in the original offer (in a common-sense application of the phrase). The offeror, within a reasonable time, had the right to reject the offeree's modifications.

The UCC also changed the New York common law rule on the method of acceptance. Outside of the UCC, the law required that strict formalities had to be followed. If **S** offered **T** by cablegram an opportunity to enter a contract, the mirror rule mandated that the acceptance could be communicated only by cablegram; the reasoning being that the offeror's selection of a particular medium suggested the medium through which he wished to be notified of the offeree's decision. Exhorting the reasonableness standard once again, the UCC permits any medium to be utilized if reasonable. Although the courts would have the final determination, a contract would be enforceable then if an offer sent via a homing pigeon were accepted and communicated by telegraph, but not so if in reverse.

Consideration

All contracts, whether or not covered by the UCC, must contain consideration, the offeree's exchange of a bargained-for detriment for the offeror's promise to act. In general, any rule applicable to contracts is viable for sales contracts. One change, however, allows for the modification of sales contracts without additional consideration. Unless the contract expresses otherwise or unless the contract falls within the purview of the Statute of Frauds, the modification need not even be in writing. In New York, other statutory provisions have eliminated the need for consideration in the typical contractual arrangement, but unlike the UCC, these provisions required a memo signed by the person against whom the change operates. Additionally, should any cause of action arise out of a breach of the contract, the UCC pre-exempts the common law pre-existing duty rule and allows for a written discharge of the claim without consideration. New York applies a similar law for non-sale contracts, but not all states have enacted the same provision.

Performance and Breach

Assuming that a contract has been duly arranged with the requisite elements of offer, acceptance and consideration, let us now look at differences in sales contracts under the UCC in regard to performance and breach. In any case, the contract will be considered satisfactorily completed as long as the substantial performance standard is met. The performing party need not comply with every detail of the agreement if the deviation from the terms of the contract does not impair the other party's position. This brings the concept of material breach into the discussion, for substantial performance and materiality of breach necessarily go hand in hand. Without the latter, the former occurs.

One factor in determining materiality, however, is whether the contract is one for goods. The UCC mandates that the tender of goods must be perfect. By this it is meant that the seller must deliver goods as specified. Partial delivery or a difference in quality or color from that specified is a breach of the contract. Since the seller retains possession of the goods until acceptance, the buyer simply rejects and then must hold and sell or return the goods to the seller. The perfect tender requirement arose because the seller was not subject to loss of his property. If, instead of a

T 1100—Bill of Sale, Short Form.

JULIUS BLUMBERG, INC., LAW BLANK PUBLISHERS
80 EXCHANGE PL. AT BROADWAY, N. Y. C. 10004

Know all Men by these Presents,

That

party of the first part, for and in consideration of the sum of

Dollars ($) lawful money

of the United States, to the party of the first part in hand paid, at or before the ensealing and delivery of these presents, by

party of the second part, the receipt whereof is hereby acknowledged, has bargained and sold, and by these present does grant and convey unto the said party of the second part, the heirs, executors, administrators, successors and assigns thereof.

To Have and to Hold the same unto the said party of the second part, the heirs, executors, administrators, successors and assigns thereof forever. And the party of the first part does covenant and agree to and with the said party of the second part, to **Warrant and Defend** the sale of the said goods and chattels hereby sold unto the said party of the second part, the heirs, executors, administrators, successors and assigns thereof, against all and every person and persons whomsoever.

Whenever the text hereof requires, the singular number used herein shall include the plural and all genders.

In Witness Whereof: the party of the first part has duly executed this bill of sale on the

day of   19

In Presence of

....(L. S.)

....(L. S.)

....(L. S.)

State of
County of
of

}ss.:

On this   day of   19   before me, the subscriber, personally

appeared

to me personally known and known to me to be the same person   described in and who executed the within Instrument,

and   he   acknowledged to me that   he   executed the same.

....

seller of goods, the promise was by a contractor who installed thousands of dollars of plumbing in an apartment complex, the loss of his property to the buyer because the pipe used was not the same as that agreed to, although comparable in quality, would result in unbearable financial hardship. Thus, in the instances of a construction contract (for a service), not under the UCC, there is no need for perfect tender, and the court would be less likely to conclude that the seller materially breached the contract.

In discussing contracts for the sale of realty, mention was made that time was not implied as being of the essence. The parties could agree that such was the case, but without an expressed provision in the contract, failure to cure a minor tax encumbrance on the day of sale would not defeat the contract. Under the UCC, time is always of the essence as an implication of law. If the parties select a specific day for completion of performance and the day passes without completion, the non-performing party is in breach.

Sometimes the buyer or seller need not wait for the day set for performance if it appears that the other party is not in a position to fulfill his commitment. This area of anticipatory breach was discussed in the introduction, but in a sales contract for goods, the UCC again imposes different rules. At common law, the issue of whether a party could hold the other in breach or suspend his own performance was conditioned upon the strength and merit of the information received. If it appeared, for example, that X would not perform, then Y could anticipate breach and hold X liable. But if it appeared that X could not perform, even though he attempted to, then Y could assume a failure of performance and withhold his own. Under the UCC, Y cannot suspend his own performance until he demands assurances from X that the latter's performance will be forthcoming. If written assurances are received within 30 days, then Y must continue fulfilling his bargain. When 30 days expires

without receipt of assurances on X's part, then Y can consider X in repudiation of the contract. Once Y does so and notifies X, or materially alters his own position (another common sense judgment), X cannot make demands by retracting the repudiation. Along these lines, Y cannot escape responsibility under the contract for such reasons as impracticality or impossibility of complying with the agreed mode of delivery. The UCC recognizes both of these impediments, but requires a drastic event to occur to invoke the doctrine of impracticality (e.g., war), and allows a reasonable substituted form of delivery if reasonable (e.g., tractor-trailer instead of freight train).

Assuming no premature breach, both parties have obligations which they must meet in order to demand return performance by, or seek UCC remedies against the other. The seller's duties vary upon whether the goods are to be delivered by a carrier or tendered at the seller's place of business. In the first situation, the contract must be looked to in order to determine if the parties contracted for the delivery of the purchased goods at the buyer's place of business or at his home. In the absence of an expressed provision, the seller need only deliver the goods to a local carrier and notify the buyer, sending him whatever carrier papers he might need to assume possession. As long as the seller acts reasonably, he will not violate the contract or the law. If delivery to the buyer is a condition of the contract, the seller must satisfy all conditions inherent in the mode of delivery. Typically, delivery contracts call for F.O.B. (free on board) or F.A.S. (free alongside delivery). F.O.B. or F.A.S. contracts can also be used both where the seller need bear the risk only until the carrier takes possession and where the seller remains liable until the goods reach their destination.

Once the seller places conforming goods at the site agreed upon by the parties, the buyer has the next move; he must pay for the goods in cash (check is considered legal tender, although possession does not transfer until the check clears) unless the contract extends credit. Again there is a distinction between carrier and non-carrier cases, but basically the buyer's duty is simply to pay when he receives the goods.

To protect the buyer, however, the UCC grants him the right to examine the goods before transfer of payment. As long as the contract does not restrict this right of inspection, the buyer can reject the goods by withholding acceptance even after delivery to him. The easiest way for the seller to curtail the right to inspect is by shipping C.O.D., thus forcing the buyer to make payment before he can examine the goods. The buyer should remember, however, that if a defect is obvious, he can reject the shipment regardless of his right to inspect.

Risk of Loss

Before discussing seller and buyer remedies, a brief note should be inserted on risk of loss. It is always possible, particularly where goods are shipped by carrier, that an unforeseen catastrophe could result in damage to or loss of the goods. In that event, one party must shoulder the financial onus of the loss. In determining which party must bear the burden, the concept of *risk of loss* has replaced that of *passage of title*.

The central factor in risk of loss is that of breach; where risk of loss might have passed from seller to buyer if the seller had fully met his obligation in tendering conforming goods, a breach on his part will hold him liable until the buyer accepts in spite of the breach or until he cures. The appropriate provision in the contract and the status of the seller also are determining factors. If the seller is a merchant, as in a retail situation, the buyer does not become liable until he assumes possession. He can purchase the goods, paying cash,

but if they are damaged before he picks them up, the seller suffers tne loss. In a non-merchant sale of goods, such as when two friends transact a sale, the selling party need only tender the goods to the buyer in order to shift the risk of loss to him. Carrier cases pose different problems, but the basic rule is that risk of loss passes when the seller places the goods at the buyer's disposal, in compliance with the contractual terms. For example, if the contract called for F.O.B. at buyer's place of business, the seller would remain liable for the goods during transit. As mentioned, breach can alter the result. Thus, if in the above example, the contract authorized F.O.B. seller's place of business, so that normally the buyer would hold the risk of loss during the shipment, the seller remains responsible throughout until he cures the defect or the buyer accepts. In the event that the buyer is the breaching culprit, then the reverse holds true. He becomes liable once the seller earmarks or identifies the goods and ships them, even though under the usual rules the risk of loss had not yet shifted to him.

Statute of Frauds

Contracts of sale are governed by a specific Statute of Frauds provision under the UCC. Briefly, it provides that the only time a transaction is required to be in writing is if the sale equals or exceeds $500. Without an acceptable writing, the contract is unenforceable. Normally, the writing must be concurrent with the contract. However, as between merchants, the UCC relaxes the law. If a writing follows an oral agreement, it satisfies the Statute of Frauds and binds the parties to its terms, unless the recipient objects within ten days.

The requirements of the writing are lenient. Terms can be incorrect or omitted and the writing still will suffice, as long as the party to be charged signs it. The one limitation is that the quantity of goods needs to be stated and the parties should realize that the contract is enforceable only up to the quantity set out in the writing.

As with all laws, there are certain exceptions. If the contract is for specially manufactured goods which are not suitable to anyone other than the buyer, if the contract is admitted to in open court or if performance is consummated, then the contract is enforceable without a writing.

Parol Evidence Rule

The parol evidence rule, likewise, is expressly provided for in the UCC. As before, if the writing is intended to be the final statement of the agreement, then neither party can introduce evidence of prior or contemporaneous oral agreements contrary to terms in the written contract. However, the Code does allow the introduction of such evidence in certain instances.

The course of dealings between the parties and common trade usage can be offered in explanation of contractual terms. This can be done even if the writing is not ambiguous. Furthermore, the parties can supplement the contract with additional terms. However, the contract cannot be complete, and the additional terms must be consistent with the writing.

Products Liability

It would be presumptuous to attempt to explain the rapidly evolving law of negligence and strict tort products liability. We should explain, however, that case law in many states is expanding the opportunities under which an injured consumer of a defective or dangerous product can recover against the seller or manufacturer of a latently defective product. The manufacturer or seller is liable to an injured party (any foreseeable party, which includes a consumer or a third party) if his lack of reasonable care caused the defect, a danger was foreseeable and the particular defect was the proximate cause of the injury. In fact, the injured party can sue not only the manufacturer of the product but anyone in the chain of distribution—e.g., middleman and retailer.

In some instances, however, the injured party need not prove that the manufacturer was negligent if he can prove that the product itself was unreasonably dangerous. Strict tort liability discards *privity of contract* and extends warranty theory to every party who might foreseeably be injured. The reasoning behind the theory is that the warranties of merchantability and fitness (to be discussed) of use are breached if an unreasonably dangerous product is manufactured. The producer cannot disclaim liability or use the defense of contributory negligence which is available to him in negligence. As in a negligence action, the injured party can sue anyone along the distributive chain.

This topic is mentioned only to alert the reader to possible actions he might have in case of injury from a defective product. Because of constant changes in product tort liability, an injured person should consult an attorney to be informed of his rights.

Warranties

Suppose that, in the hypothetical purchase situation, Henry's lamp failed to work after a short period of time. In disgust, Henry would most likely return to the store and demand repair, replacement or recompense. But suppose that the store refused to satisfy Henry's claim and flatly stated that it was its policy not to stand behind its products. In short, Henry is informed that he has been taken.

W 310—Bill of Sale for Motor Vehicle, Airplane, etc., with Affidavit. (Individual or Corporation.)

COPYRIGHT 1969 BY JULIUS BLUMBERG, INC., LAW BLANK PUBLISHERS
80 EXCHANGE PLACE AT BROADWAY, NEW YORK

Know all Men by these Presents,

That
the Seller,

whose address is

for and in consideration of the sum of $ paid by

the Buyer, whose address is

have bargained, sold, granted and conveyed and by these presents do bargain, sell, grant and convey unto the Buyer, and Buyer's successors (heirs, executors, administrators) and assigns, one

Model   Factory No.   Motor No.

To Have and to Hold the same unto the Buyer and Buyer's successors (heirs, executors, administrators) and assigns forever, and the Seller covenants and agrees to warrant and defend the said described motor vehicle hereby sold against all and every person or persons whomsoever.

☐ The motor vehicle purports to have been operated, as appears by the odometer,   miles.

☐ The Seller knows that the mileage indicated on the odometer is beyond its designed mechanical limits; the true cumulative mileage is   miles.

☐ The odometer mileage is known to the Seller to be less than the motor vehicle has travelled; the true mileage is unknown.

The Seller also certifies that the Seller owned the vehicle since   19

until the date of this Bill of Sale.

In Witness Whereof, the Seller has set his hand and seal or caused these presents to be signed by its proper corporate officers and caused its proper corporate seal to be hereto affixed, the

day of   19

Signed, Sealed and Delivered
in the Presence of

....
Seller

ASSIGNMENT OF BILL OF SALE BY INDIVIDUAL

I,   of the

, County of   , and State of

for and in consideration of the sum of $ to me in hand paid do hereby sell, assigns,

transfer and set over unto   of
(city or town)

County of   and State of   the motor vehicle

described in the attached Bill of Sale.

IN WITNESS WHEREOF, I have hereunto set my hand and seal this

day of   , 19

WITNESSES

....

....

185

ASSIGNMENT OF BILL OF SALE BY INDIVIDUAL

I,   of the

          , County of   , and State of

for and in consideration of the sum of $ to me in hand paid do hereby sell, assigns,

transfer and set over unto   of

                                                                    (city or town)

County of   and State of   the motor vehicle

described in the attached Bill of Sale.

    IN WITNESS WHEREOF, I have hereunto set my hand and seal this

day of   , 19

WITNESSES

....

....

ASSIGNMENT OF BILL OF SALE BY CORPORATION

                                                                    a corporation of the State of

(name of corporation)

                    for and in consideration of the sum of $ to it in hand

paid does hereby sell, assign, transfer and set over unto

of

the motor vehicle described in the attached Bill of Sale.

    IN WITNESS WHEREOF, the said corporation has caused these presents to be signed by its

president, attested by its secretary and its corporate seal affixed hereto the   day of

                    , 19

Attest:

....

           Secretary   Corporate Name

                                  -...

                                             President

STATE OF   } ss.:
COUNTY OF   }

                    being duly sworn, deposes and says, that he resides at

    That he is the same person who executed the within bill of sale.

    That he is the sole and absolute owner of the property described in said bill of sale, and has full

right to sell and transfer the same.

    That the said property, and each and every part thereof, is free and clear of any liens, mortgages,

debts or other incumbrances of whatsoever kind and nature, except

    That there are no judgments existing against him, in any Court, nor are there any replevins, attach-

ments or executions issued against him now in force; nor has any petition in bankruptcy been filed by or

against him.

    That this affidavit is made for the purpose and with the intent of inducing

to purchase the property described in said bill of sale, knowing that he will rely thereon and pay a good

and valuable consideration therefor.

Sworn to before me this

    day of   19   }   ....

....

           Notary Public

STATE OF
COUNTY OF   } *ss.:*

, being duly sworn deposes and says:

     That he is   *of*
a corporation organized under the Laws of the State of   *, and having its*
principal office at

     That the corporation is now the sole owner of the property described in the foregoing bill of sale.

     That your deponent states that there are no mortgages, liens, conditional sales agreement or other encumbrances of whatever nature or description affecting the property herein sold and that it is absolutely free and clear thereof, except

     That there are no actions pending against the corporation in any court; nor are there any replevins, judgments or executions outstanding against the corporation now in force; nor has any petition in bankruptcy been filed by or against the corporation.

     That this affidavit is made for the express purpose and with the intent of inducing

to purchase the property set forth and described in the foregoing bill of sale, knowing full well that
    h   will rely upon this affidavit and pay a good and valuable consideration.

   Sworn to before me this
        } ....

      day of   *19*

....
        Notary Public

State of
County of   } *ss.:*

     On the   *day of*   *, nineteen hundred and*
before me came   *to me known, who,*
being by me duly sworn, did depose and say that   *he resides in*

that   *he is the*   *of*

the corporation described in, and which executed the foregoing Bill of Sale; that   *he knows the seal of said corporation; that the seal affixed to said Bill of Sale is such corporate seal; that it was so affixed by the order of the board of*   *of said corporation; and that*   *he signed*
h   *name thereto by like order.*

State of
County of   } *ss.:*

     On the   *day of*   *in the year one*
thousand nine hundred and   *before me personally came*

to me known, and known to me to be the individual   *described in, and who executed the foregoing*
Bill of Sale, and   *acknowledged to me that*   *he executed the same.*

The reader may feel that Henry has no recourse, except to refrain from further patronization of the store. He had received no verbal assurances or written guarantees and seemingly has no viable cause of action. However, this is not true, for the authors of the UCC included within its provisions implied warranties which every merchant or seller makes to the consumer. Unless these warranties are disclaimed in ways defined by statute, they operate to hold the seller liable for failure of the product.

The warranty of merchantability is implied in every merchant sale so as to protect the consumer against problems such as those incurred by Henry. Several criteria exist in explanation of merchantability, but it can be simply stated: the goods must do that which they are supposed to do. If Henry bought the lamp for lighting, then light it must; similarly a toaster must toast and a vacuum cleaner must clean by vacuuming. Goods must be "fit for the ordinary purposes for which such goods are used." The statutory warranty further contains requirements that packaging and labeling must meet contractual terms (in a merchant situation); substitute goods must be acceptable as like goods in the trade; goods must not vary considerably within prescribed units and must not differ from promises expressed on the label.

Although all goods under the UCC carry the implied warranty of merchantability, a buyer must be cautious that the merchant has not disclaimed his liability. To accomplish this end, the merchant must meet two statutory requirements; first he must specifically mention the term merchantability, and secondly, if the disclaimer is in writing (an oral disclaimer is effective), it must be conspicuous. The buyer also can lose the warranty by examining and failing to object to faults or by refusing to inspect the goods. If the defects are ones that would be uncovered by such inspection, the warranty is waived as of then. The warranty is also disclaimed by language stating that the buyer is taking the goods "as is" or "with faults."

In certain situations, a seller, whether a merchant or not, extends an additional warranty, one of fitness. In contrast with the generic warranty of merchantability, the warranty of fitness applies to a specific purpose. To exist, the seller must be aware of a particular or special need of the buyer, and in return, the buyer must purchase the goods in reliance on the seller's affirmations. Again, in the hypothetical case of Henry and the lamp, if Henry needed a lamp capable of functioning with a 500-watt light bulb for prolonged periods, the warranty for fitness for a particular purpose would attach if Henry explained his need to the seller and bought a lamp which the seller selected for him.

The seller can likewise disclaim this warranty, but unlike the disclaimer of merchantability, he must do so in writing and it must be conspicuous. The disclaimer need not make a direct reference to the warranty, and thus, it can be stated in general terms. Identical with the warranty of merchantability, the implied warranty of fitness is defeated in those situations of buyer inspections or when expressions are included that the goods are taken "as is."

In addition, a seller may pass on to buyer any other warranty which he expressly makes, either orally or in writing. The buyer must prove that he could have relied on the seller's statements in purchasing the goods. However, if the buyer in fact does not rely on his statement, the warranty does not apply. Additionally, the seller cannot make an expressed warranty and attempt to negate its effectiveness by conduct or statements that are unreasonably contradictory.

The next question any buyer logically asks is: What is the impact of a breach of a warranty? The UCC expressly provides for the recovery of consequential damages as the result of a breach of warranty when no disclaimer exists, or if it does, is ineffective.

Basically consequential damages include losses arising from failure of the goods to meet a buyer's requirements of which the seller was aware and personal injury or property damages which proximately result. To avoid the burden of such extensive damages, sellers frequently attempt to restrict their liability or to provide for liquidated damages. These limitations are permissible unless they prove to be *unconscionable*, in which case the limitations will not be enforced by the courts. In one specific situation, the restriction is presumed to be unconscionable: A seller of consumer goods cannot waive liability for personal injury to the buyer or third parties who reasonably come into contact with the goods. However, there is no presumption of unconscionability of a limitation of commercial loss. Thus, parties can prearrange a fixed schedule of damages for failure of goods if it applies to such items as lost profits.

Remedies

Besides breaching warranties, a defaulting party can find himself in breach of the contract. When such a breach occurs, the other party naturally wishes to make himself whole by seeking and procuring one of the several remedies available to him under the UCC.

Which options are open to either the seller or the buyer is contingent upon whether or not the buyer has formally accepted the goods. From the perspective of both parties, one option has been discussed earlier in this chapter. Where the buyer or seller, through actions or words, casts doubt on his performance, the other may demand written assurances and suspend his own performance until the assurances are received. Unlike contract law, repudiation is not immediate in a case of anticipatory breach; however, if the assurances are not forthcoming within 30 days, the aggrieved party may then treat the contract as breached. If the conduct or words of the defaulting party do more than cast doubt—that is, make it certain that he will not perform, then the contract can be considered breached as of that time and the wronged party can pursue any remedy he wishes without requesting assurances.

Seller Remedies

The remaining remedies, which come into play only after one party has in fact failed on his promise, are particular to one party or the other. Since the reader is more frequently in the buyer's position, the seller's remedies will be discussed only briefly. Before the buyer has accepted and come into possession of the goods, the seller can usually recover his goods. If they are in transit, for example, he can halt delivery by so ordering the carrier or the holder (such as a warehouseman) of the goods. He has this right up until the time that whoever has the goods notifies the buyer that they are being held for him or until the buyer receives a negotiable bill of sale. These rights belong to the seller and are not a breach on his part where the buyer breaches (such as in *anticipatory breach* or by failure to pay) or becomes insolvent. Once the buyer receives the goods the seller may still (1) recover the goods within ten days if he discovers that the buyer is insolvent, (2) or at any time if the buyer is insolvent and has also led the seller to believe otherwise.

Of course, in most instances, the seller does not want to recover his goods as much as he wants to receive his money. The question of damages is complicated and turns on the specific facts of the case. In general, the seller can demand the buyer to take the goods and pay the contract price, only if the risk of loss has shifted to the buyer and the goods are lost, ruined or if the seller cannot find another ready buyer. If those situations do not exist, the seller has an option between three different measures: he can select *cover*, a UCC remedy, which is the difference between the price set in the contract and the price that the seller was able to obtain for the goods in a subsequent sale; or *common law damages*, which is the difference between the contract price and the market price (or going rate of same or similar goods); and finally, if neither of these two measures makes the seller whole, then lost profits. The last measure is based primarily on the seller's cost as offset against the agreed-upon price. The seller also must take into account specific selling expenses which were eliminated since the sale fell through. At no time must he further decrease his recovery by subtracting whatever general overhead costs are attributable to the goods covered by the breached contract. Other expenses which the seller incurred because the buyer breached his obligations can be tacked on to the final damages.

Buyer's Remedies

Most people, however, are usually in the shoes of the buyer. Therefore, it would be more worthwhile and rewarding to examine the buyer's remedies in depth. Perhaps the best approach would be to review the law and then list its practicalities to the buyer-consumer.

Once again, acceptance is the crucial element in determining the remedies available to the buyer. Under the UCC, the buyer has the right of rejecting nonconforming goods prior to acceptance and a right of revocation after acceptance. In the latter situation, the right is qualified, it being required that the defect substantially impairs the value of the goods to the buyer. What constitutes acceptance? For the most part, the buyer is not deemed to have accepted tendered goods unless he (1) notifies the seller that all is well or that he will keep the goods despite defects (as will be seen, he can still seek damages for the defects); (2) exercises acts of ownership adverse to that of

the seller; or (3) delays in rejecting defective goods. Acceptance can occur, in other words, either expressly through actual notification to the seller of the buyer's intent or impliedly by the buyer's failure to reject effectively (as evidenced by conduct inconsistent with the seller's ownership or retention of the goods). Up until the occurrence of any of these events, the buyer retains the right to reject nonconforming goods.

Acceptance, however, is conditioned on the buyer's right of inspection. Where the buyer has not had a reasonable opportunity to inspect the goods, his acts, which normally would be acceptance on his part, are negated. Thus, even a buyer who tells the seller, "Yes, I will take these goods," and who tenders payment, has not formally accepted the goods under the UCC. Upon later inspection and discovery of the defects or nonconformities, the buyer can reject and seek all available remedies.

Assuming that the buyer has not accepted, when and how can he reject the seller's goods? Basically, whenever the seller fails to meet the *perfect tender rule* under the UCC, the buyer can elect between either rejection or acceptance, in whole or in part. (The buyer should remember that whenever he rejects, accepts or revokes acceptance, he retains all his other remedies against the seller for breach of the contract.) Rejection, however, must be within a reasonable time after the buyer has had his opportunity to inspect. The seller also cannot unconscionably shorten this period of rejection by a provision in the sales contract. For the most part, the right to reject arises where the goods are not personally satisfactory to the buyer.

The buyer rejects by taking affirmative action. The UCC calls for the seller to be seasonably notified by the buyer. In addition, the buyer must particularize any and all defects determinable by reasonable inspection on which he bases his rejection. This requirement is highly important for the buyer,

T 1103—Bill of Sale of Boat

JULIUS BLUMBERG, INC., LAW BLANK PUBLISHERS
80 EXCHANGE PLACE AT BROADWAY, NEW YORK

𝔎now all 𝔐en by these 𝔓resents,

THAT   as Seller,

·of   County of

State of   for and in consideration of the sum of $ paid by

                                         as Buyer,

residing at   County of

State of   has bargained, sold, granted and conveyed and by these presents does bargain, sell, grant and convey unto the said Buyer and the Buyer's successors (heirs, executors, administrators) and assigns, the Boat hereinafter described.

YEAR BUILT	MAKE AND MODEL	NEW OR USED	LENGTH OVERALL	MAKE AND H.P. OF ENGINE(S)	ENGINE(S) NUMBER(S)	NAME OF BOAT AND REGISTRATION NUMBER

List extra equipment.

TO HAVE AND TO HOLD the same unto the said Buyer and the Buyer's successors (heirs, executors, administrators) and assigns forever; and the Seller covenants and agrees to and with the said Buyer to warrant and defend the said described Boat against all and every person or persons whomsoever.

IN WITNESS WHEREOF, the Seller has set his hand and seal or caused these presents to be signed by its proper corporate officers and caused its proper corporate seal to be hereto affixed, the day of   19

Signed, Sealed and Delivered
in the Presence of   }

....

....

STATE OF   } ss.:
COUNTY OF

   On the   day of   19
before me, the subscriber, personally appeared

to me known, who, being by me duly sworn, did depose
and say that   he resides at

that   he is the
of
the corporation described in and which executed, the foregoing Bill of Sale; that   he knows the seal of said corporation; that the seal affixed to said instrument is such
corporate seal; that it was so affixed by order of the
Board of Directors of said corporation; that   he signed
h   name thereto by like order.

STATE OF   } ss.:
COUNTY OF

   On the   day of   19
before me, the subscriber, personally appeared

to me known to be the individual   described in, and who
executed the foregoing Bill of Sale, and acknowledged
that   he executed the same.

ASSIGNMENT OF BILL OF SALE

    I, ...

of ....

County of .... and State of .... for and in consideration

of the sum of $ .... to me in hand paid, hereby sell, assign, transfer and set over unto

....

of .... County of ....

State of .... the said Boat described in the attached Bill of Sale.

    IN WITNESS WHEREOF, I have hereunto set my hand and seal this ....

day of .... 19 ....

Witness:

....

....

because if he fails to state the grounds for his rejection, he waives his right to justify his rejection on those bases. Since the seller has a right to cure the defects in the goods, the buyer cannot defeat this right by misleading or withholding information from the seller. As between merchants, a merchant-buyer must be more specific in listing his objections to nonconforming goods, but only after the seller requests such specifications in writing. In all arrangements, the buyer does not waive his right to base rejection or an action for breach on a defect which he cannot ascertain through reasonable inspection.

After rejection, the UCC imposes certain duties upon the buyer in his handling of the goods. Since the buyer rejected, the seller still owns the goods, and thus the buyer must take reasonable care of them until the seller can effect reacquisition. The UCC again differentiates between consumers and merchant-buyers, thrusting the greater duty upon merchant-buyers. The typical consumer is cast in a role of a bailee or custodian, but otherwise has no duty to return the goods. The merchant-buyer likewise has no duty to return the goods, but he must comply with reasonable instructions sent to him by the seller if the seller has no local agent. If the seller does not advise the buyer how to handle the goods, the buyer can return, sell, or store them as long as his actions are reasonable. The buyer has a security interest in the goods and can enforce that interest to recover expenses and costs incurred in dealing with justifiably rejected goods.

Assuming that, after inspecting the goods, the buyer accepts, either expressly or impliedly, what is his position? Immediately upon acceptance, the buyer is bound to pay the seller the agreed upon price. He can no longer reject the goods per se, since he has already accepted, but rather must move under rules for revocation of acceptance if he is not satisfied. If, after acceptance, the buyer is unable to revoke or does not wish to revoke, he is not precluded from asserting claims for breach of the contract or expressed or implied warranties. The mere acceptance, in other words, does not signify that the seller has satisfied all his obligations and that no breach has occurred. The buyer is only precluded from objecting to those defects of which he knew or should have known (opportunity to inspect) when he accepted the goods. However, where the defect is latent or the seller procured the buyer's acceptance by assuring him that the defects would be cured, the buyer retains his right to assert those claims.

To assert any claim, the buyer must notify the seller of breach within a reasonable time, although such notice is not applicable where the buyer's claim is based on a tort theory, (i.e., negligence or strict tort products liability). As with notification of defects under rejection, failure to notify the seller of breaches bars the buyer from recovering on those particular claims. If the seller sues the buyer, for example, to recover the purchase price, the buyer can then assert his claim for breach against the seller.

Unable to reject because he has already accepted, the buyer does have a right, although not absolute, to revoke his acceptance. In order to revoke justifiably, the buyer must show that his value in the goods was substantially impaired by a nonconformity. In addition, he must show that he had no knowledge of the defect of which he complains, unless, as mentioned earlier, the seller coaxed his acceptance through assurances that the problem would be cured. Thus, he cannot revoke if he fails to inspect the goods, and the defect is one which would have been ascertained upon such inspection. In addition, he cannot revoke if he accepts knowing of the defect and without being assured by the seller that the defect will be cured. Finally, and perhaps most importantly to both parties, the buyer cannot revoke if the seller in fact cures the problem within a reasonable time.

For the revocation to be effective, the buyer must notify the seller within a reasonable time after he discovers, or should have discovered, the defect. Mere suspicion does not require the buyer to act. Also the buyer can effectuate the revocation without returning the goods to the seller. In fact, the buyer possesses a security interest in the goods as he does under rejection, and thus he can retain the goods in order to assure enforcement without endangering his right to revoke. The buyer, however, should be careful not to use the goods or act in any way inconsistent with the seller's ownership, or he may be barred from revoking his acceptance.

The next question which must be asked is, what are the remedies which the buyer can seek when an incurable breach occurs? The buyer's remedies are the same whether the seller fails to deliver or repudiates, or whether the buyer rightfully rejects or revokes acceptance. The buyer is in an enviable position, for he has several options available to him which he can select concurrently. First, the buyer may cancel the contract upon notification to the seller. Unlike rejection or revocation, such action terminates the underlying contract. Whether the buyer cancels or not, he is entitled to recover any part of the purchase price which he has paid and money damages for the seller's breach. Secondly, where the breach is repudiation or nondelivery, the buyer may also obtain a court decree for specific performance if the goods are unique or *replevin* if the goods are identified and *cover* (or replacement) cannot be procured. In essence, this means that because he needs the goods, the buyer wants to keep the contract in force and compel the seller to make delivery. In the situation where the buyer is in possession and has justifiably rejected or revoked, he has a security interest and can recover his costs and expenses. If the seller refuses to reimburse him for these incurred costs, the buyer can resell the goods to enforce his interest.

Two different measures of damages are set out in the UCC for such situations. The first measure is based on the cost of replacement goods or "cover." The buyer's efforts to obtain cover must occur within a reasonable time and must be in good faith. Once the cost of cover is ascertained, the buyer's damages are the difference between it and the contract price. Thus, if the contract called for a price of $100 and an adequate substitute cost $105, the damages would amount to $5.00. The second measure does not require any positive action on the buyer's part and is the difference between the *going market price* as of the time of discovery of the breach and the *contract price*. Again, as a reminder, these measures are optional, and so the buyer should determine which affords him the greatest recovery before electing. In addition, the buyer also may recover any incidental or consequential damages as explained under seller's damages.

Where the buyer has accepted the goods and cannot rightfully revoke, his remedy is different. Upon the seller's breach of warranty or his failure to satisfy all of his obligations, the buyer cannot cancel the contract, but can collect damages, if he gives the seller reasonable notice of the problem. In a nonconformity situation, these damages amount to the loss sustained in the ordinary course of events, plus all incidental and consequential damages allowed under the UCC. Where the seller breaches either an expressed or implied warranty, the buyer can recover the difference in the value of the goods as they should have been (if properly tendered) and as they were when delivered (price based on the time and place of acceptance), and again incidental and consequential damages. These measurements do not bar a higher recovery if in fact the buyer's loss was greater and the seller had been informed of the possibility at the formation of the contract. The buyer, however, cannot increase his recovery by using goods which he realizes are defective and thereby incurring further personal injuries or property damages.

Bills of Sale

This section contains no forms other than three special bills of sale. Although it applies to all purchases, whether goods or realty, the bill of sale is inserted here for the sake of convenience. Because many sales transactions include the transfer of a bill of sale, we should briefly explain the document, its requisites and effects.

The primary function of a bill of sale is to evidence a transfer of title. The document itself does not necessarily create immediate rights in the buyer. But neither does its absence defeat the buyer's title, once certain conditions have been met. Ostensibly, the bill of sale is not essential to the transfer of property. In the case of goods, for example, once the buyer accepts the seller's goods, he becomes the owner of the goods, whether or not a bill of sale is delivered to him. The only time that a bill of sale is mandatory is when both parties contract to provide for its execution and delivery, or when statutory law requires a bill of sale.

If a bill of sale is not essential, then why use one? Just as a diploma is not an essential part of a college education, it nevertheless serves its function in representing and evidencing a person's qualifications. In like manner, a bill of sale aids in establishing rights in property by depicting the transfer of ownership. The bill of sale is a tangible symbol of the intentions of two persons to transfer title in a property or quantity of goods.

What are the requisites of a bill of sale? Like a contract, it must be grounded in good *consideration*. The property involved should be adequately identified so as to avoid later problems. When items such as taxi cabs, boats, planes, etc., are being transferred, registration numbers should be included in the description, along with color, make, model and other details.

The bill of sale must also state a present intent to transfer. It need not affirm delivery of the item. Delivery can be made at a preceding or succeeding time. The bill of sale must be duly executed; this includes signing by the transferor and delivery of the document to the transferee. As a rule, the bill of sale accomplishes whatever the parties intend, since their intentions prevail.

In conclusion, usually a sale is covered by more than one document—a bill of sale and a *contract for sale*. Each has its own particular features and final results. The parties should note, however, that whereas a bill of sale is executed *after* the contract for sale, if the former is to be controlling, it should cover all matter and terms of the contract. Otherwise, for provisions not covered, the contract for sale remains effective and enforceable.

Commentary

So what does all this legalese mean to the consumer? Returning to the hypothetical case of Henry, who purchases a lamp from a retail store and back home discovers its defects, there are certain actions that Henry can pursue and certain dangers which he should be alerted to from the start. It might be helpful to list some of these rights, some hints and some possible pitfalls:

(1) If there is a sales contract, read it carefully. Beware of provisions which (a) limit remedies or (b) change the measure of damages allowed by law. Such restrictions are permissible as long as they offer a reasonable remedy; such as liquidated damages. Parties can contract as they wish, and the buyer might unknowingly agree to a set sum, in case of damages. Again, these liquidated damages must not violate the rules of reasonability or conscionability.

(2) Remember that the consumer always has a right to inspect the goods before acceptance.

(3) If possible, always inspect and never accept goods which are known to be defective, unless the seller's assurances of cure are in writing.

(4) Remember that revocation of acceptance is unavailable for nonconforming goods known to the buyer at the time of acceptance; therefore, failure to inspect where the opportunity is present can lead to waiver of warranties.

(5) Signs of statements by sales personnel can lead to the conclusion that the consumer has been advised of his rights of inspection and has had his opportunity. In fact, without ever examining the goods (they could still be sealed in the box), the buyer could be deemed to have inspected and to have accepted the merchandise.

(6) If the goods are nonconforming or if a breach of warranty occurs, be sure to notify the seller as soon as possible.

(7) Always remember that although the law protects the buyer with implied warranties, it also makes provision for warranty disclaimer. The buyer should be wary not to waive any of his rights by accepting goods on which the warranties have been disclaimed. Avoid purchases which are labeled "as is" or "with all faults."

(8) Where goods are defective, return them to the store and ask for cure or an adjustment. Remember that the seller has a right to make a curative tender within a reasonable time. Other damages for breach are not available to the buyer until the seller fails to cure.

(9) Remember that if the seller does offer a curative tender, a consumer who improperly refuses to accept it (whether repair, replacement or credit) is not entitled to damages for breach of contract.

(10) If the consumer has made a down payment and attempts to get out of the contract, he has a right to the return of any amount exceeding 20% of the purchase price, or $500, whichever is smaller. Seller is allowed to deduct from the excess the cost of any benefit bestowed upon the consumer or any damages which he incurs as a result of the breach.

(11) If damages are incurred, the buyer has options with the measure of damages. Make the most of the election.

(12) Overall, the UCC is couched in terms of good faith and reasonability. It is its general policy not to grant absolute rights to either party. Thus, where one party reserves an absolute right which seems oppressive and unreasonable, instead of being cowed, seek legal counsel in order to be advised fully of your rights.

(13) Always act in good faith.

CHAPTER 9

Buying On Credit

Introduction

In this day and age, economic stability seems to be a major concern of most people. Many of us are walking in a daze resulting from high prices and no money. The dollar that purchased a sandwich and beer a couple of years ago entitles you to only the beer today. What is the solution? There might be many answers to the prevailing cash shortage which plagues everyone, but two of the more frequently used and least understood vehicles which manufacture instant cash are the credit card and the retail installment agreement.

Many of the people who use these methods of payment do not fully understand the contractual ramifications of these transactions. What they do know is that they want a television and do not have the money to purchase it. The solution is to buy it with plastic money—the credit card; or if the person does not have one, the retailer will gladly suggest that he can pay for the television on time. Why not, the consumer reasons. Pay $50.00 down and $25.00 monthly for three years. Who thinks even of one year from now, much less three years? Out comes an agreement, the signatures are scribed, and suddenly potential problems loom.

Like many contractual situations, entering into a credit agreement is much easier than

getting out of it. The beautiful television set appears to be there for the taking; the dotted line invites the signature; and, what the hell, economic times are bound to get better. This logic is normal and, as a result, most people frequently engage in this type of contractual credit agreement. This section is not intended to discourage the use of credit cards and retail installment agreements. If understood and used properly, both are an effective means by which one can purchase goods. Our main concern is to present the consumer with a guide explaining his rights and obligations under such agreements. Three statutes will be examined:

(1) Article 10 of New York Personal Property Law, § 401–419 (Retail Installment Agreements)

(2) Public Law 30–321, 82 Stat 146, 15USC § 1601–1681 (Consumer Credit Protection Act)

(3) Public Law 93–495, 88 Stat 1500, Title 111, § 301, effective October, 1975 (The Depository Institution Act)

Article 10 of the Personal Property Law is applicable to New York State only. The other two statutes are federal law, and therefore are applicable on a national basis. Not every section of the three statutes will be discussed. Instead, they will be interwoven to allow the consumer to understand their basic tenor. When discussing Article 10, it will be cited as such, so that the reader will know it is applicable only to New York State.

Definitions

A model Retail Installment Agreement and credit card applications abound with references to terms to which the consumer agrees when he signs. (Hopefully, the next time he sees that television on sale—and they are always on sale—and temptation is overwhelming the will, he will hesitate for a moment and think about the headaches he might be purchasing along with that television.) Where necessary, the statute will be quoted with the code cites for future reference. The following are some basic definitions which apply to all consumer credit transactions. 15 U.S.C. 1602 (Consumer Credit Protection Act) defines certain terms as follows:

"(e)   The term 'credit' means the right granted by a creditor to a debtor to defer payment of debt or to insure debt and defer its payment.

(f)   The term 'creditor' refers only to creditors who regularly extend, or arrange for the extension of credit which is payable by agreement in more than four installments or for which the payment of a finance charge is or may be required, whether in connection with loans, sales of property or services, or otherwise . . . the term 'creditor' shall also include card issuers whether or not the amount due is payable by agreement in more than four installments or the payment of a finance charge is or may

be required . . . ." (This is an amendment, enacted by Public Law 93–495, 88 Stat 1500, Title 111, § 303.)

(g)   The term 'credit sale' refers to any sale with respect to which credit is extended or arranged by the seller . . .

(h)   The adjective 'consumer,' used with reference to a credit transaction, characterizes the transaction as one in which the party to whom credit is offered or extended is a natural person, and the money, property, or services which are the subject of the transaction are primarily for personal, family, household, or agricultural purposes.

(i)   The term 'open end credit plan' refers to a plan prescribing the terms of credit transactions which may be thereunder from time to time and under the terms of which a finance charge may be computed on the outstanding unpaid balance from time to time thereunder. (Credit cards or open end credit plans.)

(k)   The term 'credit card' means any card, plate, coupon book, or other credit device existing for the purpose of obtaining money, property, labor, or services on credit.

(m)   The term 'cardholder' means any person to whom a credit card is issued or any person who has agreed with the card issuer to pay obligations arising from the issuance of a credit card to another person.

(o)   The term 'unauthorized user,' as used in § 7644 of the title, means a use of a credit card by a person other than the card holder and who does not have actual, implied, or apparent authority for such use and from which the cardholder receives no benefit. (E.g., a person's wife is considered to have apparent authority if she does not have actual authority.)"

These definitions are taken from the Consumer Credit Protection Act.

Credit Transactions In General

In a credit transaction there is a general requirement of disclosure. This requirement is imposed upon any creditor who extends credit to a consumer and upon which a finance charge is or may be imposed. The disclosure must be clear and conspicious, containing all information required under the Act. (Disclosure requirements will not be discussed.) In cases of consumer credit transactions where a security interest is in real property, the obligor (consumer) shall have the right to rescind the transaction within three days of the transaction or the delivery of the disclosures required by the Act. Recision is made by notification to the creditor of the obligor's intention to do so. The creditor is obligated to disclose clearly and conspicuously this right to the obligor (in these types of transactions) and give the obligor adequate opportunity to exercise his right to negate the transaction. If the obligor exercises this right of recision, he is not liable for any finance or other charge, and any security interest becomes void. The creditor, within ten days of notice, must return to the obligor any money or property given as a down payment and do all that is necessary to terminate the security interest that was created. Once the creditor has performed these duties, the obligor must give back any property received from him. If it is impractical for the obligor to do so, he shall tender back its reasonable value. If the creditor does not take possession of the property within ten days after tender by the obligor, ownership in the property is deemed to be in the obligor with no further duty of payment.

The two most basic and popular forms for the extension of credit are credit cards and what are commonly known as retail installment agreements (time payment accounts).

Credit Cards (Open End Credit Agreement)

Under federal law, credit cards fall within the category of *open end credit agreements*. Simply stated, an open end credit agreement is one in which the purchaser (cardholder) agrees to pay the card issuer for the debt incurred on a monthly basis until his account is paid in full. Normally, this involves a minimum monthly payment. The end result of this type of credit is that there is no pre-set number of months, payments or amounts which is intended to clear the account. Stated another way, one month a cardholder might put $15.00 towards his $75.00 purchase and the next month pay $35.00, depending upon his means. The interest charged the cardholder is determined on the basis of his average outstanding balance for the previous billing period (which by law is one month, but not necessarily one calendar month).

Periodic Statements

What must be contained in the periodic statements that are sent to the cardholder? Section 1637 and 1638 of the Consumer Credit Protection Act deal with these requirements. These sections are summarized as briefly as possible.

Before opening any account under an open end consumer credit plan (i.e., obtaining a credit card), the creditor shall disclose to the person to whom the credit is being extended the conditions under which a finance charge may be imposed, including the time period, if any, that the credit may be repaid without incurring any finance charge; how the balance is computed; the method of determining the finance charge; the periodic rates that may be used to compute finance charges and the balance ranges to which the rates apply; conditions under which any other charges may be imposed; conditions by which a creditor may

S 149—Loan Disclosure Statement: Truth In Lending Act: Federal Reserve Regulation Z: 7-1-69.

LOAN DISCLOSURE STATEMENT

The statements herein contained are for disclosure only and do not in any way change, modify or vary the terms and conditions of any note, security instrument or other document relative to this loan:

LOAN APPLICANT:

Application No._____

Date_____19___

(1) Total of Payments $_____
(2) Interest/discount $_____
    Creditor insurance
    (include if a man-
    datory charge)   _____

(3) **FINANCE CHARGE**
    sum of items in (2) $_____
(4) Amount financed
    (1) minus (3) $_____
(5) Other charges:
    filing fees (if any) $_____
                          $_____
                          $_____
(6) Loan Proceeds
    (4) minus (5) $_____
(7) **ANNUAL PERCENTAGE RATE** _____%

THE TOTAL OF PAYMENTS IS PAYABLE:

☐ on demand of Lender
☐ _____ days after date
☐ _____ months after date
☐ in _____ equal consecutively monthly installments of $_____ each.

The **FINANCE CHARGE** begins to accrue from the date that the loan proceeds are disbursed.

SECURITY INTEREST

☐ None
☐ Lender shall have a security interest in the collateral security described immediately below which collateral shall secure the loan identified and all other obligations of Loan Applicant, present or future.

☐ collateral described as follows_____

☐ collateral described in Collateral Receipt No._____ a copy of which has been furnished either heretofore or simultaneously herewith to Loan Applicant

and Lender shall have a continuing lien and/or right of set-off as collateral security for the payment of the loan identified above and for any and all obligations of Loan Applicant to Lender whether present or future upon any and all moneys, securities and all other property of any kind, nature or description, including general or special deposits, now or hereafter held, received or coming into possession of Lender whether for pledge, safe keeping, custody or collection or placed in a safe deposit box leased by Lender to Loan Applicant.

DEFAULT CHARGE If any installment is not paid within 10 days after it is due, a charge will be payable by Loan Applicant as follows: **5%** of the unpaid installment or **$5** whichever is less.

PREPAYMENT IN FULL Upon prepayment in full Loan Applicant is entitled to a rebate of the **FINANCE CHARGE** calculated by the Rule of 78ths or Sum of the Digits methods (subject to a minimum retention charge as provided by law).

Disclosure statements pursuant to State law that are inconsistent with the Federal Truth in Lending Act:_____

IF THIS LOAN DISCLOSURE STATEMENT IS BEING FURNISHED WITH THE LOAN PROCEEDS CHECK, AND THEY DO NOT MEET WITH YOUR APPROVAL, PLEASE RETURN THE CHECK TO US FORTHWITH.

_____ Lending Officer

_____ Lender

_____ Address

199

acquire a security interest in any property which is to secure payment of the credit extended; and a description of the interest acquired.

It should be noted that in New York State, § 413 (12) of the Personal Property Law prohibits the creation of a security interest in any personal or real property (including any goods sold under such agreement) to secure payment of the buyer's outstanding indebtedness under such open end credit transactions. This statute further provides that while the security interest which the seller attempts to impose is void, the credit agreement is not otherwise impaired. Also, in New York State, an agreement between a purchaser and a retail seller for the purchase of a particular item [goods or services], the payment for which is to be made in equal, pre-set, monthly installments, is called a retail installment contract. Basically, this is a one-shot deal between a buyer and a seller for a particular item; here, all terms of payment are expressly set forth at the time of purchase. Federal law refers to this type of agreement as a *closed end credit agreement*.

Where the purchase of goods or services is contracted for through the use of an accepted credit card (this term means any credit card which the cardholder has requested and received or has signed, used, or authorized another to use, for the purpose of obtaining money, property, labor or services on credit), and the terms of payment call for varying monthly amounts over an extended period of time, with the imposition of finance charges based upon average outstanding monthly accounts, New York State labels this type of transaction a *retail installment credit agreement*. Under federal law, this is termed an open end credit agreement.

Under an open end consumer credit plan, the creditor must transmit to the obligor a statement containing the following items: the outstanding balance on the account; amount and dates when credit was extended and a brief description of the involved transaction; the amount credited to the account during the period; the finance charge applicable to the period billed for; the balance on which the finance charge was computed and how the balance was determined; the balance of the account at the end of the period; and the date on which payment may be made to avoid further finance charge. In the case of an open end consumer credit plan, these items shall be disclosed in a notice mailed or delivered to the obligor not later than thirty days after last billing.

If the purchase order is made by phone or mail without solicitation through a catalogue, advertisement or other matter printed by the creditor, the cash price and terms of the financing may be made at any time not later than the date the first payment is due.

If the creditor fails in his disclosure requirements, he can be civilly liable for his misconduct, unless he remedies his failure within fifteen days after discovery of the error. A creditor must also make all appropriate adjustments to the account which are necessary to insure that the person will not pay finance charges at a rate in excess of the percentage rate actually disclosed. There will be no purpose in discussing the potential liabilities of the creditor, since, if the reader is confronted with this problem, an attorney should be consulted and must be consulted if he wants to institute legal action.

Public Law 93–495: Credit Billing

Public Law 93–495 amends the Consumer Credit Protection Act by adding a complete new chapter entitled Credit Billing. This amendment became effective in October, 1975 and will be touched upon only briefly. If the obligor has a mistake in his bill, he must immediately send a written notice of the mistake (must be within 60 days of billing date) to

Application for a Master Charge

Firm Name or Employer	Telephone No.	Years There	Type of Business

Address (Number & Street)	Department	Employee Number

City, State & Zip Code	Position	Annual Income $

Name & Address of Previous Employer (If above less than 2 years)	Years There

Spouse's Employer and/or Source of Other Income	Annual Other Income $

Checking Account—Bank Name & Branch Address ☐ Regular ☐ Special ☐ Business	Account Number
Savings Account—Bank Name & Branch Address	Account Number

Real Estate Owned—Describe ☐ Home ☐ Other	Rent/Mortgage Payment $	Have you borrowed from Chemical ☐ No ☐ Yes—When

Indebtedness (List all current debts—attach additional sheet if necessary)

Name and address of Creditor	Account No.	Original Bal.	Unpaid Bal.	Monthly Pmt.

I represent that all the statements made by me in this application are true and correct, and authorize Chemical Bank to exchange credit information with others in connection with this application. I understand that the use of the Master Charge Card issued by Chemical Bank is subject to the terms and conditions of the Chemical Bank Master Charge Agreement, a **New York Retail Instalment Credit Agreement.**

Date _____   Signature _____

For Bank Use Only	Loan Control	Credit $	☐ SI ☐ DIS	Approved	Verified	Date

- - - - - - - - - - - - - - - - - - - Detach Here - - - - - - - - - - - - - - - - - - -

Here's the Information on Master Charge costs:

PURCHASES

There is no **Finance Charge** on new purchases if you pay your indebtedness within **25** days of your billing date.

Payments may be extended by paying at least **1/36th** of the "new balance" shown on your Master Charge Statement or **$5**, whichever is the greater together with the **Finance Charge** included in the new balance each month. (The "new balance" is the total of the current month's purchases and any unpaid balance from previous months, less any "payments and credits" and plus any "debit adjustments" to your account, plus a **Finance Charge**.) A minimum payment is rounded up to the next highest dollar. A **Finance Charge** is imposed on the average unpaid principal amount of the previous month's new balance from time to time outstanding (an "average daily balance"), computed separately (i) for daily balances of **$500** or less at a periodic rate of **0.04831%** per day, for an **Annual Percentage Rate** of **18%**, and (ii) for daily balances in excess thereof at a period rate of **0.03287%** per day, for an **Annual Percentage Rate** of **12%**. The minimum **Finance Charge** in any billing period is **50¢** except that no **Finance Charge** is imposed on an average daily balance of less than **$5**.

COLLECTION

In the event your account is referred to an attorney for collection, a reasonable attorney's fee, not to exceed **20%** will be added to the amount due.

ADVANCES

You may repay advances on an extended basis by paying the instalment of (a) not less than **1/36th** of the total unpaid amount of advances (including **Finance Charges** and fines, if any) outstanding computed as of the time of the most recent advance or **$5**, whichever is greater, (b) a **Finance Charge** at a rate of **0.03287%** per day on the average unpaid principal amount of the advances from time to time outstanding from the date each written request therefor is posted to your account or, if made by check, after mailing thereof, and (c) a service fee of **25¢**, included in the **Finance Charge**, for each cash advance. A minimum payment is rounded up to the next highest dollar. A **Finance Charge** (including the service fee) as described above, is due whether or not payments are extended. The **Annual Percentage Rate** on an advance is **12%**.

the creditor. In this notice the consumer should state his name and account number, give the amount that he believes is in error, and set forth the reasons for his belief. Once that is done, he has met his obligations to put the creditor on notice. The burden to act now shifts to the creditor, who must pursue the proper steps. First, he must send acknowledgement within thirty days of receipt of the notice. He then has a choice of procedures, one of which he must follow to rectify the complaint. These will not be discussed since they are not applicable to the consumer. He has complied with his obligations to notify the creditor, who now must take the next step.

A ''billing error'' consists of a number of items which the Federal statute required as of October, 1975; most of these items are grounded in common sense. Basically, it is when the obligor gets billed for an amount that he did not charge. However, one classification of a billing error that should be noted is the following as quoted from the statute:

> "§ 161 (G) (3): A reflection on a statement of goods or services not accepted by the obligor or his designee or not delivered to the obligor or his designee in accordance with the agreement made at the time of a transaction.''

This particular item is pointed out because it is important for the reader to make sure that if he purchases a television or any other goods or services with a credit card, and he either does not receive them or they are defective, he should immediately write to the credit card institution and put it on notice. This notice, which is clarified as a billing error notice, must be sent to the creditor within sixty days of the statement which contains the contested charges. If the obligor (consumer) does not get proper notice to the creditor, he might encounter major problems later. Even if he has put the creditor, in the case of a credit card transaction, on notice of his billing error, the consumer might be confronted with some

problems (discussed in the chapter on sales). However, to have a fighting chance to negate the obligation to pay for the defective goods, written notice is necessary. It is not hard to do and only costs the price of a stamp. This notice must be mailed separately and is invalid if made on the billing statement or stub. In fact, no part of the statement that the creditor sends the obligor should be returned in the notice. If the obligor wants to strengthen his position, the notice can be sent by registered mail with a return receipt requested. He should just make sure that he gets written notice to the creditor within sixty days of receipt of the erroneous billing statement.

In relation to the notice of billing error, the obligor need not worry that his future credit rating will be ruined. The new Act provides that a creditor or his agent may not report anything that would adversely affect the obligor's credit rating or credit standing because of his failure to pay a questioned amount. Only after the creditor satisfies his duties under the Act, and the amount in question is resolved, does the obligor become bound to make payment. Once made, these payments must be promptly credited to the obligor's account. No finance costs may be charged to the obligor's account, if payment is made within the time period agreed to between the parties. If excess payments are made (oh, to be that fortunate!) in an open end consumer credit account, the creditor must refund the money upon request of the obligor or credit the obligor's account to the extent of the overpayment.

If a consumer uses a credit card to purchase goods or services and the seller allows for a return or debit, the consumer should make sure that the seller notifies the card issuer and sends a credit statement, if in fact the goods are returned. The credit card issuer must then credit the account. This duty is imposed upon the seller by statute, but it would benefit the consumer to remind him. It just might eliminate later hassles and save the consumer the trouble of having to notify the card issuer of a subsequent "billing error."

Another interesting note that is covered under the statute (P.L. 93–495) deals with the prohibition against offsets (§ 169). It is important, since many people who own credit cards also have checking and savings accounts at the same bank that issues the card. In essence, this section prohibits a bank from using the bank account funds to make payments on credit card obligations. Such action is expressly prohibited unless the card holder authorized it in writing. Thus, if the card holder in initiating his credit plan agrees that the card issuer may pay debts that are incurred through the use of the credit card by deducting all or a portion of such debt from the cardholder's deposit account, the bank is empowered to act. In conjunction with this provision, a card issuer cannot take action dealing with an outstanding disputed amount upon a request by cardholder. Of course, the card issuer can attach a cardholder's funds held on deposit with the card issuer, if that remedy is constitutionally available to creditors generally.

Cardholder Rights

The next area of discussion is of such importance that the actual section of the statute needs to be recited. Each and every credit cardholder should know his rights as spelled out by federal law. Any language that is confusing will be discussed after the citation of the statute.

170. Rights of credit card customers.
"(a) Subject to the limitation contained in subsection (b) a card issuer who has issued a credit card to a cardholder pursuant to an open end consumer credit plan shall be subject to all claims (other than tort claims) and defenses arising out of any transaction in which the credit card is used as a method of payment or extension of credit if (1) the ob-

ligor has made a good faith attempt to obtain satisfactory resolution of a disagreement or problem relative to the transaction from the person honoring the credit card; (2) the amount of the initial transaction exceeds $50; and (3) the place where the initial transaction occurred was in the same State as the mailing address previously provided by the cardholder or was within 100 miles from such address, except that the limitations set forth in clauses (2) and (3) with respect to an obligor's right to assert claims and defenses against a card issuer shall not be applicable to any transaction in which the person honoring the credit card (A) is the same person as the card issuer, (B) is controlled by the card issuer, (C) is under direct or indirect common control with the card issuer, (D) is a franchised dealer in the card issuer's products or services, or (E) has obtained the order for such transaction through a mail solicitation made by or participated in by the card issuer in which the cardholder is solicited to enter into such transaction by using the credit card issued by the card issuer.

"(b) The amount of claims or defenses asserted by the cardholder may not exceed the amount of credit outstanding with respect to such transaction at the time the cardholder first notifies the card issuer or the person honoring the credit card of such claim or defense. For the purpose of determining the amount of credit outstanding in the preceding sentence, payments and credits to the cardholder's account are deemed to have been applied, in the order indicated, to the payment of: (1) late charges in the order of their entry to the account; (2) finance charges in order of their entry to the account; and (3) debits to the account other than those set forth above, in the order in which each debit entry to the account was made." [P.L. 93–495, 88 Stat 1500, C. 4, Credit Billing.]

Upon close examination of this section, the reader can understand the importance of its meaning. It protects the cardholder from getting taken by shady sellers. Let us set up an example: The cardholder buys a $400 television from Sam Shadlay's Television and Appliance Store. The purchase is made through the use of an accepted credit card (e.g., Master Charge). The purchaser takes the television home and turns it on. Unfortunately, no picture appears; in fact, nothing happens. The television is not worth the box it came in. The purchaser returns to Sammy only to find that Sammy has closed for the day. Actually, Sammy has closed for good and has gone to Venezuela. The purchaser has a television that does not work and soon will receive a bill from the credit card company for $400, plus finance charges. Is he out of luck? No, because by law, all of his defenses that would have been good against Sammy for non-payment (such as breach of warranty of merchantability) are valid against the credit issuer. The purchaser does not have to pay the card issuer and can assert his defenses against the creditor (card issuer) as a result of this statute. This is quite different from the provisions of earlier laws and should be noted. One qualification, however, is that in any case, the purchaser must make a good-faith attempt to obtain satisfactory resolution of the disagreement or problem arising from the transaction from the person honoring the credit card. If his attempted resolution fails, he may then assert his defenses against the card issuer by informing him in writing that a billing error exists and the reasons why. This notification must occur upon receipt of the billing statement which includes the cost of the television. This law, which became effective in October, 1975, protects consumers from paying for defective goods.

Cardholder Liabilities

The rights of a credit cardholder have now been reviewed. What about the liability of a credit cardholder? A cardholder shall be liable for the debts incurred through the use of the credit card by him or a person whom he au-

thorizes to use the card. This is obvious. If the card is lost or stolen however, a different situation arises and the liability imposed is greatly reduced. A cardholder shall be liable for the unauthorized use of a credit card only if it is an accepted credit card and then only to a maximum of $50 (this is actually stated on the back of the credit card). The cardholder is not held liable for any amount, even up to the $50 ceiling, that results from unauthorized use after the card issuer has been placed on notice by the cardholder that the card is lost, stolen, mislaid or otherwise. The key element to remember here is that liability is limited to $50 for the unauthorized use. However, the card issuer should be notified promptly when the card is missing, and the $50 might be saved if the card has not been used yet.

If the card issuer attempts to enforce liability for the use of a credit card, the burden of proof is upon the card issuer to show that the use was authorized. If the use was unauthorized, the burden of proof is still on the issuer, and he must prove that the conditions of liability for the unauthorized use of a credit card have been met. These conditions are:

(1) The card is an accepted credit card;

(2) The liability is not in excess of $50;

(3) The card issuer gave adequate notice to the cardholder of the potential liability;

(4) The card issuer has provided the cardholder with a self-addressed, prestamped notification to be mailed by the cardholder in the event of the loss or theft of the credit card; and

(5) The unauthorized use occurs before the cardholder has notified the card issuer that an unauthorized use of the credit card has occurred, or may occur as the result of loss, theft or otherwise.

If these prerequisites are not met by the card issuer, the cardholder is not liable for even the $50.

The fraudulent use of a credit card can result in serious liability. One can be fined up to $10,000 or be imprisoned up to 10 years, or both. The fraudulent use of a credit card is a federal offense under this section.

Retail Installment Contract (Closed End Credit Agreement)

As stated previously, this is your run-of-the-mill consumer credit transaction. It is more commonly known as the "buy now, pay later" route to happiness. What distinguishes this type of transaction from a credit card purchase is the fact that at the time of the purchase, the seller must inform the consumer as to "total" cost of the purchase. "Total" means the purchase price, additional charges and finance charges. Normally, payments are in equal monthly installments and extend over a pre-agreed length of time. Each monthly installment is intended to pay part of the purchase price and part of the finance charge. When the last payment is made, the account is closed, and the goods or services purchased belong exclusively to the purchaser.

Security Interest and Default

In transactions of this type, the seller retains an interest in the goods purchased, and if the purchaser fails to make one of the prearranged payments, the seller may under certain circumstances take back the goods sold. This interest is technically a *security interest* or lien.

A security interest is generally defined as an interest in personal property (or fixtures) which secures payment or performance of an obligation. In non-legal terms, this essentially means that the seller retains a legal interest or right in the property which he sells and delivers to the obligor until he has made his final payment. If he fails to pay as agreed, the seller has a legal right to take back that property in order to satisfy the debt (i.e., the purchase price plus finance charges up to the time of payment).

There is no express definition of "default" in the Uniform Commercial Code. Generally, those acts which will constitute the purchaser's default will be defined in the retail installment contract which he enters into with the seller. The consumer should be aware of the terms constituting a default before he enters into such an agreement. The law favors the creditor in protecting his rights once a default has occurred. If obligor finds himself in this position, the aid of an attorney is highly recommended.

Once the purchaser has paid more than 60% of the cash price of the goods secured, he is deemed to have an equitable interest in the goods and is entitled to notice from the seller of the manner in which those goods will be disposed to satisfy the debt. Unless otherwise agreed, the debtor may redeem the goods by tending full payment sufficient to meet the balance of the debt due and owing, plus any expenses reasonably incurred by the seller. Once the seller has disposed of the goods, he must notify the debtor as to the amount received for such goods. If the amount received is in excess of the balance due and owing, the debtor is entitled to the difference, less reasonable expenses incurred by the seller. If the amount recovered is less than the balance due and owing, the debtor continues to remain obligated for that difference. In actuality, the disposition of goods after a default never results in a surplus. The debtor is always responsible for something more.

In light of the foregoing, the obligor should be sure of the terms and amounts to be paid, how they are to be paid, the definition of default, and if he has the financial means to meet his contractual obligation. If he does not follow these precautions explicitly, he is exposing himself to unimagined heartaches and legal entanglements. The law protects the buyer before he takes the goods home, and the seller after that.

Disclosure Requirements

If the sale is under a closed end credit agreement, the creditor must disclose the following: cash price of the property or services purchased; down payment credited; other charges that are part of credit extended but not part of the finance charge; total amount to be financed (purchase price plus other charges, less down payment); amount of finance charge in an annual percentage (except when finance charge does not exceed $5 and the amount financed does not exceed $75; or finance charge does not exceed $7.50 and amount financed exceeds $75); the number, amount, and due dates of payments for repayment; terms of default, delinquency, or similar charges payable in the event of late payments; a description of any security interest held or to be acquired by the creditor; and a clear identification of the property to which the security interest will apply. A creditor may not divide a consumer credit sale into two or more sales to avoid the disclosure of an annual percentage rate. The above disclosure must be made to the obligor before the credit is extended. This information may be contained in the contract which evidences the indebtedness of the purchaser. The obligor should be sure that he reads the retail installment contract carefully before signing it. If what is stated is unclear he should ask for an explanation. He should not sign the retail installment contract until he is certain of its terms and conditions.

The purchaser also is entitled to a filled-in copy of the retail installment contract. If it is not delivered to him at the time of the sale, it must be mailed to him at the address stated in the contract. Until the seller does so, the buyer who has not received the goods or services has an unconditional right to cancel and to receive an immediate refund of all payments made (New York Personal Property Law, 405). Most contracts of this type state on their face as follows, "I acknowledge receipt of a copy of this agreement." The obligor should be certain that he receives a completed copy signed by the seller. This acknowledgment means that he is presumed to have received a completed copy of the contract.

When the obligor has finished making all of the payments under the contract, and there is no balance outstanding, he may request in writing that the seller send him a release. This will acknowledge full payment and release of all security interests in the property.

Prohibited Terms and Conditions

There are certain terms and conditions which the seller may not include in the retail installment contract. If any one of the following clauses appears, the law considers it void; however, it does not invalidate the remainder of the contract. These clauses are as follows:

(1) The holder (seller) may not arbitrarily, and without reasonable cause, accelerate the amount owed in the absence of the buyer's default.

(2) The seller may not require a power of attorney to confess judgment or assign wages.

(3) The seller or holder of the contract is not given authority to enter upon the purchaser's premises unlawfully or to commit any breach of the peace in the repossession of the goods.

(4) The purchaser is not required to waive or give up any right of action against seller or holder for any illegal act committed in the collection of payments or repossession of the goods.

(5) The purchaser is not required to give a power of attorney naming the seller or holder as the purchaser's agent in either collection of payments or repossession of the goods.

(6) The purchaser is not required to relieve the seller from any liability for any legal remedies which the purchaser may have against the seller.

Assignment

There may be occasions when the seller chooses to assign or sell the retail installment contract to a third person. Generally speaking, this is perfectly legal. However, the *assignee* (third party purchaser of the installment contract) must notify the obligor of the assignment. There are two important points he should keep in mind upon receipt of this notification. First, he is thereafter required to make his monthly payments to the assignee, since he now owns the contract. Also, if the obligor pays the original seller by mistake, he loses his money if he cannot locate the original seller and must still pay the assignee. (Don't throw away the notification of assignment.) Second, upon notification of the assignment, the purchaser has ten days to notify the assignee in writing of any defects of the goods received from the seller or of the seller's incomplete performance of all his agreements with the purchaser. If the purchaser does not do this, he is obligated to pay the assignee the full price regardless of whether or not the goods or services received were defective. (New York Personal Property Law, 403 (3)(a).

Door-to-Door Sales

Section 425 of the Personal Property Law of the State of New York deals with home solicitation sales. This is defined as a consumer transaction in which the payment of the purchase price is deferred over time and the seller or his representative is a person who does business by means of personal solicitation at a place other than the place of business of the seller or his representative.

In a transaction of this nature, the purchaser has the right to cancel the sale up until midnight of the third business day after the day on which he signs the agreement. The cancellation must be in writing, properly addressed with prepaid postage and deposited in a mailbox. This right of cancellation does not exist where the purchaser has requested the seller to provide the goods without delay because of an emergency, and where seller has commenced performance of the contract in good faith, before notice of cancellation is received. In the case of goods which cannot be returned to the seller in substantially the same condition as when received by the purchaser, the purchaser must reimburse the seller for the reasonable value of the goods. The seller must also provide the purchaser with a printed card which the purchaser may use to cancel the sale.

The purchaser is entitled to a return of his down payment. Under certain circumstances, the seller is entitled to a cancellation fee of 5% of the cash (purchase) price, but not to exceed the amount of the cash down payment.

The purchaser is required to return any goods received if the seller so requests after cancellation, but the purchaser need not deliver them at any place other than his residence. The purchaser must also take reasonable care of those goods for a reasonable time (defined as forty days).

Credit Card Application

This is an application for an open end credit agreement, commonly known as a credit card application. Most of the terms and provisions are self-explanatory.

In any of these applications the obligor should always remember two things:

(1) They are designed to protect the credit card issuer.

(2) Whatever information the obligor fills in should be as accurate as possible. Organizations that issue credit cards generally trade information on credit status and background. If he is dishonest, the issuer will probably discover it, and he will never again be considered for a credit card.

Page (1) is strictly informational and needs no explanation. Page (2) is the meat of the agreement.

No finance charge may be computed if the full amount of the purchase (indebtedness) is paid within the time stated. In this case, it is 25 days. This is a good example of wise use of a credit card. Having already been extended 25 days credit free, the obligor, through proper management of his finances can take full advantage of a prolonged period of credit.

Usually the obligor must make a minimum monthly payment, as stated in the particular contract which he has entered into. In this case, the minimum monthly payment must be $\frac{1}{36}$th of the new balance or $5, whichever is greater, plus the finance charge.

The finance charge is determined on the basis of the average unpaid balance from the previous month. This is computed as follows: In New York State the charge may be:

(1) 0.04931% per day which is an annual percentage of 18% on an average daily balance of $500 or less; and

(2) 0.03287% per day which is annual percentage rate of 12% per annum on the average daily balance in excess of $500.

The minimum finance charge is 50¢ if the average daily balance is more than $5.

The attorney's fees which may be collected from you in the event your account is referred to an attorney for collection may be a maximum of 20% of the amount due and are to be added to that value.

In the event of a cash advance, the credit card issuer may levy a finance charge of 0.03287% per day (12% yearly) from the date of the advance, regardless of when it is repaid. In this instance, there is no grace period and interest will be charged from the moment the cash is advanced.

If the obligor defaults in any payment of a cash advance, the credit card issuer may charge a fine not in excess of 4¢ per dollar on the amount unpaid for a period in excess of ten days. In no event is the fine to exceed $5, and any fine imposed is, or will be, in addition to the finance charge.

Upon signature of the application and delivery to the credit card issuer, the obligor makes an offer. Upon receipt and signing of the credit card, the obligor accepts all of the conditions stated in the credit card application. This now becomes a binding contract. None of the terms are negatable. If the card is not returned, the obligor is bound by all terms and provisions.

Retail Installment Contract (Security Agreement)

This is the standard "buy now, pay later" time installment contract.

Page (1) begins with the identity of the parties to the contract. The clause begins with, "Buyer hereby purchases . . . and grants a security interest," to the seller in the property listed on the blank lines. The security interest discussed earlier is subject to the terms and conditions contained within this contract.

The clause beginning with the statement "This contract is not . . ." is the essence of a retail installment contract. It recites the buyer's obligation to pay the seller the total

JULIUS BLUMBERG, INC., PUBLISHER, NYC 10013

RETAIL INSTALMENT CONTRACT (SECURITY AGREEMENT)

PROVISIONS ON REVERSE SIDE ARE PART OF THIS AGREEMENT

Buyer..

Seller..

....

....

street address (residence) ....

street address ....

city & state .... zip .... telephone

city & state .... zip .... telephone

This agreement, including the provisions on the other side, covers my instalment purchase from you of the property described below. In this agreement, the words **I, me** and **my** mean the buyer. **You** and **your** refer to the seller.

Assignment   I understand that you will assign this agreement to...

address..

and I will make my instalment payments directly to them. I also understand that anyone else who signs this agreement will be responsible, individually and together, to the same extent that I am.

Property   I hereby purchase the following described property..

....

....

....

....

....

....

....

....

....

....

In this agreement the word **property** refers to the above described property and accessories and any additions and replacements.

Total payment   After deducting my downpayment in cash and trade-ins, I promise to make a **total of payments** of $........................

This represents an **ANNUAL PERCENTAGE RATE** of............%, includes the cost of insurance and other charges we have agreed on.

Instalments   I will pay this amount described below in item 9 in............................equal monthly instalments of $..............................each, plus a final unequal instalment of $............................which payment ☐ is ☐ is not a BALLOON PAYMENT (a final payment is a balloon payment if it is more than twice the amount of the equal monthly instalment). My instalments will be due the same day every month starting on

....

The **finance charge** will begin when you assign this contract. You estimate that this will be approximately **5 days** after I sign it.

Itemization of obligation

1 Cash price $........................
2 Sales tax   ....
3 Total cash price (1+2) $........................
4 Downpayment
  (a) Trade-in ....
      Less unpaid balance on
      open lien ....
      Net allowance   ....
  (b) Cash downpayment   ....
      Total downpayment   ....
5 Unpaid balance of cash price (3–4)   ....
6 Charges
  (a) Credit life insurance   ....
  (b) Joint credit life insurance ....
  (c) Credit accident and health
      insurance   ....
  (d) Other charges ....
      ....
7 Unpaid balance/Amount financed (5+6) ....
8 **FINANCE CHARGE**   ....
9 Total of payments ((7+8) $........................
10 Deferred payment price (3+6+8) $........................
   ANNUAL PERCENTAGE RATE ....%

*Insurance protection   If I want either credit life or credit accident and health insurance, you can provide me with this coverage through an insurance company you select. I understand that this insurance is not required.

→ I do ☐ do not ☐ want credit life insurance. The maximum coverage is $........................ and the premium is $........................ for the term of the loan.

→ I do ☐ do not ☐ want joint credit life insurance with my spouse. (My spouse must also be a buyer.) The maximum coverage is $........................ and the premium is $........................ for the term of the loan.

→ I do ☐ do not ☐ want credit accident and health insurance. The maximum coverage is $........................ but no more than $........................ a month. The premium is $........................ for the term of the loan.

....
Buyer's signature   Date

....
Buyer's signature (Spouse)   Date

I understand you do not provide liability insurance for bodily injury and property damage caused to others.

Applicable law   This agreement will be governed by the law of the State of ....

→

amount due under the contract. It breaks the payments down into equal monthly installments, with the first installment due and payable one month from the date of the transaction. Generally, a balloon payment will be the last payment due on the contract. Simply said, the final payment is a balloon payment, if it is more than twice as large as the normal monthly payment. The governing calculations appear in the box on the right hand side of page (1).

The seller has a right to require that insurance be obtained to protect the seller in the event of damage or loss of the goods, although the buyer may choose the insurance carrier.

In this particular contract, there is a default charge in the event of late payment. This provision is inherent in most installment agreements and usually cannot be avoided.

As for prepayment rebates, if the purchaser (buyer) pays the total outstanding amount due before the time required by the contract, he is entitled to recover from the seller a pro-rated rebate of the finance charge for that period of time when credit was offered but not used.

The Federal Truth In Lending Act, referred to under disclosure, is in fact, the Consumer Credit Protection Act, discussed previously.

If a person is asked to sign as a guarantor, he must remember that he becomes equally liable on the contract. In fact, the seller may recover from him alone without having to attempt collection from the buyer. It is recommended that a person does not sign as guarantor unless he personally knows the buyer and can be reasonably sure of his financial stability and responsibility.

Page (2):

Clause 1 and 2 are self-explanatory.

Clause 3 is clear and legally enforceable, with the exception of that portion relating to appointment of the seller as attorney in fact. In New York, for example, that portion has been invalidated by statute. If the purchaser (buyer) defaults in the insurance premiums required to insure the property, the seller may pay such premiums and charge the buyer.

Clause 4 deals with assignment of the retail installment contract. The obligor should remember that he has 10 days after notification of the assignment to inform the assignee in writing of any defects in the goods or failure of the seller to perform the contract.

Clause 5 is self-explanatory.

Clause 6 requires that the buyer care for the goods as if they belonged to the seller. In effect, they do. Remember, the seller has a legal interest in the goods until they are fully paid for. If any damage does occur to the goods, the buyer must notify the seller promptly.

Clause 7 requires honesty. When a person trades in something in order to buy something else, he is required to make sure that no one else has any interest in those goods.

Clause 8 is an acceleration clause. In essence, it states that if the buyer does not live up to his obligations called for in the contract, the entire unpaid balance shall, at the option of the seller, without demand or notice of any kind, become immediately due and payable. Other charges will be assessed to the buyer in the execution of this acceleration procedure. Other events listed in Clause 8 may also cause acceleration of payment (e.g., if the collateral is impaired). However, the main obligation of the buyer is to make payments as agreed. Failure to do this is the major reason behind defaults.

Clause 9 is self-explanatory and has been discussed previously.

Clause 10 allows the seller to accept one late payment without waiving his right to accelerate the debt if a late payment occurs again.

Oral agreements made before the contract is signed but not incorporated into the final contract are not legally enforceable and are useless. Oral agreements made after the contract is signed are just as useless. If the parties want a modification or change, it should be put in writing and the seller and buyer should sign it.

The first sentence of Clause 11 has been dealt with previously. To summarize briefly, it states that any clause which might be prohibited or invalidated by later law will not affect the validity of the remainder of the contract. That clause, and only that clause, will be invalid. There is some question as to whether or not the second sentence of Clause 11 is valid as it presently appears, however warranties in sales contracts are discussed in another chapter of the book.

CHAPTER 10

Assignments, Proxies, and Power of Attorney

Introduction to Assignments

One day, in need of a widget or two, Billie Buyer shuffles down to Willie's Widget Store and agrees with Willie that if he will deliver widgets, Billie will remit payment to him. A fortnight or two later, upon receipt of the first batch of widgets, Billie drafts a check payable to Willie only to be informed that Willie has assigned his rights to Cary's Collection Agency and that his check instead should be made out to Cary. Must he do so? What if the widgets do not meet up to his expectations? Must he even pay at all? In short, what is an *assignment* and how does it affect the involved parties, Billie, the debtor, Willie, the creditor or assignor, and Cary, the assignee?

It is always satisfying to have an historical perspective in attempting to understand any concept. At common law, assignments were invalid, the reasoning being that contracts were personal to the parties making them and one party should not find himself liable to a third party with whom he had not initially dealt. Eventually, a method was devised to circumvent the law by granting a prospective assignee a *power of attorney* (an agency relationship which will be explained shortly) to act as the assignor's collecting agent. The granting of the power gained further characteristics of modern day assignment when the courts began to consider the power irrevoca-ble and the attorney an irrevocable agent of the creditor.

Today an assignment creates a definite legal interest which cannot be denied or go unrecognized. It is easily created by stating that, "I, Willie, assign to Cary all my rights in my contract with Billie." In some instances, the assignment must be in writing, such as where the assignee is succeeding to rights in a signed security agreement, collateral or contract covering goods exceeding $5,000 in value. In essence, an assignment simply transfers rights from one party to another; as between the assignor and assignee, a transaction is as final as a sale. After the event, the assignee has all of the rights that the assignor previously had, and the assignor becomes totally divested of rights.

Assignments of Rights

To be final, an assignment must meet certain requirements of a contract. If the assignor transfers a right to the assignee, it logically follows that in return the assignor should be compensated for its loss. As in a contract, the assignor must receive consideration which consummates the assignment and makes it irrevocable. An assignment can be made by gift, if delivery of some object signifying the right is made to the assignee who thereby acquires dominion and control over the object.

This control signals the irrevocability of the act, an essential element of an assignment. Thus, if a person wishes to assign a life insurance policy gratuitously, the assignment will not be complete until the assignee receives the policy.

In order for a person to assign a right which he possesses, the right must be an assignable one. What is an assignable right? As in the widget case, the right that has been created is usually the result of a creditor-debtor relationship. The creditor has a right to payment which he can freely transfer to a third party, since by so doing the debtor's rights and duties are not affected. This test is administered to an assignment to determine whether or not it is valid. If the debtor's position is affected in any way, then the assignment fails. Examples of non-assignable rights are where the exercise of the right is personal, where the assignment materially changes the duty of the other party or varies his risk or where the other party's chance of receiving his bargained-for return performance is materially impaired. Additionally, the parties can prohibit assignments at the outset, thus making all rights under the contract nonassignable. A mere promise not to assign, however, does not prohibit the assignment, but instead results in a breach of the contract in the event of such a transaction.

Delegation of Duties

A companion concept of the assignment of rights is the *delegation of duties*. Usually the possession of a right carries with it a concomitant obligation which must be fulfilled. In the widget case, Willie's right to receive payment is extinguished, if he fails in his duty to supply the quantity and type of widgets agreed upon.

The next question is whether the assignor in parting with his rights has also transferred his duties to the assignee. This does not mean that all duties can be delegated, for similar to rights, a duty cannot be delegated if it is personal to the assignor, mandatory under the original contract or substantially alters the performance to be received by one of the initial parties. For example, if the act alters the performance required of the assignor which involves specific skills or is based on a relationship of trust, it will not be delegable. Duties that are otherwise nondelegable can become so once the initial party to the contract agrees to the delegation or waives his right to object by accepting the assignee's services or goods.

Rights and Liabilities

Only the positions of assignor and assignee are affected by a valid assignment. As between themselves, the assignor confers implied warranties upon the assignee for value. These warranties are breached where the assignor did not possess the enforceable or genuine right that he claimed to have. In addition, the assignor cannot interfere with the assignee's newly acquired rights. Should the assignor intercede and receive payments which belong to the assignee as a result of the assignment, the assignee has several courses of action available to him in order to recover his due. An attorney can always guide a wronged assignee, assisting him in realizing his interest through an action for conversion, for restitution or breach of the warranties mentioned above.

The assignor and assignee both assume further responsibilities other than those to each other. If along with all rights, the assignor transfers his duties to the assignee, the assignee becomes liable for failure of performance to both his assignor and the other contracting party. This position occurs only where the assignee, now a delegatee, expressly assumes the duty. This assumption is implied, however, where the contract assigned is one dealing with personal property. Otherwise, the general rule followed in New York and the majority of states is that no automatic assumption of duties results from an assignment.

Throughout the transaction, the assignor remains liable to the party with whom he contracted. The assignee may be bound to perform all of the duties to which the assignor agreed, but the assignor is still not released from his obligation. A *novation*, or complete discharge, can free the assignor from all responsibility and create a contract as between the original contracting party and the assignee, but only if the former agrees to the substitution.

Suppose in the widget case, Willie failed to perform as agreed and Cary began to demand payment; what rights does Billie have? In general, Billie should remember that the assignee has no greater rights than his assignor. Since non-performance would have been a successful defense against Willie, it likewise would be a good defense against his assignee. This does not permit Billie to pay Willie after he knows about the assignment and claim fulfillment of his duties under the contract when Cary sues for payment. Failure of consideration, fraud or lack of an essential element which would lead to a defect in the contract between the original parties, will result in the same defect with the assignee as a party. The problem becomes overly complicated where the claim against Willie asserted by Billie is not one arising from the contractual arrangement itself, and is being used to reduce or offset the assignee's claim. Local law varies and legal counsel would be able to explain the viability of one's position in a particular situation.

This discussion of assignments is a brief overview. At best, the reader now has some knowledge of what occurs as a result of an assignment and, in particular, some of the rights and liabilities of the parties. The list is by no means exhaustive and was offered in an effort to give more credibility to the documents. The specific examples of assignments shown in the text are also brief and for the most part follow the general rules outlined. This is not to say that the law governing the substantive transaction is not intricate and massive, for each assignment mentioned carries with it legal implications beyond the range of this book. Still, a basic comprehension and review of the forms should benefit the reader.

Examples of Assignment

General Assignment

The general assignment is the example of Willie, Billie and Cary and the purported assignment between the latter parties. The declaration of an intent to assign is sufficient and the transfer of the right is "for value," thereby becoming irrevocable. The form embellishes upon the basic concept only to the extent that the assignee appoints another person to be attorney-in-fact, to demand, receive and perform "all and every act . . . necessary" to meet the purpose of the assignment.

Mortgage Assignment

A mortgage is like other rights under law or choses in action in that it may be freely assigned in most instances. One problem with mortgages, however, is that they are either equitable or legal land interests and, as such, state law may require them to be in writing. In New York, statutes outline other essentials, illustrate short form mortgage assignments and dictate rules of construction such as the words of assignment in a mortgage and bond or note which grant the assignee full power of attorney to act in the assignor's stead. Other states require that the assignment meet all the formalities of deeds.

This particular mortgage assignment states the parties involved in the immediate transaction, the assignor and assignee, the maker of the mortgage initially, and the information identifying it:

(1) amount of original mortgage with interest;

(2) date of execution;

(3) date and place of recordation; and

(4) description of encumbered property.

Additionally, since the debt and mortgage in many jurisdictions, such as New York, must follow one another, reference is made to the assignment of the "note or obligation described in said mortgage." Finally, the assignor warrants that the amount of the current mortgage is accurate. A breach of such warranty would give the assignee a cause of action for damages.

Lease Assignment

A lease assignment is explained adequately in the discussion of leases. Examination of the form reveals the essentials: the entirety of the lease term is covered, and the assignee accepts all covenants and conditions of the assignor's lease. The assignor also makes several warranties to both the lessor and assignee which are independent covenants having no impact on the efficacy of the assignment.

Assignment of Wages

The assignment of wages, salaries or other forms of earnings or compensation has been held to be assignable, since, generally, the assignor has vested interest in the payment. The vested interest and assignability disappear where payment is conditional and no current contract evidences the obligation out of which the interest rises or no existing arrangement indicates the availability of a pool of funds to satisfy the interests.

As for wages, theory holds that the right to one's income is assignable although it is a right which for many unexpected reasons may not vest. Obviously, if the assignor terminates his employment at any time and terminates his income, the assignee possesses a hollow right. An employment contract will avoid the dilemma by vesting the otherwise potential interest.

An assignment of wages in a state which does not regulate the practice can have a debilitating effect on the welfare of the assignor if he is unable to manage his affairs on the lower income. Most states, fortunately, protect wage earners from possible myopia by limiting the assignment to a particular amount or percentage of the total salary or wage income. Other statutes void assignments for failure to stand up to statutory requirements.

The assignment form is straightforward, but the assignor should be certain to distinctly identify the goods and clearly describe the transactions involved, so as not to authorize the employer to pay out money to other potential creditors. Beyond that, the laws of most states have erected sufficient safeguards for the consumer-wage earner.

Assignment For the Benefit of Creditors

It would be hoped that no one need ever be in a position to make a general or special assignment for the benefit of creditors. In such an assignment, an assignor transfers rights to an assignee, the rights are in specific properties of the assignor and the assignee acts as trustee holding the property or proceeds for the benefit of the assignor's creditors. In short, it is a method by which a debtor can repay his creditors voluntarily without submitting to bankruptcy. Once the property is put in trust with the assignee, title passes irrevocably and the assignor retains no rights.

The law governing assignments for the benefit of creditors is too involved for discussion in this book, but examination and explanation of the form should answer minor questions which the reader may have. Since the final step is drastic and final, an attorney should always be consulted before the commitment is made.

Statutory law, for the most part, controls the operation of assignments for the benefit of creditors. Generally, the lack of exact compliance with the governing statute will not defeat the conveyance to the trustee unless the statute so dictates. In New York, the assignment must be in strict accordance with the statute and the law mandates that the entire instrument must be in writing, although other states permit oral assignments. In any case, the statutes must be checked for specific requirements.

The form allows for the identification of the parties, the assignor and assignee, and mention of the debtor's business and location. The creditors need not be included in the form and are not parties to the assignment unless so expressed. The area of concern is in the description of the property conveyed. If the property passing into the trust is to be only partnership property, for example, the assignor should be cautious not to be ambiguous and risk inclusion of personal property which he did not intend to assign. Such partial assignment, however, may not be a general assignment as covered by the form, since in most states a vital element of the assignment, whether executed under statute or common law, is that the transaction must divest the debtor of substantially his entire property and close out his current estate. Certain of debtor's property is exempt under the statutes, so this voluntary act, like forced bankruptcy, allows a person to retain some of his necessities for living such as clothes and working tools.

The trust arrangement is an explanation of the assignee's powers as trustee. These powers are generally spelled out by statute. The assignee must receive all property, give an accurate accounting to all those having a direct interest in the trust and then discharge the assignor's debts as set out in the agreement.

At this juncture, the assignor must list all debts and demands against him, making such provisions for preferences between creditors as the statutes permit. Whether preferences are prohibited within the assignment itself or within a specified time period prior to the assignment, are questions whose answers are so varied by local law that even general statements would be insufficient. Reference to local law in all of these instances is necessary. Once the preferential creditors are repaid, the remainder is used to pay remaining creditors in whole or ratably, depending on the amount of available funds.

The remainder of the instrument provides for a return of all unused proceeds or property to the assignor and appointment of the assignee as attorney-in-fact under a power of attorney for the assignor.

Powers of Attorney

In order to explain fully powers of attorney, one would have to run the gamut of agency laws. Such an endeavor would be impractical and not entirely necessary. Basically, a power is the authority to do that which the grantor of the power could legally do. Without it, the donee of the power does not have any right, actual, apparent or inherent, to perform the act for the grantor.

You may be confused by the mention of actual, apparent, or inherent authority. Suffice it to say for our purpose that a power of attorney is a form of actual authority in that the grantor formally expresses the agency relationship within a written agreement with the donee. Actual authority can be divided itself into expressed and implied authority; the

JULIUS BLUMBERG, INC., LAW BLANK PUBLISHERS
80 EXCHANGE PL. AT BROADWAY. N. Y. C. 10004

Know all Men by these Presents,

THAT

of

assignor(s),

in consideration of $ *, the receipt whereof is hereby acknowledged, has sold and by these presents*
does grant, assign and convey unto

of

assignee(s)

the following:

TO HAVE AND TO HOLD *the same unto the said assignee(s) executors, administrators and assigns forever,*
to and for the use of the assignee(s), hereby constituting and appointing said assignee(s) true and lawful
attorney(s) irrevocable, in assignor's name, place and stead, for the purposes aforesaid, to ask, demand, sue for,
attach, levy, recover and receive all such sum and sums of money which now are, or may hereafter become due,
owing and payable for, or on account of all or any of the accounts, dues, debts, and demands above assigned, and
giving and granting unto the said attorney(s) full power and authority to do and perform all and every act and
thing whatsoever requisite and necessary, as fully, to all intents and purposes, as assignor's might or could do,
if personally present, with full power of substitution and revocation, hereby ratifying and confirming all that
the said attorney(s) or attorney's substitute shall lawfully do, or cause to be done by virtue hereof.

IN WITNESS WHEREOF, *the undersigned has hereunto set* hand(s) and seal(s) the
day of 19

SIGNED, SEALED AND DELIVERED
IN THE PRESENCE OF

....L.S.

....L.S.

STATE OF
COUNTY OF } *ss.:*

On the day of , nineteen hundred and
before me came

to me known and known to me to be the individual(s) described in, and who executed, the foregoing instru-
ment, and acknowledged to me that he *executed the same.*

STATE OF
COUNTY OF } *ss.:*

On the day of , nineteen hundred and
before me came *to me known, who,*
being by me duly sworn, did depose and say that he *resides in*

that he is the of

the corporation described in, and which executed, the foregoing instrument; that he *knows the seal of*
said corporation; that the seal affixed to said instrument is such corporate seal; that it was so affixed by
order of the board of *of said corporation; and that* he *signed h*
name thereto by like order.

217

JULIUS BLUMBERG, INC., LAW BLANK PUBLISHERS
80 EXCHANGE PL. AT BROADWAY, N. Y. C. 10004

Know all Men by these Presents, That

Whereas,

in and by   Letter of Attorney, bearing date the   day of

one thousand nine hundred and   did make, constitute and appoint

as by the aforesaid Letter of Attorney may more fully and at large appear.

Now know ye, That   the said

have revoked, countermanded, annulled and made void, and by these presents do revoke, countermand annul and make void the said Letter of Attorney above mentioned, and all power and authority thereby given, or intended to be given, to the said

In Witness Whereof,   have hereunto set   hand   and seal the

day of   one thousand nine hundred and

Sealed and delivered in the presence of   ....

STATE OF

                    of   ss.:

County of

          On the   day of   in the year

one thousand nine hundred and   before me personally came

to me known, and known to me to be the individual   described in, and who executed the foregoing

instrument, and   acknowledged to me that   he   executed the same.

Know all Men by these Presents,

That *I*..

do hereby constitute and appoint..

Attorney and Agent for me and in my name, place and stead, to vote as my proxy at any election

....

according to the number of votes I should be entitled to cast if then personally present.

In Witness Whereof, *I have hereunto set my hand and seal this*......................................*day*

of..*one thousand nine hundred and*

Sealed and delivered in the presence of

....

former being the actual communication between the principal or grantor and agent or donee of the power; the latter being the extent of that power as the agent views it. Implied authority, in other words, is the agent's power to pursue all reasonable channels which in his estimation are necessary to fulfill the expressed authority.

A power of attorney, then, is delineated by the expressed grant of authority which the principal confers on the agent. These expressions of authority are construed just as all other contract provisions. The major difference with a power of attorney, however, is that the agency created is a special power and as such is restricted for all practical purposes to the four corners of the agency agreement. The reason for this is that the primary function of the written power is to evidence the existence and scope of the agent's authority to third parties. In his dealings with the agent, then, the third person should request to examine the written power in order to determine for himself whether the agent is within his authority. This becomes more apparent when the third party realizes that he is charged with full knowledge of the power of attorney regardless if he reads it or not.

Looking at the power of attorney in the text, the reader first notices the reference to New York law. Besides the general rules offered here, statutory law further defines the limits of granted powers in most states. Before granting an agent any authority, the principal should consider the extent of his own words.

Next, the two parties, the principal and agent, are named. As the note suggests, if two attorneys-in-fact are designated, the principal should be careful to specify whether the power is to be exercised jointly or independently. This can be accomplished by inserting the word "severally" or "jointly" after the words "to act."

Little guidance can be offered in completing the next section. How much authority the principal wishes to confer upon the agent is up to him. He should remember, however, to keep an eye on the statute and if any questions exist, to seek legal advice. Where the principal desires to restrict the power as to any subdivision, he should be explicit in the blank space in explaining the restrictions. The principal should also consider if he wishes to allow the agent to delegate further the power to subagents. The final paragraph simply states that once the third party acts in response to the power of attorney, he may continue to act under its authority in confidence of its validity until he receives an expressed revocation of the power.

While on the subject of powers of attorney,

one additional form should be noted—the revocation of the power form. Since man often likes to undo that which he has previously done, the general rule is that a principal can always revoke his grant of authority and leave the agent or attorney-in-fact powerless. The two basic exceptions exist where the authority was originally given as security or where the agent has an interest in the subject matter. If either situation prevails, the authority as a matter of law is irrevocable.

The power to revoke and the right to revoke are not synonymous. Thus, if the granting of a power of attorney or any analogous agency relationship was established under contractual agreement, the principal still would have the power to revoke, but simultaneously would breach his contract.

As for the method of revocation, the principal may exploit any medium at his disposal to convey to the agent and third parties that the agent's power has been terminated. In New York, revocation is complete if the manner unequivocally communicates the intended result. The form here accomplishes this requirement by first citing the source of the agent's power (the "Letter of Attorney") and then averring that the principal does "revoke, countermand, annul and make void the said Letter of Attorney . . ." The principal should remember that although the revocation terminates the agency relationship, he remains liable to third parties who transact business with the agent prior to being notified of the revocation.

Proxy

Even in these times of economic uncertainty, many people continue to invest in the stock market. Regardless of the sanity of such a financial program, shareholders of voting stock are always the recipients of proxy solicitations. With an important shareholders' meeting imminent, factions within the corpo-

P 644—Statutory Short Form of General Power of Attorney: Disability Clause. With Affidavit of Attorney. Gen. Obl. Law §5-1501 : 7-77

JULIUS BLUMBERG, INC., LAW BLANK PUBLISHERS
80 EXCHANGE PL. AT BROADWAY. N. Y. C. 10004

Notice: The powers granted by this document are broad and sweeping. They are defined in New York General Obligations Law, Article 5, sections 5-1502A through 5-1503, which expressly permits the use of any other or different form of power of attorney desired by the parties concerned.

𝕶𝖓𝖔𝖜 𝕬𝖑𝖑 𝕸𝖊𝖓 𝖇𝖞 𝕿𝖍𝖊𝖘𝖊 𝕻𝖗𝖊𝖘𝖊𝖓𝖙𝖘, *which are intended to constitute a GENERAL POWER OF ATTORNEY pursuant to Article 5, Title 15 of the New York General Obligations Law:*

That I
(insert name and address of the principal)

do hereby appoint
(insert name and address of the agent, or each agent, if more than one is designated)

my attorney(s)-in-fact TO ACT

(a) If more than one agent is designated and the principal wishes each agent alone to be able to exercise the power conferred, insert in this blank the word "severally". Failure to make any insertion or the insertion of the word "jointly" will require the agents to act jointly.

First: in my name, place and stead in any way which I myself could do, if I were personally present, with respect to the following matters as each of them is defined in Title 15 of Article 5 of the New York General Obligations Law to the extent that I am permitted by law to act through an agent:

[Strike out and initial in the opposite box any one or more of the subdivisions as to which the principal does NOT desire to give the agent authority. Such elimination of any one or more of subdivisions (A) to (K), inclusive, shall automatically constitute an elimination also of subdivision (L).]

To strike out any subdivision the principal must draw a line through the text of that subdivision AND write his initials in the box opposite.

(A) real estate transactions; ....[   ]
(B) chattel and goods transactions; ....[   ]
(C) bond, share and commodity transactions; ....[   ]
(D) banking transactions; ....[   ]
(E) business operating transactions; ....[   ]
(F) insurance transactions; ....[   ]
(G) estate transactions; ....[   ]
(H) claims and litigation; ....[   ]
(I) personal relationships and affairs; ....[   ]
(J) benefits from military service; ....[   ]
(K) records, reports and statements; ....[   ]
(L) all other matters; ....[   ]

[Special provisions and limitations may be included in the statutory short form power of attorney only if they conform to the requirements of section 5-1503 of the New York General Obligations Law.]

Second: with full and unqualified authority to delegate any or all of the foregoing powers to any person or persons whom my attorney(s)-in-fact shall select.

Third: This power of attorney shall not be affected by the subsequent disability or incompetence of the principal.

Fourth: To induce any third party to act hereunder, I hereby agree that any third party receiving a duly executed copy or facsimile of this instrument may act hereunder, and that revocation or termination hereof shall be ineffective as to such third party unless and until actual notice or knowledge of such revocation shall have been received by such third party, and I for myself and for my heirs, executors, legal representatives and assigns, hereby agree to indemnify and hold harmless any such third party from and against any and all claims that may arise against such third party by reason of such third party having relied on the provisions of this instrument.

𝕴𝖓 𝖂𝖎𝖙𝖓𝖊𝖘𝖘 𝖂𝖍𝖊𝖗𝖊𝖔𝖋, *I have hereunto signed my name and affixed my seal this* ....
day of ...., 19...........

....*(Seal)*
(Signature of Principal)

STATE OF   , COUNTY OF   ss.:

On   19   before me personally came

to me known, and known to me to be the individual   described in, and who executed the foregoing
instrument, and   he   acknowledged to me that   he   executed the same.

....

AFFIDAVIT AS TO POWER OF ATTORNEY BEING IN FULL FORCE

STATE OF   , COUNTY OF   ss.:

being duly sworn, deposes and says:

    THAT   as principal,
who resides at
did, in writing, on   19   appoint me as the true and lawful attorney of the principal,
and that annexed hereto, and hereby made a part hereof, is a true copy of said power of attorney.

    THAT, as attorney in fact of said principal and under and by virtue of the said power of attorney,
I have this day executed the following described instrument

    THAT at the time of executing the above described instrument I had no actual knowledge or actual
notice of revocation or termination of the aforesaid power of attorney by death or otherwise, or notice of
any facts indicating the same. I further represent that the said principal is now alive; has not, at any time,
revoked or repudiated the said power of attorney; and the said power of attorney still is in full force and
effect.
    THAT I make this affidavit for the purpose of inducing

to accept delivery of the above described instrument, as executed by me in my capacity of attorney in fact
of the said principal, with the full knowledge that this affidavit will be relied upon in accepting the execution and delivery of the aforesaid instrument and in paying a good and valuable consideration therefor.

Sworn to before me on   19   ....

ration, in efforts to secure the upper hand, or even congenial groups within the power structure wishing to attain the necessary majority, must solicit proxy authorizations from those holders who otherwise would not attend the meeting.

Many of the corporate law consequences of proxies are of little importance for our purpose. Still, a general background would be worthwhile to shed light on the "whys" and "whats" of your action in signing a proxy statement.

Authority to vote by proxy is usually conferred by statute or by the corporate charter. Whether a by-law can grant the same power is a question which can only be answered by reference to local law. Once the right is conferred, no further attempts by corporate officials to restrict the power can prevail.

If a person is the legal holder of the stock, meaning that he has requisite legal title on the corporate transfer books, he alone can appoint a proxy. Rules vary, contingent upon the holder's status (i.e., corporation, infant, executor, etc), but for our purposes, it is settled that the holder of title on the date of record possesses the right to vote and concurrently the right to vote by proxy. By satisfying all formal requisites, the shareholder may confer his voting rights onto another shareholder or any other legally competent person in the absence of a statute to the contrary.

What then are the formal requirements? In essence, all the shareholder is doing is appointing an agent to act on his behalf. The writing, then, should state unequivocally both the legal owner of stock and the person who is

W 277—General Assignment for Benefit of Creditors.
With or Without Preferences.

JULIUS BLUMBERG, INC., LAW BLANK PUBLISHERS
80 EXCHANGE PLACE AT BROADWAY, NEW YORK

𝕿𝖍𝖎𝖘 𝕴𝖓𝖉𝖊𝖓𝖙𝖚𝖗𝖊,

Made the   *day of*   *in the year one thousand*
nine hundred and

BETWEEN

having   *principal place of business at*

         part   *of the first part*

and

         part   *of the second part*

WITNESSETH:

WHEREAS *the part*   *of the first part ha*   *carried on and now*   *engaged in the*
business of
at No.

WHEREAS *the part*   *of the first part*   *indebted to divers persons in sundry sums of*
money, which   *unable to pay in full, and*   *desirous of pro-*
viding for the payment of the same, so far as it is possible by a general assignment of all
property for that purpose:

NOW, THEREFORE, *the part*   *of the first part, in consideration of the premises and of the*
sum of one dollar paid by the part   *of the second part, upon the ensealing and delivery of these*
presents, the receipt whereof is hereby acknowledged, ha   *granted, bargained, sold, assigned, trans-*
ferred and set over, and by these presents do   *grant, bargain, sell, assign, transfer and set over, unto*
the part   *of the second part*   *successors and assigns, all and singular the lands, tenements,*
hereditaments, appurtenances, goods, chattels, stock, promissory notes, claims, demands, property and
effects of every description belonging to the part   *of the first part, wherever the same may be,*
except such property as is exempt by law from levy and sale under an execution.

TO HAVE AND TO HOLD *the same, and every part thereof, unto the said part*   *of the*
second part,   *successors and assigns.*

IN TRUST, NEVERTHELESS, *to take possession of the same, and to sell the same with all*
reasonable dispatch, and to convert the same into money, and also to collect all such debts and demands
hereby assigned as may be collectible, and out of all the proceeds of such sales and collections, to pay
and discharge all the just and reasonable expenses, costs and disbursements in connection with the execu-
tion of this assignment and the discharge of the trust hereby created, together with the lawful com-
missions or allowances of the part   *of the second part for*   *services in executing said*
trust; THEN

AND *then to pay and discharge in full, if the residue of said proceeds is sufficient for that purpose, all the debts and liabilities now due or to grow due from the said part of the first part, with all interest moneys due or to grow due thereon; and if the residue of said proceeds shall not be sufficient to pay the said debts and liabilities and interest thereon in full, then to apply the said residue of said proceeds to the payment of said debts and liabilities ratably and in proportion.*

AND *if, after the payment of all the said debts and liabilities in full, there shall be any remainder or residue of said property or proceeds, to repay and return the same to the said part of the first part, executors, administrators or assigns.*

AND, *in furtherance of the premises, the said part of the first part do hereby make, constitute and appoint the said part of the second part true and lawful attorney , irrevocable, with full power and authority to do all acts and things which may be necessary in the premises to the full execution of the trust hereby created, and to ask, demand, recover and receive of and from all and every person or persons all property, debts and demands due, owing and belonging to the said part of the first part, and to give acquittances and discharges for the same; to sue, prosecute, defend and implead for the same; and to execute, acknowledge, and deliver all necessary deeds, instruments and conveyances: and for any of the purposes aforesaid to make, constitute and appoint one or more attorneys under him and at his pleasure to revoke the said appointments, hereby ratifying and confirming whatever the said part of the second part or substitutes shall lawfully do in the premises.*

AND *the said part of the first part hereby authorize the said part of the second part to sign the name of the said part of the first part to any check, draft, promissory note or other instrument in writing which is payable to the order of the said part of the first part, or to sign the name of the part of the first part to any instrument in writing, whenever it shall be necessary so to do, to carry into effect the object, design and purpose of this trust.*

THE *said part of the second part do hereby accept the trust created and reposed in by this instrument, and covenant and agree to and with the said part of the first part that will faithfully and without delay execute the said trust, according to the best of skill, knowledge and ability.*

IN WITNESS WHEREOF, *the parties hereto have hereunto set their hands and seals the day and year first above written.*

....
Assignor

....
Assignee

STATE OF

COUNTY OF   } *ss.:*

  On the   *day of*   *, nineteen hundred and*
before me came

to me known and known to me to be the individual described in, and who executed, the foregoing instrument, and acknowledged to me that he executed the same.

STATE OF

COUNTY OF   } *ss.:*

  On the   *day of*   *, nineteen hundred and*
before me came   *to me known, who,*
being by me duly sworn, did depose and say that he resides in

that he is the   *of*

the corporation described in, and which executed, the foregoing instrument; that he knows the seal of said corporation; that the seal affixed to said instrument is such corporate seal; that it was so affixed by order of the board of   of said corporation; and that he signed h name thereto by like order.

to act as proxy, as well as the declaration of the creation of an agency relationship and the delegation of power. As the proxy ballot indicates, the latter requirement is satisfied by the words "do hereby constitute and appoint." The shareholder should then sign his name at the end. As long as the proxy meets these requirements and on its face is free from illegality, the proxy becomes effective, unless local laws mandate additional requisites. These additional directions, for example, might include the name of the corporation, the date, acknowledgment by one or more subscribing witnesses, a seal and filing the proxy with powers to be. Once completed, the proxy is vested with all powers that the stockholder legally enjoyed and can exercise them in accordance with whatever general or special authority was granted.

One final note on the finality of a proxy. Laws differ among the many jurisdictions. Generally, a proxy is revocable at any time up until it is exercised, unless the authorization declares the proxy irrevocable or the proxy is considered coupled with an interest such as payment of valuable consideration. Should this question ever arise, advice of counsel should be sought.

T 602— Assignment of Wages

COPYRIGHT 1966 BY JULIUS BLUMBERG, INC., LAW BLANK PUBLISHERS
80 EXCHANGE PLACE AT BROADWAY, NEW YORK

ASSIGNMENT OF WAGES, SALARY, COMMISSIONS OR OTHER COMPENSATION FOR SERVICES

KNOW ALL MEN BY THESE PRESENTS, THAT, I

being over 21 years of age, residing at

do hereby transfer, assign and set over unto

having a principal place of business at No.

herein referred to as "Assignee", and to said Assignee's legal representatives, successors and assigns, all of my salary, wages, commissions and compensation for services now or hereafter due and payable to me from

of   my present employer
and from any future or other employer, to the extent of 10 per centum thereof, payable on
of each *week, month,* until the obligation herein below described shall have been fully paid, satisfied and discharged, together with all lawful charges and interest thereon and I hereby authorize my said employer to pay 10 per centum of my salary, wages, or compensation as and when the same would become due and payable to me.

At present, I receive compensation in the sum of $ per

The consideration for this assignment and the transaction out of which it arises and to which it relates, together with a description of the goods sold or services rendered or other basis of indebtedness and the date on and place at which payments are to be made, is as follows:

This assignment is security only for above described transaction or series of transactions and no other assignment or order for the payment of my salary, wages, commissions or other compensation for services is subject to payment or exists in connection with same transaction or series of transactions, or in connection with any other transaction, and no levy on execution against said salary, wages, commissions or other compensation is in force.

I hereby acknowledge receipt of a copy of this assignment and of all papers executed by me attached to said assignment, together with a copy of all papers executed by me pertaining to the transaction or series of transactions herein described. This instrument may not be changed orally.

IN WITNESS WHEREOF, I have hereunto executed this assignment this   day of
19

This is an Assignment of Wages, Salary, Commissions or Other Compensation for Services.

Witness:

....
Assignor

STATE OF   COUNTY OF   ss.:

On this   day of   19   , before me personally appeared
to me known and known to me to be the individual described in
and who executed the foregoing assignment and   he duly acknowledged to me that   he executed the same.

The foregoing is a true and accurate copy of an original assignment duly executed by said
on   19   now in possession
of   and I so certify under my hand and seal this
day of   19

....
Notary

....
....N. Y.

Gentlemen:
You are hereby notified that   has heretofore executed and delivered to me the assignment, a copy of which duly authenticated, is hereto annexed.

Demand is hereby made that you pay over to the undersigned 10 per centum of any and all salary, wages, commissions or other compensation for services which may become due to the said

from the date of the service upon you of this notice of assignment, until the sum of $ with interest from 19 has been fully paid.

You are advised that a copy of this assignment properly authenticated has been filed with the Clerk of the County of on the day of 19

Dated.. ....

STATEMENT OF AMOUNT DUE:

Take notice that the following is an itemized statement of the amount now due to

the assignee above named:

Full amount of obligation set forth in foregoing assignment .... $..........................

Interest from 19 to 19 ...... $..........................

Total $..........................

PAYMENTS ON ACCOUNT

on...............19...... $..........................	on...............19...... $..........................
on...............19...... $..........................	on...............19...... $..........................
on...............19...... $..........................	on...............19...... $..........................
on...............19...... $..........................	on...............19...... $..........................
on...............19...... $..........................	on...............19...... $..........................
on...............19...... $..........................	on...............19...... $..........................
on...............19...... $..........................	on...............19...... $..........................
on...............19...... $..........................	on...............19...... $..........................
on...............19...... $..........................	on...............19...... $..........................
on...............19...... $..........................	on...............19...... $..........................

Total Payments on Account...................................... $..........................

Balance Due...................................... $..........................

Summary of Sections 46-c, e, f, 48, 48-a, b, c and 49 of the Personal Property Law of New York

SEC. 46-c—No assignment of future earnings, securing or relating to any indebtedness aggregating less than one thousand dollars shall be valid for any purpose unless: (a) it is contained in a separate written instrument in type of the size specified, and contains specified designations of instrument in the title and before the signature, (b) it identifies specifically and describes the transaction to which it relates, including name and address of assignee, basis of indebtedness, date on and place at which payments to be made, and contains a summary of Sections 46-c, e, f, 48, 48-a, b, c and 49 of Personal Property Law, (c) such assignment is security only for transaction or series or renewal thereof described therein, and no other valid assignment exists in connection therewith, except that under specified conditions assignment securing a guarantee of payment of goods amounting to fifteen hundred dollars or less shall be valid.

SEC. 46-e—No assignment of future earnings shall be valid unless personally executed by assignor and copy thereof with any papers attached, together with copies of any papers executed by assignor pertaining to transaction are delivered to assignor.

SEC. 46-f—Except as in Article IX of the Banking Law no person shall receive for the use and sale of his personal credit or for making or continuing a loan in anticipation of earnings assigned outright or on the security of an assignment of earnings a greater sum than 18% per annum as interest or otherwise, except the charges permitted by Section 380 of the General Business Law. Provides penalties for violation of Section.

SEC. 48—No assignment of future earnings except to bank, trust company or credit union to be filed with employer until ten days have elapsed after written notice mailed to assignor, addressed as prescribed, stating that unless amounts in default are paid within ten days from date of mailing, assignment will be filed with assignor's employer; but such notice not to be mailed by assignee until twenty-one days have elapsed after default of payment by assignor, and contains substantially following language; "Bring this notice with you when making any payment on account of your indebtedness and have payment endorsed on this notice"; if payment accepted by assignee after such notice given, and if noted by assignee at time of acceptance, assignor no longer considered in default for purpose of filing assignment with employer, but on subsequent default assignment may be filed on compliance with same prescribed provisions.

SEC. 48-a—Earnings, as payable, covered by any assignment, commencing with first payment after expiration of ten days from date of filing with employer of true copy of assignment, properly authenticated and setting forth prescribed information. Amount collectible not to exceed 10% of earnings on assignment relating to indebtedness less than one thousand dollars, such assignment effective if at time of filing no other assignment, or garnishment against earnings or no order under Section 793 of Civil Practice Act is in force. While such assignment in effect, no other deductions shall be made from earnings on any such subsequent assignment or garnishment.

SEC. 48-b—No assignment effective unless earnings of assignor at least thirty dollars per week if assignor employed in city of two hundred and fifty thousand or more population and at least twenty-five dollars per week if assignor employed elsewhere.

SEC. 48-c—Validity of any assignment not affected by unemployment, cessation of employment or by changes of employers. If the assignor is re-employed by the same employer before the expiration of ninety days from the termination of employment, the assignment shall continue to be collectible without further filing of papers. If the employee is re-employed on or after the expiration of such ninety days, the assignment shall again become collectible from the employer as provided in section forty-eight-a only after copies of the assignment and the other documents specified in such section have been filed with the employer following the re-employment.

SEC. 49—Delay and demand provisions of Section 48 and public filing requirements of Section 47 shall not apply to assignments taken by banks, trust companies and credit unions where such assignments contain specified language.

CHAPTER 11

Conclusion

Various rights, obligations and remedies involved within particular transactions already have been discussed. We hope the reader has been helped by those explanations. For the most part, in the text we only have scratched the surface of the subject, because the law dealing with these particular contracts is both expansive and intricate; in particular transactions (e.g., forming a partnership), an attorney should be consulted, if at all possible. Nonetheless, some knowledge of the law can be helpful if applied with caution. This chapter will deal with three different, but related areas of contract law—breaches, remedies, discharges of a contract and theories based on general common law. It should aid the reader to develop a full picture of a contractual transaction from start to finish. The chapter will close with some general comments.

Breach of Contract

A breach of contract is an unjustifiable failure to comply with the obligation assumed by a party to the contract. Simply, it means that one party, the promisor, does not honor his promise to the other person, the promisee. Breach of contract may occur in three basic ways: (1) non-performance of the duty imposed by the contract; (2) repudiation (disavowal); and (3) hindrance or prevention of performance by one party upon the other. Breach of contract is not a difficult concept, or at least not as difficult a concept in contract law as some discussed earlier in the book. Breaches of contract are very common. Here are brief explanations of a number of contractual transactions to help you understand the concept of breach.

Conditions

Failure to perform a contractual duty can be confused with the failure of the occurrence of a condition, that creates liability. There is ure of a condition by one party does not create a liability. It is breach of a promise, not of a condition, that creates liability. There is no problem with understanding breach of promise. If the contracting party fails to perform the promise contracted for, the promisee has an action for breach of the contract. However, many contracts contain conditions, the breach of which may not constitute a breach of contract; rather, it allows the other party the right to non-performance without incurring liability.

Conditions are sub-divided into three classes: *condition precedent, subsequent,* and *concurrent*. A quick look at each will bring the point home.

A condition precedent is a fact or event which must occur before a duty of performance becomes mandatory. Let us illustrate: "In consideration of your taking me to the game, I will buy you a beer if the Knicks win," is an example of a condition precedent. If the Knicks do, in fact, win, then I have to buy you a beer; the condition precedent, that is, the Knicks winning, has been satisfied and that condition precedent is now elevated to an unconditional duty. If I do not buy you a beer, I have breached the contract. If the Knicks do not win, I have no duty to perform and, hence, no contractual liability.

A condition subsequent is very rare. When it exists, a condition subsequent terminates the obligation to perform the contract and the possibility of incurring liability for any breach. In essence, it discharges a previous absolute duty of performance. For example, an obligation agreed to in a contract may be subject to a condition of notification within a period of time, such as an insured notifying the insurance company of a loss within twelve months. If he fails to satisfy the condition, the insurance company's obligation is terminated because the condition subsequent in the contract has occurred. It discharges any obligation of performance under it.

A condition concurrent must be in existence at the time when both parties are required to perform their obligations. An example: You purchase a motorcycle at Mike's Motorcycle Shop. The motorcycle is to be delivered C.O.D., (cash on delivery). Thus, payment is conditional on delivery, and delivery is conditional on payment.

Express conditions, which can be any of the above three, are created by agreement of the parties to the contract. The reader should look for words or phrases like "on condition that," "provided," "if," etc. Also, a condition may be reasonably implied.

What should be noted by the reader is to be on the lookout for conditions in a contract. Remember, a breach of a condition is not a breach of the contract. The condition must occur to impose a duty to perform, and it is the non-performance of that duty which creates a breach of the contract.

Repudiation (Anticipatory Breach)

Repudiation is a statement by a promisor that he will not undertake his promised future performance. There are a number of ways that breach of contract by repudiation may be effectuated. A positive statement issued by the promisor to the promisee, proclaiming that the promisor does not intend to perform, results in a breach of contract. A simple example will illustrate the point: "I will sell you my car on June 5, 1980 for $500." You accept my offer and are ready to tender the $500. We have a contract. On June 1, I tell you, "I am not going to sell the car to you." You are mad, but also wise. You consult an attorney and sue for damages. You win. There was a breach of contract. (Damages are discussed later.)

A voluntary act on the part of the promisor which makes rendering performance impossible, or apparently so, is a form of repudiation and gives rise to breach of contract. Consider another example: instead of informing you on June 1 that I will not sell the car, I sell the car to Paul, a third party, who does not know of our deal. Is this a breach of contract? Yes, and you may sue for damages for breach of contract on the theory that performance is now impossible because of the sale to Paul.

A repudiating party always has an opportunity to retract the repudiation if it is done before the promisee (you) has sued or changed his position in reliance on the repudiation. An example will illustrate the point. On December 1, a contract is entered into between X and Y for the sale of X's car to Y for $500. It is in writing and duly executed. The date of performance is December 25. On December 15, X tells Y that he is not going to perform. Y does nothing about this. (Y could sue then if he wishes, but chooses not to.) On December 20, X notifies Y that he intends to perform the contract as agreed to. This retraction is effective, the contract is reinstated and the parties,

X and Y, are both bound by its terms. Y's inaction allows X to retract the repudiation and perform as required under the contract's terms.

There are other remedies available to a promisee after promisor's repudiation (anticipatory breach). It has been mentioned that the promisee may sue for damages immediately upon the issuance of the repudiation. The promisee may accept the promisor's repudiation as a discharge of his own contractual obligation and simultaneously recover for his own performance in restitution (discussed later), or the promisee may wait until the actual date that performance was to take place and, upon non-performance, sue the promisor then. And, finally, the promisee may always attempt to urge the promisor to perform.

The common law concept of anticipatory breach (repudiation) has been incorporated into the Uniform Commercial Code with respect to sales. This theory was discussed in the chapter on sales and an explanation was developed there. It is worth noting that a repudiation is not considered a breach when the defendant (promisor) is under a unilateral obligation to pay a sum of money at a future date. The repudiation of the obligation does not give rise to a course of action, and the doctrine of anticipatory breach cannot be used to accelerate payment of a debt (e.g., installment payments). Therefore, the party who suffers as a result of this type of repudiation must wait until the due date of payment and then sue for non-performance.

Prevention of Performance

One party's hindering or preventing the performance of the other party is self-explanatory. X and Y contract for the sale of X's car to Y on December 25 for $500. On December 15, Y destroys X's car. X obviously cannot perform; however, since Y caused X's non-performance, Y cannot sue for breach of contract. More accurately stated, Y could sue for breach of contract, but X would have a valid defense to non-performance.

Remarks

This concludes the discussion of breach of contract. For all practical purposes, the reader will know when a breach occurs. It is not difficult to know when you have been wronged. The key questions to ask when negotiating a contract are:

(1) Are there any conditions contained in the contract?

(2) When do these conditions occur?

(3) After occurrence, what legal obligations arise under the contract?

Another key point to note is that in the event of a repudiation, the wronged party has many courses of action, all of which should be acted upon immediately, with aid of legal counsel. Examination of remedies is our next task, since it is important that a party realizes what can be done when a contract is, in fact, breached.

Remedies for Breach

After one party has breached his duties, the other has three alternative recourses available to him which he can pursue in order to be *made whole*. These three basic remedies are damages, restitution and specific performance.

Damages

As a general statement, the purpose for remedies for breach of contract is to put the injured party in the same position after the breach as he would have been had the other party fully performed. The most common means to accomplish this end is to award the

231

aggrieved party money damages in an amount sufficient to offset the losses incurred. The only difficulty in achieving this just result is in the measurement of damages.

Different legal theorists attach different labels to the types of damages recoverable by an aggrieved party. As a general rule, the party is allowed the difference between the price called for in the contract and the cost of his own performance. These damages are strictly compensatory and are recoverable only to the extent foreseeable by the breaching party at the time of the formation of the contract.

Extraordinary or consequential damages, which proximately arise as a result of the breach, can be recovered only where the breaching party can reasonably foresee their occurrence. Example: X agrees to sell Y 100 widgets. On the day set for performance Y fails to accept delivery of the widgets, and X sells them elsewhere, at a lower price. Obviously X has a right to be compensated for his lost profits and whatever additional incidental costs are incurred from selling the widgets to a third party. If the later sale results in a price greater than that agreed to in the contract and X suffers no pecuniary loss, then he is entitled to nominal costs at best.

To illustrate extraordinary damages, let us assume that X breaches, and because of this non-delivery, Y is unable to complete a deal from which he would have made an unusually high profit. In addition to the compensatory damages, is X liable for Y's loss of these high profits. The answer is no, unless X had knowledge of Y's subsequent deal at the time of contracting. The determining factor again is foreseeability, and since X could not be reasonably expected to foresee the later contract, calling for an incredibly high profit level, he is not liable to Y for that particular loss.

In order to recover at all, the injured party must be able to calculate damages with some certainty. If his measure of damages is purely conjecture, at best he can recover nominal damages (a token amount) or his costs in performing his part of the bargain. One additional burden on the injured party is that he must attempt to mitigate. Even after proving damages with utmost certainty, he cannot recover any damages that he could reasonably avoid. In the above example where Y refused to accept delivery of the widgets, X has a duty to sell the widgets to another party. If to do so would require an unreasonable effort (e.g., if the only other user and purchaser of widgets was three thousand miles away), then he is excused. Where he does act to mitigate the damages, he is allowed to recover for any costs which he incurs.

Restitution

Restitution is a remedy for an aggrieved party who has not fully performed his side of the bargain before learning of the other party's breach, and when the other party's duty requires something else or more than an agreed price. To seek restitution, a valid contract must be in existence, one party must totally breach it and the aggrieved party must be in a position to rescind. Since the injured party has not given his full consideration as stated in the contract, he is unable to seek damages—a calculation in which the contract price is always a factor. Still, he has suffered a measurable loss for which he should be compensated. In short, he should be restored to the position he was in before partially performing under the contract.

The measure of damages for restitution is limited to the actual cost of the partial performance which the injured party has rendered, less whatever value of returned performance he has received. If X pays Y $1,000 for a super widget, which is capable of doing more tasks than an everyday widget, and uses it in performing everyday tasks for several weeks only to have it fail in its first extraordinary job, X can recover his $1,000 less the value received from the widget in its normal duties. One highlight in the area of restitution is that the contract price does not restrict recovery, as it does under damages. Thus, even though an aggrieved party would have lost money under the original contract price, he can profit in an action for restitution—because the court is not limited to an award based on the agreed to price.

Specific Performance

One final remedy is specific performance or *specific restitution*. Sometimes, money damages will not make an injured party whole. In such an instance, he naturally would like a court to mandate that the contract be performed or, in the alternative, that the specific object of the contract (e.g., a section of realty) be returned. If money damages are not satisfactory, the court will so order as long as it can supervise the performance, and its decision does not unjustly prejudice the other party. It should be remembered that a court can grant specific performance at its discretion and if it decides not to do so, the other remedies remain available to the injured party.

Discharge

Discharge is the end of the line. The parties, in effect, state that they are happy with each other and everything has been performed as agreed to. Performance is the usual method by which discharge becomes effective.

There are many methods of discharge. Methods of discharge of a contractual liability may take the following forms:

(1) new agreement

(2) substituted contract and novation

(3) accord and satisfaction

(4) cancellation and rescission

(5) merger

(6) release and covenant not to sue

(7) occurrence of a condition subsequent

(8) payment

(9) discharge by operation of law

Method (3), accord and satisfaction, and (7), occurrence of a condition subsequent, were discussed previously. Let us begin discussion with (1), a new agreement.

A *new agreement* has to be in the same form as the original contract. If the original contract was in writing, the new agreement must also be in writing, if required by the terms of the original contract or by law. The new agreement should state that the parties discharge each other from any contractual liability arising out of the original contract.

A *novation* involves the substitution of a new party into the contract with a discharge of one of the original parties. The other original party, however, must agree to this substitution. In essence, a new contract is executed between the new party and the old party with all the same terms of the original contract. For example, **X** and **Y** have a valid contract. **Y** decides to substitute **Z** in his stead. If **X** accepts this substitution, a novation has occurred, and **Y** is relieved of his liability. A novation results as long as all the parties, in this case **X**, **Y** and **Z**, are involved in the new agreement and **Y**'s original liability is extinguished.

In a two-party situation, an original contract can be discharged with the substitution of a new contract. This can be effectuated either by an express intention in the new contract to that effect or by a new contract which is inconsistent with the original one. The former situation discharges through an expressed provision. The latter situation discharges impliedly.

Recision of a contract, by mutual agreement of the parties, discharges their respective obligations and liabilities. The parties, in essence, are restored to their original status. Cancellation is the destruction of a document (e.g., a note which is the debt—and not merely evidence of the debt—is destroyed by the party owed the money) or its surrender to the party subject to the duty or to someone on his behalf.

A *merger* involves a discharge of the contractual obligation by operation of law. Basically, a merger is the acceptance by one party of a higher contractual right, such as a judgment, which by law, discharges the lesser right (contract right) by incorporation into the judgment.

A *release* or a covenant not to sue, unlike recision, involves the surrender of a right by only one party under the contract. In return, therefore, the other party must supply good consideration in return for that surrender.

Payment is simply meeting one's obligation under the contract. X owes Y $100 on the contract. X pays Y $100. X is discharged.

Discharge by operation of law, includes not only merger, but certain actions of the parties, such as a material alteration of a negotiable note or a specific proceeding of law, such as bankruptcy, which acts as a discharge by preventing the obligee to recover.

A Reader's Checklist

We hope the text has been helpful in illuminating pitfalls which the layman may confront in the daily management of his affairs and in suggesting remedies which he can seek. In all honesty, the book was written in that spirit. Time and again, it has been suggested that advice of an attorney is the best solution to any contractual problem. In some areas, such as wills, mortgages and partnerships, only a skeleton of the law was offered because of the intricacies involved. In all likelihood, a person will and should consult an attorney before executing these agreements or documents. It should be remembered that knowing how to "handle your own contract" at times can mean knowing when to seek counsel.

Other topics covered, however, are those confronted much more frequently and in which consultation with a lawyer would prove impractical. For example, the layman cannot be expected to seek legal advice in ordinary contractual transactions such as signing a lease, applying for credit, buying on time and purchasing personal use goods.

It is in these areas that the book has been focused in depth. In conclusion, a reiteration, in checklist form, is presented here for use when engaging in any contractual situation. If the reader remains alert and follows these 15 bits of advice, he may detect these latent dangers and avoid them where possible (and as a result he will not sell his soul, as did Doctor Faustus).

(1) Always receive a copy of every document involved in the transaction that is signed by either party.

(2) Retain all receipts, envelopes, and any other tangible evidence of communication between the parties until satisfaction.

(3) Preferably pay by check—this, in itself, is a record of payment.

(4) Never sign a contract that contains blanks that could possibly be filled in at a later date.

(5) Remember, everyone has a right to a completed copy of the agreement.

(6) Carefully read every contract and search for certain clauses that might prove detrimental. Examples are: (a) a waiver clause; (b) a wage assignment clause; (c) provision for cooling-off periods; (d) an acceleration clause; (e) power-of-attorney; (f) submission to particular court jurisdiction or compulsive arbitration; (g) waiver of right to trial by jury.

(7) In a contract for services to be performed in the future (e.g., health spas, dancing schools, vocational schools, judo classes, etc.) determine what cancellation privileges exist.

(8) In retail installment agreements, always determine who is financing the credit extended to you. Is it the seller or a third party? If it is a third party, determine who it is.

(9) In any consumer transaction, generally beware of certain rights that you as the consumer might forfeit by signing the agreement.

(10) Goods should never be purchased through a post office box. However, if you are·"taken" and the post office box is used for commercial purposes, you can find the company's true name and address through the post office.

(11) Not all contracts are enforceable. Numerous provisions in contracts are determined to be unconscionable, illegal, etc., and therefore unenforceable. Whenever this problem arises, an attorney should be consulted.

(12) Certain public agencies exist in most metropolitan areas whose primary functions are to deal with unfair practices in the consumer market. Although these agencies do not adjudicate rights, they may expedite an equitable resolution. These organizations and agencies, such as the Better Business Bureau, American Arbitration Association, Federal Trade Commission, Consumer Protection Agency, etc., should be utilized by the consumer; these agencies were created for your use and protection; do not hesitate to use them. This list of organizations and agencies is incomplete— each locality may have one or more of these, or other agencies which perform similar functions.

(13) Consultation with an attorney has been recommended throughout the book. However, many people lack the monetary means to avail themselves of personal legal advice. In many communities, excellent organizations such as Legal Aid, Inc. and Legal Services (Community Action for Legal Services) were created to aid those with minimal or no income. These organizations were founded on the theory that every person deserves to have his legal rights adjudicated properly. Do not hesitate to use them.

(14) In New York (and possibly in your state) there is a small claims court. The main purpose of this division of the state court system is to offer the aggrieved party a forum to present his "side of the story." In New York the claim cannot exceed $1,000, and the remedies available are refunds and damages. A point to be noted is that the action can be brought cheaply (under $5.00) and will be heard generally within one month after filing. Also, representation by an attorney is not necessary. Informality is the tenor of the proceeding.

(15) In transactions for the purchase of goods in which the goods prove to be unsatisfactory, a course of action not often used, but sometimes effectual, is a personal letter to the president of the corporation. Do not discard this recommendation as frivolous, since the price of a stamp might bring an equitable solution to the problem.

In closing, one point is emphasized: this book is meant to be an aid to the layman in contractual situations; it is not intended to be used as an affirmative tool with which to negotiate in bad faith. If a flaw is discovered in a contract, it should be made known to the other party and not be used later to avoid the legal obligation. There is no substitute for fairness and honesty in contractual dealings.

Bibliography

Anderson, R. Anderson on the Uniform Commercial Code, Vols. I and II. Rochester: Lawyers Cooperative Publishing Co., 1971.

Benden, Richard Roy and Rohan, Patrick J. Powell on Real Property. New York: Matthew Bender and Co., 1968.

Bicks, A. Contract for the Sale of Realty. Student Edition (as revised). New York: Practicing Law Institute, 1972.

Black, H. C. Law Dictionary. Fourth Edition. St. Paul: West Publishing Co., 1951.

Bromberg, Alan R. Crane and Bromberg on Partnership (Hornbook Services). St. Paul: West Publishing Co., 1968.

Burby, William E. Handbook of the Law of Real Property. Third Edition (Hornbook Services). St. Paul: West Publishing Co., 1965.

Calamari, John D. The Law of Contracts (Hornbook Services). St. Paul: West Publishing Co., 1970.

Casey, W. J. Estate Planning. New York: Institute for Business Planning, Inc., 1973.

Consumers Report, A Guide for Renters, Pts. 1–111, Vols. 39, No. 10; 39, No. 11; 40, No. 1. Consumers Union of the United States, Inc., Mount Vernon, New York, 1974.

Corbin, Arthur Linton. Corbin on Contracts. St. Paul: West Publishing Co., 1952.

Corpus Juris Secundum. Agency, Vol. 3; Assignment, Vol. 6; Assignment for the Benefit of Creditors, Vol. 6; Compensation and Salaries, Vol. 15; Contracts, Vol. 17; Contracts, Vol. 17A; Deeds, Vols. 26–28; Landlord and Tenant, Vols. 52–53; Mortgages, Vol. 68; Sales, Vols. 77–78; Wills, Vols. 94–96. Brooklyn: The American Law Book Co., 1936 to date.

Ferser, Merton. Principles of Agency. Brooklyn: Foundation Press, 1954.

Friedman, Milton R. Contracts and Conveyances of Real Property, and cumulative supplement (1972). Second Edition. New York: Practicing Law Institute.

Friedman, Milton R. Friedman on Leases. New York: Practicing Law Institute, 1974.

Hawland, William Dennis. A Transactional Guide to the UCC. Philadelphia: Joint Committee on the Continuing Legal Education of the American Lawyers Institute and American Bar Association, 1964.

Kratovil, Robert. Modern Mortgage Law and Practice. Englewood Cliffs, N.J.: Prentice-Hall, 1972.

LeBlanc, Nancy E. A Handbook of Landlord-Tenant Procedure and Law with Forms. Third Edition. New York: MRY Legal Services, Inc., 1966.

Mandel, Ludwig. The Preparation of Commercial Agreements. New York: Practicing Law Institute, 1973.

Marks, Edward; Maloney, Richard J. and Paperno, Lloyd. Mortgages and Mortgage Foreclosure in New York. Massapequa Park, N.Y.: Acme Book Co., 1961.

McKinney's Consolidated Laws of New York Annotated. Real Property Law, Bk 49. St. Paul: West Publishing Co., 1968.

Moynihan, C. J. Introduction to the Law of Real Property (Hornbook Services). St. Paul: West Publishing Co., 1962.

New York State Bar Association. Basic Real Estate Practice in New York. Albany, N.Y. 1978.

Nordstrom, Robert J. Handbook of the Law of Sales. St. Paul: West Publishing Co., 1970.

Osborne, George Edward. Handbook on the Law of Mortgages (Hornbook Services). St. Paul: West Publishing Co., 1970.

Restatement of the Law. Agency, Vols. 1, 2. Second Edition. St. Paul: American Law Institute Publishers, 1958.

Rowley, Scott and Sive, David. Rowley on Partnership. Second Edition. Indianapolis: Bobbs-Merrill Co., 1960.

Scoles, E. F. Problems and Materials on Decedents' Estates and Trusts. Second Edition.

Boston/Toronto: Little, Brown and Company, 1973.

Seavey, Warren Abner. Handbook of the Law of Agency (Hornbook Services). St. Paul: West Publishing Co., 1964.

Simpson, L. P. Handbook of the Law of Contracts. Second Edition (Hornbook Services). St. Paul: West Publishing Co., 1965.

Sorizno, Nicholas M. Handling Your House Closing. A Practical Guide. White Plains, N.Y. Penchant Press, Inc. 1974.

Sugarman, Robert Reuben. The Law of Partnership. Second Edition. Brooklyn, 1947.

United States Code Annotated. Commerce and Trade. Title 15. St. Paul: West Publishing Co., 1974.

United States Code Congressional and Administrative News. 93rd Congress. Second Session. No. 12, Dec. 25, 1974. St. Paul: West Publishing Co., 1974.

Walsh, W. F. A Treatise on the Law of Property. Second Edition. New York: Baker, Voorhis and Co., 1937.

Williston, S. A Treatise on the Law of Contracts, Vols. 1–15. Third Edition. Mount Kisco, N.Y.: Baker, Voorhis and Co., Inc., 1957.

Wincor, Richard. The Law of Contracts. Dobbs Ferry, New York: Oceana Publications, 1970.

Glossary

ACCEPTANCE—One of the elements needed for a contract. A contract is binding after one party has made an offer, and another party has *accepted* that offer, provided there has been *mutual assent*; i.e., a meeting of the minds.

ACCELERATION OF PAYMENT CLAUSE—A contract clause which accelerates the time when a legal obligation becomes due because the obligor failed to meet certain conditions.

ACCORD AND SATISFACTION—An agreement whereby parties to an earlier agreement consent to its discharge.

ANTICIPATORY BREACH—A breach which occurs when one party to a contract unequivocally, by action or words, renounces the contract and refuses to perform in advance of any requirement to do so.

APPURTENANCE—An appurtenance is an appendage to property which is regarded as being permanent. For most practical purposes there is no legal distinction between the terms: *appurtenance*, *personalty* and *fixtures*.

BLUE SKY LAW—State statutes providing for the regulation and supervision of investment companies and the issuance of stock.

"BOILERPLATE" CLAUSES—Standard provisions which, in substance, are found in all contracts (particularly pre-printed forms) of similar purpose.

BREACH OF CONTRACT—Failure to perform a promise (covenant) which is an intrinsic element of a contract.

CAPACITY TO CONTRACT—A term that has many meanings in legal contexts. In a contract, capacity refers to the signer's or signee's ability to carry out the obligations as stated in the contract. Capacity is frequently used to determine whether a contract is void or voidable. For example, a minor may have the capacity to fulfill his contractual obligations, which would make the contract void, but his being underage would, in most states, release him from the contract or render the contract voidable.

COMMON LAW—Common Law refers to that system of law and juristic theory which originated in England and arises from usage and custom instead of from legislative action.

CONSIDERATION—One of the elements needed for a contract. Consideration is a return promise or performance, and it takes the form of a legal benefit to the promisor or a legal detriment to the promisee.

CONTRACT—A contract is a promise, or a set of promises, for breach of which the law gives a remedy, or for the performance of which the law in some way recognizes a duty. The six elements required for a contract are: 1) offer, 2) acceptance, 3) consideration, 4) legal capacity of the parties to the contract, 5) legal subject matter, 6) a writing if required by law.

COVENANT—Covenants (promises) are the contractual elements of an agreement and, as such, can be both expressed within the provisions of the agreement or implied as a matter of law.

CONDITION—A contingency which, according to the agreement, must arise or fail to arise before performance is required.

CREDIT—The right granted by a creditor to a debtor to defer payment of debt or to issue debt and defer its payment.

DEED—The instrument of conveyance for all land interests, regardless of whether they are partial rights or complete title, either commencing now or in the future.

EASEMENT—The right to make a specified use of land belonging to someone else.

EXECUTORY CONTRACT—A contract that remains to be carried out. The opposite would be an executed contract.

EXPRESS TRUST—An express trust is a fiduciary relationship by which an owner of property, known as the grantor or settlor, conveys legal title in trust to a trustee for the benefit of a third person; the beneficiary, who holds equitable title to the property. See also *Inter Vivos* and *Testamentary Trust*.

"FINE PRINT"—A misnomer whereby some people equate legal interpretation of a contract with legal loopholes or legal entrapment. Actually, "fine print" refers to the legal interpretation of a contract's bold-faced language.

FORECLOSURE ON MORTGAGE—An action brought by the mortgagee (usually the bank) upon any default on a mortgage debt payment to gain full title to the mortgaged property.

GRANTING CLAUSE—In a will, the granting clause expresses the grantor's intent to grant or give an estate to another. This clause is usually coupled with a habendum clause.

HABENDUM CLAUSE—In a will, the habendum clause defines further the ownership of an estate, as granted under the granting clause.

IDENTITY CLAUSE—This clause is found in most contracts. Its purpose is to identify the parties involved and thus initiate a contract. Specific problems can occur when all of the parties are not identified. See *Contract for the Sale of Property*, Chapter Three.

IMPOSSIBILITY OF PERFORMANCE—Sometimes a party will enter into a contract only to discover that through no fault of his own he cannot fulfill his obligations. Should this occur the party may have a legal defense for release from the contract. For a full discussion of this legal defense see *Impossibility of Performance*, Chapter One.

INTESTACY—Where the deceased has either no will, or had drawn up a will with part of his estate or property left undisposed. See *Dying Intestate*.

INTER VIVOS TRUST—Literally translated means "living trust." *Inter vivos* is a trust which is created to take effect during the lifetime of the grantor or settlor, whereas a testamentary trust does not become operative until the death of the grantor.

LEASE—An agreement, usually in writing, which gives rise to a landlord-tenant relationship whereby the tenant has the right to use and occupancy of a premises for a specified period of time.

LEGAL SUBJECT MATTER—One of the elements needed for a contract. Essentially what is meant by "legal subject matter" is that two parties cannot contract to do something illegal otherwise the contract is unenforceable.

LIEN—A monetary charge against, security interest in or incumbrance upon property.

LIVERY—In English law meant delivery of property; today the term is known as delivery of the deed.

MATERIAL BREACH—A breach of such significance that it defeats the purpose of a contract.

MUTUAL ASSENT—When *acceptance* of an *offer* has been met then a contract can be formed. Mutual assent is the concept that the person making the offer and the person giving the acceptance have a *common* understanding of what they are agreeing to.

NOVATION—See *Accord and Satisfaction*. The substitution of a new contract for a previous valid one. The parties to the new contract can be the same or different ones to the prior contract.

OBLIGOR—See *Realty Mortgages*, Chapter Four. An obligor is literally someone who has engaged to perform some obligation.

OFFER—An offer is a promise conditional upon an act, forebearance or return promise, which is being given in exchange for the promise of its performance.

OPEN-END CREDIT PLAN—Under Federal Law, credit cards fall into this category. This is an agreement in which the purchaser (cardholder) agrees to pay the card issuer for the debt incurred on a monthly basis until his account is paid in full.

ORAL AGREEMENT—Verbal offer and acceptance can form a binding contract, unless the *Statute of Frauds* requires a written agreement.

PAROL EVIDENCE RULE—Parol evidence means, literally, oral or verbal evidence. The purpose of the parol evidence rule is to make sure that a written contract cannot be contradicted or modified by oral agreements prior to or simultaneous with the written document.

PARTNERSHIP—An association of two or more competent persons to carry on a business as co-owners for profit.

PERFECT TENDER RULE—Allows a buyer of merchandise to reject or accept, either in whole or in part, a seller's merchandise, if goods delivered are not exactly consonant with the goods as described in the purchase contract. See *Buyer's Remedies*, Chapter Eight.

PERSONALTY—Personal Property. See *Appurtenances*.

PROCEDURAL LAW—Those laws which prescribe methods of enforcing rights or obtaining redress of their invasion.

RESCISSION—The annulling of a contract and restoring partners to their original status.

RECORDING STATUTE—Laws enacted in many states which provide for the official recording of deeds, mortgages, liens, easements, etc. Such central recording provides prospective purchasers an opportunity to be on notice of encumbrances.

RESTITUTION—A legal remedy for an aggrieved party which has the effect of making him whole either by making good on the contract or providing equivalent merchandise.

REVOCATION—The annulling or recalling of an offer prior to its acceptance.

STATUTE OF FRAUDS—A statute governing the requirement of a written document in certain contractual situations. Where a written instrument is required, an oral contract is unenforceable.

STATUTE OF LIMITATIONS—A statute restricting the period of time within which a lawsuit can be maintained.

SURETY—See also *Obligor*. One who insures a debt or obligation of another person and, as such, is primarily liable.

TESTAMENTARY TRUST—A trust that does not become operative until the death of the grantor.

TITLE SEARCH—A review of all local public records to develop a history of a given property.

UNIFORM COMMERCIAL CODE—A nine-article statute governing commercial transactions (sales, secured interests, negotiable instruments, et al.) which has been uniformly adopted (with minor changes) in all states.

Index of Contracts

ABOUT THE AUTHORS

JACK WITHIAM, JR., graduated from Hamilton College in Clinton, New York in May of 1971 with an A.B. degree in economics. He then attended the Albany Law School of Union University in Albany, New York and received a J.D. degree in June, 1974. Currently residing in New York City, he has been an attorney for the Mutual Life Insurance Company of New York, Citibank, N.A., and now is General Counsel for Little Brothers Shows, Inc., and George Little Management, Inc., companies which produce and manage trade shows in the United States. He has been admitted to the practice of law in New York State since 1975.

CHRISTOPHER NEUBERT attended the University of Notre Dame in South Bend, Indiana, graduating with a degree in Business Administration in June of 1970. Thereafter, he attended New York Law School in Manhattan and was awarded his J.D. degree in June, 1974. Chris lives in Boston, Massachusetts, and works for the Mutual Life Insurance Company of New York. Mr. Neubert is admitted to the practice of law in the states of New York and Massachusetts.